BLACKS IN THE NEW WORLD
August Meier, Series Editor

A list of the books in the series appears at the end of this volume.

Religious Philanthropy
and
Colonial Slavery

Religious Philanthropy
and
Colonial Slavery

The
American Correspondence
of the
Associates of Dr. Bray,
1717–1777

Edited with an Introduction by
John C. Van Horne

University of Illinois Press
Urbana and Chicago

Publication of this work was supported in part by a grant
from the National Historical Publications and Records Commission.

LIBRARY OF CONGRESS CATALOGING IN PUBLICATION DATA

Main entry under title:

Religious philanthropy and colonial slavery.

    Includes bibliographical references and index.
    1. Missions to Afro-Americans—History—18th century—
Sources.   2. Afro-Americans—Education—History—18th
century—Sources.   I. Van Horne, John C.   II. Associates of
Dr. Bray (Organization)
BV2783.R45   1985   266'.023'41008996073   84-2766
ISBN 0-252-01142-2 (alk. paper)

To
HARRIET CHAMBERLIN VAN HORNE
my grandmother and namesake

*Collect to be used by the Associates
when They begin to Do Business.*

Most Gracious God, who hast been pleased
to offer Salvation to all Mankind, We adore thy
infinite Goodness which hath brought the Light
of the Gospel to these Kingdoms. O, may We
shew our Sense of this inestimable Benefit by
walking as Children of Light, & by compassion-
ating the Miseries of those that Still sit in Darkness: To this End We humbly beseech Thee to
prosper the Undertaking of this Society; make
Us zealous & diligent in the good work in which
we are engaged, give Us Wisdom to discern the
best & most proper Means of promoting it,
Courage & Resolution to pursue it, & by Unity &
Affection in our Consultations & by thy Blessing
on our Endeavours the Happiness to effect it,
thro' Jesus Christ our Lord. Amen.

Minutes, 1 : 164 (meeting of 3 December 1761).

CONTENTS

APPENDIXES

ACKNOWLEDGMENTS

During the years that I have been working on this project I have enjoyed the assistance of many individuals and institutions. I should especially like to thank Professor George H. Reese, formerly director of the Center for Textual and Editorial Studies in Humanistic Sources at the University of Virginia, and Professor William W. Abbot, editor of The Papers of George Washington at the same institution, for supervising the preparation of an earlier version of this book.

The bulk of the documents in this collection are among the manuscripts of the Associates of the late Rev. Dr. Bray, now housed in the archives of the United Society for the Propagation of the Gospel, in London. I am indebted to Mrs. Brenda Hough and Mr. Ian Pearson, former and current archivists at U.S.P.G., for providing me with photocopies of documents and for answering my numerous queries concerning the collection. For permission to reproduce transcriptions of documents in the Associates' manuscript collection I thank D. F. Fromings, secretary to the Managing Associates. For permission to reproduce transcriptions of documents in other collections I thank Mr. William H. Runge, curator of the Tracy W. McGregor Library, University of Virginia (for eleven items from the McGregor Library); the American Philosophical Society, Philadelphia (for eight items from the Society's Benjamin Franklin Papers); and His Grace the Archbishop of Canterbury and the Trustees of Lambeth Palace Library (for three items from the Fulham Papers).

I must also gratefully acknowledge the financial assistance of the Center for Textual and Editorial Studies as well as a research grant from the Johnson Fund of the American Philosophical Society that allowed me to travel to England in the spring of 1980 to study several manuscript collections that were otherwise inaccessible. Edward C. Carter II, editor of The Papers of Benjamin Henry Latrobe, generously granted me a one-month leave of absence from my position as associate editor of the Latrobe Papers so that I could undertake the trip to England.

At the University of Illinois Press I benefitted from the efforts of Donald Jackson, formerly consulting editor, who first expressed an interest in this work; August Meier, editor of the Blacks in the New World Series, who helped me give the book (and particularly the Introduction) its present shape; and Cynthia Mitchell, who provided a close and careful reading of the manuscript.

Portions of the Introduction appeared, in a different form, as "Impediments to the Christianization and Education of Blacks in Colonial America: The Case of the Associates of Dr. Bray," in *The Historical Magazine of the Protestant Episcopal Church* 50 (1981): 243–69. I am grateful to the editor, Dr. John F. Woolverton, for permission to reprint it here.

The publication of this book has been aided by a generous subvention from the National Historical Publications and Records Commission.

My wife, Christine, has provided constant support and encouragement, and her helpful suggestions have left their positive imprint on this work.

INTRODUCTION

The turn of the eighteenth century witnessed the first stirrings of a concerted effort by adherents of the Church of England to ameliorate the condition of black slaves in the New World. This concern for the spiritual and temporal welfare of blacks, though important, was but part of a missionary and philanthropic movement of much greater scope within the Established Church. New organizations such as the Society for Promoting Christian Knowledge (S.P.C.K.), established in 1699; the Society for the Propagation of the Gospel in Foreign Parts (S.P.G.), established in 1701; and the Associates of the Late Rev. Dr. Bray, established in 1723/24 and reorganized in 1729/30, began to carry the message of Anglicanism to the outer reaches of the British Empire.

This volume deals with the work in the American colonies of the Associates of Dr. Bray, an organization concerned with the conversion and education of blacks, both slave and free, in the American colonies; with the establishment of libraries and the distribution of books both in the British Isles and in the colonies; and, for a time, with the founding of the colony of Georgia. The Associates continued their work in America—primarily among blacks—until 1777, when they temporarily ceased their activities there because of the disruptions caused by the American Revolution.

The documents that comprise this collection of correspondence are mostly letters from the American representatives of the Associates to the secretaries of the organization in London, and they deal primarily with the Americans' efforts to convert and educate colonial blacks. The letters are important in that they detail the several methods the Associates used over the years to prosecute their design, and because they chronicle the difficulties the Americans encountered in forwarding this work—impediments that in the end were cumulatively of such weight as to crush almost any hope of widespread or long-term success.

1

Despite the rather meager results of the Associates' enterprise, the records the organization left are a source of illuminating information about early America. We learn something of the nature of eighteenth-century Anglo-American philanthropy, and the letters from the Americans constitute important accounts of colonial American slavery, education, religion, and society. In all, this collection of documents should afford historians of various backgrounds and interests new insights into colonial America.

Thomas Bray's Plan

The Rev. Thomas Bray (1658–1729/30) was the chief architect of and the prime mover behind the formation of all three of the missionary and philanthropic organizations mentioned above. A native of Marton, Shropshire, Bray entered All Souls College, Oxford, as *puer pauper* in March 1674/75.[1] There he "became a considerable Proficient in Theological Studies" and took an A.B. in November 1678.[2] Meager finances prevented Bray from remaining longer at Oxford, and he probably returned home, for when he entered into holy orders three years later, he became curate of Bridgnorth in his native county. Soon after, Bray moved to Warwickshire as private chaplain to Sir Thomas Price of Park Hall and as vicar of Marston. With this move, Bray began to enjoy the patronage of wealthy and influential men who would promote both his clerical career and his missionary and philanthropic schemes. His presence in Warwickshire and "his exemplary Behaviour and distinguished Diligence in his Calling" brought Bray to the attention of Simon, Lord Digby, who recommended the young clergyman to his brother and heir, William. William first presented Bray to the vicarage of Over Whitacre and then, in 1690, to the vacant rectory of Sheldon, also in Warwickshire. While at Sheldon, Bray composed his famous catechetical lectures, "the first Fruits of his Piety and Learning," which were published in 1696 as *A Course of Lectures upon the Church Catechism*.[3]

Bray's initial contact with colonial affairs came in the fall of 1695, when Henry Compton, the bishop of London, selected Bray to be his commissary in Maryland.[4] Bray accepted the office, but he did not sail for Maryland for four years. In the meantime he appointed a curate for Sheldon and moved to London, where his ideas began to coalesce and the missionary and philanthropic enterprises he later founded began to take shape in his mind. After failing in 1697 to secure Parliamentary assistance "for the Propagation of the true Religion in the Plantations,"[5] Bray drew up "A General Plan of the Constitution of a Protestant Congregation or Society for Propagating

Christian Knowledge."[6] Bray envisioned an organization whose goals were to supply the colonies with missionaries, provide parochial libraries for the missionaries abroad and the clergy at home, and establish charity schools at home "for the Education of poor Children in Reading, Writing, and more Especially in the Principles of the Christian Religion." At this early date, before Bray had yet visited America, he expressed particular concern for Indians and blacks. In his plan he proposed granting pensions as rewards to those missionaries who "most hazard their persons in Attempting the Conversion of the Negroes or Native Indians." Although this society did not materialize immediately, the plan contained the seeds of the activities that would later occupy the S.P.C.K., the S.P.G., and the Associates of Dr. Bray.

Since a royal charter for his "Protestant Congregation" could not then be obtained, Bray formed a voluntary society dedicated to much the same ends. On 8 March 1698/99 Bray and four laymen held the first meeting of the Society for Promoting Christian Knowledge.[7] The new society took as its province most of the projects outlined by Bray in his "General Plan." In addition, the members hoped to stem the tide of atheism and Quakerism (virtually synonymous!), found lending libraries throughout England and Wales, print and distribute books, reform prison conditions, and combat profaneness and immorality. With regard to the American colonies, the new Society was determined to support Bray's plans to send missionaries and libraries. At their first meeting they asked Bray to submit a "Scheme for Promoting Religion in the Plantations," which he did two months later at the meeting of 4 May 1699. In addition to providing missionaries and libraries, Bray's plans called for establishing free catechetical schools for the children of poor planters, establishing plantations "stock'd with some Negroes" to provide additional maintenance for married clergymen, bringing back "the Quakers, who are so numerous in those parts, to the Christian Faith," and converting the Indians by educating some of their youth in the Christian religion and sending them back to convert their tribes.[8]

The one aspect of Bray's "General Plan" of which the S.P.C.K. took no notice was that concerning the conversion of blacks. Bray, however, had already conceived the plans that would ultimately result in the foundation of an organization devoted to that cause—the Associates of Dr. Bray. In 1699, while in Holland "to solicit King William's Protection and Encouragement to his good Designs," Bray encountered Abel Tassin, Sieur D'Allone, of the Hague. D'Allone was a French Huguenot refugee who became secretary to Princess Mary of Orange in 1680 and continued to be her secretary after she became queen of England in 1689. He was William III's secretary for Dutch affairs from 1698.[9] Bray confided his plans for the conversion of blacks to D'Allone, who was so taken with the idea that a correspondence on the subject developed between them that was to bear great fruit.

By 1699, then, Bray had explored the possibilities for several types of missionary and philanthropic enterprise—establishing libraries and charity schools at home, sending missionaries and books to the colonies, and providing for the conversion and education of America's Indians and blacks. By 1699, also, it was time for Bray (now Dr. Bray, he having taken B.D. and D.D. degrees) to gain a firsthand knowledge of life in the colonies, or at least one colony. He embarked for Maryland in December 1699 and arrived in the colony the following March, but his stay in Maryland was to be short. Bray helped secure the passage of an act establishing the Church of England in the colony that May, and he returned to England shortly thereafter to seek royal assent to the bill. The Board of Trade objected to certain particulars of the act, and Bray drafted a bill according to their instructions, with the understanding that it would be confirmed if passed in Maryland. The colonial assembly passed the new bill in March 1701/2.[10]

Although Bray was never again to set foot in America, his influence there was only beginning to be felt. Soon after his return to England he realized the inadequacy of the S.P.C.K. in dealing with the manifold duties it had undertaken, and he petitioned the crown to charter a missionary society. The charter, granted by William III on 16 June 1701, established the Society for the Propagation of the Gospel in Foreign Parts, an organization that complemented the S.P.C.K. by taking over responsibility for furnishing the plantations with missionaries. Thereafter the S.P.C.K. devoted itself to educational endeavors at home and had only tenuous connections with the colonies. The S.P.G. charter enjoined the Society not only to minister to the spiritual needs of the colonists, but also to make "such other Provision . . . as may be necessary for the Propagation of the Gospell in those Parts."[11] Although this clause was interpreted to mean the conversion of the heathen, such work was not the highest priority of the S.P.G. Thus Bray's efforts on behalf of America's Indians and blacks, particularly the latter, did not take institutional form until the establishment of the Associates of Dr. Bray in 1723/24.

Bray and D'Allone's Bequest

Earlier work among blacks grew out of the partnership formed by Bray and D'Allone in 1699. Little is known of their relationship during the eighteen-year period between that first meeting in Holland

and 1717, when D'Allone gave Bray and Robert Hales, a friend of Bray and a clerk of the Privy Council, £100 to make "an Experiment of what cou'd be done in forwarding so good a work [i.e., converting blacks]."[12] After consulting with some gentlemen from South Carolina to determine that Charleston would be a proper place to undertake such work, Bray and Hales sent a Mr. Clifford to South Carolina, the first of many missionaries, catechists, schoolmasters, and schoolmistresses that Bray, and later his Associates, employed to convert and educate American blacks.[13]

D'Allone must have been pleased with Bray's efforts, for his will, written on 1 July 1721, stipulated that one-tenth of his English estate, as well as arrears due him from a pension from the crown, were "to be deliver'd to the Revd. Dr. Thomas Bray & his Associates that a Capital fund or Stock may be made thereof together with that little he has recd. from me before & that the yearly Income or proceed thereof be bestowed & employed in the Erecting a School or Schools for the thorough Instructing in the Christian Religion the Young Children of Negro Slaves & such of their Parents as shew themselves inclinable & desirous to be so instructed."[14] After D'Allone's death in 1723, Bray learned that the bequest amounted to £900, but there was some initial uncertainty as to who would administer the fund. Who in fact *were* "Dr. Thomas Bray & his Associates"?

Around Christmas 1723 Bray was so dangerously ill that his life was despaired of. In order to put the D'Allone bequest on a firm legal footing in the event of Bray's death, Henry Temple, first Viscount Palmerston, one of the executors of D'Allone's will, "was pleas'd to intimate, that it would be requisite he [Bray] should nominate and appoint, by Deed, such as he would desire to have Associates with him in the Disposition of the Legacy."[15] This Bray did in an instrument dated 15 January 1723/24, by which he appointed John, Viscount Percival, later first earl of Egmont of the Irish peerage; Robert Hales; Hales's brother, the Rev. Stephen Hales; and William Belitha.[16] Bray soon recovered from his illness, but the exigency had prompted the establishment, by deed, of trustees of D'Allone's legacy—the first "Associates."

Bray's action was challenged just one year later, when the S.P.G. learned that the D'Allone legacies were to be settled. In February 1724/25 the Society referred the matter to its standing committee and agreed that Bray "and the other Persons concern'd have Notice that the Committee have directions to receive any Evidence they [Bray and the men he had named] can produce, that the said Bequest does belong to Dr. Bray and those Gentlemen nominated by him and not this Society."[17] In short, the S.P.G. was contending that the phrase "Bray &

his Associates" could be construed as meaning the S.P.G. itself, and the Society placed the burden of proof on Bray to provide evidence to the contrary.

Bray obliged the S.P.G., five days later submitting his evidence. He was apparently not even certain himself what D'Allone intended when he bequeathed the funds, for when Palmerston informed him of the bequest, Bray attempted "to come at the meaning of Mr. D'Allone in those General words of his will (To Dr. Bray & his Associates)." Bray had to read over letters and other papers that had passed between himself, D'Allone, and Robert Hales regarding the conversion of blacks before he was able to conclude that D'Allone "had never given the least Intimation or hint by Lettre or otherwise to the Dr. of his Intentions to have the [S.P.G.] Consulted or concerned in that affair."[18] In March the standing committee examined Bray's evidence and acknowledged that he and his four Associates had indeed been entrusted with the bequest, and the Society at large concurred in the committee's assessment.[19]

D'Allone's will makes it clear that Bray and his Associates were to use the legacy exclusively for the "Instructing in the Christian Religion" of blacks, but it was difficult for Bray, who had long conceived both blacks and Indians to be the "heathen" of America, to restrict his activities to blacks alone.[20] He had written in 1698 that "it would . . . become the Professors of so Excellent a Religion as ours, to have a Provision made in one or two Schools at leastwise, in every Province, for the Instruction of half a dozen _Indian_ Youth, to be sent afterwards amongst their own People, to civilize and convert them,"[21] and in 1727 Bray still asserted that such work was a legitimate secondary concern of the D'Allone trustees.[22] However, the Associates sent books to only a few Indian missionaries and supported only one school for Indians in the American colonies, and that for a short time;[23] they directed the vast majority of their efforts in colonial America toward the conversion and education of blacks, both slave and free.

Bray's own ideas about blacks were not equivocal. He considered them barbarous and heathen, and he accepted the institution of slavery. His concern was for the blacks' immortal souls, not their temporal condition. We have seen that in his 1699 "Scheme for Promoting Religion in the Plantations" Bray called for supporting clergymen through the labor of slaves. In April 1701, in sending Gabriel D'Emilian to Maryland as a missionary, Bray granted him £133.12.10 "for his own Subsistense & to purchase 2 Negroes to Stock his Glebe he having a Family."[24] And in February 1701/2, in "A Memorial Shewing the Necessity of one to Superintend the Church and Clergy in Mary Land," Bray proposed to raise an adequate stipend for a commissary by purchasing 500 acres of good land to be worked by twenty slaves in order to raise tobacco and other commodities.[25]

Bray's initial plans for dispensing the D'Allone bequest called for granting a small annual allowance to missionaries going to the colonies or ministers already settled there who would instruct blacks in Christianity. Since the fund at first yielded less than £40 per annum, Bray realized that he could not send missionaries to convert blacks solely on the Associates' account. His hope therefore was to enlist the colonial clergy in his enterprise by "Giving five or ten pounds when it can be afforded, as an Addition to their other Income," so that "a hundred pounds a Year will provide Ten or Twenty Instructors, & those the best Qualify'd, whereas Five hundred or a Thousand pounds per Anna must be expended in maintaining the same Number of Catechists sent on purpose having none other Maintenance than what can be provided from hence."[26] Three Maryland clergymen had earlier assured him that the parochial clergy were "the most proper Persons to whose Care and Conduct this Affair should be Committed," provided they were supplied with books.[27] This early method devised by Bray—of securing the assistance of the colonial clergy and supplying only a small allowance and books with which to instruct blacks— enjoyed the prospect of reaching a great number of potential converts at a relatively small cost.

Little is known of the Associates' activities during the six years between their foundation in January 1723/24 and Bray's death on 15 February 1729/30, but we know that Bray's method of dispensing the fund was being implemented. One month before his death Bray stated that he and his Associates had, in accordance with D'Allone's will, "employed and supply'd with necessary Books both for Catechists and Catechumens about twenty Missionaries together with direccions how to have the Negroes and Heathens [i.e., Indians] instructed in the Christian Religion in the English Plantations."[28]

There was, however, some disagreement among the Associates as to the most effective means of using the D'Allone funds. Bray's approach was not without its critics, especially Percival, whose relationship with Bray greatly influenced the course of events during the early years of the Associates. Percival was known as a prideful man who was "conscious of his own dignity" and "pompous and egotistical."[29] His secondary role in the disposition of the D'Allone legacy and his inability to determine the fate of the fund no doubt led to his disaffection from Bray and the early Associates.

When Bray first approached Percival, probably around Christmas of 1723, regarding the D'Allone legacy and the creation of a trust to administer it, Percival "absolutely refused to be Concerned with" it, though "prest to it by Dr. Bray & others from him." Bray apparently appointed Percival a trustee in the instrument of 15 January 1723/24 without his prior permission and, having done so, failed to inform him of the action, for Percival claimed to have only accidentally learned of his inclusion in the trust in mid-February 1724/25, more than a year later. Upon learning of his appointment, and being uncertain of the nature of the new organization, Percival wrote to the secretary of the S.P.G., stating that other avocations and his family's ill health prevented him from participating in the affairs of the D'Allone trustees and requesting that Bray "may be moved to raise out my Name."[30] The S.P.G. forwarded the letter to Bray, but Percival's resignation was not effected.

Early in 1725/26, Percival changed his mind and accepted the D'Allone trust in the hope of forwarding a scheme of his friend the Rev. George Berkeley, dean of Derry. Berkeley's plan, outlined in his *Proposal for the Better Supplying of Churches in Our Foreign Plantations*, was to establish a college in Bermuda for training missionaries and converting North American Indians, but he was willing to add to that the duty of "breeding up young Negroes agreeable to Mr. Delons will" in order to qualify to receive the £900 legacy.[31] According to Berkeley and Daniel Dering, a Dublin cousin of Percival, all of the Associates except Bray himself favored this method of disposing of the D'Allone bequest,[32] so Percival agreed to take on the trust. As he explained to Dering: "I did not intend to concern my self with Mr. Dalones Legacy, and accordingly gave Dr. Bray a positive Refusàl, but since there is a disposition in the other Associates to give the money to Dean Berkeley's Colledge I will on that Condition Act."[33]

Despite the fact that his four Associates looked favorably on the dean's chimerical scheme, Bray did not consent to such a drastic alteration in the disposition of the fund. In fact, although ill, he marshalled his strength in an effort to defeat Berkeley's entire plan. His opposition to Berkeley's proposed college was based on more than the knowledge that it threatened Bray's own plans for the use of the D'Allone legacy. The dean's *Proposal* had cast aspersions on the quality of the colonial clergy, asserting that they "have proved, too many of them, very meanly qualified both in Learning and morals for the Discharge of their Office," and that many of them "quit their native Country on no other Motive, than that they are not able to procure a Livelihood in it." Bray took such charges as an indictment of his long-term efforts to provide well-educated and dedicated clergymen for the colonies. He bitterly resented Berkeley's insinuations, and he was not quick to forgive.[34]

In reply Bray in 1727 published *Missionalia; or, A Collection of Mis-*

sionary Pieces Relating to the Conversion of the Heathen; Both the African Negroes and American Indians, part of which dealt with Berkeley's *Proposal* point by point, demonstrating the absurdity of attempting to convert Indians far from their native country. Because of Bray's vehement defense of his own plans for utilizing the D'Allone bequest, the effort to divert the fund to Berkeley's proposed college was as unsuccessful as the dean's scheme itself proved to be. Bray retained control of the bequest, and Percival, no doubt mortified by Bray's vitriolic attack on his friend, was left as he had been before his acceptance of the trust—an unwilling member of an organization with whose leader he disagreed.

The Formation of the Associates of Dr. Bray and the Georgia Trustees

At this juncture several important occurrences coincided to produce a major alteration in the structure and aims of the Associates. The resulting enlargement and reorganization of the Associates facilitated the founding of Georgia and laid the groundwork for the most active period in the Associates' work among American blacks. In 1727 a friend of Bray's, after a visit to Whitechapel Prison in London, represented to Bray the dreadful state of the prisoners and the miserable conditions in which they were confined. At this Bray "immediately apply'd himself to solicit Benefactions, in order to relieve them," and soon he was able to provide bread, beef, and broth on Sundays.[35] Early in 1729 the House of Commons also interested themselves in ameliorating prison conditions. On a motion by James Edward Oglethorpe, the Commons on 25 February 1728/29 appointed a committee "to enquire into the State of the Gaols of the Kingdom."[36] One result of the work of the committee was a proposal to release thousands of debtors from prison and, later, a plan to settle them in America. Thus Bray and Oglethorpe shared an interest in improving the plight of prisoners.[37]

They shared as well an interest in a £15,000 charitable legacy left by Joseph King, a London haberdasher. King's bequest was to be disposed of by three trustees: a Mr. Gordon, his heir; Thomas Carpenter; and a Mr. Smith of one of the Inns of Court. For several years before his own death in February 1729/30, Bray had drawn up various memorials and proposals in order to insure the "proper Application" of the bequest.[38] Bray's efforts, however, were unsuccessful because the three trustees could not agree on the disposition of the funds. Carpenter and Smith were seventy years old, and Gordon, the heir, hoped to outlive the elder trustees and apply the funds to his own use.

9

This dispute among the trustees set the scene for Oglethorpe's involvement in the affair. The two old gentlemen hoped to place the legacy in the hands of a master in Chancery pending the appointment of new trustees. When Gordon challenged this attempt, Oglethorpe represented Carpenter and Smith in court. He won the suit, and on appeal by Gordon, the initial decision was upheld by the Lord Chancellor. Carpenter and Smith then proposed to give £5,000 of the legacy to Oglethorpe and a charitable colony trust, provided "that the trust should be annexed to some trusteeship already in being."[39]

The imposition of such a condition forced Oglethorpe to seek out a charitable organization that would be willing to take on the added responsibility of establishing a colony. As it happened, Bray, in poor health and with only a few months to live, was then casting about for some way to enlarge the number and increase the scope of his organization to insure that it would survive his passing. Colonization appeared to be an appropriate means to accomplish that end. Bray's own interest in colonization dated from the early 1720s, when he encouraged the schemes of Captain Thomas Coram and Jean Pierre Purry of Neuchâtel.[40] In fact, according to Coram, Bray had worked out his own plan for a charitable colony independently of Oglethorpe. As Coram later explained:

> a little before Christmas 1729 his Death he found drew near for he was sure by his continued decay he should not live out the Winter yet he would before he dyed find out a way to have a Settlement made for the Releife of such honest poor Distressed Families from hence as by Losses, want of Employment or otherwise are reduced to poverty and such who were persecuted for their professing the protestant Religion abroad, to be happy by their Labour and Industry in some part of His Majesties Dominions in America.[41]

In the winter of 1729/30, then, Bray and Oglethorpe fortuitously came together. Both wished to relieve debtors; both favored the establishment of a charitable colony; both sought funds from the King bequest; and Bray was seeking to enlarge the Associates and guarantee their continued existence at the same time Oglethorpe sought to annex his charitable colony trust to an established organization. Bray and three of the four original Associates therefore executed a legal document on 15 January 1729/30, exactly six years after Bray's deed naming the four original D'Allone trustees and exactly one month before his death, which devolved the authority to administer the D'Allone legacy upon a larger body of men.[42]

The document named twenty-eight new Associates: the Rev.

Digby Cotes, the Rev. Arthur Bedford, the Rev. Samuel Smith, the Rev. Richard Bundy, the Rev. John Burton, Edward Digby, Edward Harley, Thomas Coram, James Oglethorpe, James Vernon, Edward Hughes, Thomas Towers, Robert Hucks, Rogers Holland, John Laroche, Charles Selwyn, Robert Moore, James Lowther, William Sloper, Oliver St. John, Adam Anderson, George Carpenter, Henry Hastings, the Rev. Richard King, John Campbell, Erasmus Philipps, Thomas Carpenter, and a Mr. Smith of one of the Inns of Court. Not all of these men participated in the enlarged Associates, however. The last five listed here—King, Campbell, Philipps, Thomas Carpenter, and Smith (the latter two no doubt the King trustees)—did not. The first twenty-three did become Associates, and their names are recorded in the minutes of the meeting of 30 July 1730 along with the names of three other members apparently elected sometime after 15 January. Those three were the Rev. Daniel Somerscales, George Heathcote, and Francis Eyles.[43]

Percival never signed the feoffment, although a space with seal was left for his signature. He was then inactive in the organization and was therefore not involved in the collaboration between Bray and Oglethorpe concerning the charitable colony project and the enlargement of the Associates. Bray and Oglethorpe apparently recognized the feoffment as legally defective, since it lacked Percival's signature. Thus on 13 February 1729/30 Oglethorpe approached Percival hoping to gain Percival's assent to the increase in the number of Associates and the adoption of the charitable colony project, thereby legalizing the enlargement and making it possible for the Associates to receive a portion of the King legacy. It was clear to Oglethorpe that Percival had virtually no interest in administering the D'Allone legacy but that his cooperation was essential for the legal enlargement of the Associates and the receipt of the promised £5,000 from the King legacy. Realizing that he might be able to arouse Percival's interest in the project to found a colony but that Percival would resist becoming involved again in the D'Allone branch of the trust, Oglethorpe told him that acceptance of responsibility for the charitable colony trust did not require acceptance of responsibility for the D'Allone legacy.[44] Percival accepted Oglethorpe's "Overture with pleasure."[45] Thus as in 1726, Percival again agreed to participate in the work of the Associates in order to forward a scheme he favored but not to administer the D'Allone bequest according to Bray's dictates.

Percival's failure to sign the feoffment once he had agreed to accept the reorganization may be attributed to his belief that the trust could not be legally enlarged by such an instrument.[46] Thus the legal defects of the feoffment obviated the need for him to sign it. The Asso-

ciates shortly thereafter reached the same conclusion as had Percival—
that a legal remedy for the defective feoffment had to be sought from
the High Court of Chancery. On 24 June 1730 Oglethorpe laid the
Associates' cause before Sir Joseph Jeckyl, Master of the Rolls, "who
spoke with Respect of the new Society formed thereby, and not only
promised it all the Encouragement, which lay in his Power, but also
gave a final Decree, the most advantageous to the Society, which could
be desired."[47]

The decree has not been discovered, but it apparently named
twenty-nine or thirty men.[48] If it named twenty-nine men, they were
presumably those whose names were recorded in the minutes of the
meeting of 30 July 1730. If it named thirty men, then one must have
died or declined the trust before 30 July. In either case, the Chancery
decree of 24 June 1730 apparently did not confirm the authority of
the men named in the feoffment, but rather confirmed the authority
of the Associates as the group existed on 24 June—that is, without
King, Campbell, Philipps, Thomas Carpenter, and Smith, and with
Somerscales, Heathcote, Eyles, and perhaps one other man.

The Associates as reorganized, then, concerned themselves with
forwarding three different designs: the conversion and education of
blacks under the D'Allone legacy; the establishment of parochial libraries by virtue of a legacy left for that purpose by Bray, who also left
a great store of books that the Associates took over and gradually distributed; and the founding of a charitable colony to be funded, it was
hoped, by the King legacy.

The project to establish a charitable colony clearly had the highest priority. At their first meeting after the enlargement, held on
21 March 1730, the Associates agreed "to do whatever shall be thought
proper for them to promote so good a Design." On 1 July 1730 they
agreed to try to "obtain a Grant of Lands in America, that such poor
Persons may be transplanted thither, who shall be willing to go beyond the Seas for their better Maintainance," and on 30 July James
Vernon laid before the Associates a draft of a petition to the king for a
grant "of certain Lands to the Southward of Carolina." The following
14 January, Percival, George Carpenter, Vernon, Heathcote, Hucks,
Towers, Eyles, Laroche, Oglethorpe, and Moore were appointed a
committee of the Associates "for Solliciting the Grant for the Lands
designed for the Charitable Colony in South Carolina in America."[49]
One year later, on 27 January 1731/32, the Privy Council approved
the charter for the group. The king signed it on 21 April, and it
passed the seals on 9 June 1732. The charter created "The Trustees
for Establishing the Colony of Georgia in America," and it named
Percival the first president of the Trustees.[50] Of the twenty-nine Asso-

ciates, twenty-one signed the petition to the crown and were named in the charter as Trustees. The eight Associates who did not sign the petition and were thus not named in the charter were Cotes, Harley, Hughes, Selwyn, Lowther, St. John, Hastings, and Somerscales. Thus although the Georgia Trust derived institutionally from the enlarged Associates, the two groups were not entirely coextensive.

The period between the granting of the Georgia charter and the official separation of the Georgia Trustees from the Associates of Dr. Bray on 31 May 1733 is important to an understanding of the evolution of the two organizations. It is clear from the Associates' Minute Book that the business of establishing the colony on a firm footing was the highest priority of the composite organization. The Minute Book records no meeting of the Associates between 6 July 1732 and 31 May 1733—an eleven-month hiatus during which the Associates met only as the Georgia Trustees and kept a separate journal.[51] As their energies were directed toward raising funds and recruiting settlers for the new colony, concern with the other two branches of their work temporarily waned, and the Georgia Trustees routinely handled the few items of non-Georgia business that arose during this period.[52]

The initial decision to concentrate on the affairs of Georgia at the expense of the other two endeavors was forced on the Trustees by the pressing nature of the first year of the Georgia enterprise. By May 1733, though, the Georgia Trustees had concluded that their charter did not authorize them to administer the D'Allone legacy for converting blacks or Bray's legacy for promoting parochial libraries.[53] They may have been brought to this conclusion by the enlargement of the Georgia Trust that occurred at the meeting of 15 March 1732/33, when seventeen new Trustees joined those named in the charter.[54] But whereas all the charter Trustees were Associates, none of the seventeen new Trustees ever became an Associate. With the personnel of the two organizations no longer so similar, the Georgia Trustees could no longer routinely conduct the Associates' business along with Georgia business, as they had been doing. Also, on 10 May 1733 the House of Commons granted £10,000 to the Trustees, the first of thirteen grants that totalled more than £136,000 over the life of the Trust.[55] This grant allowed the Trustees the financial means necessary to pursue their objective independently of the Associates. The separation of 31 May 1733, then, seems to have resulted from the changes in membership and financing of the Georgia Trust.[56]

Not all the Associates accepted the separation as inevitable and beneficial. To some it was tantamount to a repudiation of the trusts for converting blacks and establishing libraries. Thomas Coram believed that most of the Associates were concerned only with Georgia affairs: "There are not many of those associates who gives themselves any Trouble about the other two Matters, but I believe I may venture to say the better sort of them do."[57] James Vernon "took it ill" that some of the young members of the Georgia Trust had "separated the Colony affairs and the members of it from the care of Mr. Dalone's legacy for converting blacks, and Dr. Bray's improvement of that design, of which others of the Trustees for Georgia are Trustees."[58] And at the time of the separation, Percival declared that the hope of receiving £5,000 from the King legacy for the Georgia project was the motive behind the enlargement of the Associates and that when nothing was received from the King legacy, "Some gentlemen desired the Two Trusts might be Separated, the One having no relation to the other."[59]

Such statements suggest the existence of "pious" and "parliamentary" groups within the Associates and raise the question of whether the contingent of Parliament men who joined the Associates in 1729/30 did so only to secure an institutional base from which to apply for support for the Georgia project from the trustees of the King legacy.[60] Albert B. Saye has asserted that the members of Parliament who became Associates in 1730 did so only nominally and took no part in the activities of the charitable society. Speaking of the members of the Parliamentary Gaols Committees who became Associates in 1730, Saye has more recently reiterated his belief, stating, "The natural conclusion seems to be that Oglethorpe brought these members into the 'new Society' for promoting his scheme of colonization, and that they became Trustees of Georgia not because they were Associates, but rather that they became Bray Associates from their interest in the Georgia project."[61]

Verner Crane adduced some evidence in an attempt to refute Saye's notion. He pointed out that William Sloper was the only member of Parliament among the enlarged Associates who never attended a meeting of the Associates. All the others, Crane stated, attended at some time, and several of them, particularly Oglethorpe himself, were active members.[62] Yet an examination of the Associates' Minute Books seems to support Saye's claim that the parliamentary Associates were only nominally interested in the conversion of blacks and the establishment of libraries. Crane's statement that all but one of the members of Parliament among the Associates attended a meeting was based on the attendance records of all the Associates' meetings after the enlargement. As we have seen, the securing of the Georgia charter and the establishment of the colony on a firm footing were high priorities of the reorganized society, and the parliamentary contingent may have attended meetings between the enlargement and the separation of the Associates from the Georgia Trustees in order to forward the Georgia scheme. A more telling test of the motives for which the members of Parliament joined the Associates is to examine their attendance at Associates' meetings held after the separation of 31 May 1733. Such an examination conclusively demonstrates that, as Saye has claimed, the members of Parliament were on the whole little interested in the trusts for the conversion of blacks and the establishment of libraries, and it corroborates the statements of Coram, Vernon, and Percival that there were in fact two factions within the enlarged Associates: those interested in all three branches of the composite society, and those interested only, or primarily, in the charitable colony project. Of the ten Associates who served on the Parliamentary Gaols Committees and became Trustees of Georgia, only five—Hucks, Laroche, Towers, Holland, and Oglethorpe—ever attended a meeting of the Associates after the separation.[63]

But Saye's critique of the parliamentary Associates, however accurate, should not obscure the existence of the group of men interested in all three branches of the composite society. We should not forget that the Georgia charter named as Trustees all the Associates who signed the petition to the crown, not just those who were members of Parliament. Thus "pious" members of the Associates played a great role in the founding of the colony and several, particularly Samuel Smith, Stephen Hales, James Vernon, Adam Anderson, Thomas Coram, Richard Bundy, and John Burton, were among the most active Georgia Trustees. It should not be assumed, therefore, that the Georgia project was entirely the result of the labors of the parliamentary Associates, for we have seen that Bray himself played a crucial role in laying the foundation for the colony, and his "pious" colleagues were deeply involved in securing the charter and administering the new colony.

While realizing that after the separation no Parliament man regularly attended the Associates' meetings, we should, nevertheless, recognize the importance of the charitable colony project to the later fortunes of the Associates. The project was the occasion of the collaboration between Bray and Oglethorpe that brought about the enlargement of the organization and was, therefore, responsible for bringing into the Associates several members who served all three branches of the society with much dedication. Although during the period from July 1732 to May 1733 the Associates' activities virtually ceased as the group was subsumed within the Georgia Trust, the Associates emerged with renewed vigor. With the removal of Georgia business from their concerns, the small group of faithful members—Vernon, Bedford, Coram, Smith, Anderson, and Hales—met regularly and devoted great energy to the two original mandates of the Associates: the conversion of blacks in America and the establishment of parochial libraries both at home and abroad. Fittingly, his memories of conflict with Bray now forgotten, Percival overcame the disaffection he had formerly felt toward the Associates and became one of the most dedicated members.

The Associates' Activities in the Colonies

After Georgia had been founded and the Trustees for the colony had become a distinct organization, the Associates concentrated their effort in the colonies on the Christianization and education of blacks. They expended the vast proportion of their funds and energies in this endeavor, and the preponderance of this work among all their activities in America is reflected in the correspondence that follows. Yet the Associates were not inactive in the American colonies with regard to the establishment of libraries and the distribution of books for purposes other than the instruction of blacks. (This was particularly true in the 1730s and early 1740s, when their efforts to promote the instruction of blacks had not yet taken shape.)

Besides the instances that are noted in the correspondence below,[64] the Associates in 1736 established a parochial library in Savannah, Georgia. In 1741 they ordered two copies of each book in their store given to Thomas Coram to be sent to Taunton, Massachusetts, toward founding a parochial library there, and in 1755 the Associates appropriated £20 to "be laid out in Books to found a Parochial Library in Pennsylvania."[65] In addition the Associates distributed books to the Rev. John Fulton, a missionary going to South Carolina in 1730, to an unidentified "Gentleman who is Going over as a Missionary to settle in Virginia" in 1733, and to the Rev. John Andrews, a clergyman going to Charleston in 1753.[66] These small catechetical libraries generally contained a variety of religious tracts, prayer books, and testaments, but sometimes the Associates sent large quantities of individual titles to the colonies for widespread distribution. Thus we find that in 1737 they sent 300 copies of *A Short and Easy Method for the Instructing of Youth in the Principles of Religion* to the Rev. John Wesley at Savannah, "to be distributed for the use of such Instruction of the Children in Georgia as he shall think best." And in 1753 they shipped 400 copies of Gilbert West's *Observations on the History and Evidence of the Resurrection of Jesus Christ* and George Lyttleton's *Observations on the Conversion and Apostleship of St. Paul, in a Letter to Gilbert West, Esq.*, bound together (London, 1747), to Virginia, Maryland, and New England.[67]

It is clear that the Associates, although overwhelmingly Anglican in membership and interested in propagating the faith according to the tenets of the Church of England, were not averse to aiding non-Anglican Protestants. The three missionaries to the New England Indians who received books from the Associates in 1735 were all Harvard graduates and ordained Congregationalist ministers, and they were supported by the Edinburgh Society for Propagating Christian Knowledge among the Indians (also known as the Scottish S.P.C.K.), a missionary arm of the Presbyterian Church of Scotland.[68] The Associates sent twenty-four copies of Erasmus's *Ecclesiastes* to New England in 1733, most of which were distributed to Congregationalist clergymen, and they gave libraries to German Protestants in Philadelphia and Virginia and to the Swiss Protestants going to settle in Purrysburg, South Carolina.[69] As will be seen, they also supported catechists to the Negroes at Purrysburg.

Yet it was to the administration of the D'Allone bequest and other contributions for the conversion and education of colonial blacks that the Associates devoted themselves. During the more than fifty years between their founding by Bray and the cessation of their activities in the American colonies because of the disruptions caused by the Revolution, the Associates utilized several methods to instruct blacks in Christianity. We have seen that Bray himself initiated two of these methods—sending catechists or missionaries to the colonies and providing books to colonial clergymen who had agreed to undertake the instruction of blacks. After Bray's death, the Associates continued to employ these two methods and supplemented them with another that was truer to the letter of D'Allone's will—supporting formally established Negro schools in the American colonies.

The sending of catechists or missionaries to the colonies proved relatively unsuccessful. The Associates sent out catechists only twice, the first attempt to South Carolina in the 1730s, near the colony of Georgia that they had recently taken an important part in founding, and the second to Georgia itself in the 1750s. The initial object of their attention was a colony of Swiss Protestant refugees at Purrysburg. The promoter of the colony was Jean Pierre Purry of Neuchâtel, who in 1724 conceived a plan to establish Swiss and other foreign Protestants on the southern frontier of the American colonies to act as a buffer against the French and Spanish and their Indian allies. Purry finally arrived in Carolina in the early part of 1731 and, within a few months, had selected for his settlement a site known as the Great Yamassee Bluff on the north bank of the Savannah River about twenty miles up-river from where the town of Savannah would be established two years later. By July 1733 Purry had settled his tract with over 250 Swiss, and by the time of his death in 1736, he is said to have imported 600 Swiss colonists.[70]

Three considerations may have induced the Associates to first send catechists to South Carolina. The most important was probably Bishop of London Edmund Gibson's opinion, rendered early in 1734/35, that the conversion of American blacks be begun in that colony.[71] Second, the Associates may have settled on Purrysburg as the initial recipient of their largesse because of Thomas Bray's own interest in Purry's scheme. In 1726, Purry's agent, Jean Watt (or Vatt), included Bray among those he described as "our friends" in England, and Bray made a bequest of £5 to Mr. John Vatt, presumably the same man.[72] It is also possible that the Associates fixed on Purrysburg because of its proximity to Georgia. They certainly felt a keen interest in Georgia, yet, as black slaves were prohibited from the new colony, funds from the D'Allone legacy could not be expended there. Purrysburg, just upriver from the Georgia capital, was the closest settlement to the new colony. This supposition is supported by a statement made by the Rev. John Burton, an Associate and Georgia Trustee, in a letter of 28 September 1735 to John Wesley, a few weeks before Wesley's departure for Georgia as a missionary appointed by the Trustees: "One end for which we were associated was the conversion of negro slaves. As yet nothing has been attempted in this way; but a door is opened, and not far from home [i.e., Georgia]. The Purryburgers have purchased slaves; they act under our influence; and Mr. Oglethorpe will think it advisable to begin there."[73]

Whatever their motivation, the Associates resolved on 3 September 1735 that a salary of £30 per annum be provided for "a Person for Instructing the Negroes in Purysburgh." They requested Oglethorpe to "Inquire for a proper Person & the best manner of Settling him at Purysburgh."[74] Egmont's diary casts more light on the Associates' commitment to Purrysburg, for it reveals that of the £40 income that the D'Allone legacy yielded annually, £30 was to be expended for the catechist's salary, the remaining £10 "we reserve for buying books and other necessaries for this purpose."[75] Until the annual income of the Associates rose, then, Purrysburg was intended to be the sole recipient of funds from the D'Allone legacy.

Oglethorpe did not act hastily in the matter. It was not until almost a year and a half later that he first met Count Nikolaus Ludwig von Zinzendorf, leader of the Moravian Brethren, or *Unitas Fratrum*. Zinzendorf had arrived in England on 20 January 1736/37, partly to meet with the Georgia Trustees concerning a settlement of Moravians that had been established in the colony. Soon after his arrival, the Associates asked Zinzendorf to provide two catechists to convert the blacks at Purrysburg. On 23 February 1736/37, Zinzendorf "agreed that two of his Moravians now settled in Georgia should reside in Purysburg, for a yearly salary of £15 to each, houses to be built for them at the cost of Dr. Bray's Associates."[76]

Despite the fact that Zinzendorf intended to remove two Moravians from Georgia to Purrysburg, he sent two men from Europe to serve as catechists—"one of my chaplains, master [Peter] Bohler," and "[George] Schulius, a Moravian brother."[77] Boehler, who had studied theology at the University of Jena and was destined to rise to the rank of bishop of the Moravian Church, arrived with Schulius in London from Germany on 18 February 1737/38. Zinzendorf ordained Boehler minister to the Brethren in Savannah, and the Associates commissioned both men to instruct the blacks of Purrysburg in Christianity. The two missionaries embarked for America on 22 May 1738, and after many delays they arrived in Savannah on 16 October 1738.[78]

The mission of Boehler and Schulius to Purrysburg could not have been successful, as there were few blacks there to be Christianized. The Associates obviously knew little of the situation at Purrysburg, nor, apparently, were they apprised of it by Zinzendorf or others. The missionaries "could do no more than take upon them the care of some Swiss colonists and their children in the town of *Purisbury*, where no Negroes lived at that time."[79] Shortly after their arrival in Purrysburg, Boehler and Schulius traveled to Charleston. There they met the Rev. Alexander Garden, who proposed that the Negro school be opened at that place rather than at Purrysburg. He pointed out that the larger black population of Charleston offered better opportunities for catechizing, and he promised the missionaries all the assistance he could give. Boehler and Schulius, impressed with the prospect of achieving greater success at Charleston than at Purrysburg, returned to Savannah to obtain Oglethorpe's permission to alter the location of the school. Oglethorpe refused to allow them to deviate from the plan for Purrysburg, and Boehler and Schulius, though they "wished themselves free to proceed without his consent, wished they had not entered into an agreement with 'the associates of the late Dr. Bray,'" nonetheless felt bound to make an attempt at Purrysburg.[80] They finally settled there in February 1738/39. Schulius soon fell ill and died on 4 August 1739, and Boehler quit Purrysburg and sailed to Philadelphia with the remnants of the Georgia Moravians in April 1740.[81]

After the failure of their mission to Purrysburg, the Associates did not again consider sending a missionary to America until 1749, when they resolved that to "promote the Conversion of the Negroes, it is necessary to endeavour to send over a proper Person as an Itinerant

Teacher in the Principles of Christianity, to go to such Colonies as he shall be appointed." Nothing came of this resolution, however. Then in 1751, shortly after the Georgia Trustees altered their policy of excluding blacks from the colony, the Associates and the S.P.G. jointly appointed Joseph Ottolenghe catechist to the Negroes in Georgia.[82] Although the renunciation of the prohibition on slavery represented a devastating setback to the efforts of the Trustees to establish a stable colony of small farmers, the Trustees did try to mitigate the effect of the introduction of slavery into the colony by the new legislation itself. Harold Davis has stated that the act "constituted the most benign slave code that Georgia had in colonial times."[83] One section of the act stipulated that slave owners who failed to require their blacks "to attend at some time on the Lords Day for Instruction in the Christian Religion" would be subject to a fine of £10 for each offense.[84]

This provision for the religious instruction of blacks, coupled with the fact that in 1750 there was only one Anglican clergyman in Georgia, undoubtedly led to the appointment of Ottolenghe. However, Ottolenghe's wide range of other activities in the colony—as superintendent of the silk culture, Savannah representative in the Commons House of Assembly, justice of the peace, vestryman, and member of numerous commissions to carry out many public responsibilities—kept him from devoting as much time to the instruction of blacks as the S.P.G. and the Associates thought necessary, and those organizations terminated his services as catechist in 1759 and 1761, respectively.[85]

Thus, both of the Associates' attempts to support catechists in the American colonies ended unsuccessfully. The venture in Purrysburg was ill conceived and ill fated from the outset; that in Savannah arose from the Associates' desire to aid both the colony they had founded and that colony's black residents. That the Georgia venture met with little success was owing partly to Ottolenghe's extra-catechetical activities and partly to the nature of the slave system itself and the existence of many impediments to the Christianization of blacks, discussed below.

The Associates' Negro Schools

The final severing of relations between the Associates and Ottolenghe in 1761 came at a time when the Associates were exploring a different approach to the instruction of blacks. Indeed, since the late 1750s the Associates had been turning their attention to the establishment of organized, formal Negro schools in the colonies. In January 1757 the Rev. John Waring, the Associates' secretary, wrote to Benjamin

Franklin concerning the work of the organization. At that time the Associates apparently had not yet thought of the establishment of a school, for Waring cited the example of the Welsh circulating schools and asked Franklin if a similar scheme could "be set on foot in Your province for the Service of the blacks?"[86] The Associates were thus thinking still in terms of itinerant schoolmasters. Since Waring's letter arrived in Philadelphia after Franklin had sailed for London, his wife showed the letter to the Rev. William Sturgeon, who since 1747 had been S.P.G. catechist to the Negroes in Philadelphia. Sturgeon in turn wrote to Franklin in August, recommending that a school be opened in Philadelphia "under the Care and Inspection of the Minister, or some other prudent Person or Persons."[87] Franklin then communicated Sturgeon's proposal to Waring in January 1758. Obviously enthusiastic about the plan, Franklin saw its importance extending beyond Philadelphia: "A separate School for Blacks, under the Care of One, of whom People should have an Opinion that he would be careful to imbue the Minds of their young Slaves with good Principles, might probably have a Number of Blacks sent to it; and if on Experience it should be found useful, and not attended with the ill Consequences commonly apprehended, the Example might be followed in the other Colonies, and encouraged by the Inhabitants in general."[88]

Upon learning of the plan the Associates hesitantly proceeded toward an implementation of Sturgeon's and Franklin's vision. At their meeting of 1 February 1758, they agreed to consider at the next meeting whether it would be proper to open a school for black children in Philadelphia, and in the meantime they commissioned Waring to "get the best Information he can of such Particulars as may enable the Associates to Judge of the Propriety & Usefulness of such a School there." Such information could of course be had most readily from Franklin himself. Waring consulted Franklin about the expediency of opening a Negro school in Philadelphia, and at their meeting of 5 April 1758 the Associates agreed to a three-year trial of such a school at a maximum expense of £20 per annum.[89]

The Philadelphia school opened on 20 November 1758, with a mistress and thirty pupils under Sturgeon's direction. Boys were to be taught to read and girls were to be taught to read, sew, knit, and embroider. The mistress was to attend church with the children every Wednesday and Friday, and "all her Endeavours are to be directed towards making them Christians." The school was immediately successful, and in June 1759 Sturgeon reported that thirty-six scholars attended regularly.[90] Perhaps because of Sturgeon's report the Associates agreed in November 1759 to consider at their next meeting whether other schools should be opened "in Some of the British Plantations in America." When the subject was raised again on 2 January 1760, the Associates agreed to open three schools "with all Convenient Speed" in the plantations. They also requested Waring to inform Franklin of the decision and to solicit Franklin's assistance in the establishment of the schools. Although the idea of establishing Negro schools was implanted in the minds of the Associates by Sturgeon and Franklin and nourished by Sturgeon's early report of success, the Associates apparently reached the decision to increase the number of schools before seeking Franklin's advice. The Associates elected Franklin a member on 2 January, however, and when he attended his first meeting fifteen days later, they readily accepted his recommendations concerning the locations of the three prospective schools and the men to superintend them. Franklin suggested that New York, Williamsburg, and Newport were the most proper places in the British plantations for the additional Negro schools, and he recommended as superintendents of the schools the Rev. Messrs. Samuel Johnson, Henry Barclay, and Samuel Auchmuty, of New York; William Hunter and the Rev. Thomas Dawson, of Williamsburg; and the Rev. Thomas Pollen, of Newport.[91] Waring then wrote to the gentlemen to inform them of the Associates' intentions and to request their assistance in forwarding the "pious Undertaking" by opening schools "with all convenient Speed." The response was quite favorable, and the schools in New York and Williamsburg opened on 22 and 29 September 1760, respectively.[92]

The superintendence of the New York school soon fell to Auchmuty, who was S.P.G. catechist to the Negroes and assistant to Barclay, the rector of Trinity Church. Johnson's responsibilities as president of King's College and Barclay's responsibilities as rector of the city's Anglican community precluded their intimate involvement with the school. With Johnson's departure for Stratford, Connecticut, in 1763 and with Barclay's death in 1764, Auchmuty became sole administrator of the school, and he carried on the work and corresponded with the Associates until he closed the school following the death of the mistress in October 1774.[93]

In Virginia, both Dawson, the rector of Bruton Parish and the president of the College of William and Mary, and Hunter, the printer of the *Virginia Gazette*, accepted the charge and succeeded in establishing the Williamsburg school, but Dawson died exactly two months after the school opened. After Dawson's death, Hunter recommended that the Associates ask Robert Carter Nicholas, the treasurer of the colony, and the Rev. William Yates, the newly elected rector of Bruton Parish, to join him in the administration of the school, which the Associates did. Hunter died in 1761, after the school had been operating less than a year, leaving it in the hands of Nicholas and Yates. The correspondence indicates that Nicholas acted as the principal administrator and that, after Yates's death in September 1764, successive rectors of Bruton Parish gave Nicholas at best only nominal aid. Nicholas carried on the correspondence with the Associates, and he administered the school until it was forced to close, like its New York counterpart, following the death of the mistress late in 1774.[94]

The Newport school did not begin its operations until 1762 because of the departure of Pollen, the minister of Trinity Church, for a parish in Jamaica. In that year, the Associates wrote to the Rev. Marmaduke Browne, Pollen's successor as minister of Trinity Church. Before the end of November 1762 Browne had hired as mistress the woman "with whom Mr. Pollen had partly agreed before his Departure" and opened the school. Browne ran the school until his death in 1771, after which the Rev. George Bisset, Browne's successor as minister of Trinity Church, continued to superintend the school until at least April 1775.[95]

The Associates opened one other Negro school, in 1765, at Fredericksburg, Virginia, under the superintendence of Fielding Lewis, a wealthy planter and burgess. The Fredericksburg school never attracted a large number of students, despite the efforts of Lewis and later of the Rev. James Marye, Jr., the minister of the parish. Marye's prediction that the small population of Fredericksburg could not sustain a school was eventually confirmed by Lewis in his letter to the Associates announcing the demise of the school in 1770 after five years of service: "A School will never succeed in a small Town with us, as the Numbers of Negro's are few."[96]

The Associates' Philadelphia Negro school, the inspiration for the opening of the four other schools, was the most long-lived of the five. Before the Revolution four mistresses and four superintendents served the school. After Sturgeon resigned his position as assistant minister of the United Congregations of Christ Church and St. Peter's (and presumably his superintendence of the Associates' Negro school) because of ill health in July 1766, the task fell to Francis Hopkinson, a lawyer, composer, and later a signer of the Declaration of Independence, and Edward Duffield, a clockmaker and watchmaker. They administered the school until 1774, when the Rev. Thomas Coombe, assistant minister of the United Congregations, took over the supervision of the school. Coombe kept the school open until at least July 1775.[97]

Thus, the schools at New York, Williamsburg, and Fredericksburg had closed by the time of the outbreak of the Revolution, and the Associates had read the last communications from Bisset at Newport and Coombe at Philadelphia at their meetings of 5 October 1775 and

7 March 1776, respectively. With their program for the American colonies effectively at an end, the Associates noted in their Minute Book on 1 April 1777:

The pious Designs of the Associates in supporting Negroe Schools on the Continent of America being at present interrupted by the unhappy Disputes between great Britain and her Colonies, and there being little Prospect of resuming the same, till an amicable Accommodation shall take place

Agreed, that in order to answer the pious Intention of our Association it will be adviseable to adopt some other Plan of Charity of a similar Nature, and this Board are of Opinion, the Establishment and Support of Schools in England for the Instruction of poor Children in such Places as shall appear to stand most in need of such charitable Institutions will best correspond with the Intentions of this Society.[98]

After the war, Hopkinson and Franklin resumed their correspondence with the Associates. Through the generosity of a wealthy English clergyman, the Associates had been able in 1774 to purchase a lot in Philadelphia for the support of the Negro school. By October of 1786 Hopkinson had let enough of the ground to enable him "to renew the Negroe Charity School according to the Designs of the Associates." The school reopened that December, and within a year's time it was again full.[99] Alone among the five Negro schools founded by the Associates, the Philadelphia school was firmly enough established and well enough endowed to have reopened following the Revolution. In fact, the success of this school provided the impetus for the later founding of two more Philadelphia Negro schools by the Associates, one of them in conjunction with the African Church of St. Thomas, the first black church in the United States.[100]

Besides the five Negro schools that were set in operation, the Associates tried unsuccessfully to open other such schools in the colonies. At various times they attempted to establish schools at Chester, Maryland; Edenton, Wilmington, and Bath, North Carolina; and Yorktown and Norfolk, Virginia.[101] But to no avail.

In addition to sending catechists to and establishing Negro schools in the colonies, the Associates had since their earliest days utilized another means to convert and educate blacks—providing books to any colonial clergyman who was willing to undertake the instruction of blacks. This approach of course derived directly from Bray's own plans for dispensing funds from the D'Allone legacy. On occasion the Associates also sent books to American laymen for use in converting blacks. Even after the establishment of the Philadelphia Negro school in 1758, the Associates continued to send books to America, and the recipients of such shipments used them to advantage in areas where the establishment of schools was not feasible.

Often the recipients distributed books to blacks who presumably could already read, for their self-edification.[102] And frequently literate blacks were used as intermediaries between the Associates' American representatives and the larger black population. In this scheme, whites educated certain blacks and then provided them with books with which to teach their fellow blacks.[103]

Colonial Opposition to the Associates' Work

Supporting catechists, establishing Negro schools, and providing books to Americans were, then, the three methods that the Associates utilized to implement their mandate to convert and educate American blacks. Success attended some of these efforts; others did not enjoy the same result. But whether successful or not, virtually all of the Americans who attempted to carry the Associates' pious designs into effect encountered obstacles that hindered their work.

Much of the correspondence that follows is given over to the recitation of these obstacles in an effort to explain the limited success the Americans enjoyed in their work on behalf of the Associates. Most of these difficulties arose from attitudes held by whites toward blacks and toward the Christianization and education of blacks. Others stemmed from the constraints imposed by the need for labor in the colonies, the language barrier that separated blacks from whites, the dearth of qualified and willing teachers, and the unwillingness of whites to share the financial burdens of the enterprise.

Opposition to the Christianization of blacks had a long history by the time the Associates began their work in the colonies. Hostility arose primarily from the widely held belief that the baptism of slaves was tantamount to the emancipation of slaves. This belief itself undoubtedly arose from the understanding that Christians could not legally be enslaved. In the Old World the institution of slavery had slowly evolved from one in which Christians held other Christians in bondage to one in which by the fifteenth century, as David Brion Davis has written, "Europeans had become increasingly prejudiced against the enslavement of men from Christian countries. . . . These scruples, however, did not extend to unbelievers, who were usually thought to be undeserving of freedom." Davis has concluded that "paganism and religious infidelity were the prime excuses for enslaving non-Europeans."[104]

Following the "discovery" of Africa by Europeans in the fifteenth and sixteenth centuries, slavery continued to be morally acceptable to whites because those enslaved were "strangers," or "infidels," who coincidentally were darker hued than the Europeans who held them captive. This distinction on the basis of religious belief posed a dilemma for devout slaveholders in the American colonies. Their Christian duty enjoined them to convert their slaves, but in so doing they would be making their slaves Christian and, therefore, incapable of being held in bondage. Early in the eighteenth century Samuel Sewall addressed this problem and concluded that Christianization did indeed bring freedom to slaves: "The Law of our Land is so far from allowing it [slavery]; that if an Infidel be brought into this Kingdom, as soon as he can give an Account of the Christian Faith and desires to be Baptized; any Charitable lawful Minister may do it, and then he is under the same Law with other Christians [i.e., he is free]."[105] Most colonial Americans, however, did not share Sewall's belief. The rationale behind the enslavement of blacks slowly and almost imperceptibly came to be based on the blacks' color rather than on their non-Christian status. Yet vestiges of the previous understanding of the basis of chattel slavery lingered in the minds of white Christian slave owners, engendering resistance to attempts to convert black bondsmen.

Actions taken both in London and in the colonies indicate that the Christianization of blacks was not being accomplished early in the colonial period. On 1 December 1660 Charles II instructed his Council for Foreign Plantations to consider how "servants or slaves may be best invited to the Christian Faith, and be made capable of being baptized thereunto; it being to the honor of our Crowne and of the Protestant Religion that all persons in any of our Dominions should be taught the knowledge of God, and be made acquainted with the misteries of Salvation."[106] Beginning twenty-two years later, royal instructions to colonial governors directed that "the best means" be found out "to facilitate and encourage the conversion of Negroes and Indians to the Christian religion."[107] Resistance to conversion nonetheless persisted, and colonial assemblies themselves attempted to overcome the ingrained fear among slaveholders that the baptism of their bondsmen would lead ultimately to freedom for blacks. Proponents of the conversion of blacks attempted to assuage the anxiety of slave owners through legislation explicitly stating that baptism did nothing to alter the temporal condition of slaves. By such means the proponents of black conversion unwittingly did much to instill and reinforce the notion that slavery was in fact based on racial, rather than religious, distinctions.

The first such act in the American colonies was the Maryland statute of 1664 that declared that all Negroes and other slaves "shall serve

Durante Vita." Although this act did not specifically mention baptism, it was brought about partly by the desire of the Assembly to enact a bill "obligeing negroes to serve durante vita they [the Assembly] thinking itt very necessary for the prevencion of the damage Masters of such Slaves may susteyne by such Slaves pretending to be Christned And soe pleade the lawe of England." While the prevention of damage to the property rights of slave owners was the reason for the passage of this first Maryland law, an act passed in 1671 was explicitly intended to encourage the conversion of blacks by removing doubts from the minds of the slave owners. Because slave owners had "neglected to instruct them in the Christian faith or to Endure or permitt them to Receive the holy Sacrament of Baptisme for the Remission of their Sinns upon a mistake and ungrounded apprehension that by becomeing Christians" the slaves and their issue would become free, the act stipulated that such conversion or baptism "is not nor shall or ought the same be denied [i.e., deemed] adjudged Construed or taken to be or to amount unto a manumicion or freeing Inlarging or discharging" the slave or his issue from bondage.[108]

New York was the second colony whose laws dealt with the issue of baptism and freedom. The section on bond slavery of the "Duke's Laws" of 1665 included a provision "that This Law shall not extend to sett at Liberty Any Negroe or Indian Servant who shall turne Christian after he shall have been bought by Any Person."[109] A New York act of 1706 was passed explicitly to encourage the baptism of black, Indian, and mulatto slaves. Since some inhabitants were willing or even wished to have their slaves baptized but were "deterred and hindered therefrom by reason of a groundless opinion" that baptism necessitated freedom, it was enacted that baptism "shall not be any cause or reason for the setting them or any of them at liberty."[110]

Virginia followed New York with an act in 1667 that held "that the conferring of baptisme doth not alter the condition of the person as to his bondage or Freedom, that divers masters, Freed from this doubt, may more carefully endeavour the propagation of Christianity, &c."[111] Three years later Carolina's Fundamental Constitutions were adopted, section 107 of which reads:

> Since Charity obliges us to wish well to the Souls of all Men, and Religion ought to alter nothing in any Man's Civil Estate or Right, it shall be lawful for Slaves, as well as others, to Enter themselves and be of what Church or Profession any of them shall think best, and thereof be as fully Members as any Freeman. But yet, no Slave shall hereby be exempted from that Civil Dominion his Master has over him, but be in all other things in the same State and Condition he was in before.[112]

In Massachusetts on 30 May 1694, a group of ministers memorialized the governor and legislature to remove "the wel-knowne Discouragement" to conversion by passing a law "which may take away all pre[tense] to Release from just servitude, by receiving of Baptisme," but no law to this effect was enacted. The New Jersey legislature passed an act in 1704 that stated that baptism "is thought by some to be a sufficient Reason to set them [slaves] at Liberty; which being a groundless Opinion, and prejudicial to the Inhabitants of this Province," therefore the baptism of a slave "shall not be any reason or cause for setting them, or any of them at Liberty." The Privy Council disallowed the act five years later.[113]

The first royal instruction concerning the conversion of blacks, issued to Governor Thomas Culpeper of Virginia in 1682, ordered Culpeper "to have a due caution and regard to the property of the inhabitants," a phrase that suggests there was an awareness in England that the slave owners in America saw the conversion of blacks as a threat to their property rights. But instructions issued to Virginia governors after 1685, and subsequent instructions to the governors of the other colonies, did not include the phrase.[114]

During the reign of Queen Anne (1702–14) someone did propose an act of Parliament that would have promoted the Christianization of blacks through a legal guarantee to slave owners that their right to their slave property would not thereby be jeopardized. "A Draught of a Bill For Converting the Negros &c. In the Plantations" by an anonymous author reflected the thinking behind many of the colonial enactments. It also apparently sought to make the Christianization of blacks imperial policy while at the same time adding the weight of an act of Parliament to the arsenal of arguments used to sway slave owners to favor, or at least to allow, such Christianization. The draft began by positing the obligation of all Christian slave owners to show "a Prudent zeal to promote & propogate" Christianity among their bondsmen, and it alleged that the neglect thereof "seems chiefly to be Occasion'd by a mistaken Opinion that the Interest of the Master in his Negro or Servant, is taken away or Lessen'd by the Negro or Servant becoming a Christian." The proposed bill then declared that to prevent such neglect, "no Negro or other Servant who shall hereafter be baptiz'd, shall be thereby Enfranchis'd, nor shall such Baptism be, or be Construed to be any Manumission . . . or in any Measure or Degree be, or be Construed to be any Diminution or Prejudice of or to any just Right or Property" claimed by the master or owner at the time of such baptism.[115]

The proposed bill never became law. Nor did a bill for establishing the African trade, passed by the House of Commons on 27 May

1712, which contained a clause stipulating that after 24 December 1712 all owners of slaves born in America "shall be obliged to cause all such negro children, within three months after their birth, to be baptized by the minister of the parish; and that no proprietor or owner of any negro shall lose his property or ownership in any negro, by such negro's professing the Christian religion, or being baptized into the same."[116] The clause may have been introduced at the instance of the S.P.G., whose secretary wrote to the Rev. Francis Le Jau in South Carolina in February 1710/11 that the Society was seeking an act of Parliament for the encouragement of the conversion of Indians and blacks.[117] Three years later the Society declared that it had

> prepared a Clause to be offer'd in Parliament, on a fair Opportunity, obliging all Masters or Owners of such *Negro Slaves*, To cause their Children to be Baptiz'd within *Three* Months after their Birth; and to permit them, when come to Years of Discretion, to be instructed in the Christian Religion on the *Lord's-Day*, by the Missionaries under whose Ministry they live; but notwithstanding such *Baptism* or *Profession* of Christianity, The respective Owners or Proprietors are to have the same Right, Title, and Property to them, as they had before, in like manner as is practised all the World over, even in Countries of the *Romish* Communion.[118]

Nothing ever came of the Society's clause. Whether there was any connection between the "Draught of a Bill for Converting the Negros &c. In the Plantations," the clause in the bill passed by Commons in 1712, and the clause sought by the S.P.G. is not known, but together they testify to the fact that early in the eighteenth century at least some Englishmen were aware of a serious impediment to the Christianization of blacks that Americans had long recognized.

The fact that colonial assemblies deemed legislation necessary and that Englishmen drafted acts of Parliament to the same effect reveals the pervasiveness and tenacity of the belief that Christians could not be enslaved. And the frequency and vehemence with which spokesmen of the Church of England reiterated the intention of these laws reflects not only their desire to bring blacks within the fold of Christianity without bringing into question the legitimacy of the institution of slavery, but also the fact that even legislation could not entirely allay the fears of slave owners. Bishop Gibson made a representative statement of the Anglican understanding of the relationship between Christianity and slavery in 1727: "Christianity, and the embracing of the Gospel, does not make the least Alteration in Civil Property, or in any of the Duties which belong to Civil Relations; but in all these Respects, it continues Persons just in the same State as it found them."[119]

The legislation and exhortations may gradually have had an effect in overcoming the aversion on the part of slave owners to the baptism of slaves on the grounds that emancipation would be the ineluctable consequence, for this concern is not voiced in any of the letters in the present collection. The success of this campaign may be partly attributed to the evolution of the institution of slavery itself, by which it came to rest firmly on racial, and not religious, foundations. Thus Christianization came to be less of a threat to the property rights of slave owners, and thus also the American representatives of the Associates were able to carry out their work free from at least overt opposition on these grounds. Yet old beliefs die hard, and hostility to the Christianization of blacks manifested itself in other guises.

Oft-mentioned was the fear that the Christianization of slaves bred egalitarian notions among bondsmen, rendering them more intractable and potentially rebellious.[120] In an attempt to overcome this belief, those who advocated the Christianization of blacks invoked the biblical injunctions to obedience and submission, and they argued that Christian slaves would in fact be better servants than non-Christian slaves.[121] The "tremendous Sanctions" of Christianity, as John Waring called them, were the biblical exhortations to submissiveness and contentment with one's lot in this world in the expectation of a greater spiritual reward in the next. And they were the passages from the Church's catechism, to be learned by all Christianized blacks, that counseled subservience. In answer to the question, "What is thy duty towards thy neighbour?" the prospective convert replied, in part, "To submit myself to all my governors, teachers, spiritual pastors, and masters. To order myself lowly and reverently to all my betters . . . and to do my duty in that state of life, unto which it shall please God to call me." These were the lessons of Christianity to be inculcated into the minds of bondsmen in order to bring them to Christianity without bringing about a concomitant rebelliousness. The Pauline injunction, "Let every man abide in the same calling wherein he was called. Art thou called being a servant? Care not for it," thus came to epitomize the attitude of those who sought to convert the blacks.[122] Paul's formula for the spiritual equality of all men, that "there is neither bond nor free . . . for ye are all one in Christ Jesus," was relegated to the background as emphasis was placed instead on acceptance of one's temporal lot.[123] As David Brion Davis has noted, "Christianity gave a certain moral dignity to servitude. For the Romans the servile character was synonymous with everything lowly and vicious; Christianity raised obedience, humility, patience, and resignation to the level of high virtues."[124]

A corollary of the fear that Christianization was inherently dangerous because it instilled unwarranted notions of pride and equality in blacks was the fear that slave literacy, which proponents of Christianization frequently viewed as both a means to and an end of conversion, was also inherently dangerous. In fact, the Associates' American correspondents found this fear rather more prevalent than the fear of Christianization itself.[125]

While proponents of black conversion could attempt to convince slave owners of the benefits to be gained thereby in the form of more obedient and faithful servants, the only argument that proponents of the secular education of blacks could adduce to support their cause was that teaching blacks to read was a necessary concomitant of a meaningful conversion and that religious and secular education had therefore to be carried on simultaneously. From the point of view of the slave owner, however, slave literacy was not necessary and had no beneficial results; it posed only a threat. It could facilitate communication among slaves and thereby increase the chance of conspiracies and insurrection.[126]

The legislative record as well as the Associates' correspondence indicates that in the colonial period whites feared slave literacy more than slave conversion. No American colony legally prohibited or restricted the baptism or catechetical instruction of slaves, but two colonies—South Carolina and Georgia—passed legislation regarding slave literacy. The South Carolina act of 1740 and the Georgia act of 1755 (passed five years after slavery was legalized there) prohibited teaching slaves to write or allowing them to be employed in writing, as such activities "may be attended with great Inconveniencys."[127] The Georgia act of 1770, in addition to repeating the injunction of the 1755 act, forbade teaching slaves to "read writing."[128] Significantly, as slave codes became more harsh in the antebellum period, several states followed the precedent of South Carolina and Georgia and restricted literacy among both slaves and free blacks, but no state attempted to hinder by law slave conversion.[129]

Although surviving evidence suggests that in the colonial period neither the Christianization nor the education of slaves was a contributing factor in any uprising, the fact that many slave owners *perceived* the Christianization and education of blacks as threats to order and security hindered the work of the Associates and other groups. There were two incidents during the colonial period in which the Christianization and education of blacks were believed to have played a part. The first was the New York City slave insurrection of 1712, during which a group of about two dozen slaves set fire to a building and attacked those who came to put out the blaze, killing nine whites and wounding several others. The frightened citizens hunted down the conspirators, tried them quickly, and brutally executed them: thirteen were hanged, one was starved to death in chains, three were burned at the stake, one was burned over a slow fire for eight to ten hours, and one was broken on the wheel.[130] Local whites at first tended to attribute the slave violence to the instruction given at a school operated by the Rev. Elias Neau, S.P.G. catechist to the Negroes, but on examination it was determined that "the guilty *Negroes*, were . . . such as never came to Mr. *Neau's* School; and what is very observable, the Persons, whose *Negroes* were found to be most guilty, were such as were the declared Opposers of making them Christians." David Humphreys, the secretary of the S.P.G., in what was undoubtedly a gross understatement, concluded that the insurrection was "a Calamity . . . which mightily discouraged this Country from promoting the Instruction of their Slaves."[131]

A second incident in which Christianization, or at least the prospect of Christianization, was implicated in a slave revolt occurred in Virginia in 1730, just a few months after the enlarged Associates began to meet. Governor William Gooch reported to the Board of Trade that slaves had gathered in many meetings and consultations "in several Parts of the Country" in order to obtain freedom. Many of the slaves were examined, but no design to rise was discovered, "only some loose discourses that His Majesty had sent Orders for setting of them free as soon as they were Christians, and that these Orders were Suppressed." Six weeks after the initial meetings were broken up, 200 slaves in Princess Anne and Norfolk counties assembled on a Sunday while whites were attending church. They chose officers to lead the intended insurrection but were discovered, and four ring leaders were executed. The Rev. James Blair, Gibson's commissary in Virginia, explained that because the slaves believed that the king intended to free all Christian slaves, they flocked to baptism faster than otherwise, and when nothing came of the design, "they grew angry and saucy," and undertook the abortive rising.[132]

It is clear that the Christianization and education of slaves in the colonial period did not in any material way contribute to slave revolts, but it cannot be disputed that Christianization and education were associated in the popular mind with slave pridefulness, arrogance, intractableness, and rebellion. Whether Christianized and educated slaves tended to be more submissive and accepting of their condition than those who remained outside the pale of the churches cannot be clearly determined, but the popular perception that the opposite was in fact the case could only have been a major hindrance to the work of the Associates.

In some situations blacks' lack of knowledge of the English language posed serious problems for the Associates' operations in the colonies. The fact that our present-day knowledge of the rate at which blacks acquired facility in English is not great renders discussion of this subject somewhat speculative. Certainly many factors would have influenced the rate at which the slaves learned English. Among them were place of birth, whether a black was born in Africa or in the West Indian or North American colonies; his age at the time of importation if born in Africa; the type of worker he was, whether field hand or house servant; the location of his master's establishment, whether rural or urban; and the relative proportions of blacks and whites in the local population. The number of possible combinations of these various factors is so great as to make it difficult to generalize concerning the slave population of any given area at any given time, yet it seems clear that a distinction can be made in general between the northern and southern colonies.

If knowledge of the English language can be considered a facet of the general acculturation of slaves to white ways, then surely it would have come more quickly and been of greater importance in the north, where slaves served in closer proximity to more whites than was often the case in the south. There is much evidence that would tend to support such a conclusion. The northern colonies drew their slave population to a greater extent than did the southern colonies from the West Indies rather than directly from Africa. Their lower demand for slave labor meant that there were fewer large influxes of unacculturated blacks. Slaves in the northern colonies more often worked in urban environments as house servants or artisans. And, as a distinct minority of the population in all the northern colonies, blacks lived and worked primarily among whites rather than blacks. Perhaps this is why none of the Associates' American correspondents from north of Delaware complained of difficulties presented by the blacks' peculiar languages or lack of knowledge of English.

Those from the middle and southern colonies, however, did complain, reporting that the blacks' peculiar language, "a wild confused medley of Negro and corrupt English," made them unintelligible to all but those accustomed to hearing it.[133] And until the blacks came to a thorough understanding of English, their repetition of words was meaningless. As Ottolenghe frankly observed, "they tho ready to repeat every Thing as they are instructed yet have very little Notion or Idea of what they thus repeat, and consequently a Parrot might as well be baptiz'd as any of them." It appears also that it took quite a few years before southern slaves could be brought to that thorough understanding, if at all.[134] The problem of a language barrier to conversion and education, then, may be seen as one that demonstrably affected the work of the Associates in the southern colonies but did not seem to have been an impediment in the northern colonies.

The African-born blacks, for whom the English language proved an obstacle, were also at another disadvantage, at least according to white Christians: the native religious beliefs they brought with them were so at odds with Christianity as to preclude their conversion. Philip Reading enumerated as one of the difficulties he encountered in his work among Delaware blacks "the prejudices of Slaves themselves. Those born in Guinea are strangely prepossessed in favour of superstition and Idolatry." Ottolenghe decried the existence of "the old Superstition of a false Religion to be combated with," and he later described Georgia's blacks as "nurs'd in extravagant Idolatry."[135] Such comments reveal little curiosity about the true nature of African religions, merely the frustration of seeing Christianity, particularly Anglicanism, make such modest inroads among African-born blacks.

Another difficulty encountered by the Associates' American representatives was that masters generally did not allow their young blacks time enough for catechetical and secular education. (Indeed many of those masters who did allow their slaves to be Christianized and educated did so not out of deep commitment, but because it was to their advantage to do so.) In an economy in which labor was in short supply and great demand, many slave owners could only afford to allow their slaves to attend instruction until they became useful and productive laborers. Thus the Associates' Negro schools were plagued by high attrition of students, with few in attendance long enough to be thoroughly trained or indoctrinated in Christian principles. The administrators of the New York, Williamsburg, and Fredericksburg schools went so far as to attempt, though unsuccessfully, to impose a minimum number of years that slave owners had to agree to leave their children in the schools.[136] This situation should not, however, be considered unique to the educational work of the Associates, or even to educational work among blacks in general. With labor of any kind dear, education even for white children was considered by many to be an unaffordable luxury.

One reason some slave owners were apathetic toward the Christianization of their slaves was that they themselves had not been baptized and were not therefore imbued with a sense of the importance of the sacrament. Clergymen and catechists from Massachusetts to Georgia lamented the lack of concern for the Church's ordinances and its effects on their attempts to convert blacks. As Ottolenghe aptly put it, "twill be no Wonder that those who have so little Concern for their immortal Souls, should not attempt the Salvation of those whom they believe to have no Souls at all!"[137] Although the extent of dis-

regard for the sacraments among whites cannot be precisely determined, it was clearly great enough to have contributed to apathy, and
even antagonism, toward the Christianization of blacks.

Shortly after the formation of the Associates, Samuel Smith foresaw a working partnership between the plantation clergy, schoolmasters, and catechists on the one hand, and slaveholders on the
other, devoted to the Christianization and education of slaves. He anticipated that "Minister and Planter will be embark'd in every Branch
of the same Undertaking, and act in Conjunction in their several Sta-
tions. . . . Every House, were that practicable, should be render'd in
some Sense a Temple, and every Planter a Priest." [138] Smith's hope that
slave owners would be brought into full participation in the Associates'
design was obviously overly sanguine. And so was Franklin's belief, ar-
ticulated almost thirty years later, that Philadelphia slave owners would
financially support the Associates' Negro school in that city. [139]

However, since many slave owners lacked enthusiasm for the
Christianization and education of their slaves and since they often
patronized the schools of the Associates only when it suited their purposes to do so, we should not be surprised to find that they were
unwilling to bear any of the financial burden of the Associates' operations in the colonies. Yet the unwillingness of slave owners to be concerned with the solvency of the Williamsburg school elicited letters of
anguish and incomprehension from London. On one occasion the
Associates' secretary was barely able to contain his outrage and in-
credulity at the penuriousness of the local slave owners: "Must it not
greatly Surprise Us," he expostulated to Nicholas, "to find that Gentlemen possessed of opulent Fortunes, as many of the Inhabitants of
Williamsburgh are, have so little Generosity and publick Spirit as to
refuse to contribute even in a small Degree to the Support of an Institution calculated purely for their benefit? . . . Indeed I am much
astonished that any persons descended from Britons, whose Characteristicks are Humanity & Benevolence shou'd so far deviate from the
Principles & Practice of their Progenitors." [140]

The harsh tack that Waring privately took with Nicholas was not
reflected in the Associates' public statements, however. Their *Account*
published in 1769, which Waring wrote, anticipated cooperation from
the slaveholding class: "They [the Associates] encourage themselves
with a well-grounded Persuasion, that what is now begun on the foot
of Charity, will soon be carried on by the Planters themselves on the
foot of Expediency and common Utility, in Proportion as they feel
the Benefit of the Experiment." [141] But the public optimism was ill
founded, as Waring well knew. Three years later Nicholas reported
that he and several other inhabitants did contribute toward the sup-

port of the school, "tho there is far from being a general Disposition to promote its' Success."[142] Nicholas's statement epitomizes Americans' attitudes toward the Associates' Negro schools: they would utilize the schools when it was to their benefit but would not be out of pocket to insure the continuance of the schools.

Allied to the problem of financing the schools was that of finding suitable teachers who would undertake the work. Teaching white children was a more prestigious and lucrative occupation, and as blacks and whites were not generally taught together, it was necessary to hire a schoolmaster or mistress who would teach only blacks. This difficulty contributed to the failure of attempts to establish Negro schools in Norfolk, Virginia, and Wilmington, North Carolina. Even for those schools that the Associates did succeed in establishing, finding and keeping qualified teachers presented difficulties, as in Philadelphia and Newport.[143] And the Williamsburg and New York Negro schools, though each was served by a diligent and faithful mistress from 1760 to 1774, both closed following the deaths of their mistresses within a month of each other late in 1774, testimony to the difficulty, or even impossibility, of replacing them.

In addition to the impediments just discussed, relating to attitudes and conditions prevalent in America, another factor that played a crucial role in determining the fate of the Associates' efforts was their own attitude toward the American colonies. There was a certain naïveté, even ignorance, concerning the colonies and their inhabitants, both black and white. The Associates were plagued by unrealistic expectations and a failure to come to terms with the realities of the colonial society and economy.

Although the Associates were willing to accept the judgment and recommendations of those more familiar with American affairs in practical questions, they retained a moral sense that was totally irreconcilable with the racial attitudes prevalent in the colonies—attitudes, as we have seen, that greatly influenced the fortunes of the Associates' efforts in the colonies. Put simply, the Associates did not comprehend the nature of the colonial slave system and the dynamics underlying American whites' attitudes toward blacks. Hence their statement, in an account of their work to be published in several London newspapers, that wealthy American planters and merchants in particular had an obligation to "sow spiritual things to them by whose servitude & labour they reap so much temporal gain." American slave owners obviously felt no such obligation, and their continued refusal to recognize such an obligation elicited the kind of invective that John Waring unleashed on Robert Carter Nicholas and Fielding Lewis in 1769.[144]

The Associates' sense of moral outrage was completely out of touch with what could reasonably and realistically have been expected of American slave owners, and it reveals that as late as 1769 the Associates were no closer to comprehending the colonial situation than they had been when they started out in their enterprise in 1730. It was as if all of the numerous letters sent to the Associates from America depicting in great detail, and often eloquently, the myriad obstacles to successful work among colonial blacks had made no impression in London.

The Associates were not alone, however, in failing to grasp the racial situation in the colonies. Naïveté concerning this subject was seemingly endemic in Englishmen in the eighteenth century. Winthrop Jordan has noted the widening breach between English ideals and colonial practices. For example, English colonial officials were shocked by the use of castration as a punishment for crimes committed by slaves. Jordan commented: "It was a measure of the gulf between Americans and Englishmen created by America's racial slavery that such laws should be passed in America and vehemently disallowed in England." [145] Americans were also altering the traditional rights of Englishmen to exclude free blacks. A 1723 Virginia statute excluding all blacks from the polls was questioned by English authorities because it treated "one *Freeman* . . . worse than another meerely upon account of his complexion." [146] After the Board of Trade finally communicated this concern to the governor in 1735, Gooch staunchly defended the act. He claimed that the act was necessary in order to maintain distinctions between blacks and whites, "to make the free-Negros sensible that a distinction ought to be made between their offspring and the Descendants of an Englishman, with whom they never were to be Accounted Equal." [147]

Jordan has observed that "though they comprehended the economics of slavery well enough, officials in England did not really quite understand, at least during the first third of the century, this logic of the racial situation in the New World." Speaking of the activities of the S.P.G., Jordan noted: "What is most revealing about these efforts is that Englishmen were far more eager to convert Negroes than Americans were. Clerical authorities in England never really understood that racial slavery had created an enormous gulf between England and her colonies, and when English bishops [or indeed the secretary of the Associates!] called upon masters in the plantations to treat their slaves as brothers by bringing them to a knowledge of Christ they showed themselves naïvely unaware of the facts of life in the plantations." [148] Waring and the Associates thus appear to have been in the mainstream, rather than on the fringes, of English thought. As one historian has aptly put it, "The zeal of the Associates outstripped their experience."[149]

Assessment of the Associates' Efforts

How, then, can we assess the work of the Associates in the American colonies? Certainly the numbers do not impress. Over the years the beneficence of the Associates reached, through Negro schools, catechists, and books, perhaps two or three thousand of colonial America's blacks. In light of the fact that there were close to half a million blacks in the colonies on the eve of the American Revolution, the number pales into insignificance. And even those few whom the Associates did reach probably did not achieve a lasting conversion or a useful degree of literacy.[150] Hindered by many and great obstacles, the Associates' enterprise failed to establish a permanent and effective means of carrying the gospel to and fostering education among America's blacks. Yet fortified by a deep sense of right and duty, the Associates pressed on in their endeavor despite the meager results and discouraging reports. Notwithstanding the larger failures, the smaller successes are testimony to the good intentions and determination of the Associates and of those who acted in their name in America to carry on the good work begun by Thomas Bray.

NOTES

1. H. P. Thompson, *Thomas Bray* (London, 1954), p. 2; Joseph Foster, *Alumni Oxonienses: The Members of the University of Oxford, 1500–1886*, 8 vols. (London, 1887–92), s.v. Bray, Thomas.

2. [Samuel Smith], *Publick Spirit, Illustrated in the Life and Designs of the Reverend Thomas Bray, D.D., Late Minister of St. Botolph without Aldgate* (London, 1746), p. 5. Bray took the M.A. from Hart Hall, Oxford, only in 1693, when he could afford the fee. He received B.D. and D.D. degrees from Magdalen College, Oxford, in 1696. Thompson, *Bray*, p. 3; Foster, *Alumni Oxonienses*.

3. [Smith], *Publick Spirit*, pp. 6–8 (quotes on pp. 7, 8). See also Thompson, *Bray*, pp. 3–4.

4. Lawrence C. Wroth, "Dr. Bray's 'Proposals for the Incouragement of Religion and Learning in the Foreign Plantations'—A Bibliographical Note," *Proceedings of the Massachusetts Historical Society* 65 (1932–36): 518–34.

5. [Smith], *Publick Spirit*, p. 18.

6. This document, along with other manuscripts and printed works that Bray bequeathed to Sion College, London, was sold at auction in 1977 and the collection was subsequently dispersed. The Library of Congress has a photostatic copy of the entire collection as it existed when Sion College owned it; the "General Plan" is fols. 342–43.

7. Samuel Clyde McCulloch, "The Foundation and Early Work of the Society for Promoting Christian Knowledge," *Historical Magazine of the Protestant Episcopal Church* 18 (1949): 3–22; W. O. B. Allen and Edmund McClure, *Two Hundred Years: The History of the Society for Promoting Christian Knowledge, 1698–1898* (London, 1898), pp. 1–60; and Edmund McClure, ed., *A Chapter in English Church History: Being the Minutes of the Society for Promoting Christian Knowledge, 1698–1704* (London, 1888).

8. Allen and McClure, *Two Hundred Years*, pp. 23–24, 26, 29.

9. [Smith], *Publick Spirit*, p. 43; David C. A. Agnew, *Protestant Exiles from France, Chiefly in the Reign of Louis XIV; or, The Huguenot Refugees and Their Descendants in Great Britain and Ireland*, 3d ed., 2 vols. ([London], 1886), 2:207–10.

10. Nelson Waite Rightmyer, *Maryland's Established Church* (Baltimore, 1956), pp. 37–54.

11. The S.P.G. charter is printed in James S. M. Anderson, *The History of the Church of England in the Colonies and Foreign Dependencies of the British Empire*, 2d ed., 4 vols. (London, 1856), 3:567–74. See also Henry P. Thompson, *Into All Lands: The History of the Society for the Propagation of the Gospel in Foreign Parts, 1701–1950* (London, 1951).

12. "Dr. Brays reasons for Vesting the bequest of Mr. D'alloune in Trustees &c.," 24 February 1724/25, Manuscripts of the S.P.G., ser. A, vol. 19, p. 18, United Society for the Propagation of the Gospel Archives, London, microfilm in Library of Congress.

13. D'Allone to Hales, 12/23 July 1717, n. 1, below.

14. "Extract out of Mr. Dallones Will," 1 July 1721, S.P.G.MSS., A19, p. 17.

15. [Smith], *Publick Spirit*, p. 44.

16. Assignment of Trustees of Mr. D'Allone's Bequest, 15 January 1729/30, below.

17. General Meeting Journals of the S.P.G., 5:33 (meeting of 19 February 1724/25), U.S.P.G. Archives, photostats in Library of Congress.

18. "Dr. Brays reasons for Vesting the bequest of Mr. D'alloune in Trustees &c.," S.P.G. MSS., A19, p. 18.

19. Standing Committee Journals of the S.P.G., 3: not paginated (meeting of 15 March 1724/25), U.S.P.G. Archives, microfilm in Library of Congress; S.P.G. Journals, 5:36–37 (meeting of 19 March 1724/25).

20. In fact, the association in Bray's mind between blacks and Indians was so strong that he once used the word *Negroes* in reference to Indians. *Missionalia; or, A Collection of Missionary Pieces Relating to the Conversion of the Heathen; Both the African Negroes and American Indians* (London, 1727), p. 77. Bray's confounding of blacks and Indians was not unique, for in the 1760s Eleazar Wheelock referred to his Indian students as his "Black" children, to his most famous pupil, Samson Occam, as his "black son," and to the frontier tribes who needed his help as the "Black Tribes." Wheelock Papers, 762516 (1762), 761304.1 (1761), Dartmouth College Library, Hanover, N.H., quoted in James Axtell, "Dr. Wheelock's Little Red School," in *The European and the Indian: Essays in the Ethnohistory of Colonial North America* (New York, 1981), pp. 87–109.

21. Bray, *Apostolick Charity, Its Nature and Excellence Consider'd, in a Discourse upon Dan. 12.3, Preached at St. Paul's, Decemb. 19. 1697* (London, 1698), preface (unpaginated).

22. Bray, *Missionalia*, pp. 13, 17–18.

23. See [Colman to Egmont, 8 July 1734] and Stewart to Waring, 1 May 1764 and enclosures, below.

24. Bray's Accounts, pt. 2, fol. 66, U.S.P.G. Archives.

25. Bray MSS., Sion College Library, fols. 209–12.

26. "A General Scheme of Laying out Mr. D'Allones Bequest or other Charities for the Conversion of the Negroes in our English Plantations to the Greatest Advantage," Christian Faith Society Papers, F/3, ff. 26–29, Lambeth Palace Library, London; "The Advantage of Conducting the Design of Converting the Negroes according to the foregoing Scheme," ibid., fols. 30–31, quotation from fol. 31.

27. Bray, *Missionalia*, dedication (unpaginated), and pp. 117–18.

28. Assignment of Trustees of Mr. D'Allone's Bequest, 15 January 1729/30, below.

29. John Percival, first earl of Egmont, *Diary of Viscount Percival, Afterwards First Earl of Egmont, 1730–1749,* ed. R. A. Roberts, 3 vols. (London, 1920–23), 1:iv (hereafter, Egmont, *Diary*); Ruth Saye and Albert B. Saye, "John Percival, First Earl of Egmont," in Horace Montgomery, ed., *Georgians in Profile: Historical Essays in Honor of Ellis Merton Coulter* (Athens, Ga., 1958), p. 9.

30. Percival to S.P.G., 23 February 1724/25, S.P.G. MSS., A18, p. 19.

31. Berkeley to Percival, 10 February 1725/26, Add. MSS. 47,031, fol. 104, British Library, London, printed in Benjamin Rand, *Berkeley and Percival: The Correspondence of George Berkeley, Afterwards Bishop of Cloyne, and Sir John Percival, Afterwards Earl of Egmont* (Cambridge, Mass., 1914), p. 230. For Berkeley's ill-fated St. Paul's College, see his *Proposal for the Better Supplying of Churches in Our Foreign Plantations, and for Converting the Savage Americans to Christianity, by a College to Be Erected in the Summer Islands, Otherwise Called the Isles of Bermuda* (London, 1725); A. A. Luce, *The Life of George Berkeley, Bishop of Cloyne* (London, 1949), chaps. 7–9; Edwin S. Gaustad, *George Berkeley in America* (New Haven, 1979), esp. chap. 2.

32. Berkeley to Percival, 10 February 1725/26; Dering to Percival, 31 January 1725/26 and 28 February 1725/26, Add. MSS. 47,031, fols. 104, 90–92, 111–13, British Library.

33. Percival to Dering, 12 February 1725/26, ibid., fols. 106–7.

34. A. A. Luce and T. E. Jessop, eds., *The Works of George Berkeley, Bishop of Cloyne,* 9 vols. (London, 1948–57), 7:346. Before the turn of the century Bray had expended some funds to procure "a List of the Scandalous Ministers about the Town [London] that I might not be Imposd upon in the Choice of those whom I send into the Plantations." "Dr. Bray's Accounts, Part I," 1695–99, fol. 39, U.S.P.G. Archives, London.

35. [Smith], *Publick Spirit*, pp. 51–52.

36. *Journals of the House of Commons* 21:237.

37. Bray's interest in prison reform actually dated from the turn of the century, when the S.P.C.K. appointed a committee to visit the prisons of Lon-

don. In a report drawn up by Bray, the committee gave a full account of the vices and immoralities prevalent. "There can be little doubt that the work, delegated, more than twenty-five years afterwards, to a Committee of the House of Commons upon this subject . . . was prompted by" the earlier efforts of the S.P.C.K. Anderson, *History of the Church* 2 : 567–69.

38. Codicil to Bray's will, 15 February 1729/30, PROB 11/636, quire 55, Public Record Office, London.

39. Egmont, *Diary* 1 : 44–45 (entry of 13 February 1729/30).

40. Verner W. Crane, *The Southern Frontier, 1670–1732* (Durham, N.C., 1928), pp. 283–87; H. B. Fant, "Picturesque Thomas Coram, Projector of Two Georgias and the Father of the London Foundling Hospital," *Georgia Historical Quarterly* 32 (1948): 77–104.

41. Coram to the Rev. Benjamin Colman, 30 April 1734, in Worthington C. Ford, ed., "Letters of Thomas Coram," *Proceedings of the Massachusetts Historical Society* 56 (1922–23): 20.

42. Assignment of Trustees of Mr. D'Allone's Bequest, below.

43. Minute Books of the Associates of Dr. Bray, 3 : 7–8, U.S.P.G. Archives, photostats in Library of Congress.

44. Egmont, *Diary* 1 : 45.

45. "Acct. of Georgea," Add. MSS. 47,000, fols. 53–55, British Library.

46. Egmont, *Diary* 1 : 90, 93 (entries of 1 April and 11 April 1730).

47. Minutes, 3 : 1, 2 (meetings of 21 March, 12 May, and 24 June 1730).

48. Ibid., 3 : 70, 1 : 136 (meetings of 4 November 1734 and 3 April 1760); Mr. Turner to C. B. Dalton, 11 October 1871, Associates MSS., U.S.P.G. Archives.

49. Minutes, 3 : 1, 4, 11, 24.

50. Kenneth Coleman, *Colonial Georgia: A History* (New York, 1976), p. 17. The charter is printed in Allen D. Candler et al., eds., *The Colonial Records of the State of Georgia*, 27 vols. to date (Atlanta, 1904–16, Athens, 1976–), 1 : 11–26.

51. The journals of the Georgia Trustees for this period are printed in *Col. Recs. Ga.* 1 : 65–119. This arrangement precluded the eight Associates who were not Georgia Trustees from participating in the Associates' business during this period.

52. They read and approved the Associates' accounts and received bank receipts for the deposit of the Associates' funds (*Col. Recs. Ga.* 1 : 84, 87, 2 : 9); and they provided books for the Rev. Joseph Bugnion, the minister going to the Swiss settlement at Purrysburg in South Carolina. Ibid., 1 : 72. This last minute was ordered struck from the Trustees' journal on 11 June 1733, shortly after the separation of the Associates from the Trustees, because it rightly belonged "to the Trust of Dr. Bray." Ibid., p. 124.

53. Egmont, *Diary* 1 : 378 (entry of 23 May 1733).

54. *Col. Recs. Ga.* 1 : 105.

55. Richard S. Dunn, "The Trustees of Georgia and the House of Commons, 1732–1752," *William and Mary Quarterly*, 3d ser. 11 (1954): 553.

56. At their meeting of 31 May 1733 the Associates reviewed their accounts and determined that £109.18.4 of their funds was in the hands of the

Georgia Trustees. The Common Council of the Trustees turned over the money on 11 June 1733, and the separation was complete. Minutes, 3 : 56–58; Egmont, *Diary* 1 : 382; *Col. Recs. Ga.* 2 : 39.

57. Coram to Colman, 30 April 1734, in Ford, ed., "Letters of Coram," p. 21.

58. Egmont, *Diary* 2 : 41 (entry of 3 March 1733/34).

59. Robert G. McPherson, ed., *The Journal of the Earl of Egmont: Abstract of the Trustees Proceedings for Establishing the Colony of Georgia, 1732–1738* (Athens, Ga., 1962), pp. 23–24.

60. Thirteen of the twenty-six new Associates listed in the minutes of the meeting of 3 July 1730—Oglethorpe, Hughes, Towers, Hucks, Holland, Laroche, Selwyn, Moore, Lowther, Campbell, Sloper, Heathcote, and Eyles— had served on the Parliamentary Gaols Committees. The first ten of these men were appointed to the original Gaols Committee. The last three were appointed to the revived Gaols Committee on 17 February 1729/30. *Journals of the House of Commons* 21 : 237, 444.

61. Albert B. Saye, *New Viewpoints in Georgia History* (Athens, Ga., 1943), p. 23, and "The Genesis of Georgia Reviewed," *Georgia Historical Quarterly* 50 (1966): 157. Saye writes of the ten members of the Parliamentary Gaols Committees who became Georgia Trustees. He does not account for Hughes, Selwyn, and Lowther, who also served on the Committees but were among the eight Associates who did not become Georgia Trustees.

62. Verner Crane, review of Saye, *New Viewpoints*, in *William and Mary Quarterly*, 3d ser. 1 (1944): 412. Crane did acknowledge, however, that the Associates who had served on the Gaols Committees were "presumably strongly committed to the cause of the charitable colony." Crane, "Dr. Thomas Bray and the Charitable Colony Project, 1730," *William and Mary Quarterly*, 3d ser. 19 (1962): 54.

63. Hucks attended only an anniversary meeting at which a sermon was given but no business conducted (17 March 1736/37; Minutes, 1 : 18). Laroche attended once (6 June 1740; ibid.: 40). Towers attended twice (6 October 1736 and 15 March 1738/39 [an anniversary meeting at which only one item of business was conducted]; ibid.: 11–12, 34). Holland attended twice (17 March 1736/37 [see above] and 4 July 1739; ibid.: 18, 36). And Oglethorpe, who was by far the most active among the parliamentary Associates, attended only ten meetings in thirty-six years following the separation (3 February 1734/35, 3 September 1735, 9 February 1736/37, 2 November 1737, 1 February 1737/38, 16 March 1737/38, 21 March 1744/45, 19 March 1746/47, 16 March 1748/49, and 4 May 1769; ibid., 3 : 74–75, 93, 1 : 14, 21–22, 25, 27, 51–53, 58–61, 66–68, and 2 : 23–24).

64. Ziegenhagen to Smith, 12 August 1735, below; Gavin to Smith, 20 October 1735, below; Bond of Arnold, 7 April 1736, below; List of Books Sent to New Haven, [c. 7 April 1736], below; Parker to Waring, 18 May 1761, below; Boucher to Waring, 31 December 1762, below; [Colman to Egmont, 8 July 1734], below; List of Books Sent to New England, 21 April 1735, below.

65. Minutes, 3 : 60, 1 : 9 (meetings of 2 July 1733 and 7 July 1736), 1 : 43, 94 (meetings of 16 November 1741 and January 1755). It is not certain that

these books were sent to Pennsylvania, for at their next meeting the Associates ordered that £20 worth of books "be applyed to found a Parochial Library in England or Wales" and resolved that James Vernon "procure the Best Advice he can from Philadelphia at what place in that Province it will be most proper to fix a parochial Library." Ibid. (meeting of 14 January 1755).

66. Minutes, 3:7, 62, 63 (meetings of 30 July 1730, 6 August and 1 October 1733), 1:83 (meeting of 17 August 1753); Fulham Papers, 34:51–52, Lambeth Palace Library.

67. Minutes, 1:21, 87 (meetings of 2 November 1737 and 16 November 1753).

68. [Colman to Egmont, 8 July 1734], below; List of Books Sent to New England, 21 April 1735, below.

69. Stirling to Coram, 10 April 1735 and enclosure, below; Ziegenhagen to [Smith], 3 May 1735 and enclosures, below; Ziegenhagen to Smith, 12 August 1735, below; Egmont, *Diary* 1:286 (entry of 20 July 1732); *Col. Recs. Ga.* 1:72.

70. Henry A. M. Smith, "Purrysburgh," *South Carolina Historical and Genealogical Magazine* 10 (1909): 187–219; Crane, *Southern Frontier*, pp. 283–87.

71. Egmont, *Diary* 2:157 (entry of 5 March 1734/35).

72. Crane, "Bray and the Charitable Colony Project," p. 58; Bray's will, 31 January 1729/30, PROB 11/636, quire 55, Public Record Office.

73. Nehemiah Curnock, ed., *The Journals of the Rev. John Wesley*, 8 vols. (London, 1909–16), 8:287.

74. Minutes, 3:93.

75. Egmont, *Diary* 2:190, 192–93 (entries of 6 August and 3 September 1735).

76. Egmont, *Diary* 2:357.

77. Adelaide L. Fries, *The Moravians in Georgia, 1735–1740* (Raleigh, N.C., 1905), p. 203.

78. David Cranz, *The Ancient and Modern History of the Brethren; or, A Succinct Narrative of the Protestant Church of the United Brethren, or Unitas Fratrum, in the Remoter Ages, and Particularly in the Present Century*, trans. and ed. by Benjamin La Trobe (London, 1780), pp. 226–27; Fries, *Moravians in Georgia*, pp. 207–8.

79. Cranz, *History of the Brethren*, p. 229.

80. Fries, *Moravians in Georgia*, pp. 210, 211.

81. William C. Reichel, ed., *Memorials of the Moravian Church*, vol. 1 (Philadelphia, 1870), p. 162. See also Minutes, 1:35, 37, 40 (meetings of 2 May 1739, 5 March 1739/40, and 6 June 1740); [Smith to Beaufain, c. 5 March 1739/40], below.

82. Minutes, 1:70, 73 (meetings of 10 April 1749 and 14 January 1750/51); S.P.G. Journals, 11:311 (meeting of 15 February 1750/51). For slavery and the colony of Georgia see Paul S. Taylor, *Georgia Plan, 1732–1752* (Berkeley, 1972); Darold D. Wax, "Georgia and the Negro before the American Revolution," *Georgia Historical Quarterly* 51 (1967): 63–77; and Betty Wood, *Slavery in Colonial Georgia, 1730–1775* (Athens, Ga., 1984).

83. Harold Davis, *The Fledgling Province: Social and Cultural Life in Colo-*

nial Georgia, 1733–1776 (Chapel Hill, N.C., 1976), p. 126. Davis also notes that there is no evidence that the draft bill was ever acted upon by the Board of Trade, the Privy Council, or George II but that "the trustees nevertheless put it into effect on their own authority."

84. *Col. Recs. Ga.* 1 : 59.

85. See pp. 344–45, below.

86. Waring to Franklin, 24 January 1757, below.

87. Franklin to Waring, 3 January 1758, enclosure, below.

88. Franklin to Waring, 3 January 1758, below.

89. Minutes, 1 : 112, 114.

90. Sturgeon to Waring, 9 November 1758, and 12 June 1759, below.

91. Minutes, 1 : 126, 129, 130–31.

92. Waring to Dawson, 29 February 1760, below. See also Johnson to [Waring], 28 July 1760, below; Pollen to [Waring], 12 August 1760, below; Auchmuty to Waring, 4 April 1761, n. 1, below; Hunter to Waring, 16 February 1761, below.

93. Auchmuty to Waring, 20 October 1774, below.

94. Hunter to Waring, 16 February 1761, below; Waring to Nicholas, 1 June 1761, below; Nicholas to Waring, 21 December 1764, 1 December 1772, and 5 January 1774, below; Waring to Johnson, 25 March 1773, below; Nicholas to Waring, 17 November 1774, below.

95. Browne to Waring, 29 November 1762, below; Bisset to [Waring], 12 April 1775, below.

96. Marye to Waring, 25 September 1764, below; Lewis to Waring, 1 February 1772, below.

97. [Hopkinson and Duffield to Waring, c. March 1768], below; [Coombe to Waring, 18 July 1775], below.

98. Minutes, 2 : 75–76, 77, 78–79.

99. Hopkinson to the Rev. Thomas Lyttleton, 24 October and 21 November 1786, Hopkinson and Franklin to Waring, 22 October 1787, Associates MSS., U.S.P.G. Archives.

100. Minutes, 2 : 235–37, 248–49, 351 (meetings of 7 January 1796, 6 February 1797, and 5 March 1804). See also Edgar L. Pennington, "The Work of the Bray Associates in Pennsylvania," *Pennsylvania Magazine of History and Biography* 58 (1934): 1–25.

101. Minutes, 1 : 147, 150, 173, 189–90, 226–27 (meetings of 5 February 1761, 7 May 1761, 4 March 1762, 7 April 1763, and 23 May 1765); Earl to Waring, 3 October 1761, below; Stewart to Waring, 12 August 1762, below; Barnett to Waring, 1 February 1766, 17 August 1767, and 9 June 1770, below; Smith to Waring, 22 September 1762, below; Rhonnald to Waring, 27 September 1762, below.

102. Reading to [Smith], 24 November 1746, below; Miller to Smith, 6 September 1748, below; Boucher to Waring, 22 January 1765, below; Barnett to Waring, 17 August 1767 and 11 June 1768, below; Baker to Waring, 23 April 1770, below.

103. [Drayton to Smith, 2 June 1736], below; Boucher to Waring, 28 April 1764 and 9 March 1767, below; Barnett to Waring, 17 August 1767, below.

104. David Brion Davis, *The Problem of Slavery in Western Culture* (Ithaca, N.Y., 1966), pp. 100, 48. The Bible also lent support to the notion that enslaving heathens was justifiable, especially Leviticus 25 :44, in which God said to the children of Israel, "Both thy bondmen, and thy bondmaids, which thou shalt have, shall be of the heathen that are round about you; of them shall ye buy bondmen and bondmaids."

105. Samuel Sewall, *Athenian Oracle* [Boston, 1705], quoted in Lawrence W. Towner, "The Sewall-Saffin Dialogue on Slavery," *William and Mary Quarterly*, 3d ser. 21 (1964): 50–51. The bracketed insertions are Towner's.

106. E. B. O'Callaghan and Berthold Fernow, eds., *Documents Relative to the Colonial History of the State of New York*, 15 vols. (Albany, 1853–87), 3 : 36.

107. Leonard W. Labaree, *Royal Instructions to British Colonial Governors, 1670–1776*, 2 vols. (New York, 1935), 2 : 505–6.

108. William H. Browne *et al.*, eds., *Archives of Maryland*, 72 vols. to date (Baltimore, 1883–), 1 : 533, 526, 2 : 272.

109. Colonial Office Papers, 5/1142, folio 33v, Public Record Office, quoted in Winthrop D. Jordan, *White over Black: American Attitudes toward the Negro, 1550–1812* (Chapel Hill, N.C., 1968), pp. 92n–93n.

110. *The Colonial Laws of New York from the Year 1664 to the Revolution*, 5 vols. (Albany, 1894–96), 1 : 597–98.

111. William Waller Hening, ed., *The Statutes at Large: Being a Collection of All the Laws of Virginia, from the First Session of the Legislature, in the Year 1619*, 13 vols. (Richmond, 1819–23), 2 : 260.

112. Mattie E. E. Parker, ed., *North Carolina Charters and Constitutions, 1578–1698* (Raleigh, N.C., 1963), p. 183.

113. *The Acts and Resolves, Public and Private, of the Province of the Massachusetts Bay*, 21 vols. (Boston, 1869–1922), 7 : 537 (manuscript mutilated at bracketed portion of word); *The Laws and Acts of the General Assembly of Her Majesties Province of Nova Caesarea or New Jersey* . . . [New York, 1709], unpaginated; W. L. Grant and James Munro, eds., *Acts of the Privy Council, Colonial Series*, 6 vols. (London, 1908–12), vol. for period 1680–1720, p. 848.

114. Labaree, *Royal Instructions* 2 : 505–6.

115. Lambeth Palace Library MSS., vol. 941, no. 72, Lambeth Palace Library, transcript in Library of Congress.

116. Leo Francis Stock, ed., *Proceedings and Debates of the British Parliaments Respecting North America*, 5 vols. (Washington, D.C., 1924–41), 3 : 295.

117. John Chamberlain to Le Jau, 20 February 1710/11, S.P.G. MSS., vol. 17, fol. 30, Lambeth Palace Library, microfilm in Library of Congress.

118. Abstract of the Proceedings of the S.P.G. for 1713/14–1714/15, appended to St. George Ashe, bishop of Clogher, *A Sermon Preached . . . on Friday the 18th of February 1714[/15]* (London, 1715), pp. 49–50.

119. [Gibson], *A Letter of the Lord Bishop of London to the Masters and Mistresses of Families in the English Plantations Abroad; Exhorting Them to Encourage and Promote the Instruction of Their Negroes in the Christian Faith* (London, 1727), in David Humphreys, *An Historical Account of the Incorporated Society for the Propagation of the Gospel in Foreign Parts* . . . (London, 1730), pp. 257–71; quotation from p. 265.

120. Ottolenghe to [Waring], 19 November 1753, below; Baker to Waring,

23 April 1770, below; Pollen to Waring, 6 July 1755, below. See also the Rev. Robert Jenney to S.P.G., 19 November 1725, S.P.G. MSS., B1, no. 78; Theodore G. Tappert and John W. Doberstein, trans. and eds., *The Journals of Henry Melchior Muhlenberg*, 3 vols. (Philadelphia, 1942–58), 1:58; and Adolph B. Benson, trans. and ed., *Peter Kalm's Travels in North America*, 2 vols. (New York, 1934), 1:209.

121. Ottolenghe to [Waring], 19 November 1753, below; Waring to Nicholas, 20 April 1768 and 25 May 1769, below; [Waring to Lewis, April 1769], below. See also Hugh Jones, *The Present State of Virginia from Whence Is Inferred a Short View of Maryland and North Carolina*, ed. Richard L. Morton (Chapel Hill, N.C., 1956; orig. publ. 1724), p. 99; [Gibson], *Letter to Masters and Mistresses*, p. 266; Stephen Hales, *Sermon Preached before the Trustees of Georgia* (London, 1734), p. 16; and George Whitefield, *Three Letters from the Reverend Mr. G. Whitefield* (Philadelphia, 1740), pp. 14–15.

122. 1 Corinthians 7:20–21, quoted in Hales, *Sermon*, p. 14. See also Titus 2:9–10, and Ephesians 6:5–9.

123. Galatians 3:28. See *A Letter to the Negroes Lately Converted to Christ in America. And Particularly to Those, Lately Called out of Darkness into God's Marvellous Light, at Mr. Jonathan Bryan's in South Carolina; or, A Welcome to the Believing Negroes, into the Household of God. By a Friend and Servant of Theirs in England* (London, 1743), pp. 20–23, 26–27.

124. Davis, *Problem of Slavery in Western Culture*, p. 85.

125. Franklin to Waring, 3 January 1758, below; Yates and Nicholas to [Waring], 30 September 1762, below; Browne to Waring, 29 November 1762 and 10 June 1768, below; and Lewis to Waring, 1 February 1772, below.

126. Eugene D. Genovese, *Roll, Jordan, Roll: The World the Slaves Made* (New York, 1974), p. 562. See also Jones, *Present State of Virginia*, p. 99.

127. Thomas Cooper and David J. McCord, eds., *The Statutes at Large of South Carolina*, 10 vols. (Columbia, 1836–41), 7:413; *Col. Recs. Ga.* 18:136. Although these laws were not always strictly enforced, they did reflect prevailing attitudes and fears.

128. *Col. Recs. Ga.* 19, pt. 1:242–43.

129. See acts of Virginia, North Carolina, and Louisiana (1830), Alabama (1832), South Carolina (1834), and Arkansas (1847), in John C. Hurd, *The Law of Freedom and Bondage in the United States*, 2 vols. (Boston, 1858–62), 2:9, 87, 162, 151, 98, 170.

130. Kenneth Scott, "The Slave Insurrection in New York in 1712," *New-York Historical Society Quarterly* 45 (1961): 43–74.

131. Humphreys, *Historical Account of the S.P.G.*, pp. 240–42. See also Henry Newman to Edmund Gibson, 31 March 1726, Christian Faith Society Papers, F/3, fols. 89–90, Lambeth Palace Library, London.

132. Gooch to Board of Trade, 14 September 1730 and 12 February 1730/31, C.O. 5/1322, fols. 158, 161–63, Public Record Office, microfilm in Library of Congress; Gooch to Gibson, 28 May 1731, Blair to Gibson, 14 May 1731, Fulham Papers, 12:169–70, 163–64, Lambeth Palace Library.

133. Reading to Smith, 10 October 1748, below.

134. Ottolenghe to Waring, 12 July 1758, below. See also Ottolenghe to

[Waring], 18 November 1754, below; Ottolenghe to Waring, 4 October 1759, below; Marye to Waring, 25 September 1764, below. See also Jones, *Present State of Virginia*, p. 99; the Rev. Thomas Hasell to S.P.G., 12 March 1712/13, S.P.G. MSS., A7, p. 401.

135. Reading to Smith, 10 October 1748, below; Ottolenghe to Waring, 18 November 1754 and 12 July 1758, below. See also [Gibson], *Letter to Masters and Mistresses*, pp. 258–59.

136. Auchmuty to Waring, 18 October 1762 and 2 May 1764, below; Yates and Nicholas to [Waring], 30 September 1762 and enclosure, below; Nicholas to Waring, 27 December 1765, below; and Lewis to Waring, 12 December 1766 and 31 October 1768, below.

137. Ottolenghe to [Waring], 4 October 1759, below. See also Pollen to [Waring], 6 July 1755, below; Boucher to Waring, 31 December 1762, below; and Browne to Waring, 1 July 1766, below.

138. Samuel Smith, *A Sermon Preach'd before the Trustees for Establishing the Colony of Georgia in America, and before the Associates of the Late Rev. Dr. Bray, for Converting the Negroes in the British Plantations, and for Other Good Purposes . . . on Tuesday February 23, 1730/31* (London, 1733), p. 19.

139. Franklin to Waring, 17 February 1758, below.

140. Waring to Nicholas, 25 May 1769, below.

141. *Account of the Designs of the Associates of the Late Dr. Bray; with An Abstract of Their Proceedings* (London, 1769), p. 10; Minutes, 2:23 (meeting of 4 May 1769).

142. Nicholas to Waring, 1 December 1772, below.

143. Franklin to Waring, 3 January 1758, below; Sturgeon to Waring, 21 August 1761, 23 November 1761, May 1762, and 6 November 1764, below; Hopkinson and Duffield to Waring, 28 May 1768, below.

144. Minutes, 1:85 (meeting of 17 August 1753); [Waring to Lewis, April 1769], below; Waring to Nicholas, 25 May 1769, below, and quoted on p. 35, above.

145. Jordan, *White over Black*, pp. 155–56.

146. Richard West to the Board of Trade, 10 January 1723/24, C.O. 5/1323, fols. 177, 181, Public Record Office, quoted in Emory G. Evans, ed., "A Question of Complexion: Documents Concerning the Negro and the Franchise in Eighteenth-Century Virginia," *Virginia Magazine of History and Biography* 71 (1963): 413.

147. Gooch to Alured Popple, 18 May 1736, C.O. 5/1324, fols. 19, 22, Public Record Office, quoted ibid., p. 414.

148. Jordan, *White over Black*, pp. 127–28, 208.

149. Mary F. Goodwin, "Christianizing and Educating the Negro in Colonial Virginia," *Historical Magazine of the Protestant Episcopal Church* 1 (1932): 152.

150. See Nicholas to Waring, 27 December 1765, below; Browne to [Waring], 10 June 1768, below.

EDITORIAL METHOD

This collection of approximately 200 documents comprises the correspondence of the Associates of Dr. Bray with the American colonies. Most of the surviving letters received by the Associates from their American correspondents are in the American Papers of the Associates of the Late Dr. Bray, a manuscript collection now in the archives of the United Society for the Propagation of the Gospel, London. A few are in the Fulham Papers, Lambeth Palace Library, London. For those letters to the Associates which have not been found I have relied on extracts from the Associates' Minute Books, which often abstracted the contents of letters received. In one instance a contemporary printed copy has been used.

As the Associates did not retain copies of their outgoing letters, this collection is necessarily composed mostly of letters to them. However, a fairly complete catalog of the outgoing letters can be compiled from acknowledgments in letters from the Americans to the Associates, and from mentions of outgoing letters in the Minute Books, often with information about their contents. Receivers' copies of some of the letters to the Associates' American correspondents have been found in American repositories and are used in the present collection. For those letters not found I have again relied on extracts from the Minute Books, if available. These extracts are generally incorporated into the bibliographic note accompanying the letter to the Associates to which the outgoing letter was a reply.

The bibliographic note immediately following the text of each document supplies such pertinent information as its nature, location, and endorsements. The following notations are used to describe the physical nature of the documents:

ALS: Autograph letter signed.
LS: Letter signed.
D: Document.

49

DS: Document signed.

Copy: Contemporary manuscript copy.

Draft: Draft of a document of which the final version is not extant.

Printed copy: Document copied from a printed source.

As the great majority of the documents in the collection are from the American Papers of the Associates of the Late Dr. Bray, no repository is listed if the document is from this source. If the document is from another repository the source is indicated immediately following the descriptive notation of the document, e.g., ALS: American Philosophical Society.

In transcribing the documents an attempt has been made to retain the original spelling, punctuation, and format. However, in the interests of clarity the following editorial changes have been made:

1. When known, the place is added to the dateline, in brackets, if omitted by the author.

2. All sentences begin with a capital letter.

3. When it cannot be determined whether upper or lower case was intended for the initial letter of a word, the author's normal usage is followed.

4. Dashes used in place of commas, semicolons, colons, or periods are replaced by the appropriate mark where necessary, and superfluous dashes are eliminated, although dashes used to set off parenthetical expressions are retained.

5. Superscript letters are lowered to the line of type, and the resulting abbreviation silently expanded if it is not easily recognizable.

6. Abbreviations are silently expanded unless they are accepted or easily recognizable. Periods are added after all remaining abbreviations.

7. Appropriate terminal punctuation is added where necessary.

8. The tilde is silently omitted and the word expanded. Thus, "comand" is rendered "command."

9. The thorn symbol (y) is replaced by "th." Thus, "y^e" is rendered "the."

10. The tailed p (℘) is rendered as either "pre," "pro," or "per," depending on its usage.

11. "X" is changed to "Christ." Thus, "X^{tian}" is rendered "Christian."

12. In some instances long sentences are broken up and appropriate punctuation added.

13. In some instances paragraphs are created where the author has used long dashes or other breaks, but continued on the same line.

14. Authors' slips of the pen, such as repetition of words or letters left out, are silently corrected.

15. Periods after numbers are omitted where they occur in the middle of a sentence. Thus, "Your letter of May 17. I received yesterday" is rendered ". . . of May 17 I received . . ."

16. The ampersand (&) is retained except if it occurs at the beginning of a sentence, in which case it is rendered "And."

17. Square brackets are used to enclose, in italics, editorial insertions such as [torn] and [illegible] and to enclose, in romans, editorial expansions, corrections, and conjectural readings. Words supplied by the editor to correct an author's omission are bracketed without comment. Words supplied by the editor to complete a sentence where the manuscript is torn, blotted, etc. are bracketed and the reason for the insertion is given in the bibliographic note following the document.

18. The names of all the months are spelled out, regardless of how abbreviated in the manuscript.

19. The complimentary closes of the letters are run together, with only the signature assigned a new line.

20. The names and addresses of recipients written as either superscriptions or subscriptions have been silently omitted.

21. Commas have been added between the members of series.

The notes following each document are intended to identify people mentioned and subjects discussed in the texts, gloss obsolete or unclear terms, etc. Biographical sketches of the correspondents represented in the collection and of recipients of shipments of books from the Associates have been gathered into a Biographical Appendix, which follows the last document.

SHORT TITLES AND ABBREVIATIONS

Berkley, "Churches and Parishes of Maryland"
Henry J. Berkley, "The Churches and Parishes of the English Establishment in the Province of Maryland," typescript, n.p., n.d., in Maryland Historical Society, Baltimore.

Boucher, *Reminiscences of an American Loyalist*
Jonathan Bouchier, ed., *Reminiscences of an American Loyalist, 1738–1789: Being the Autobiography of the Revd. Jonathan Boucher, Rector of Annapolis in Maryland and Afterwards Vicar of Epsom, Surrey, England.* Boston, 1925.

Bray MSS., McGregor Collection, U.Va.
Manuscripts of the Associates of Dr. Bray, The Tracy W. McGregor Library, University of Virginia.

Bridenbaugh, *Mitre and Sceptre*
Carl Bridenbaugh, *Mitre and Sceptre: Transatlantic Faiths, Ideas, Personalities, and Politics, 1689–1775.* New York, 1962.

Brock, *Huguenot Emigration to Virginia*
R. A. Brock, *Documents, Chiefly Unpublished, Relating to the Huguenot Emigration to Virginia, and to the Settlement at Manakin-Town, Collections of the Virginia Historical Society,* new series 5 (Richmond, 1886).

Brydon, *Virginia's Mother Church*
George M. Brydon, *Virginia's Mother Church and the Political Conditions under Which It Grew.* 2 vols. Richmond, 1947–52.

Burton, *Annals of Henrico Parish*
Lewis W. Burton, *Annals of Henrico Parish, Diocese of Virginia.* Richmond, 1904.

"Catalog of Books"
"Catalog of Books for Home and Foreign Libraries, 1753–1817," Manuscripts of the Associates of Dr. Bray, archives of the United Society for the Propagation of the Gospel, London; photostats in Library of Congress.

53

C.O.
Colonial Office Papers, Public Record Office, London.
Coleman, *Colonial Georgia*
Kenneth Coleman, *Colonial Georgia: A History.* New York, 1976.
DAB
Dictionary of American Biography.
Davis, *Fledgling Province*
Harold E. Davis, *The Fledgling Province: Social and Cultural Life in Colonial Georgia, 1733–1776.* Chapel Hill, N.C., 1976.
Dexter, *Yale Graduates*
Franklin Bowditch Dexter, *Biographical Sketches of the Graduates of Yale College, with Annals of the College History.* 2 vols. New York, 1885–96.
DNB
Dictionary of National Biography.
Dorr, *Historical Account of Christ Church*
Benjamin Dorr, *A Historical Account of Christ Church, Philadelphia.* Philadelphia, 1841.
Egmont, *Diary*
John Percival, first earl of Egmont, *Diary of Viscount Percival, Afterwards First Earl of Egmont, 1730–1749.* 3 vols. London, 1920–23.
Executive Journals of the Council
H. R. McIlwaine et al., eds., *Executive Journals of the Council of Colonial Virginia, 1680–1775.* 6 vols. Richmond, 1925–66.
Foster, *Alumni Oxonienses*
Joseph Foster, *Alumni Oxonienses: The Members of the University of Oxford, 1500–1886: Their Parentage, Birthplace, and Year of Birth, with a Record of Their Degrees.* 8 vols. London, 1887–92.
Franklin Papers
Leonard W. Labaree et al., eds., *The Papers of Benjamin Franklin.* 25 vols. to date. New Haven, Conn., 1959– .
Fulham Papers
Fulham Papers, Lambeth Palace Library, London; microfilm in Library of Congress. Calendared in William Wilson Manross, comp., *The Fulham Papers in the Lambeth Palace Library: American Colonial Section, Calendar and Indexes.* Oxford, 1965.
Ga. Col. Recs.
Allen D. Candler et al., eds., *The Colonial Records of the State of Georgia.* 27 vols. to date. Atlanta, 1904–16, Athens, 1976– .
Ga. Col. Recs., unpub.
Georgia Colonial Records, vols. 20, 29–39, typescripts in Georgia Department of Archives and History, Atlanta; microfilm in Library of Congress.

GHQ
  Georgia Historical Quarterly.
Goodwin, *Historical Sketch of Bruton Church*
  W. A. R. Goodwin, *Historical Sketch of Bruton Church, Williamsburg, Virginia.* Petersburg, Va., 1903.
Goodwin, *Record of Bruton Parish Church*
  W. A. R. Goodwin, *The Record of Bruton Parish Church.* Richmond, 1941.
Greene, *Quest for Power*
  Jack P. Greene, *The Quest for Power: The Lower Houses of Assembly in the Southern Royal Colonies, 1689–1776.* Chapel Hill, N.C., 1963.
Gundersen, "Anglican Ministry in Virginia"
  Joan R. Gundersen, "The Anglican Ministry in Virginia, 1723–1776: A Study of a Social Class." Ph.D. dissertation, Notre Dame University, 1972.
Hening, *Statutes*
  William Waller Hening, ed., *The Statutes at Large: Being a Collection of All the Laws of Virginia, from the First Session of the Legislature, in the Year 1619.* 13 vols. Richmond, 1819–23.
HMPEC
  Historical Magazine of the Protestant Episcopal Church.
James, *Colonial Rhode Island*
  Sydney V. James, *Colonial Rhode Island: A History.* New York, 1975.
JHB
  H. R. McIlwaine and John P. Kennedy, eds., *Journals of the House of Burgesses of Virginia, 1619–1776.* 13 vols. Richmond, 1905–15.
John Norton & Sons
  Frances Norton Mason, ed., *John Norton & Sons: Merchants of London and Virginia.* Richmond, 1937.
Journals of the Board of Trade
  Journals of the Commissioners for Trade and Plantations, 1704–1782. 14 vols. London, 1920–38.
Laugher, *Thomas Bray's Grand Design*
  Charles T. Laugher, *Thomas Bray's Grand Design: Libraries of the Church of England in America, 1695–1785.* Chicago, 1973.
Malone, "North Carolina Anglican Clergy"
  Michael T. Malone, "Sketches of the Anglican Clergy Who Served in North Carolina during the Period 1765–1776," *HMPEC* 39 (1970): 137–61 (part 1), 399–438 (part 2).
Mason, *Annals of Trinity Church*
  George Champlin Mason, *Annals of Trinity Church, Newport, Rhode Island, 1698–1821.* Newport, 1890.

Mason Papers
Robert A. Rutland, ed., *The Papers of George Mason, 1725–1792.* 3 vols. Chapel Hill, N.C., 1970.
Meade, *Old Churches*
William Meade, *Old Churches, Ministers, and Families of Virginia.* 2 vols. Philadelphia, 1857.
Minutes
Minute Books of the Associates of Dr. Bray [volume 1 (1735–1768); volume 2 (1768–1808); volume 3 (1729–1735)], archives of the United Society for the Propagation of the Gospel, London; photostats in Library of Congress.
Morgan and Morgan, *Stamp Act Crisis*
Edmund S. and Helen M. Morgan, *The Stamp Act Crisis: Prologue to Revolution.* Revised ed., New York, 1962.
N.C. Col. Recs.
William L. Saunders, ed., *The Colonial Records of North Carolina.* 10 vols. Raleigh, N.C., 1886–90.
N.C. State Recs.
Walter Clark, ed., *The State Records of North Carolina.* 16 vols. Winston and Goldsboro, N.C., 1895–1905.
OED
Oxford English Dictionary
Perry, *Historical Collections, Pennsylvania*
William Stevens Perry, ed., *Historical Collections Relating to the American Colonial Church.* Volume 2, *Pennsylvania.* Hartford, Conn., 1871.
Perry, *Historical Collections, Virginia*
William Stevens Perry, ed., *Historical Collections Relating to the American Colonial Church.* Volume 1, *Virginia.* Hartford, Conn., 1870.
PMHB
Pennsylvania Magazine of History and Biography.
P.R.O.
Public Record Office, London.
Rightmyer, *Maryland's Established Church*
Nelson Waite Rightmyer, *Maryland's Established Church.* Baltimore, 1956.
SCHGM
South Carolina Historical and Genealogical Magazine.
Schneider and Schneider, *Samuel Johnson*
Herbert Schneider and Carol Schneider, eds., *Samuel Johnson, President of King's College: His Career and Writings.* 4 vols. New York, 1929.

Sibley and Shipton, *Harvard Graduates*
    John L. Sibley and Clifford K. Shipton, *Sibley's Harvard Graduates: Biographical Sketches of Those Who Attended Harvard College*. Cambridge, Mass., 1873– .
Smith, *Life and Correspondence of Smith*
    Horace W. Smith, *Life and Correspondence of the Reverend William Smith, D.D.* 2 vols. Philadelphia, 1879.
S.P.C.K.
    Society for Promoting Christian Knowledge.
S.P.G.
    Society for the Propagation of the Gospel in Foreign Parts.
S.P.G. Journals
    General Meeting Journals of the S.P.G., archives of the United Society for the Propagation of the Gospel, London; photostats in Library of Congress.
S.P.G. MSS.
    Manuscripts of the S.P.G., archives of the United Society for the Propagation of the Gospel, London; microfilm in Library of Congress.
Stephenson, "Negro School in Williamsburg"
    Mary A. Stephenson, "Notes on the Negro School in Williamsburg, 1760–1774," typescript, 1963, in Research Department, Colonial Williamsburg, Inc.
Stiles, *Literary Diary*
    Franklin Bowditch Dexter, ed., *The Literary Diary of Ezra Stiles, D.D., LL.D.* 3 vols. New York, 1901.
Strickland, *Religion and the State in Georgia*
    Reba C. Strickland, *Religion and the State in Georgia in the Eighteenth Century*. New York, 1939.
Tyler's Quarterly
    Tyler's Quarterly Historical and Genealogical Magazine.
Venn, *Alumni Cantabrigienses*
    John Venn and J. A. Venn, comps., *Alumni Cantabrigienses: A Biographical List of All Known Students, Graduates and Holders of Office at the University of Cambridge, from the Earliest Times to 1900*. 10 vols. Cambridge, Eng., 1922–54.
VMHB
    Virginia Magazine of History and Biography.
Weis, *Colonial Clergy Md., Del., Ga.*
    Frederick Lewis Weis, *The Colonial Clergy of Maryland, Delaware, and Georgia*. Lancaster, Mass., 1950.
Weis, *Colonial Clergy Middle Colonies*
    Frederick Lewis Weis, *The Colonial Clergy of the Middle Colonies:*

New York, New Jersey, and Pennsylvania, 1628–1776. Worcester, Mass., 1957. Originally published in *Proceedings of the American Antiquarian Society* 66 (1956): 167–351.

Weis, *Colonial Clergy New England*
Frederick Lewis Weis, *The Colonial Clergy and the Colonial Churches of New England, 1620–1776.* Lancaster, Mass., 1936.

Weis, *Colonial Clergy Va., N.C., S.C.*
Frederick Lewis Weis, *The Colonial Clergy of Virginia, North Carolina and South Carolina.* Boston, 1955.

WMQ
William and Mary Quarterly.

The
American Correspondence
of the
Associates of Dr. Bray,
1717–1777

Abel Tassin, Sieur D'Allone to
Robert Hales (Extract)

Hague July 12/13th [i.e., 12/23] 1717.

That which Occasions my Writing to You at present is that whereas You may remember when You wer' here discoursing together of Converting Negroes & other West Indian Slaves and their Children I told that when I wer' paid the Arrears of my Pension of the late Queen I wou'd out of it Contribute something towards so Charitable an undertaking. So I have now to desire You to deliver my Inclosed to Your Friend the most worthy Dr. Bray wherein is a Bill of 100 lb. which Mr. Henry Temple of East Sheen will pay him upon sight.[1] I recd. the greatest part of those Arrears some months ago when I got notice at the same time that the remainder thereof was like to be paid too. But it having faild me till now I find my Self in Circumstances that I can do it another way. I confess 'tis but a very small matter what I do towards so great a good Work, but I doubt not that if the Undertaking of it be found practicable and duely begun with many too wou'd more plentifully Contribute to its management and performance.

I do leave to You Sir to discourse at large about the same with Your Friend whom I do refer to what I write to You on the Subject that I may not needless be troublesome to him, In hopes that either He or You will let me know what difficultys there are or may be met with in the Execucon of that project On which I shall perhaps have some notions to offer.[2]

Extract. S.P.G. MSS., ser. A, vol. 19, pp. 22–23.

1. Henry Temple (c. 1673–1757) was the eldest surviving son of Sir John Temple, speaker of the Irish House of Commons. He was created Baron Temple and Viscount Palmerston in the Irish peerage in March 1722/23. Palmerston, who was the executor of D'Allone's English estate, sat in the English House of Commons from 1727 to 1747. *DNB*.

2. After receiving the £100 gift, Bray and Hales "found out a person proper and Well disposed to the Work and advising with some Gent. of South Carolina whether Charles Town wou'd not be a proper place to send a School-

master or Catechist to, by Way of Experiment [they] did in Conjunction send Mr. Clifford to wait upon Mr. D'Alloune at the Hague for his Approbation and Instructions who was so well pleased with him as to add 30 lb. more towards furnishing him with books and gave him 5 lb. in his pocket to defray his Charges to and from Holland. . . . Mr. Clifford being immediately upon his return from Holland fully Equip'd for his Mission as far as Mr. D'Allonnes Benefaction wou'd reach and sent to Carolina, and Judge [Nicholas] Trott a person well known to and highly Esteemed by Dr. Bray being then one of the chief in the Government there the said Clifford was recommended to his Protection and Encouragement." "Dr. Brays reasons for Vesting the bequest of Mr. D'alloune in Trustees &c.," 24 February 1724/25, S.P.G. MSS., A19, p. 19.

Assignment of Trustees of Mr. D'Allone's Bequest

[London, 15 January 1729/30]

To all People to whom these Presents shall come The Reverend Thomas Bray of St. Buttolph's without Aldgate London Doctor of Divinity and his Associates (Vizt:) The Right honourable the Lord Viscount Percival of the Kingdom of Ireland, Robert Hales Esqr. late Clerk of his Majesty's most Honourable Privy Counsel, the Reverend Stephen Hales of Teddington in the County of Middlesex Clerk, and William Belitha of London Esqr. send Greeting.[1] Whereas Mr. Abel Tassin D'Allone late of the Hague in Holland deceased in and by his last Will and Testament in Writing bearing Date the first day of July (new Stile) which was in the year of our Lord One thousand seven hundred twenty and one Did (amongst other things) will declare order and direct that the fifth part or portion of his English Estate should be divided into two equal parts one part thereof to be delivered to the said Reverend Doctor Thomas Bray and his Associates That a Capital Fund or Stock might be made thereof and that the yearly Income or Produce thereof should be bestowed and imployed in the Erecting a School or Schools for the thorough instructing in the Christian Religion the young Children of the Negroe Slaves and such of their parents as should show themselves inclinable and desirous of such Instruction in some one or other part of the English plantations in the West Indies according to such a Scheme as should be made. And did thereby further bequeath unto the said Doctor Thomas Bray and his Associates to and for the same Purposes therein and herein before expressed all the Arrears of his Pension from his late Majesty that should be owing to him at the time of his Decease and of his said Will made Henry Temple Esqr. who has since been created Lord Viscount Palmerston of the Kingdom of Ireland and Harrold Johannes Pels Esqr. and Robert Pierre Chilton Seigneur De la Daviere of Holland[2] Executors and on or about the thirteenth Day of October One Thousand Seven Hundred Twenty and Three (old Stile) the said Mr. D'Allone departed this Life in Holland. And the said Lord Viscount Palmerston hath since proved the said Will alone in the prerogative Court of Canterbury[3] and taken upon himself the Execution of the said Will which relates only to the Testators Estate which he was possessed of in Great Britain as by the said Will and Probate thereof Relation being thereunto had may more fully appear. And Whereas the said Doctor Thomas Bray to the Intent and purpose that the aforesaid Legacies might be had and received of and from the said Lord Viscount Palmerston and that he might be legally discharged from the same and that the said Legacies might be faithfully and honestly applied and disposed of according to the true Intent and meaning of the said Testators Will The said Doctor Thomas Bray by a Deed bearing Date the fifteenth day of January Anno Domini One thousand Seven Hundred and Twenty and three Did declare the said Lord Viscount Percival, Robert Hales, Stephen Hales, and William Belitha his Associates and Fellow Trustees of the aforesaid Bequests for the use Intent and Purposes mentioned in the said Will. And for that purpose the said Doctor Thomas Bray did thereby assign transfer and set over unto himself and his said Associates Vizt. the said Lord Viscount Percival, Robert Hales, Stephen Hales, and William Belitha and unto the Survivors and Survivor of them and unto the Executors and Administrators of such Survivor the aforesaid Legacies or Sums of Money given and bequeathed or ordered willed and directed to be paid or delivered unto the said Doctor Thomas Bray in and by the said recited Will to be applied bestowed and employed to such Uses Intents and Purposes as are therein specified and expressed. And the said Doctor Thomas Bray in case of his Death Inability or Absence did further by the said Deed give and grant unto his said Associates Lord Viscount Percival, Robert Hales, Stephen Hales, and William Belitha and the Survivors and Survivor of them his full power Right Title and Authority to act in the Premisses as fully and amply to all intents and purposes as he the said Doctor Thomas Bray might or could do therein by Virtue of the said recited Will. And Whereas the said Doctor Thomas Bray and his said Associates have in pursuance of the Direccions of the said Will employed and supply'd with necessary Books both for Catechists and Catechumens about twenty Missionaries together with direccions how to have the Negroes and Heathens instructed in the Christian Religion in the English Plantations according to the true purport and meaning of the said Will. And Whereas the said Doctor Thomas Bray and his said Associates find themselves under great Difficulties in pursuing the said Design by reason of the

Smallness of their Number, And Whereas the said Robert Hales on account of diverse Affairs which may probably require his presence in parts beyond the Seas is desirous to render up and be discharged from the Execution of the said Trust and the other Associates are by their Family occasions often called to a distance from London, And Whereas the said Doctor Thomas Bray findeth himself in a declining State of Health which he doubteth may soon disable him from performing the said Trust and the said Doctor Thomas Bray and his said Associates fearing so good and pious a Design should be dropt for want of a sufficient Number of proper persons to carry on so laudable and laborious an Undertaking find it necessary to increase the Number of their Associates, Now Know Ye that to the End Intent and purpose that the said Robert Hales may according to his Desire be legally discharged of and from Executing the said Trust and that so laudable an Undertaking may not be frustrated for want of a sufficient Number of persons proper to carry it on and that the said Legacies or Sums of Money may continue to be faithfully and honestly applied according to the true Intent and meaning of the said Testator's Will The said Reverend Doctor Thomas Bray, Lord Viscount Percival, Robert Hales, Stephen Hales, and William Belitha do hereby Declare The honourable Edward Digby Esqr., The honourable Colonell George Carpenter, James Oglethorpe of Westbrook Place in the County of Surrey Esqr., The honourable Edward Harley Esqr. one of the Auditors of his Majesties Exchequer, The honourable James Vernon Esqr. one of the Clerks of his Majesty's most honourable Privy Counsel, Edward Hughes Esqr. Judge Advocate of his Majesty's Court Martial, Robert Hucks of the Parish of St. Gyles's in the Fields Esqr., Thomas Towers of the Inner Temple Esqr., Rogers Holland of Chippenham in Wilts Esqr., John Laroche of Milgate in Kent Esqr., Major Charles Selwyn of Richmond in the County of Surrey, Robert More of Bishops Castle in the County of Salop Esqr., Erasmus Philips of St. Andrew Holbourn Esqr., John Campbell of St. George in the Fields in County Middlesex Esqr., James Lowther of Whitehaven Esqr., William Sloper of St. James's Esqr., [blank in MS] St. John of Soho Esqr., Henry Hastings of Westminster Esqr., Mr. Thomas Carpenter of Friday Street, [blank in MS] Smith of the [blank in MS] Temple Esqr., [blank in MS] Anderson [blank in MS], Captain Thomas Coram, [The] Reverend Digby Cotes Principal of Magdalen Hall M.A. University Orator, The Reverend Mr. Arthur Bedford, The Reverend Mr. Samuel Smith Lecturer of St. Alban Woodstreet, The Reverend Mr. Bundy, The Reverend Mr. Richard King Vicar of Topsham in the County of Devon, The Reverend John Burton M.A. their Associates or Fellow Trustees of the aforesaid Legacies or Sums of Money for the Uses Intents and purposes mentioned in the said Will and therefore the said Doctor Thomas Bray and his said Associates Vizt. The Lord Viscount Percival, Robert Hales, Stephen Hales, and William Belitha Do and each of them Doth hereby assign transfer and [set] over unto themselves the said Doctor Thomas Bray, Lord Viscount Percival, Stephen Hales, and William Belitha and unto the said Edward Digby, Colonel George Carpenter, James Oglethorpe, Edward Harley, James Vernon, Edward Hughes, Robert Hucks, Thomas Towers, Rogers Holland, John Laroche, Major Charles Selwyn, Robert More, Erasmus Philips, John Campbell, James Lowther, William Sloper, [blank in MS] St. John, Henry Hastings, Thomas Carpenter, [blank in MS] Smith, [blank in MS] Anderson, Captain Thomas Coram, Digby Cotes, Arthur Bedford, Samuel Smith, [blank in MS] Bundy, Richard King, John Burton and the Survivors or Survivor of them and the Assigns of such Survivor the aforesaid Legacies or Sums of Money be the same more or less given and bequeathed or ordered willed or directed to be paid or delivered unto the said Doctor Thomas Bray in and by the said recited Will and every part and parcell thereof to be apply'd bestowed and employed as they the said Doctor Thomas Bray, Lord Viscount Percival, Stephen Hales, and William Belitha, Edward Digby, Colonel George Carpenter, James Oglethorpe, Edward Harley, James Vernon, Edward Hughes, Robert Hucks, Thomas Towers, Rogers Holland, John Laroche, Major Charles Selwyn, Robert More, Erasmus Philips, John Campbell, James Lowther, William Sloper, [blank in MS] St. John, Henry Hastings, Thomas Carpenter, [blank in MS] Smith, [blank in MS] Anderson, Captain Thomas Coram, Digby Cotes, Arthur Bedford, Samuel Smith, [blank in MS] Bundy, Richard King, John Burton or the major part of them or of the Survivors of them shall order direct and appoint and do further give and grant unto them the said Trustees and Associates to and for such Uses Intents and Purposes as are mentioned and expressed in the said Mr. D'Allone's Will according to the true Intent and meaning thereof: all their Right Power and Authority to act and do in the Premisses as fully and amply to all Intents Constructions and purposes as the said Doctor Thomas Bray, Lord Viscount Percival, Stephen Hales, and William Belitha might or could do therein by virtue of the said Will and before recited Deed. And the said Doctor Thomas Bray, Lord Viscount Percival, Stephen Hales, and William Belitha Do by these Presents give and grant unto themselves and the said Edward Digby, Colonel George Carpenter, James Oglethorpe, Edward Harley, James Vernon, Edward Hughes, Robert Hucks, Thomas Towers, Rogers Holland, John Laroche, Major Charles Selwyn, Robert More, Erasmus Philips, John Campbell, James Lowther, William Sloper, [blank in MS] St. John,

Henry Hastings, Thomas Carpenter, [*blank in MS*] Smith, [*blank in MS*] Anderson, Captain Thomas Coram, Digby Cotes, Arthur Bedford, Samuel Smith, [*blank in MS*] Bundy, Richard King, John Burton and the major part of them and the Survivors of them and the major part of them full power right and Authority to elect nominate and appoint by way of Balloting any new Associate or Associates who shall and may have the like power vested in them as to act in the said Trust Except to the Election of new Members which is hereby reserved to those only above mentioned. And further that this good Work may be kept on Foot in Case of Mortality of some of us the said Doctor Thomas Bray, Lord Viscount Percival, Stephen Hales, William Belitha, Edward Digby, Colonel George Carpenter, James Oglethorpe, Edward Harley, James Vernon, Edward Hughes, Robert Hucks, Thomas Towers, Rogers Holland, John Laroche, Major Charles Selwyn, Robert More, Erasmus Philips, John Campbell, James Lowther, William Sloper, [*blank in MS*] St. John, Henry Hastings, Thomas Carpenter, [*blank in MS*] Smith, [*blank in MS*] Anderson, Captain Thomas Coram, Digby Cotes, Arthur Bedford, Samuel Smith, [*blank in MS*] Bundy, Richard King, John Burton and [*blank in MS*] do hereby for themselves severally and respectively agree when or before (as occasion shall require) the number of the Survivors of the said Associates and Trustees shall be reduced to Five to Elect nominate and appoint other Trustees and Associates vested with the same powers right and authority. Lastly they the said Doctor Thomas Bray, Lord Viscount Percival, Stephen Hales, William Belitha, Edward Digby, Colonel George Carpenter, James Oglethorpe, Edward Harley, James Vernon, Edward Hughes, Robert Hucks, Thomas Towers, Rogers Holland, John Laroche, Major Charles Selwyn, Robert More, Erasmus Philips, John Campbell, James Lowther, William Sloper, [*blank in MS*] St. John, Henry Hastings, Thomas Carpenter, [*blank in MS*] Smith, [*blank in MS*] Anderson, Captain Thomas Coram, Digby Cotes, Arthur Bedford, Samuel Smith, [*blank in MS*] Bundy, Richard King, John Burton and [*blank in MS*] do and each of them for himself his Heirs Executors and Administrators doth hereby declare and make known that they will not nor any of them or the heirs Executors and Administrators of them or any of them shall or will be answerable or accountable for the Acts Deeds Receipts Payments or Defaults of the other of them but Each for himself and his own Acts Deeds Receipts Payments and Defaults only nor shall or will any of them respectively be answerable for any money but what shall be actually received by them respectively. In Witness whereof We have hereunto set our hands and Seals the Fifteenth day of January in the third year of the Reign of our Sovereign Lord George the Second of Great Britain France and

Ireland King Defender of the Faith Anno Domini One thousand Seven hundred and Twenty Nine.

LS   Thomas Bray
LS
LS   Robert Hales
LS   Stephen Hales
LS   Wm: Belitha

DS. This document, formally engrossed on parchment, is endorsed "Assignment of Trustees of Mr. D'Allone's Bequest." Beneath this endorsement is a pencilled notation that reads "Useless. See Chancery Proceedings." There are ribbons and spaces for the seals and signatures of twenty-five additional men. For an extended discussion of this document, see pp. 10–12, above.

1. For Percival, Stephen Hales, and Robert Hales, see Biographical Appendix. William Belitha (d. post-1744) was a subscribing member of the S.P.C.K. from 1722. *An Account of the Society for Promoting Christian Knowledge* (London, 1745), p. 38.

2. In his will D'Allone described Pels and Chilton as "a Dutchman and a Frenchman now living at the Hague in Holland." David C. A. Agnew, *Protestant Exiles from France, Chiefly in the Reign of Louis XIV; or, The Huguenot Refugees and Their Descendants in Great Britain and Ireland*, 3d ed., 2 vols. ([London], 1886), 2:208.

3. Palmerston proved the will on 23 December 1723. Ibid., p. 210.

[Rev. Jacob Henderson to Rev. Samuel Smith]

[Prince Georges County, Maryland, c. 1731]

Two Letters from the Commissary of Maryland to Sam. Smith were read wherein were inclos'd his Address to the Clergy of that Province at his late Visitation & his Proceedings in relation to the Conversion of the Negroes.[1]

Letters not found. Extract from Minutes, 3:43 (meeting of 15 January 1731/32). After reading these letters the Associates

Agreed that a Parcel of the Bishop of London his Letters to the Masters & Mistresses of Families & to the Value of five Pounds be sent to the Commissary.

Agreed that Sam Smith do prepare an Answer to the Commissary his Letter to be lay'd before the Associates at their next Meeting.

Smith's reply, which has not been found, was approved and ordered to be sent at the meeting of 27 January 1731/32. Minutes, 3:44. At the meeting of 10 February 1731/32 Smith reported sending to Henderson 250 copies of [Edmund Gibson], *Two Letters of the Lord Bishop of London: The First, to the Mas-*

ters and Mistresses of Families in the English Plantations Abroad; Exhorting Them to Encourage and Promote the Instruction of Their Negroes in the Christian Faith. The Second, to the Missionaries There; Directing Them to Distribute the Said Letter, and Exhorting Them to Give Their Assistance towards the Instruction of the Negroes within Their Several Parishes (London, 1727). Minutes, 3 : 46.

1. Enclosures not found. They were most likely copies of the records of Henderson's visitations of and addresses to the clergy of the Eastern Shore of Maryland, 24 June 1730, and of the Western Shore, 15 July 1730. Fulham Papers, 3 : 134–41.

Rev. Arthur Holt to Rev. Samuel Smith

[All Faith's Parish,
St. Mary's County, Maryland, 21 May 1734]

Reverend Sir,

Since I wrote to You last,[1] the want of health obliged me to remove, with my Family to the Northward, having My Lord of Londons[2] recommendation and My Lord Howe's[3] License to absent for Twelve Months from Barbadoes.

Finding health restored to my Family in Maryland, we all desired rather to settle here than venture again over the dreadful deep to Barbadoes whose torrid Clime we had reason to believe wou'd soon deprive Us again of that health which with great Risques and expence we have so lately acquired.

I apply'd my Self to the Governor of Maryland,[4] who receiv'd me kindly and has placed me for the present in the Rectory of All-Faith in the County of St. Mary, where I have a People to Serve different from those in Barbadoes.

My Parish abounds with Papists. There are several Priests and several Places where they convene their people at their Pleasure. Their Priests are of the Jesuit Order.

The Protestants seem very inclinable to hear and practice their Duty. My Labour is very great amongst them; my Parish being near 60 Miles long and very mountainous; but to my great Joy my Churches are fill'd and many are forced to Crowd at the Out Side of the Doors and windows.

I have had already upwards of 90 Communicants in one Church and above 50 at the other.[5] I have Baptiz'd several Negroes since I came hither. The People are much more easily persuaded to have their Slaves Christians than the Inhabitants of Barbadoes, nor indeed is the Task so hard here this Colony being but Yet in its Infancy and the Number of Slaves but small.

I catechise every Lords Day except on Communion days and read Dr. Newton's Exposition of the Catechism,[6] being one of the Books I received from Doctor Bray, which with the other Books he sent to me, tho they were not so acceptable to the Barbadians as might have been expected, will I hope sufficiently answer the end here, where they are highly necessary.[7] I shall still keep them under my own Care, except otherwise ordered by those pious Associates who succeed Doctor Bray, whose Commands I shall when honoured therewith be ever ready to obey.

I have reason to believe that the Publick Libraries of this Province woud if examin'd into be found to stand much in need of some regulation.[8]

Pray give my Duty to your honourable Society. If they are at Leisure and are dispos'd to extend their Favours to the people of this Place I'm persuaded they will have a happy Effect. Some of those small pieces dissuasive from and defensive against Popery, woud be a very Charitable Present in this parish where Romish Pamphlets are diligently dispers'd up & down & where during my Predecessors incapacity many years thro' Lameness & Sickness &c. the Romish Priests made a plentiful Harvest.[9] Many Families amongst us are but half Protestant the husband of one and the Wife of the other Persuasion. The Women who are Papists and intermarry with Protestant Husbands, make it a part of their contract that all their Daughters shall be brought up in the Romish Faith. The Number of Papists we suppose now to exceed the protestants at least 3 to one in this County.

I shou'd be very glad to be honoured with your Correspondence in Mary Land who am Revd. Sir Your most obedient humble Servant

Art. Holt.

All-Faith, St. Mary's County Maryland
May 21. 1734.

Copy: Fulham Papers, 3:174–75, Lambeth Palace Library, London. At the meeting of 4 November 1734 "Mr. Smith acquainted the Associates That he had recd. a Letter from Mr. Holt a former Correspondent of the Associates at Barbados who is now Settled at Maryland, desiring a small Present of Books for the Instruction of his Negroes. Agreed That the same be prepared and sent accordingly." Minutes, 3:71.

1. Letter not found.

2. The Rt. Rev. Edmund Gibson (1669–1748) was bishop of London from 1723 until his death. *DNB*.

3. Emanuel Scrope Howe (c. 1698–1735), second Viscount Howe in the Irish peerage, was governor of Barbados from 1733 until his death. He was the father of Admiral Richard Lord Howe and General Sir William Howe. Sir Robert H. Schomburgk, *The History of Barbados* (London, 1848), pp. 320, 322; *DNB*, s.v. Richard Howe.

4. Samuel Ogle (c. 1702–1752) was governor of Maryland from 1731 to 1732, from 1733 to 1742, and from 1747 until his death. *DAB.*

5. The church of All Faith's Parish was at present-day Mechanicsville. The chapel, known as Four-Mile Run Church, became the parish church of St. Andrew's Parish. Berkley, "Churches and Parishes of Maryland," pp. 30–31; Percy G. Skirven, *The First Parishes of the Province of Maryland* (Baltimore, 1923), p. 177.

6. This work has not been identified.

7. On 1 March 1727/28 Bray sent to Holt in Barbados "a Catechetical Library in Embrio . . . to instruct the Negroes," book presses in which to keep the volumes, and "Books for the Instruction of the Negroes to Read, & in the Principles of the Christian Religion." "Dr. Bray's Account of Receipts & Disbursements . . . ," 28 Feb. 1727/28 to Nov. 1729, U.S.P.G. Archives, London.

8. This is a reference to the laymen's libraries established in Maryland by Thomas Bray. These lending libraries, containing primarily religious tracts, were intended to be kept in the vestry of each parish and lent out at the discretion of the minister. In 1701 eleven such libraries were sent to Maryland. Thomas Bray, *The Layman's Library: Being a Lending Library for the Use of the Laity* [London, 1700]; Joseph Towne Wheeler, "The Laymen's Libraries and the Provincial Library," *Maryland Historical Magazine* 35 (1940): 60–73.

9. Holt's predecessor in All Faith's Parish was the Rev. Robert Scott (d. 1734) of Kent, England, who served the parish from 1708 until his death. Weis, *Colonial Clergy Md., Del., Ga.*, p. 63.

[Rev. Benjamin Colman to the Earl of Egmont]

[Boston, 8 July 1734]

My Lord,

Mr. Coram, who has the Honour to be one of the late Rev. Dr. Bray's Associates, having informed me of his communicating my Letter to him of September 1733, and that the Honourable and Reverend Associates had shewn that Regard to it as to order it on their File; and that he had asked for a small Parcel of Books for the three Missionaries and their Successors, Mr. Stephen Parker at Richmond Fort, Mr. Ebenezer Hinsdel at Fort Dummer, and Mr. Joseph Secomb at St. Georges River, all on the Borders of his Majesty's Province of the Massachusetts-Bay in New-England, and that the Honourable Associates had declared their Will to give some Books as desired, provided a proper Application were made for them; I am therefore directed by his Excellency Jonathan Belcher Esq; our Governour, who is ever ready unto every good Work, and first in the pious Care for the Missions aforesaid, to give your Lordship the Trouble of this Line, and let the Honourable Gentlemen Associates know in what need of proper

Books the Missionaries aforesaid are, and how acceptable your Charity and Bounty to them would be to the Commissioners here who have the Oversight of these Missions.[1]

It is now thirty-eight Years ago, that the Rev. Dr. Bray himself informed me, at his Chamber in White-Hall, that he was projecting his extensive Charity of Parochial Libraries, when I could little have thought of addressing your Lordship on this Occasion at such a Distance of Time and Place. The Dr. like a true Minister of Jesus Christ, went about doing good, and his Works follow him, his Praise remains in all the Churches.

In particular I would ask by your Lordship's Favour, for each Missionary a Copy of the Rev. Mr. Smith's most worthy Sermon preached to the Trustees and Associates *Anno* 1730,1, it being wonderfully calculated to instruct and animate Persons imployed in such a Service.[2]

It only remains now to ask your Lordship's Pardon for the Freedom I have taken, to add my hearty Prayers for the best of Blessings on the Gentlemen Associates, and to do my self the Honour of subscribing, My Lord, Your very obedient Humble Servant.

Printed copy: Ebenezer Turell, *The Life and Character of the Reverend Benjamin Colman, D.D.* (Boston, 1749), pp. 145–46. Following the text of the letter Turell wrote, "To this Letter the Right Honourable the Earl returned a kind Answer." The reply has not been found.

1. For Thomas Coram see Biographical Appendix. Colman's letter to Coram, dated 19 September 1733, has not been found.

Coram received from his sister-in-law, Elizabeth (Waite) Stirling (see Biographical Appendix), an extract from the *Boston Weekly News-Letter* of 13 December 1733 announcing the ordination in Boston of three missionaries to the Indians. Coram laid Colman's letter before the Associates and requested books for the missionaries on 1 April 1734. The missionaries were Stephen Parker (c. 1706–1744) at Fort Richmond, Maine; Ebenezer Hinsdell (1706–63) at Fort Dummer (now Brattleboro, Vermont); and Joseph Seccomb (1706–60) at Fort St. George's (now St. George, Maine). They were supported by the Edinburgh Society for Propagating Christian Knowledge among the Indians, of which Colman was an American commissioner. Jonathan Belcher (1681/82–1757), governor of Massachusetts and also a commissioner of the Scottish S.P.C.K., evidently requested Colman to make application to the Associates for books for the missionaries. At their meeting of 9 October 1734 the Associates agreed to send £10 worth of books to the missionaries, "which is a present we make to them for carrying on that good work." For the books sent, see List of Books Sent to New England, 21 April 1735, below. Egmont, *Diary* 2 : 129; Coram to Colman, 30 April 1734, Colman Papers, Massachusetts Historical Society, printed in *Proceedings of the Massachusetts Historical Society* 56 (1922–23): 19–24; *Boston News-Letter*, 6–13 March, 10–17 April 1735; Sibley and Shipton, *Harvard Graduates* 8 : 141–48, 246–47, 9 : 87–96.

2. Samuel Smith preached the first anniversary sermon before the Asso-

ciates on 23 February 1730/31. After the chartering of the Georgia Trustees
in 1732 (all of whom were Associates), Smith's sermon was published under
the title *A Sermon Preach'd before the Trustees for Establishing the Colony of Georgia
in America, and Before the Associates of the Late Rev. Dr. Thomas Bray, for Converting the Negroes in the British Plantations, and for Other Good Purposes* (London,
1733).

[Hugh Bryan to Rev. Samuel Smith]

[Port Royal, South Carolina, 4 March 1734/35]

Read a Letter from Mr. Hugh Bryan of Port Royal in So. Carolina dated 4 March 1735 acknowledging the Rect. of the Books sent
him for Converting his Negroes.[1]

Letter not found. Extract from Minutes, 3:91 (meeting of 6 August 1735).

1. At their meeting of 4 November 1734 "Mr. Verelst [see Biographical
Appendix] acquainted the Associates that he had sent to the Care of Mr.
[Thomas] Causton at Savanah in Georgia three Parcels of Books containing in
each 3 Bibles, 30 Primmers, 30 small Spelling Books, 30 Horn Books, 20 Testaments & 30 Psalters. Directed to Mrs. Hague, Mrs. Drayton, & Mr. Bryan at
Charles Town in South Carolina for Instruction of their Negroes, for him
to send by the first Opportunity. Mr. Smith was desired to send Letters to
Charles Town acquainting them of the said Books being so sent by the Associates." Minutes, 3:70–71. Smith's letters have not been found. See [Drayton
to Smith, 2 June 1736], below. Mrs. Lilia Hague (or Haigue) was a sister of
Alexander Skene, who had served in the South Carolina Commons House
of Assembly and in 1719 led a successful attempt to overthrow the Proprie-
tary government and make South Carolina a royal colony. Mrs. Hague, who
owned thirty-one slaves in January 1725/26, took "great pains to have [her]
negros instructed in the Christian religion." Frank J. Klingberg, *An Appraisal
of the Negro in Colonial South Carolina: A Study in Americanization* (Washington,
D.C., 1941), pp. 40–43, 55n, 59.

Rev. Charles Chauncy to Thomas Coram

[Boston, 8 April 1735]

Sir,

My natural backwardness to writing, together with being a
stranger to you, is the best excuse I am able to make for not expressing before now the gratefull sense I have of your favour, thrô the
hands of your Sister. I had never before seen *Erasmus's Ecclesiastes*;
and heartily thank you for a book, wearing a name of so great figure
in the learned world.[1]

Be pleased also to accept of my acknowledgments for the handsome notice, the honorable Associates to the late Rev. Dr. Bray, have taken of the three *Indian Missionaries*, upon Dr. Williams's foundation.[2] And as your kindness and goodwill discovered to this Country, in the exhibition, of which I have been a partaker, first gave occasion to, and your good services afterwards made way for, this donation; you will not esteem yourself flatterd, or any of the honorable associates dishonord, if we hold our selves especially obligd to you, and are particular in our returns of love and gratitude.

By the trust reposed in you as one of the honorable Associates of Dr. Bray, you have it in your power of being instrumental of doing extensive service. I question not your inclination to act fully up to your power in endeavours to do good: And as we in this Country have had already a signal specimen of it, we encourage our selves to expect your further notice and regards as there may be occasion.

I heartily wish that you and all associated with you may be always under the Divine Influence and direction, and be made great blessings in the wise and faithfull management of the trust committed to you: which, together with salutations as due to your self and spouse and family, is all at present, from, Sir, Your obliged and most humble servant

Charles Chauncy

Boston Aprill. 8th. 1735.

ALS. Sent "per Capt. Cary."

    1. See Stirling to Coram, 10 April 1735, note 1, below.

    2. Dr. Williams's Foundation was the Edinburgh Society for Propagating Christian Knowledge among the Indians. Daniel Williams (1643?–1716), an English Nonconformist divine and philanthropist, left the bulk of his estate (estimated at £50,000) to charitable causes. He bequeathed £56 sterling per annum to the Society towards the support of three qualified missionaries "that should Labour in the Instruction and Conviction of Infidel People perishing in Ignorance of Christ: The Honourable Society choose to make the poor Heathenish People about *New-England* the first Objects of their Care" (*New-England Weekly Journal* [Boston], 17 December 1733). See [Colman to Egmont, 8 July 1734], note 1, above. *DNB*.

Elizabeth Stirling to Thomas Coram

[Boston, 10 April 1735]

Sir

I now write on purpose to Remitt to you an Account of the books you put into my hands, with derections how I should dispose of them.

They ware all of one Sort Entitled Erasmi Ecclesiastes, and mounted in Number to 24.[1] The persons they have been given to with their Names Characters & places of abode are on the other Side. I delivered them my Self to most & Received from their own mouths their greatfull Acknowlegments to you, (I have Reason to think it was generaly very acceptable) & that all desire to Remember you with honour.

You have Reason to be offended at my Neglect of not giving you an Account of their disposal before & therfore am willinger to Ask pardon then Excuse my fault Especialy Since I know your Readyness to overlook Those offenc's that ware not designed Such, in Expectation of which I Remain Dear Brother Your Affectionate Sister & Servant

Eliza: Stirling

Boston Aprill 10. 1735

ALS.

1. Stirling is acknowledging receipt of copies of Desiderius Erasmus (d. 1536), *Ecclesiastes, sive Concionator evangelicus. Liber primus. De dignitate, difficultate, pietate, puritate, prudentia caeterisque virtutibus ecclesiastae. Cui praesigitur dissertatio praeliminaris*, ed. Thomas Bray (London, 1730). The copyright of this work passed to the Associates on Bray's death. They presented a copy of the book to all men of Oxford and Cambridge who were to be ordained, and the book was included in nearly all the libraries established by the Associates in England and America. Laugher, *Thomas Bray's Grand Design*, p. 15.

At their meeting of 2 July 1733 the Associates "Agreed That twenty four of Erasmus's Ecclesiastes be deliver'd to Capt. Coram to be sent to New England." Minutes, 3:60.

Enclosure
List of Recipients of Books

The Revd. President & fellows of Harvard College in Cambridge[1]			6
	Dr. Cuttler		
	Dr. Coleman		
	Dr. Sewall		
	Mr. Price		
All Ministers in the town of Boston[2]	Dr. Harwood	Each 1 is	10
	Mr. Prince		
	Mr. Foxcroft		
	Mr. Checkley		
	Mr. Chauncy		
	Mr. Byles		

Mr. MacSparren of Naraganset
Mr. Brown of Providence
Mr. Cotton 1st. ordaind Missionary of Providence   5
   In the Colony of Rhode Island
Mr. Billins of Millton
Mr. Miller of Brantrey
The 3 Indian Missionaries Hinsdel, Parker, & Secomb[3]   3
            The whole Amount   24
                          E.S.

ADS. At their meeting of 4 February 1733/34 the Associates read several letters "from the Ministers of New England expressing their great Value of & Acknowledgement for those Erasmus's Ecclesiastes that had been presented to them, by the hands of Captain Coram." Minutes, 3 : 65.

1. The president of Harvard College was Benjamin Wadsworth (1669/70–1736/37). The five fellows were Henry Flynt (1675–1760), Joseph Sewall (1688–1769), Nathaniel Appleton (1693–1784), Edward Wigglesworth (c. 1693–1765), and Nathan Prince (1698–1748). *Historical Register of Harvard University, 1636–1936* (Cambridge, 1937), p. 7.

2. These Boston ministers were Timothy Cutler (1684–1765) of Christ Church (Anglican); Benjamin Colman (see Biographical Appendix); Joseph Sewall of Old South Church (Congregational); Roger Price (1696–1762) of King's Chapel (Anglican) and commissary of the bishop of London for New England; Thomas Harward (1700–36), king's lecturer at King's Chapel; Thomas Prince (1687–1758) of Old South Church; Thomas Foxcroft (1696/97–1769) of First Church (Congregational); Samuel Checkley (1695/96–1769) of New South Church (Congregational); Charles Chauncy (see Biographical Appendix); and Mather Byles (1706/07–1788) of Hollis Street Church (Congregational). Sibley and Shipton, *Harvard Graduates* 5 : 45–66, 341–68, 376–93; 6 : 47–58, 74–78; 7 : 464–93; Weis, *Colonial Clergy New England*, p. 102.

3. The Rev. James McSparran (d. 1757) was S.P.G. missionary to Kingston, Rhode Island, and minister of St. Paul's Church, Kingston. The Rev. Arthur Browne (1699–1773) was S.P.G. missionary to Providence, Rhode Island, and minister of King's Chapel, Providence. He was the father of the Rev. Marmaduke Browne, the administrator of the Associates' Negro school at Newport. The Rev. Josiah Cotton (1703–80) was minister of the First Congregational Church, Providence. Mr. Billins has not been identified. For Ebenezer Miller see Biographical Appendix. For Hinsdell, Parker, and Seccomb see [Colman to Egmont, 8 July 1734], note 1, above. Weis, *Colonial Clergy New England*, pp. 42, 63, 132.

List of Books Sent to New England

[Boston, 21 April 1735]

Books given by the Honble. & Revd. Associates of the late Excellent Dr. Bray of London, for the Use of the three Missions on the Borders of New-England, on St. Georges River, at Richmond Fort & at Fort Dummer.

Received by me Benja. Colman of Boston, & as equally divided by me as I am able, to be forwarded to the three Revd. Missionaries, Mr. Stephen Parker, Mr. Ebenezer Hinsdel & Mr. Joseph Seccombe.

Mr. Burkit on the New Testament	three
Papal Usurpations, History of Waldenses, with Dr. Bray's Visitation, Acts, &c.	three
Dr. Bray's Catechetical Lectures, with Kettlewels practical Beleiver	three
Dr. Mores Theological Works	one
The Works of Mr. William Allen, in 13 distinct Tracts	one
Mr. Smiths Sermon before the Trustees	six
Dr. Hopkins 17 Sermons	three
Erasmi Ecclesiastes	three
Bp. Worcesters Charge, Bibliotheca Catechetica, &c.	one
Life of Bernard Gilpin, Missionalia	three
Animadversion on Sir Isaac Newtons Chronology	two
Dr. Hicks Apologetical Vindication, & Spinckes Trust in God	three
Bp. Londons pastoral Letter, Christs Sermon on Mount, paraphrased, & Scriptural Catechism &c.	three
Refutation of principal Errors, Address to Godfathers, right keeping Christmas &c.	three
Collection of Psalms proper &c.	two
Method of family Religion, of instructing youth, Bedfords Sermons, Extirpation of Popery, Laws against Hereticks, &c.	three
Dr. Kennets Sermon, Apothegmata curiosa, Primordia Bibliothecaria	three
Dr. Bray on the Baptismal Covenant	three
Dr. Mores Enchiridion Ethicum	three
Dr. Clark on Baptism, Confirmation & Repentance	three
Mr. Lewis Church Catechism explaind	one
The great Importance of a religious Life	three
Dr. Watt's Preservative, with Setts of Catechisms	six
Dr. Hales Admonition to the Drinkers of Brandy, fifty, to be distributed by the Honble. Commissioners here	
Stanhope Concio ad Clerum, preventive Charity &c., Miscell.	one

76

Serious Address to Godfathers, Dissuasive from Gaming,
    A.B.C. Catechism, persuasive to keep the Lords day
Boston. April. 21. 1735.

D. This document is in Colman's hand. It may have been enclosed in a letter to the Associates now lost, for at the meeting of 25 June 1735 the Associates "Read a Letter from New England from Dr. Coleman containing an Acknowledgement of having recd. the Books for the Library for the Missionaries, and also a Bible for Mr. Joseph Seccomb one of the said Missionaries." Minutes, 3 : 88. The books were sent to New England on board the *Union*, Capt. Homans, which sailed from London on 15 February 1734/35. Minutes, 3 : 76 (meeting of 3 March 1734/35). At their meeting of 3 September 1735 the Associates "Read a 2d. Letter from Dr. Coleman giving an Acct. that he had distributed two Dividends of the Books for the Library for the Missionaries at New England, & recd. the Receipts for the said Dividends. And also a Letter from Govr. Belcher to Mr. Smith acknowledging the Receipt of the said Books. And Mr. Smith was desired to acknowledge the Rect. of the Letters." Minutes, 3 : 93. None of the letters has been found. Hinsdell's receipt (not found) for his portion of the library, presumably forwarded to the Associates by Colman, was read by the Associates at their meeting of 3 December 1735. Minutes, 3 : 96. Seccomb acknowledged receipt of his books in a letter to Egmont dated 21 June 1735 (not found), which was read by the Associates at their meeting of 7 January 1735/36. Minutes, 1 : 2.

Rev. Frederick Michael Ziegenhagen to [Rev. Samuel Smith]

Kensington May the 3d, 1735.

Reverend and Dear Sir

    According to my Duty and Promise, I should have wrote to you long before this, but I have had this winter till now so much bussiness upon my Hands, that I have not been able to go through it, much less to do each of it in its Time, and so I hope you will excuse the long Delay of my not writing to you. I send you hereby the List of Books for the use of the Protestant German Congregation in Virginia and Philadelphia, bought for the twenty Pounds sterling you was pleased to pay to me from an unknown Benefactor.[1] As the People in Virginia are in greater want of them, than in Philadelphia, I have, with your and the kind Benefactor's Leave, given them the greatest share of the Books, viz: two thirds. I can't but acquaint you with a very providential thing that happen'd just when the Books were upon the Road from Hall,[2] it is this, that three Deputies from the above said Congregation in Virginia unexpectedly arrived in London at the same Time, in order to sollicit here and in Germany for some charitable assistance for the maintenance of a Minister, and the building of a church &&.[3] The Honorble. William Gooche Deputy-Governour of Virginia, and the Ministre of the english Congregation there, the Revd. Mr. Patrik Henry[4] hath attested by a proper Certificate and Letter the poor conditions and Circumstances of this German Congregation. I beg leave to inclose with this the Governour's Certificate and the Minister's recommendatory Letter.[5] Our Friend Mr. James Vernon,[6] and Mr. William Sharp, Clarck of the privy Council,[7] hath been extraordinary kind to the Deputies, both in Words and Deeds. Reverend Sir, as Providence hath been pleased to make you a blessed instrument to get and procure good, religious Books for whole Congregations, I hope you will excuse it, if I should knock at your Door in behalf of the good Mr. Stoever, Minister of the Virginian Congregation, who is himself one of the Deputies, and now in London. The poor Man is in great want of good Books. I have wrote to Hall and interceded with the Revd. Professor Franck for Him, who hath promised to send him some german and latin Books. But he wants a Hebrew Bible, a Hebrew Dictionary and of good practical english Books he hath nothing at all. Pool's Annotations on the Bible[8] would be of great use to Him, etc. I am certainly ashamed to trouble you with more things, after you have been so good to the Salzburgers, and the People in Virginia and Philadelphia, but relying on your goodness, I can't help to lay Mr. Stoever's Case before you. Who knows, the Lord may inable you to supply its want also. Wishing you grace and happiness from the Lord I remain with sincere estim Revd. Sir Your much obliged humble servant

Fred: Mich: Ziegenhagen

ALS.

1. The list has not been found.

2. Halle, a city on the Saale River in present-day East Germany, was the center of German pietism and the home of the Francke Institutes, which included an orphanage, a dispensary, and a publishing house.

3. The Rev. John Caspar Stoever, Sr., (1685–1739) of Frankenberg, Hesse, was from 1733 to 1739 minister of Old Hebron Lutheran Church, near Madison, Virginia. Stoever arrived in Philadelphia in September 1728 and moved to the Lutheran settlement in Virginia shortly thereafter. In 1733 he agreed to become the minister and traveled to Pennsylvania to be ordained by the Rev. John Christian Schulz. The following year Stoever, along with Michael Smith, an elder, and Michael Holt, a member of the congregation, went to Europe to collect funds for a church, a glebe, books, and a schoolhouse. They also hoped to return with an ordained minister to serve as Stoever's assistant. Although Stoever died on the return voyage, he did succeed in raising nearly £3,000 and in hiring the Rev. George Samuel Klug as assistant pastor. Councillor Koehler, of Kolberg, Pomerania, wrote to Professor Gotthilf Francke, of the University of Halle, on 11 May 1736 of Stoever's plans:

He has the intention . . . on his return, to buy twelve negroes as slaves, with whom he intends to clear enough land so that he together with another minister and assistant could live on it, without being a burden to the congregation. He is now paid a salary of 3,000 pounds of tobacco by the congregation. If these slaves be kept better than those among the English people, and be instructed in the Christian religion he thinks that thereby hundred, nay even thousands of slaves, who are compelled to work for Englishmen, will be brought from heathen ignorance to Christ, indeed that much good could thereby be accomplished among the English. (*VMHB* 14 [1906–7]: 144–45)

Weis, *Colonial Clergy Va., N.C., S.C.*, p. 49; Klaus G. Wust, *The Virginia Germans* (Charlottesville, 1969), p. 44; W. P. Huddle, *History of the Hebron Lutheran Church, Madison County, Virginia, from 1717–1907* (New Market, Va., 1908), pp. 20–30.

4. For Gooch and Henry see Biographical Appendix.

5. See the enclosures to this letter, below.

6. James Vernon (d. 1756) was an original member of both the Georgia Trustees and the Associates. He was the son of Secretary of State James Vernon (1646–1727) and the older brother of Admiral Edward Vernon (1684–1757). Vernon was clerk of the Privy Council in extraordinary 1701–2, envoy extraordinary to the king of Denmark 1702–6, M.P. for Cricklade, Wiltshire, 1708–10, commissioner of the excise 1710–56, and clerk of the Privy Council in ordinary 1715–56. Vernon was also a member of the S.P.G. and the S.P.C.K., and often acted as intermediary between those organizations and the Georgia Trustees. *DNB*; Strickland, *Religion and the State in Georgia*, pp. 33–35.

7. William Sharpe (d. 1767) was clerk of the Privy Council in extraordinary 1722–30 and in ordinary 1730–67. *Acts of the Privy Council of England. Colonial Series*, 6 vols. (London, 1908–12), 5:683, 690, 743; *Gentleman's Magazine* 37 (1767): 430.

8. Matthew Poole, or Pool (1624–79), *Annotations upon the Holy Bible*, 2 vols. (London, 1683–85).

Enclosure

Rev. Patrick Henry to Rev. [John Peter] Stehelin

St. Martins parish Hanover County. Virginia
September 4. 1734.

Revd. Sir.

I gladly embrace this opportunity of writing you to whom I am so much obliged, and do gratefully acknowledge the favours I receivd of you. The sense I have of the obligations I am under to you. I should by this bearer have given you a full account of my affairs, but seeing he knows as much of my circumstances & situation as is worth your knowing, I refer you to his account of me. The occasion of the present trouble is to recommend to your favour the Reverend Johannes Casparus Stoeverus Minister of a German Congregation in this Colony. I have recommended him to some friends in Scotland whither he sails directly & from there goes for Holland & returns by London. His bussines is to endeavour to obtain some charitable Contributions for building a Church for the use of his Congregation, purchasing Glebe Land for him, their present incumbent & his successors and raising a fund for their better subsistence, the people being so poor that they cannot give more towards their ministers support than 3000# of tabacco. What I earnestly desire of you is that you would please communicate this to my worthy friend the Reverend Dr. Hay of St. Stephens Coleman street[1] and see if any thing can be done towards the above design & I would further beg of you to introduce the bearer to my Lord of London & St. Davids,[2] as hoping their Lordships upon having his own account of the circumstances of his Congregation may be inclinable to do something towards his support. I do from my own personall knowledge of him declare, that I believe him to be a man of very good morals, and especially very diligent in the business of his function and the general character of his Congregation is that they are Men of honesty & integrity. There has been some money raised in this Colony for the above mentioned purposes, but all that has hitherto been contributed comes vastly short of what would be necessary for purchasing Glebe Land & building a Church & glebe house, not to speak of the fund for the ministers subsistence. I do entreat of you Sir to use your interest to forward this matter which I have reason to hope will tend to the advancement of religion among this people who really seem to be devoutly disposed. The bearer is in great hopes that if he could find a way of applying to the Queen[3] her Majesty would probably be graciously enclined to consider his and Congregations circumstances, but I refer that to your prudent management. I heartily wish you & family as much happiness as you can desire & I am very Sincerely Revd. Sir Your most obliged humble Servant

Patrick Henry

ALS.

1. The Rev. John Hay (d. 1753). *Gentleman's Magazine* 23 (1753): 540.

2. The Rt. Rev. Edmund Gibson (1669–1748) was bishop of London from 1723 until his death. The Rt. Rev. Nicholas Clagett (d. 1746) was bishop of St. David's from 1731 to 1742. *DNB.*

3. Caroline of Ansbach (1683–1737) was queen consort of George II. *DNB.*

Enclosure

Certificate of Governor William Gooch

[Williamsburg, 18 September 1734 O.S.]

Virginia

William Gooch Esqr. his Majestys Lieutenant
Governor and Commander in Chief of the Colony
and Dominion of Virginia

To all to whom these Presents shall come greeting. At the Request of Michael Holt, & diverse other German Protestants, Inhabitants near the great Mountains in the County of Spotsilvania in this Dominion. I do hereby certifie; that the said Inhabitants do at their own proper Charge keep and maintain a Minister of the Gospel, of their own Persuasion (to wit) the Reverend Caspar Stover, for whom they have already purchased a Glebe, and built a Mansion House, and are now building a Church for their Congregation,[1] which is well attested to me. And also that the said Inhabitants are of low Circumstances, and not able to defray the Expenses of the Finishing the said Church, without some Assistance from others. And that in Order to obtain some Relief and Assistance from their Countryman in the Empire of Germany towards the Finishing the said Church, and the Maintenance and Support of the Minister. They are now Sending thiter their said Minister, Mr. Stoever together with the said Michael Holt and Michael Smith. And that their said Message & Negotiation in the Premisses, may recieve Credit in that Empire, I have given this Certificate, and caused the Seal of this Colony to be affixed to the same. At Williamsburgh this Eighteenth Day of September (old stile) in the Eight Year of the Reign of our Soverain Lord George the Second, King of Great Brittain, France and Ireland, Defender of the Faith, &c. Annoq. Domini MDCCXXXIV.

William Gooch.

L.S.

Copy. At their meeting of 25 June 1735 the Associates "Read a Certificate from the Govr. of Virginia giving a Character of the Revd. Caspar Stover. Agreed, That a Collection of Books be sent towards founding a Parochial Library, for the use of him & the succeeding Ministers of the Palatine Congregation in Virginia." Minutes, 1:88.

1. In 1733 the Lutherans acquired 193 acres for church and school purposes. Hebron Church was completed in 1740. Philip Slaughter, *A History of*

St. Mark's Parish, Culpeper County, Virginia (Baltimore, 1887), p. 104; *VMHB* 14 (1906–7): 155.

Rev. Frederick Michael Ziegenhagen to Rev. Samuel Smith

Kensington Square August 12. 1735.

Revd. Sir

The favour of yours August the 5th, with the inclosed catalogue of the Books, which the Associates of Dr. Bray have been pleased to give for the use of Mr. Stoever and his successors in Virginia,[1] came the same day to my hands, but my drinking for several weeks some mineral waters is the reason of the delay of my answer, which I beg you will excuse. Looking over the said catalogue, I agree entirely with you, Revd. Sir, that this collection, by the blessing of God, will be of great service and advantage to the present and succeding Ministers as well, as to the Congregation of the Palatines in Virginia. May the Lord bless and reward the kind and generous Benefactors for it. I shall aquaint Mr. Stoever very soon with this good news, and on his return from Hamborough[2] he will not fail to give his most humble tanks to the Associates, and assure them, that their Books given him shall be preserved and appropriated in the manner they intend. For the trouble, Revd. Sir, you have been more particularly at upon account of these Books, I wish Mr. Stoever and myself could make any suitable Return to you, and I should be very glad of any opportunity to do you acceptable service, meanwhile I remain Revd. Sir your much obliged and humble servant

Fred: Mich: Ziegenhagen

ALS. Endorsed with what appears to be "Barllin," although neither the spelling nor the meaning is clear. This letter was read by the Associates at their meeting of 3 September 1735. Minutes, 3:93.

1. Smith's letter and its enclosure have not been found.
2. Hamburg, West Germany.

[Rev. Benjamin Colman to the Associates of Dr. Bray]

[Boston, 17 September 1735]

A letter was read from Dr. Coleman in New England acquainting us that there is very little hope of converting the Indians to whom the three Scotch missioners had last year been sent, but that to the westward of that Government there is great prospect of succeeding among the Hussatachonack Indians, who received one Mr. Serjent of Yale College to teach them with joy.[1] Enclosed was this Mr. Serjent's first speech to them on the 3rd October 1735, which seems wonderfully well calculated to prevail on those people.[2]

Letter not found. Extract from John Percival, first earl of Egmont, *Diary of Viscount Percival, Afterwards First Earl of Egmont, 1730–1749*, ed. R. A. Roberts, 3 vols. (London, 1920–23), 2:207 (entry for 3 December 1735). The Associates' Minute Book also records the reading of this letter on 3 December 1735 and notes the date of the letter. Minutes, 3:96.

   1. The Rev. John Sergeant (1710–49), of Newark, New Jersey, graduated from Yale College in 1729. After acting as a tutor at Yale from 1731 to 1735, Sergeant settled as a missionary among the Housatonic Indians in western Massachusetts under the auspices of the Society for Propagating the Gospel among the Indians in New England. He remained there until his death. Dexter, *Yale Graduates* 1:394–97.
   2. The speech has not been found.

Rev. Anthony Gavin to Rev. Samuel Smith

Williamsburgh October the 20, 1735.

Revd. Sir.

   After a Passage of eleven Weecks we were forced to Annapolis in Maryland from Whence I Came to Virginia, and was presented and received by the Vestry in Henrico's Parish on James River. The Allowance of the Parish is 16000 [pounds] of Tabaco, small Perquisits, a House and 150 Acers of good Land: But I shall not receive any Tabacos till this time come 12 months. And I shall be obliged to buy slaves & other Necessaries to work and get some Help from the Land, Which will Keep me in Arrears 2 or 3 years, as I am Informed; & then I may begin, with the assistance of God, to be easy, & live Comfortably. I give you this account to shew the Impossibility I shall meet with of furnishing myself with Books; and the Necessity of accepting the charitable Grant of your Board;[1] However if God bless my Endeavours, I shall, as soon as possible, send in money to you the Value of the Collection of Books which you should send me, if the Honourable Board would give me Credit & time for it; for I find there will be a Charity misemployed to furnish with Books Clergymen of this Countrey, since their Parishes Allowance is Sufficient to Maintain them very decently and leave Something to Supply themselves with Books; tho' at present my Case is different.

I have 2 Churches in the Parish 20 Miles distant one from the other and a Chapel; & I am to serve a bordering Parish now vacant so that, according to Costum, once every 3 weeks in every Church, and in the Week in the next Parish.[2] However the Clark of every Church reads Prayers, when I dont preach, and reads a Sermon. And I shall want a Collection of the best Sermons you Can find in the Stock of your Society, and Some funeral Sermons. An Expositor & Commentator, and a Dictionary English and Latin, and besides these any other Books which you should think useful for the discharge of my Duty. Which you may deliver to Mr. Philip Smith Marchant in King's Arms yard Coleman Street[3] & he will take Care to send them safe by the first ship.

I beg of you to do me the favour to buy a Second hand Summer Gown, & to put it in the Box at the Top of the Books; & the price of it, and I do promise you to send order to Mr. Smith to pay you by the first next Springs Tabacos; for the Gown I brought was so spoiled a Board, that I have been obliged to make a riding Gown of it.

If you Know of any Sober Clergyman, and will take the Trouble of reccommending him to My Lord Bishop of London, you shall do a great Service to this Countrey, for there are now Several Parishes Vacant, with the same Allowance, House & Glebe, and good Company. The Lord be thanked, I have not heard an Oath as yet in this Colony, and we have so good Governor & so Exemplary that all Vice and Immoral Actions are almost banished out of the Colony; and it is a Pleasure for a Clergyman to live among sober, religious People.

We have a Colege here for the Education of Youth[4] and by this Means, the Parishes in a few years since will be furnished with Clergymen of the Countrey Bread, of which there is five already in this Province of a good Life & Conversation.

Pardon the Teadiousness of this Letter, and pray, favour me with an other of a greater Length, and with any new printed Papers that may divert & instruct a Country Clergyman, and whatever you should lay out in this, I shall repay you with Pleasure. I am with true Esteem and Respect Your most obedient affectionate humble Servant & Brother Revd. Sir

Ant: Gavin

Be pleased to direct to me to be left at Col. William Randolph in Henrico's Parish on James River in Virginia.[5]

ALS. Endorsed as read 7 January 1735/36. At that meeting the Associates "Agreed That a Collection of Books be sent him out of the Store on the Terms he desired them, That is to say, To repay the Expence thereof." Minutes, 1 : 1.

1. Before his departure from England Gavin had asked the Associates for a small collection of books for the instruction of slaves and for the discharge of his parochial duties. At their meeting of 5 May 1735 the Associates "Agreed That Mr. Gavin be acquainted That in relation to the Books for the Instruction of Black Slaves That he will be furnished with them by the Society for Propagating the Gospel And that when he is Settled in Virginia The Associates will Consider of furnishing a small Collection for the use of himself & Successors." Minutes, 3:84. The Associates must have sent Gavin some books after his departure, for on 12 November 1735 they "Agreed That another Parcel be bound for the use of Mr. Gavin to be sent him If the Associates receive a Satisfactory Account from him in Virginia." Minutes, 3:95.

2. The two churches in Gavin's parish were Curle's Church, or Four-Mile Creek Church, on the north side of the James River, and Jefferson's Church, near Rock Hall on the south side of the James. The chapel was the Falls Chapel at the Falls of the James. Burton, *Annals of Henrico Parish*, pp. 12–14. It is not clear whether Gavin visited the bordering parish every fourth Sunday or served the two churches and the chapel on successive Sundays and visited the bordering parish during the week.

3. Not further identified.

4. The College of William and Mary.

5. William Randolph II of Turkey Island (1681–1742) was a member of the Council 1728–42 and a vestryman of Henrico Parish. *VMHB* 3 (1895–96): 261–62; Burton, *Annals of Henrico Parish*.

Bond of Rev. Jonathan Arnold

[London, 7 April 1736]

Know all Men by these Presents, that I Jonathan Arnold Clerke of the Parish of Newhaven in the Colony of Connecticut in New England, am bound and firmly obliged to the Right honourable John Earl of Egmont, and the Honourable James Vernon Esquire, in the Summe of ten Pounds of lawful Mony of England, to be paid to them or either of them, or to their or either of their Heirs, Executors, Administrators or Assigns; for which Payment well and truly to be made I bind my self, my Heirs, Executors Administrators and Assigns firmly by these Presents. Witness my Hand and Seal this seventh Day of April in the Year of our Lord one thousand seven hundred and thirty six.

The Condition of this present obligation is such, that whereas the said Jonathan Arnold hath received some Books, consisting of two Folio's two Quarto's and eleven Octavos or twelves for a Parochial Library for the Parish of Newhaven, as appears by Titles to them annexed.[1] If therefore the said Jonathan Arnold shall present the said

Books, and after his Death or Removal shall leave them to the said Use for ever, then this Obligation shall be void and of no Effect, or else it shall stand in full Power, Force and Virtue.

Jona. Arnold

Signed, sealed and delivered in the Presence of,
    Eleanor Willis
    Arthur Bedford.[2]

DS. This document is in the hand of Arthur Bedford. At their meeting of 5 April 1736 the Associates "Read a Letter from Mr. Smith recommending the Revd. Mr. Jonathan Arnold Missionary from the incorporated Society to Newhaven in Connecticut in New England, to have a small Collection of Books given him out of the Store belonging to the Associates.

"Agreed, That a Collection of Books be delivered to the Said Mr. Arnold out of the Store for the use of himself and his Successors Missionarys at Newhaven aforesaid." (Minutes, 1 : 6)

This bond was delivered to the Associates at their meeting of 5 May 1736. See bibliographic note to the following document.

    1. See following document.

    2. Eleanor Willis has not been identified. The Rev. Arthur Bedford (1668–1745) was a graduate of Brasenose College, Oxford (A.B. 1687/88, A.M. 1691), and was ordained in 1688. Bedford was one of the original Associates and served as secretary (with the Rev. Samuel Smith) from 1 July 1730 to 8 July 1731. He was the author of many works, the most well known being *A Serious Remonstrance in Behalf of the Christian Religion against the Horrid Blasphemies and Impieties Which Are Still Used in the English Playhouses* (London, 1719). Minutes, 3 : 3, 7–8, 33; *DNB*.

Catalogue of Books Sent to New Haven

[c. 7 April 1736]

A Catalogue of the Books for a Parochial Library ordered to be sent to the Parish of Newhaven in the County [1] of Connecticut in New England.

Folio

Num. 1.

1 Dr. Bray's Martyrology.
2 Dr. Bray's Martyrological Letters.
3 Dr. Brays Circular Letters to the Clergy of Maryland.

4 Dr. Bray's Proposal for a Collection of Psalms.
5 Chronological Tables.

Num. 2.

1 Dr. Bray's Catechetical Lectures.
2 Kettlewell's Practical Believer.

Quarto

Num. 1.

1 A Catalogue for a Parochial Library.
2 Act of Queen Anne for Parochial Libraries.
3 Rules for preserving Parochial Libraries.

Num. 2.

1 Mr. Smith's Sermon before the Associates of Dr. Bray.
2 Mr. Burton's Sermon. Ditto.
3 Bishop of Lincoln's Sermon for Charity Schools.
4 Bishop of Litchfield's Sermon for Reformation of Manners.
5 A Vindication of Informers.
6 A Perswasive to the Observance of the Lord's Day.
7 A Caution to Swearers.

Octavo.

Num. 1.

Worthingtons three Treatises.

Num. 2.

1 Erasmus his Ecclesiastes.
2 Popish Laws against Hereticks.

Num. 3.

More's Enchiridium Ethicum.

Num. 4.

Dr. Bray on the Baptismal Covenant.

Num. 5.

Missionalia, Viz.
1 An Epistle to D'allone's Trustees.
2 A Dedication to Mr. King.
3 The Life of Gilpin.
4 The Life of Rawlett.
5 Letter to Henderson and Wilkinson.
6 Memorial for Converting the Indians.
7 A Letter from Mr. Tustian.
8 Erasmus de Enuntiando Evangelio.
9 A Letter to the Clergy of Maryland.
10 Primordia Bibliothecaria Missionalia.

Num. 6.

1 Hickes his Apology for the Church of England.
2 Apophthegmata curiosa.
3 Blaire's Paraphrase of Christ's Sermon on the Mount.
4 Kennet's Sermon for Propagating the Gospel.
5 A short and easy Method to extirpate Popery.
6 An easy Method for Instructing Youth.

Num. 7.

Dr. Clarke's three Treatises.

Num. 8.

Bedford against Sir Isaak Newton.

Num. 9.

1 To the Clergy of mean Cures.
2 A Letter to a Clergy Man in the Country.
3 An Advertisement for Catechizing.
4 A Preface Ditto.
5 An Introduction. Ditto.
6 An Introduction for Libraries.
7 The Church Catechism with apposite Texts.
8 An Exposition on the Preliminary Questions of the Church Catechism.
9 An Advertisement for Libraries.
10 A Memorial for Libraries.
11 Apparatus Bibliothecarius.

12 Primordia Bibliothecaria.
13 Primordia Bibliothecaria, or Bibliotheca minima.
14 Proposals for Printing Tracts out of Erasmus.

Num. 10.

1 The Bishop of London's Pastoral Letter.
2 The Bishop of Lincoln's Sermon for Charity Schools.
3 The Bishop of Chester. Ditto.
4 The Whole Duty of Man, or a Scriptural Catechism.
5 A short and plain Account of Religion.
6 A Collection of Psalms.
7 Bedfords Assize Sermon at Taunton.
8 Ditto at Welles.
9 Bedford's Sermon against the Play House.
10 A second Advertisement against the Play House.
11 Letters concerning the Arabick Psalter and Testament.

Num. 11.

1 A Disswasive from Perjury.
2 An easy Method of family Religion.

Num. 12.

1 The Manner of Keeping Christmass.
2 The Church Catechism.
3 An Address to Godfathers.
4 A Disswasive from Drunkenness.
5 A Rebuke to Uncleanness.
6 A Letter from the Society for Promoting Christian Knowledge.

73

Memorandum, That Num. 12, was not sent, but left behind at the Bookbinder's by Mistake.

D. This document is in the hand of Arthur Bedford. At the Associates' meeting of 5 May 1736 "Mr. Bedford delivered a Catalogue of the Books delivered to Mr. Arnold for a Parochial Library for Newhaven in Connecticut in New England, and also delivered Mr. Arnold's Bond for preserving the same, & to his Successors." Minutes, 1 : 7.

    1. The word *Colony* was apparently intended here.

Rev. Arthur Holt to Rev. Samuel Smith

[Chester River in Maryland, 28 May 1736]

Revd. Sir

Yours of May the 6th. I have receiv'd with the Box of Books.[1] I return you thanks for your good office in obtaining that valuable Present for me. I'll do my Endeavour that the good Design both of your self & of that Honble. Society from whom you have obtain'd those Books may be answer'd. I beg your Care of the inclos'd to Mr. Newman.[2]

I return you thanks for your good Wishes in my Behalf; I have now a large Parish, & a well inclin'd People, free from the Distractions of Barbadoes, or the industrious & artful Insinuations of the Jesuits which made me uneasie in my last Parish and which do abound in most of my neighbouring Parishes. The only Seperatists that are considerable amongst us are Quakers, some of which of both sexes, & of advanc'd Years, I have had the joyful success to receive by publick Baptism into the Church & I find them constant at the Lords Table since.[3]

The Number of Communicants encreases Monthly. I have now betwixt *70 & 80** at my Parish Church & about 40 at my Chappel.[4] I seldom omit to Catechise but when other Labours are too great, & I constantly read after Catechising, a Lecture out of Dr. Newtons Exposition which my People are very well pleas'd with & I'm sensible its of great service to them. My Church & Chappel are generally full; I often go to different Parts of my Parish (chiefly on week Days) about thirteen Miles from home, where I always find large Congregations, & a great Number of Children to be baptiz'd which can not conveniently be brought to the Parish Church. My People shew them selves on all Occasions, very affectionate towards me, which gives me Hopes that I shall be the more serviceable to them in my Station.

The Number of Negroes is yet but small in these Parts, the Planters have hitherto chiefly purchas'd white servants, & rais'd up orphan Children to work for them: but they now seem inclinable to encourage the Negroe Trade & in all probability will have considerable Numbers of them here in a short Time.

My Register of the Negroes Christned by me was consumd with several of my Books by a Fire which happened in my House in the dead of Night.

If any thing offers wherein I can be servicable to your Society, if they please to lay their Commands upon me, I shall with all dutyfulness obey them. I desire my best Service may be acceptable to them

& to your self, which will give a great deal of Pleasure to, Revd. Sir your most obedient Humble Servant

Art Holt.

Chester R. in Maryland
May. 28th. 1736

ALS. A marginal note opposite the asterisk in the third paragraph reads: "The next Communion Day after this was written, I had 93 Communicants, several new ones being added the last Month." This letter was read by the Associates at their meeting of 6 October 1736. Minutes, 1 : 12.

1. Letter not found. For the books Holt requested see his letter to Smith of 21 May 1734, above.

2. Henry Newman (1670–1743), a native of Massachusetts and a graduate of Harvard College (A.B. 1687, A.M. 1690), moved to London about 1703. He was the secretary of the Society for Promoting Christian Knowledge from 1708 until his death. Holt's letter has not been found. *DAB*.

3. For the history of the Quakers in this region, see Kenneth Carroll, *Quakerism on the Eastern Shore* (Baltimore, 1970).

4. The Church of St. Luke's Parish was St. Luke's Church, at Church Hill. The chapel was the Chapel of St. Andrew's, one half mile from present-day Sudlersville. Berkley, "Churches and Parishes of Maryland," pp. 211–12.

[Ann Drayton to Rev. Samuel Smith]

[Charleston, South Carolina, 2 June 1736]

Received a Letter from Mrs. Ann Drayton which she sent to Mr. Smith from Charles Town 2 June 1736 acknowledging the Receipt of the Books sent her.[1]

Letter not found. Extract from Minutes, 1 : 12 (meeting of 6 October 1736). Mrs. Drayton has not been identified. Egmont recorded in his diary entry of 6 October: "A letter was read from a gentlewoman in Carolina to Mr. Smith, giving an account that all her negroes were instructed in the Christian religion, some of whom could read and instructed others, and she thanked us for the parcel of books we sent her." Egmont, *Diary* 2 : 300.

1. See [Bryan to Smith, 4 March 1734/35], note 1, above.

[Rev. John Wesley to the Associates of Dr. Bray]

[Savannah, c. 25 February 1736/37]

By Mr. Ingham[1] I writ to Dr. Bray's Associates, who had sent a Parochial Library to Savannah.[2] It is expected of the Ministers who receive these, to send an Account to their Benefactors of the Method they use in catechizing the Children, and instructing the Youth of their respective Parishes. That Part of the Letter was as follows:

'Our General Method is this: A young Gentleman who came with me,[3] teaches between Thirty and Forty Children, to read, write and cast Accounts. Before School in the Morning, and after School in the Afternoon, he catechises the Lowest Class, and endeavours to fix something of what was said, in their Understandings as well as their Memories. In the Evening he instructs the Larger Children. On Saturday in the Afternoon I catechise them all. The same I do on Sunday before the Evening Service. And in the Church, immediately after the Second Lesson, a select Number of them having repeated the Catechism and been examin'd in some Part of it, I endeavour to explain at large, and to inforce that Part, both on them and the Congregation.

'Some time after the Evening Service, as many of my Parishioners as desire it, meet at my House (as they do also on Wednesday Evening) and spend about an Hour in Prayer, Singing and mutual Exhortation. A smaller Number (mostly those who design to communicate the next Day) meet here on Saturd. Evening: And a few of these come to me on the other Evenings, and pass half an Hour in the same Employment.'

Letter not found. Extract from John Wesley, *An Extract of the Rev. Mr. John Wesley's Journal from His Embarking for Georgia to His Return to London* (Bristol, [1739]), p. 36.

1. The Rev. Benjamin Ingham (1712–72), of Yorkshire, was educated at Queen's College, Oxford (A.B. 1734), where he was an active member of John and Charles Wesley's Holy Club. He was ordained in June 1735 and sailed with the Wesleys to Georgia in October 1735, arriving in Savannah in early February 1735/36. Ingham was involved in missionary work among the Yamacraw Indians, among whom he lived for several months. On 24 February 1736/37 Ingham and John Wesley decided that Ingham should return to England to "endeavour to bring over, if it should please God, some of our friends [i.e., ministers] to strengthen our hands in this work." He left Savannah on 26 February but never returned to Georgia. Ingham became a Moravian and an active member of the Brethren's Society for the Furtherance of the Gospel among the Heathen, and he eventually broke with the Wesleys. Frank Baker, *From Wesley to Asbury: Studies in Early American Methodism* (Durham, N.C., 1976), pp. 5, 8–9, 12; Wesley, *An Extract of Mr. Wesley's Journal*, p. 35; Luke Tyerman, *The Oxford Methodists: Memoirs of the Rev. Messrs. Clayton, Ingham, Gambold, Hervey, and Broughton, with Biographical Notices of Others* (London, 1873), pp. 57–154; *DNB*.

2. The Associates gave a parochial library for Savannah to the Georgia Trustees on 2 June 1736; the Trustees sent the library to Georgia later that month. *Ga. Col. Recs.* 3:130; Minutes, 1:9 (meeting of 7 July 1736).

3. Charles Delamotte (1714–90), son of a London magistrate, was a sugar

merchant and a member of the Wesleys' Holy Club in Oxford. Delamotte "had a mind to leave the world, and give himself up entirely to God." He emigrated to Georgia at his own expense and taught school in Savannah from his arrival in February 1735/36 until his departure for England in mid-1738. Delamotte later became a Moravian. Tyerman, *Oxford Methodists*, pp. 67–68; Baker, *From Wesley to Asbury*, pp. 4–5, 12; Davis, *Fledgling Province*, pp. 234–35; *DNB*, s.v. Wesley, John.

[Rev. Samuel Smith to Hector Berenger de Beaufain]

[London, c. 5 March 1739/40]

Resolved, That a Letter be sent to Mr. Beaufain at Purysburgh to know whether Mr. Peter Boehler & Mr. George Schoeleus the Catechists sent for converting the Negroes do reside at Purysburgh and what Progress they have made in that good Work, and do desire their sending the Associates an Acct. thereof.[1]

Letter not found. Extract from Minutes, 1 : 37 (meeting of 5 March 1739/40).

1. The Associates first decided to support a catechist for instructing the blacks in Purrysburg, South Carolina, on 3 September 1735. At that meeting they appropriated £30 per annum for a salary and asked James Oglethorpe "to Inquire for a proper Person & the best manner of Settling him at Purysburgh." Minutes, 3 : 93. More than a year later two Moravian Brethren from Frankfort were procured as catechists by Count Nikolaus von Zinzendorf. The men were Peter Boehler (1712–75), later bishop of the Moravian Church, and George Schulius (c. 1712–1739). They arrived in South Carolina in October 1738, but their mission was unsuccessful as there were few blacks near Purrysburg. Schulius died shortly after they arrived, and Boehler led the Moravian migration from Georgia to Pennsylvania in 1740. Minutes, 1 : 16, 27, 35, 40 (meetings of 2 March 1736/37, 16 March 1737/38, 2 May 1739, and 6 June 1740); *DAB*.

Rev. Alexander Garden to Rev. Samuel Smith

Duplicate   [Charleston, 24 September 1742]

Sir,

By the Reverend Mr. Quincy[1] I have received your Letter of 24th. March, with the No. of Books therein mentioned, which I shall carefully disperse in the best Method I can for answering the good End of the pious & worthy Author & Donor.[2]

They are come over very seasonably, as the Society are about settling some Negroe-Schools in these Parts, in which they will be of the greatest Service.[3] And as on the settling of such Schools, there will be Occasion for Nos. of spelling Books, Psalters, Testaments, Bibles &ca., The Worthy Associates, We hope, will also afford their Charitable Assistance, towards the supplying with these. Meantime with hearty thanks and Respects, I remain Reverend Sir, Your most Obedient Humble Servant

A. Garden.

South Carolina, Charles Town
September 24th. 1742.

LS. Sent "per Capt. Gregory Q.D.C." The meaning of the abbreviation is not clear, but it may stand for *Quem Deus Custodiat*, or "Whom God Keep." This letter was read by the Associates at their meeting of 18 April 1743, at which time they "Resolved, That Five pounds be laid out in said Books & sent to Mr. Garden Commissary in South Carolina residing at Charles Town as he desires." Minutes, 1:46. Several years later the Associates again agreed to write to Garden "to acquaint him with the Nature of this Charity; And to desire he would accept of being a Corresponding Member with the Associates, and would transmit to them his Opinion on what the Associates could do to promote the Instruction of the Negroes in South Carolina." Minutes, 1:60 (meeting of 19 March 1746/47). Neither a letter to Garden nor a reply has been found.

The Associates considered Charleston again on 6 October 1763, when they "Agreed to consider at the Next Meeting whether Charles Town S. Carolina may not be a proper Place for a Negroe School." Minutes, 1:194. They appear to have been unaware that the S.P.G. supported a Negro school in Charleston until 1764 (see note 3 to this letter), for at their meeting of 3 November 1763

> Mr. Waring reported that there is a Negroe School at Charles Town S. Carolina, which he believes, is Supported by the Inhabitants, under the Direction of the Revd. Mr. [Robert] Smith.
> Agreed that Mr. Waring do write to the Revd. Mr. Smith to ask his Opinion how the religious Instruction of the Negroes may be most effectualy promoted in that Province. (Minutes, 1:194)

Neither a letter to Smith nor a reply has been found.

1. The Rev. Samuel Quincy, a native of Boston, was ordained a priest by the bishop of Carlisle in 1730. He was appointed S.P.G. missionary to Savannah in 1733, but as he did not keep the Georgia Trustees informed of his activities, and as General Oglethorpe thought he was not diligent in performing his duties, the Trustees revoked his license and appointed John Wesley to succeed him on 10 October 1735. Quincy then spent several years in England and arrived in South Carolina in June 1742 as missionary to St. John's Parish, Colleton District. He served that parish until his resignation in 1745. From 1746 to 1747 he was rector of St. George's Parish, Dorchester District, and

from July 1747 to 1749 he was assistant to Garden at St. Philip's Church, Charleston. Quincy resigned to return to Boston. Weis, *Colonial Clergy Va., N.C., S.C.*, p. 88; Weis, *Colonial Clergy Md., Del., Ga.*, p. 91; Frederick Dalcho, *An Historical Account of the Protestant Episcopal Church, in South-Carolina, from the First Settlement of the Province, to the War of the Revolution* (Charleston, 1820), pp. 161, 163, 349, 361; Coleman, *Colonial Georgia*, p. 148.

2. Smith's letter has not been found. The books were fifty copies of Thomas Wilson (1663–1755), bishop of Sodor and Man, *The Knowledge and Practice of Christianity Made Easy to the Meanest Capacities; or, An Essay towards an Instruction for the Indians* (London, 1740). Minutes, 1:46.

3. More than two years before writing this letter Garden proposed to the S.P.G. a plan for the instruction of Negroes whereby two Negro boys were to be purchased and trained as teachers at the expense of the Society. The Society approved the plan, and on 12 September 1743, after the two young blacks had been trained, the school at Charleston was opened by Garden, with the object of teaching blacks to be instructors of other blacks. The school continued in operation until 1764. S.P.G. Papers in Lambeth Palace Library, 4: 31–40, 143–44, Lambeth Palace Library, London, microfilm in Library of Congress; Frank J. Klingberg, *An Appraisal of the Negro in Colonial South Carolina: A Study in Americanization* (Washington, D.C., 1941), pp. 101–22.

Rev. John Thompson to Rev. Samuel Smith

Orange [County, Virginia], August 25th. 1743

Revd. Sir,

I receiv'd your kind letter of the 2d. of February 1741, with a Present of books from the venerable Society for promoting Christian Knowledge, as also a Benefaction from the Associates of the late Dr. Bray;[1] for which, I desire the favour of you, Sir, to return them my hearty & unfeigned Thanks; hoping that I shall make such a good Use of their repeated Favours, as to answer, in some measure, their pious & laudable Designs. My Parish was so extensive, as to admit of a Division, & a new one erected;[2] but notwithstanding, my labour & diligence is nothing abated, having, still, three Places of Worship to preach at; & give the Sacrament at each place three times in the year; where I have a considerable number of Communicants, & to my great comfort, perceive, their number yearly increasing. The people seem better dispos'd, & to have more of the christian Temper, than when I first settled amongst them. I baptiz'd, this last year, 298 white children, 13 Negroes & a Mulatto; & hope, in a short time, to have several Negroes, so far instructed, as to be fit to come to the Lord's Table. I have taken all possible care for the Encouragement of Schools in my Parish, of which, now, we have a good number; & have distributed amongst them Lewis's Catechism, & Lessons for children &c.[3] which I received from the Society. Practical pieces of Divinity wou'd be of great Use here; but as I have already receiv'd many Favours from my good Friends, shall not intrude any further upon their good Nature; but whenever they think proper, to present me with a few Books, they shall be receiv'd with all thankfulness, & converted to a proper Use. Sir, I have nothing of moment, to acquaint you with, but gratefully acknowledge the obligations I am under to you, & remain, with the profoundest Veneration & Respect, Reverend Sir, Your most Obliged Humble Servant

Jno. Thompson

P.S. Pray give my very humble Service to my good Friend, Mr. Henry Newman: I thank him for his kind Letter, & readiness to serve me.[4] Present my Respects to your good Lady. Commissary Blair is dead, & left a fine Character behind him.[5]

ALS. This letter was read by the Associates at their meeting of 18 February 1745/46, when they resolved to send testaments and small tracts to Thompson. Minutes, 1:54.

1. Upon reading a letter from Thompson to Smith of 18 April 1741 thanking the S.P.C.K. for a packet of books sent in 1741, the S.P.C.K. agreed to send another packet gratis to Thompson. They shipped 106 books in July 1741. S.P.C.K. Minutes, 19:64 (meeting of 7 July 1741).

Smith's letter of 2 February 1741 (perhaps 1741/42) has not been found. On 18 April 1743 Smith reported to the Associates that he had sent fifty copies of Thomas Wilson (1663–1755), bishop of Sodor and Man, *The Knowledge and Practice of Christianity Made Easy to the Meanest Capacities; or, An Essay Towards an Instruction for the Indians* (London, 1740) to Thompson. Minutes, 1:46.

2. St. Mark's was divided on 1 November 1740 into St. Mark's and St. Thomas's parishes. Hening, *Statutes* 5:96–97.

3. The Rev. John Lewis (1675–1746), *The Church Catechism Explain'd by Way of Question and Answer, and Confirm'd by Scripture Proofs* (London, 1700); *Lessons for Children, Historical and Practical; to Which Are Added Some Prayers, and the Chief Rules of Spelling and Dividing Words into Syllables. Drawn Up for the Use of a Charity School in the Country* (London, 1734).

4. Newman died on 26 June 1743, two months before Thompson's letter was written. Newman's letter to Thompson was dated 18 September 1741. CN 2/8, pp. 20–21, S.P.C.K. Archives, London.

5. The Rev. James Blair (1655–1743) was rector of Bruton Parish Church, president of the College of William and Mary, member of the Council, and commissary of the bishop of London in Virginia. He died on 18 April 1743. *DAB*.

Rev. Philip Reading to [Rev. Samuel Smith]

Apoquinimy in the County of New Castle on Delawar
November 24th. 1746.

Reverend and Worthy Sir,

I take this opportunity to acquaint you of my safe arrival here in July last, after a passage of about eight weeks. Upon my coming to this place I applied myself as soon as possible to dispose of the books you was pleased to put in my hands for the use of the Negro Slaves.[1] After having made proper enquiry, I thought it most serviceable to put about one third into the hands of the Commissary at Philadelphia,[2] another third into the hands of the Missionary at Perquihoma,[3] and the remainder I kept to be disposed of in these parts where those Slaves are very numerous. The two above-named Gentlemen have given me hopes of doing service with them in their districts, and such Masters and Mistresses as I have discoursed with in these parts, promise to encourage the goo[d work with] hearty concurrence. But having been visited with a long fit of Sickness, I have not been able to make any late enquiries, but hope by the next opportunity to be more perfect and satisfactory in my account. If the worthy associates are inclined to put any more books into my hands, no endeavours shall be wanting on my part to do them faithful service. I believe a few Common Prayer books, with about one dozen of the History of the Old and New Testament[4] interspersed with Cuts for the younger sort might be of use.

My situation here is not disagreeable, nor yet free from very great inconveniences. One of my Churches being twelve miles distant from the place where I lodge,[5] and the congregation very widely dispersed obliges me to be often on horseback. This circumstance is frequently attended with unhealthy consequences: for being forced to go much abroad, and to stay whole nights in the remote parts of my district, and being generally ill-provided with lodging, subjects me to colds and many other disorders. This climate in Autumn is very unhealthy, and most families, especially those of the Europeans, are subject to intermitting fevers. I am just recovered from one, which kept me in confinement ten weeks, and was a great embarrassment to me in my private affairs. I have hinted this last article in my letter to the Society,[6] but have gone no farther than the ba[re] mention of it. If however, any thing should be proposed for my relief, I presume to flatter myself that you [will] promote it with your kind assistance. I am, with sincere respects to your self and good family,

Philip Reading

ALS. The bracketed portions of the text are conjectural readings, the manuscript being torn. This letter was read by the Associates at their meeting of 19 March 1746/47. Minutes, 1 : 60.

1. The Associates resolved to give testaments and tracts to Reading at their meeting of 18 February 1745/46. Minutes, 1 : 54.

2. The Rev. Robert Jenney, for whom see Sturgeon to Waring, 1 July 1762, note 3, below.

3. The Rev. William Currie (1710–1803) was S.P.G. missionary at Perkiomen, Montgomery County, Pennsylvania, from 1737 until his resignation in 1776. Weis, *Colonial Clergy Middle Colonies*, p. 202; *The History of Old St. David's Church, Radnor, in Delaware County, Pennsylvania* (Philadelphia, 1907), p. 44.

4. Reading was probably requesting copies of the Rev. Samuel Craddock (1621?–1706), *The History of the Old Testament Methodiz'd According to the Order and Series of Time Wherein the Several Things Therein Mentioned Were Transacted. In Which the Difficult Passages are Paraphras'd. The Seeming Contradictions Reconcil'd. The Rights and Customs of the Jews Opened and Explain'd. To Which is Annex'd A Short History of the Jewish Affairs from the End of the Old Testament to the Birth of Our Saviour . . .* (London, 1683).

5. Reading served Duck Creek, the church twelve miles south of Appoquinimy, from 1746 until the arrival of the Rev. Hugh Neill (d. 1781) in 1750. Nelson Waite Rightmyer, *The Anglican Church in Delaware* (Philadelphia, 1947), p. 41.

6. Reading to the Rev. Philip Bearcroft, secretary of the S.P.G., 14 November 1746, S.P.G. MSS., B14, no. 207. Reading wrote that he had "been sick of an intermitting fever (the Epidemical Distemper of this Country) from the middle of August 'till the latter end of October, which prevented my officiating among my people, and visiting them in the manner I proposed."

Rev. Ebenezer Miller to Rev. Samuel Smith

[Braintree, Massachusetts, 6 September 1748]

Revd. Sir

I arriv'd at Piscataqua about seventy Miles from hence on the 13th. of August after a pleasant tho long Passage for we saild from Portsmouth the 9th. of June. The Books from the Associates of Dr. Bray I brought with me, & some of them I have already distributed to Negroes.[1] To such as coud read, I gave the Prayer:Books. And to such as were learning to read, I gave the Testaments & Catechetical Discourses, & promised them Prayer:Books as soon as they were able to make Use of them, which I thought wou'd quicken them in their learning to read. The poor Creatures seem'd much pleased that Gentlemen at so great a Distance, & who coud receive no Advantage from them, shoud have such a Concern for their Instruction in Christian Principles. I shall dispose of what remain, in such a Manner, as I think, will best Serve the charitable Purposes of the worthy Associates, & shall always take Pleasure in being their Almoner. My Compliments to your Lady & Sister[2] & all that enquire after me.

I am, Revd. Sir, your affectionate Brother & obliged humble Servant

E. Miller

Braintree in New:England
September 6th. 1748.

ALS. This letter was read by the Associates at their meeting of 18 April 1749. Minutes, 1:69.

1. At their meeting of 13 February 1747/48 the Associates "Resolved, That Five pounds worth of Books be given to Dr. Miller of Braintree for promoting the Instruction of the Negroes in his Parish and Neighbourhood in New England." Minutes, 1:62.
2. Not identified.

Rev. Philip Reading to Rev. Samuel Smith

Apoquiniminck [Delaware] October 10th. 1748.

Reverend Worthy Sir,

Yours of August 25th. 1747[1] came safe to hand, together with a box containing 50 Common Prayer Books, and 12 Copies of the History of the O. and N. Testament, for which, in the name of the poor Slaves, I am to return thanks to the pious Associates. The Ship, by which your Box was sent, did not arrive here 'till the latter end of last March, and I have been obliged to wait ever since for opportunity to return an answer, but as we have great probability of peace, the Correspondance on my part, will, I hope, for the future be less interrupted and more punctual.[2]

It is with great willingness that I ingage in promoting the good work which the Associates pursue: the case of the Negroes among us is truly deplorable, and must excite the concern of every serious, considerate person. The Gentlemen, in whose hands I left parcels of the first Cargo of Books, inform that they have disposed of part of them, as they hope, to good purpose. The work is truly slow in its success, which according to my best observation seems to be owing to the following difficulties.

The first is, the great prejudices of Masters. Many of them are destitute of common humanity, and differ in nothing but complexion and free estate from the most abject slave: their hearts are set upon nothing but gain, and they are so far from promoting instruction of any kind, that if you should offer the best means of it to one of their own children gratis, they would certainly refuse it, provided you took the child from the plow or the cart. What then can be expected in behalf of a poor slave from such as want natural affection even to their own flesh and blood?

The second is, the slow apprehension and difficulty of conversing with the Majority of Negroes themselves: they seem to be of a species quite different from the whites, have no abstracted ideas, cannot comprehend the meaning of faith in Christ, the nature of the fall of man, the necessity of a redeemer, with other essentials of the Christian scheme. Besides this, they have a language peculiar to themselves, a wild confused medley of Negro and corrupt English, which makes them very unintelligible except to those who have conversed with them for many years.

Our third difficulty is, the prejudices of Slaves themselves. Those born in Guinea are strangely prepossessed in favour of superstition and Idolatry. They have a notion, that when they die, they are translated to their own countrey, there to live in their former free condition: of this they are so fond, that many of them upon a slight affront (especially the nation called Keromantees) will lay violent hands upon themselves with great calmness and deliberation.[3] Here we may add, that all, without exception, where they are pinched in food and raiment, will employ themselves on Sundays in raising potatoes, pease, melons &c. for their own use, with which they purchase cloaths, drink and other necessaries.

These, Sir, are our present difficulties: but amidst these I have some glimmering of hope. At my first coming upon this Mission, there were not more than 2 or 3 Negroes who attended the service of our Church: but now betwixt 12 and 20 are constant hearers, 2 of them are strict communicants, and a third will be admitted next Christmas.[4] I have prevailed on many to bring their children to baptism, and some, who come to Church, use their Common Prayer Books with great propriety and devotion. Thus, considering the difficulties before-mentioned, we have, by the Grace of God, as good success, as for the time could be expected.

Upon the receit of the last box of books, I sent the greater part of them to two neighbouring Clergymen in Maryland, to which province Dr. Bray seems to have had a particular eye, when he first took the instruction of Negroes into his consideration: since the distribution of those books, I have received an invitation from the Revd. Messrs.

Jones, Forester, Sterling, Hamilton and Harrison (Ministers of Parishes in Maryland) to become a member of a monthly Society, which, as I understand, is to be formed for the Service of religion,[5] and hope to ingage those Gentlemen to assist the Associates in their laudable undertakings.

As to my own part, I shall ever be ready to obey their Commands, and shall on all occasions give them the best assistance of which I am capable.

I am, with assurances of respect to that pious Body, Revd. Sir, Your very obedient very humble Servant

Philip Reading.

ALS. This letter was read by the Associates at their meeting of 18 April 1749. Minutes, 1:69.

1. Letter not found.

2. The Treaty of Aix-la-Chapelle, ending the four-year War of the Austrian Succession (called King George's War in America), was signed on 18 October 1748.

3. See William D. Piersen, "White Cannibals, Black Martyrs: Fear, Depression, and Religious Faith as Causes of Suicide among New Slaves," *Journal of Negro History* 62 (1977): 147–59.

4. Two years later Reading reported to the S.P.G. that there were 367 non-Christian Negro slaves in his parish. Reading to the Rev. Philip Bearcroft, secretary of the S.P.G., 25 June 1750, S.P.G. MSS., B18, no. 164.

5. These ministers were the Rev. Hugh Jones (1671–1760) of North Sassafras and Augustine parishes, Cecil County; the Rev. George William Forester (d. 1774) of Shrewsbury Parish, Kent County; the Rev. James Sterling, for whom see Biographical Appendix; the Rev. John Hamilton (1706–73) of St. Mary Anne Parish, Cecil County; and the Rev. Richard Harrison (d. 1763) of St. Luke's Parish, Queen Anne's County. Weis, *Colonial Clergy Md., Del., Ga.*, pp. 43, 45, 50, 64; Rightmyer, *Maryland's Established Church*, pp. 187–88. The society, if it was ever organized, has not been traced.

Rev. Stephen Hales to Harman Verelst

Teddington [England] June 21. 1749

Sir

I intirely agree with Mr. Smith to send Dr. Crows Library to Georgia by Mr. Zeuberbuhler, for a Publick Library there.[1] Pray my Complements to Mr. Zeuberbuhler wishing him a prosperous Voyage, & all desired Success in his Mission. As there are some usefull Gentlemen lately chosen into the Trust who reside much in London, I conclude you will have no occasion for me.[2] But in case you should, I shall be constantly here, ready at a Call. I being detained here by very important Affairs relating to the getting Ventilators into Ships, for the better preservation not only of the Health & Lives of many, but also of the Provisions & Goods, & even the Timber of Ships, both in Voyages, & layed up in time of Peace. I am now forwarding this Affair apace by means of Lord Hallifax, who has put Ventilators into five of the Nova Scotia Ships, & says there ought to be a law to oblige all slave Ships to have Ventilators. He has prevailed with Mr. Pen to put 'em into all the Ships, for the future, which carry Germans to Pensilvania. My Lord H: is fully convinced that the Fires, are a mere Nothing.[3] I hear lately that the East India Company have ordered them to be put into all their Trading Ships, they haveing lately received an Account, of the good Effects of Ventilators in all the Men of War there.

I have had thoughts of writing to you to have Ventilators in the Ship that Carries our 70 Moravians, but then I thought the number of 'em was not so great, as to make it necessary, especially if they should go in several Ships.[4] They cost about 15 or £17, & are made by Mr. Stibbs Carpenter in Fore-Street London Wall. I make no doubt but they would be of great Service, not only in preserving the Provisions, but also any kinds of Perishable Goods the Ship shall return with, if they were worked only half an Hour twice every day as they return. This Lord Hallifax has desired, the owners of the five *Nova Scotia* Ships, to have done at my Request.

I am Sir Your humble Servant

Stephen Hales.

ALS.

1. The Rev. William Crowe (d. 1743) was educated at Trinity College, Cambridge (A.B. 1714, A.M. 1717, honorary D.D. 1728), and was ordained a priest in 1716. He was rector of St. Botolph, Bishopsgate, and Finchley, Middlesex, and was chaplain to George II. Dr. Crowe left his library to Hales and the Rev. Samuel Smith to dispose of either for parochial libraries in England or for the use of the colony of Georgia. The Associates resolved on 15 March 1743/44 that the books should be sent to Georgia. On 4 July 1749 the Georgia Trustees agreed and arranged for the library to be sent over with the Rev. Bartholomew Zouberbuhler, the minister at Savannah who had returned to England for a visit in 1748. Minutes, 1:49 (meeting of 15 March 1743/44); Venn, *Alumni Cantabrigienses; Ga. Col. Recs.* 1:534–35. For Zouberbuhler see Biographical Appendix.

2. "The Trust" could be a reference either to the Associates or to the Georgia Trustees. Both groups elected new members on 16 March 1748/49. The four new Associates were the Rev. John Berriman (1691–1768), rector of St. Alban's, Wood Street, and of St. Olave's, Silver Street, London; the

Rev. William Best, D.D. (b. 1695), vicar of St. Laurence Jewry and rector of St. Mary Magdalen, Milk Street, London; the Rev. Thomas Skinner, M.A. (born c. 1716); and the Rev. John Waring (c. 1716–94), later secretary of the Associates (see Biographical Appendix). Minutes, 1:68; Foster, *Alumni Oxonienses*; *DNB*.

The six men elected Georgia Trustees on 16 March 1748/49 were John Percival (1711–70), second earl of Egmont; Anthony Ewer; Edward Hooper; Sir John Cust (1718–70), baronet, speaker of the House of Commons; and Slingsby Bethell and Stephen Theodore Janssen, aldermen of the City of London. *Ga. Col. Recs.* 1:529; *DNB*.

3. George Montagu Dunk (1716–71), second earl of Halifax, was president of the Board of Trade 1748–61 and secretary of state for the northern department from January 1771 until his death the following June. He was influential in the founding of Nova Scotia; the town of Halifax was named after him. At the meeting of 6 April 1749, with Halifax presiding, the Board of Trade agreed to install ventilators in four of the twelve ships then being fitted out to carry settlers to Nova Scotia. Ventilators may have been installed on a fifth ship later. Hales's ventilators were operated manually on a bellows principle. "The Fires, are a mere Nothing" is probably a reference to the older, less successful method of ventilating ships by means of fire-pipes, or metal pipes about two-and-a-half inches in diameter, through which fresh air was drawn when the mouth was placed near the ship's fire, or through which air was expelled when the pipes were placed in the fire, "thereby causing a small Draught, by rarifying the Air in the Pipes." Halifax was present at one trial of the fire-pipes, when "the In-draught of the Air was so weak, that only one of them extinguished the flame of a Candle." Hales, *Treatise on Ventilators*, p. 114. The use of the bellows type of ventilator on the Nova Scotia ships was so successful that Halifax reported to Hales that twelve times as many passengers died in unventilated as in ventilated ships. *Journals of the Board of Trade* 8:402; Hales, *A Treatise on Ventilators* (London, 1758), pt. 2, pp. 95–96, 112–18; D. Fraser Harris, "Stephen Hales, the Pioneer in the Hygiene of Ventilation," *Scientific Monthly* 3 (1916): 440–54; *DNB*.

"Mr. Pen" was either Thomas (1702–75) or Richard (1706–71), sons of William Penn and proprietors of Pennsylvania. Hales wrote, in his *Treatise on Ventilators*, that Mr. Penn proposed to the Pennsylvania Assembly "the Making of a Law, to lay a great Penalty on every Ship that has not Ventilators onboard, and do not work them frequently" (p. 85). No evidence of any communication from either Thomas or Richard Penn to the Assembly concerning ventilators has been discovered, nor has a Pennsylvania law requiring ventilators on ships been found. The Assembly passed, on 27 January 1750, "An Act for Prohibiting the Importation of Germans or Other Passengers in Too Great Numbers in Any One Vessel." This act, however, did not mention ventilators, and it was first proposed to the Assembly in November 1749 in a petition from "sundry Inhabitants of the City of Philadelphia," not by one of the proprietors. James T. Mitchell and Henry Flanders, comps., *The Statutes at Large of Pennsylvania, from 1682 to 1801* 5 (Harrisburg, 1898): 94–97; *Pennsylvania Archives*, 8th ser. 4 (Harrisburg, 1931): 3287–88; *DAB*.

4. The minutes of the Common Council of the Trustees for the meeting of 29 May 1749 record that Mr. Balthazar Zoller and several other German Protestants attended, "and alleg'd, that they had been prevail'd on by one Mr. Riemensperger to leave their Habitations in Germany, and come over at their own Expences to England, in order to go and settle in South Carolina; And they, not being provided for by him as they expected, are left in great Distress, and therefore pray the Trustees will send them to Georgia as Servants." *Ga. Col. Recs.* 2:495. The Common Council resolved that, as the number of Germans was only seventy, their passage would be paid. The Germans were to be maintained until their voyage, and they were to serve for four years as servants. Apparently not all of the seventy Germans ultimately sailed for Georgia, for the accounts of the Trustees show that passage was paid in that year for only sixty-three "Foreign Protestants." *Ga. Col. Recs.* 3:340.

Joseph Ottolenghe to [Rev. Samuel Smith]

[Savannah, 4 December 1751]

Revd. Sir

In my last sent you by the Charming Martha I took the Liberty to acquaint you with my safe Arrival to Georgia.[1] I shall now proceed & lay before you the Method which I have taken to discharge that awfull Office which God was pleased to call me to, & the Honorable Associates, to place me in. As soon as the Fatigue of the Voyage permited it, I desir'd the Revd. Mr. Zouberbuyler[2] that he would be so good to give the People Notice in the Church that I would instruct their Negros three Days in the Week, viz. Sundays, Tuesdays & Thursdays, which he accordingly did; & that I might make it easie to the Masters of these unhappy Creatures, I have appointed the Time of their coming to me to be at Night, when their daily Labour is done. When we meet, I make them go to Prayers with me, having composd for that Purpose a few Prayers, suitable (I hope) to the Occasion. Having thus reccommended our Selves to the Protection of Heaven, & for his Blessing, on our Undertaking; I instruct them to Read, that they may be able in Time to comfort themselves in reading the Book of God. After this is done, I make them repeat the Lords Prayer, & the Belief,[3] & a Short Portion of the Catechism, explaining to them in as easie & Familiar a Manner as I can the Meaning of what they repeat, & before I part with them, I make a Discourse to them on the Being of a God, or the Life & Death of our Adorable Redeemer, or upon some of the Precepts of the Holy Gospel, generally introducing some Event or Story, taken out of the Bible, suitable to the Discourse in Hand; & in order to get their Love, I use them with all the Kindness & endearing Words that [I] am capable of, which makes them willing to come to me, & ready to follow my Advice, & as Rewards are Springs that sets less selfish Minds than these unhappy Creatures possess, on Motion, I have therefore promis'd to reward the Industrious & Deligent,[4] & hope thro' Christ's Grace, that twill have its due Effect. These then Dear Sir, are the Methods, these the Path, that I have chalk'd out in order to discharge my Duty. If right & agreable to your Better Judgment, I shall continue in them, if not, I shall be very ready to put in Practice any other Method, which you shall please to prescribe.

I hope that the Great God of Heaven will bless this poor Colony, but as Solomon Says, That the Throne is establish'd by Righteousness,[5] I do not at all doubt but that you'll agree with me, that no Community or Society of Men, can ever be establish'd without a due Sense of Religion, so necessary to the Well Being of every Individual that composes it. And yet how lamantable the Reports, how deplorable the Accounts, which daily grieves my Heart, upon the Situation of many in this Colony, who live at a great distance from the Church, & from all Spiritual Helps. The Ignorance of some is surprising & Heathenism of others is Shocking! What can good Mr. Zouberbuyler do in this Case? Shall he feed them & starve us? Will he not neglect us if he administers to them? Besides their Distance from him makes it impracticable to be of any Service to them. What Profit could they reap from his being with them, at the most 3 or 4 Times in a Year? While experience points us out a certain Analogy subsisting betwixt Body & Soul, & that as the one would be starved if not often fed, the latter must perish if seldom nourished with Spiritual Food. I own this to be a disagreable Subject, & what makes it the more afflictive to me is, that I can'nt afford it a Remedy. I had tis true pressing Messages from these scatterd Sheep, to go & preach the Gospel among them, upon a foolish Report which prevaild in this Colony, that I was a Clergyman in Cog: however after some talk had with them I beat them out of this Silly Notion. But this would not serve them, but I must commence a strolling Preacher forsooth, because they have heard that in England, & in most of the American Colonies itinerant Lay-Preachers were Common, & that much Good is done by them. But to this I answer'd them that Irregularities were never to be drawn into a Precedent, & that if the Number of these Ramblers, had been ever so great, yet since that Practice was in itself Sinful, & our Blessed Saviour has declar'd that all such as enterd not by the Door into the Sheepfold, but climbeth up some other way, the same was a Thief & a Robber;[6] & St. Paul expressly assures that Thieves do not inherit the Kingdom of Heaven.[7] And therefore were ever my Talents so well fitted for the Ministry, as they are not, & my Inclinations never so great to comply with their Desire, yet, as by my commencing an unlawful Minister, I begin a Thief, & by Preaching the Gospel of the Kingdom to them, I shut my self out of that very Kingdom, are Considerations too great &

Motives too strong to deter me from granting their Requests.[8] I gave therefore to some of them Books, to comfort them, & desir'd them to wait on Mr. Zouberbuyler, for some Instructions how to govern themselves till God shall be pleas'd to send among them a Lawful Minister.

I wish that I had some Thing better to entertain you with, than what went before. I know my Deficiency, & want only the Sense to follow Solomon's Advice both to hold my Tongue & Scribbling, an Itch which torments every empty Nodles,[9] but I trust for Pardon from your candid & generous Nature, which I will hasten to relieve from this Task, by drawing to a Conclusion, & only beg the Favour of you to stand my Friend, & to endeavour to persuade the Honble. the Trustees to find some Means to encrease my present Stipend, which indeed cann't maintain me especially under the Disadvantages of every Thing's being extremely dear, & my Wife constantly Ill. I should be very thankfull to you (if my Petition is Reasonable if not to let it die) to use your Interest with the Honble. the Trustees to make me a Present of a Couple of Horses. The granting of my Petition would be of great service to me, & no great detriment to that Honble. Body, since that I understand that they have a good Stock of them. The use which I intend to make of them beside the putting of them to do such Business for me as I cann't do without them, I intend also God willing to visit gradually the Plantations in this Colony in order to spur them on as well as to advice them how to carry on the Silk-Manufactory which if well attended to, & rightly managed, will by God's Blessing be of great Moment to this Colony, so well situated for it;[10] as also to introduce among them as God shall enable me, a little more Sense of Religion, than they have at present, & I hope so to demean my self in this last particular as to give no Offence. I should have petition'd but for one Horse, but as tis impracticable for a single Person & a Stranger, to travel thro' Woods without Danger, I shall be oblig'd to have always a Person to guide me.

And now I beg of you a Thousand Pardon for these Liberties which I have taken, & may the God of all Consolation Bless you & protect you & make you Happy in this Life & eternally Bless'd in the Next. With these my earnest Prayers you have the sincere Respects due to you from Revd. Sir Your most Obedient Humble Servant

J. Ottolenghe

Savannah December 4th. 1751
P.S. Youll receive a Letter of advice for a Bill drawn upon you, for my half a Year's Sallary. Mr. Copp whom the Honble. the Trustees settled to be a Minister at Augusta, has accepted of a Parish in South Carolina & will quit the Former next Spring.[11]

ALS. This letter was read by the Associates at their meeting of 10 July 1752, at which time they

> Resolved, That Mr. Smith be desired to send him Seven pounds and ten shillings on this Occasion as a Relief in his present Distress. Resolved, That an Answer be sent to Mr. Ottolenghe desiring his sending an Account of the Number of Negroes he instructs, and to acquaint him the Associates approve of his Method of Proceeding therein; and That though the Associates have the Instruction of Negroes solely in View as their Trust, they should be glad he would encourage White Children inclined to partake of the same Knowledge; And also That in any thing he can assist Mr. Zouberbuhlers Ministry in the Instruction of distant People preparatory for the Sacraments it will be a charitable & good Office. And That the Application to the Trustees for a Couple of Horses cannot be considered unless their should happen any Remainder of the Money granted for Discharging the Services incurred to Midsummer last, and That he do write to the Associates as often as opportunity will permit. (Minutes, 1:78–79)

The letter to Ottolenghe has not been found.

1. Letter not found. Ottolenghe arrived in Georgia in July 1751 aboard the *Charming Martha*, Captain John Leslie. The ship sailed from Georgia for England in September 1751 with Ottolenghe's missing letter on board. *Ga. Col. Recs.* 26:91, 107, 257, 302, 340. Smith laid the letter, dated in July 1751, before the Georgia Trustees

> who are very sorry to find, that you have taken up other Thoughts, and enter'd into other Views, than what you set out with from England. It will not be in the Trustees Power to put you into any other Employment, than what you have undertaken, nor will it be to Enable you to keep any Servants for the Cultivation of Lands for you, They having Surrender'd their Trust into the hands of his Majesty; But They will recommend you to the Associates of the late Dr. Bray, who are intrusted with the good Work of instructing the Negroes, and sent you for that purpose to Georgia. This requiring a perpetual travelling from Plantation to Plantation, where the Negroes reside, is utterly inconsistent with your Scheme of Sitting down at Savanah in a good Employment, or with an Estate. (Benjamin Martyn to Ottolenghe, 23 January 1751/52, Ga. Col. Recs., unpub., 31:546–47)

For Martyn see Ottolenghe to [Smith], 8 June 1752, note 2, below.

2. For Bartholomew Zouberbuhler see Biographical Appendix.

3. The Apostles' Creed.

4. Obsolete form of diligent. *OED*.

5. It is an abomination to kings to commit wickedness: for the throne is established by righteousness. Proverbs 16:12.

6. Verily, verily, I say unto you, He that entereth not by the door into the sheepfold, but climbeth up some other way, the same is a thief and a robber. John 10:1.

7. Nor thieves, nor covetous, nor drunkards, nor revilers, nor extortioners, shall inherit the kingdom of God. 1 Corinthians 6:10.

8. Ottolenghe meant that the considerations were so great and the motives were so strong as to deter him from granting their requests.

9. Ottolenghe seems to have confused two separate passages. The allusion to Solomon's advice to hold the tongue is probably a reference to Proverbs 21:23: "Whoso keepeth his mouth and tongue keepeth his soul from troubles." The allusion to an itch for scribbling is a reference to Juvenal, Satire 7, line 51: "An incurable itch for scribbling takes possession of many, and grows inveterate in their insane breasts."

10. One of the Georgia Trustees' principal motives for founding the colony was to play an important role in Britain's trade policy by producing such commodities as wine and silk, for which Britain was dependent on foreign markets. Parliament encouraged the production of silk in Georgia through bounties, but the industry never developed as had been hoped. Production reached a peak of 1,084 pounds in 1766 but fell to 290 pounds by 1770. After Parliament eliminated the bounty in 1771, silk culture in Georgia was virtually abandoned, and the filature in Savannah discontinued operations. See Trevor R. Reese, *Colonial Georgia: A Study in British Imperial Policy in the Eighteenth Century* (Athens, Ga., 1963), pp. 121–25; Mary T. McKinstry, "Silk Culture in Colonial Georgia," *GHQ* 14 (1930): 225–35; Marguerite B. Hamer, "The Foundation and Failure of the Silk Industry in Provincial Georgia," *North Carolina Historical Review* 12 (1935): 125–48; Davis, *Fledgling Province*, p. 8.

11. The Rev. Jonathan Copp (1725–62), of Connecticut, graduated from Yale College in 1744. He converted to Anglicanism in 1747 while serving as master of the New London grammar school and travelled to England for ordination three years later. While Copp was in England the Associates gave him twelve copies of Gilbert West, *Observations on the History and Evidence of the Resurrection of Jesus Christ*, and George Lyttleton, *Observations on the Conversion and Apostleship of St. Paul, in a Letter to Gilbert West, Esq.*, bound together (London, 1747). Since the charter was to expire in 1752, the Trustees asked the S.P.G. to appoint a missionary for Augusta. Copp then returned to America early in 1751 as S.P.G. missionary to Augusta, Georgia, and the only Anglican minister in Georgia not appointed by the Trustees. Although Ottolenghe believed he would leave in 1752, Copp did not depart Augusta for South Carolina until 1755. He was rector of St. John's Parish, Colleton District, South Carolina, from January 1756 until his death. Minutes, 1:76 (meeting of 21 March 1750/51); Dexter, *Yale Graduates* 1:756–57; Strickland, *Religion and the State in Georgia*, p. 85.

Joseph Ottolenghe to [Rev. Samuel Smith]

[Savannah, 8 June 1752]

Revd. Sir

In my last I acquainted you with the Method I took in order to discharge my Duty in the Instruction of the Negros.[1] In this, I shall with much Pleasure & Satisfaction assure you, that God has been very

Merciful to me in Blessing my poor Endeavours with good Success. Most of them are gone thro' the Catechism, & several begin to read tolerably well, and every one of them are capable to repeat by Heart such Prayers as their Temporal & Spiritual State stands in need of obtaining from Heaven. They are able likewise to answer Questions touching our holy Religion, as are requisite for them to know, & I hope that during that Period of Life which the Author of it shall please to grant me, & with his holy Assistance to give no room whatever of Complaint against the Discharge of my Office.

Kind Mr. Martyn in his last to me, makes me hope that the Associates will give me some farther Proof of their Benevolent Disposition towards me, which shall ever be return'd with all Gratitude & Prayers for their Prosperity.[2] At Present my Duty waits on them, the Like be pleas'd to accept from him who in all Christian Duties can sincerely subscribe himself Your most obedient Humble Servant

J. Ottolenghe

Savannah in Georgia
June 8th. 1752

ALS.

    1. Dated 4 December 1751, above.

    2. Benjamin Martyn (1699–1763) was secretary of the Georgia Trustees from October 1732 until the surrender of the charter to the crown in June 1752, and was agent of the crown for the colony from February 1753 until 1763. Martyn was the author of *Reasons for Establishing the Colony of Georgia with Regard to the Trade of Great Britain . . . with Some Account of the Country, and the Design of the Trustees* (London, 1733); *An Impartial Inquiry into the State and Utility of the Province* (London, 1741); and *An Account Showing the Progress of the Colony of Georgia* (London, 1741). Martyn was also the author of a tragedy called *Timoleon*, which played with success in 1730, and he was an original member of the Society for the Encouragement of Learning (founded 1736). For his letter to Ottolenghe see Ottolenghe to [Smith], 4 December 1751, note 1, above. *Ga. Col. Recs.* 2 : 5; Trevor R. Reese, "Benjamin Martyn, Secretary of the Trustees of Georgia," *GHQ* 38 (1954): 142–47; Greene, *Quest for Power*, p. 284.

[Joseph Ottolenghe to Rev. Samuel Smith]

[Savannah, 19 January 1752/53]

    Read a Letter from Mr. Ottolenghe dated January 19: 1752 directed [to] Mr. Smith acquainting him with a Draught upon him for [£]7 : 10, & likewise Representing the great Advantages which the proper Encouragement of the Growth of Silk in Georgia may be of to this Kingdom. Resolv'd that a Copy of Mr. Ottolenghe's Letter be sent to the Lords of Trade.[1]

Letter not found. Extract from Minutes, 1:80 (meeting of 8 June 1753).

1. The journals of the Board of Trade do not record the reading of this letter, although on 1 February 1753/54 Martyn laid before them a letter he had received from Ottolenghe relating to the current state of the silk culture in Georgia and containing proposals of what would be further necessary for the ensuing season. *Journals of the Board of Trade* 10:9.

Joseph Ottolenghe to [Rev. John Waring]

[Savannah, 19 November 1753]

Sir

I found my self favour'd, with your kind Letter datet August the 11th, which came safe to me the 8br. 16th.[1] I was extremely pleas'd with it, not only on Account of its Contents, but also because it being the First, which I have been favour'd with from any concern'd in the Association of the late Dr. Bray, altho 2 Years & half employd (tho' unworthy) to execute that pious Man's Design. As for yours which you say to have been sent me, in May or June passd, I never had the Pleasure of seeing it, & consequently must have miscarryied.

Before I attempt to give you an Answer to that which reachd my Hands, I must beg of you to Pardon me if I should mistake in my Address to you, because I know not in what Station of Life you Shine. And tho' I think it my Duty to give Honour to whom Honour is due, yet in this my State of Ignorance I have chosen the plain Way of Address, as knowing that an humble Mind will at any Time rather loose, than take what does not belong to it. This Point settled, I shall proceed, as far as my Health (which at present is very much impair'd) will permit, to answer your Letter, as it lies now before me.

And First I must beg of you that you'll return my most sincere Thanks in behalf of the poor of this Colony; White, as well as Black, a Present so Valuable that it will do more Good than if twice its Value in Money had been sent to be distributed among them. The Contents laid down in the Catalogue are all in the Box, & there is not one Book among them except the Prayer Books, (because of the Old Version of the Psalm) but that by God's Blessing will answer the Pious Ends of them that sent them.[2] I shall take care to distribute them with the same Caution, which I do with those which I have last Year Recd. from that most Pious & most Useful Society for promoting Christian Knowledge.[3] And tho' I can not lay down the Various Methods which I take to assure my self that the Person or Persons on whom I bestow any Books, deserves the Favour. However I would have this to be understood in a restrain'd Sense, because I am a Man & liable to many Errors.

I shall continue to draw as usual, only this Time, I must draw for more than I commonly did. For Mr. Loyd in one of his Letters Dated September 18th. 1752[4] acquainted me that he had an Order from the Revd. Mr. Smith to pay me £7 : 10 & that he had wrote to his Correspondent to pay me the said Sum of 7 : 10.0. But as the Design why the said sum was sent me, I was not then acquainted with, till now that you are so Good to explain it to me; and therefore as I was then in the Dark, & not knowing how to behave my self without giving Offence, I resolved not to draw for the full Sallary of half a Year due Christmas last 1752, but by a Bill upon the Revd. Mr. Smith, in Favour of Messrs. Smith & Gordon,[5] of £7 : 10. The Matter remain'd uncertain till now, for in my second Draught of Midsummer last 1753, I drew as usual for £12 : 10. So that now I must draw for £18 : 10.[6] And afterwards I shall continue to draw as usual. Immediately upon the Rect. of the 7 : 10 caus'd to be paid by Mr. Lloyd, I desir'd the Revd. Mr. Smith to return my sincere Thanks, together with my due Respects to the Associates for their Favour, which I now repeat, & desire that you'll be so good to tender the same to them.

I shall proceed to comply with your Commands, in giving you an Account of my Proceeding with the Negroes, & tho tis what I have already done in some of Mines to the Revd. Mr. Smith, yet I will repeat it again. But first take this as a certain Truth, & beg that you'll not rely upon my bare assertion, but that a strict Enquiery may be made into it that the Associates may be fully convinc'd that I do not impose upon them. And that is that from the Time of my Arrival here, I never upon any Account Whatever, Sickness excepted, omitted the discharging of my Duty towards these unhappy Souls, Committed to my Charge. And tho' during the Time of making the Silk I have been employd by the Public to direct that Business; yet at Night (which is the Time which Im oblig'd to fix for the Instruction of the Negroes because then they have finish'd their daily Task & some Masters will suffer them to come to me) how much fatigu'd soever I find my self, I never neglect my Duty. And tho' the being employ'd in the Silk Business for about two Months in year, has been a Means to help me toward my Maintainance, which my Sallary could never do, in a Country where every Things are excessiv'ly Dear, yet had this, or any other engagements that should interfer with the Instructions of the Negroes I would immediately drop it.

111

I bless my God that I have all the Success with these Poor Creatures that their Circumstances & Station in Life, can well admit of. I
have a good Many that can say the Catechism perfectly well, & as I
take all the Care imaginable to explain to them in as familiar a Manner as I can adapt to their low Capacity; I find upon Examining them,
which I do once a Week, that by the Blessing of God they daily improve in the knowledge of our Holy Religion. It is true that their
Number is not so great as I could Wish, by reason of their penurious
Masters, who thinks that they should be great Loosser should they
permit their Slaves to learn what they must do to be saved. Not Considering that he would be a greater Gainer if his Servant should become a true follower of the Blessed Jesus, for in such a Case, he would
have instead of an immoral dishonest Domestic a faithful Servant.
Others again, especially those who resort to us from the West Indies,
will upon no Account whatever suffer their Slaves to be instructed in
the Christian Religion, alledging that tis a just observation (of the
Devil's framing I suppose) that a Slave is ten times worse when a Christian, than in his State of Paganism; but they must mean such as practice Christianity as they do, for tis Certain that such as we have amongst
us, are as great Heathen as their Slaves, & what wonder is then that
they take all Methods & use so many sophistical Arguments to obstruct
the Instruction of their Servants, for should these Poor Souls come to
behold the Beauty of the Christian Religion & observe that tho their
Masters call themselves by the glorious Name of Christians, & yet are a
Scandal not only to human Nature but to our Holy Profession, they
would despise such wretched Masters. However I bless God that I
have at Times more than my present little House will contain, & as I
ever treat them with familiarity & kind Words (the only Place perhaps
where they are civily used) they endeavour to find all the Time which
they can spare to be with me. As the First Thing we do is to pray to
God for his Protection & Blessing on our undertaking, few of them
can but repeat them by Heart. Their Behaviour is devout, & at Church,
demean themselves as becomes Christians. As I generally sing a Psalm
with them, such as are us'd at Church, several of them who have really
good Voices, having learn'd the Words & Tune at Schole, join the Congregation at Church. I generally explain to them their Duty acquaint
them as far as their Capacity will permit, with the Historical & Moral
Part of our holy Religion, & against any of our Solemn Festivals, explain to them the Nature & Reason of their institution, & how they
ought to be observ'd. I gradually teach them Prayers fitting their Conditions, & Capacities, to be used by them Morning & Evening, as well
such as they are to use before & after Meal. Thus far is my Method
with them, but if any Advice shall come to me from you or any good
Christians for my better Conduct towards the discharging of my Duty;

I shall with all Thankfulness put in Practice what ever I shall be advis'd with.

As the Town is poorly suppli'd with Instructors for our White People, I have invited any one that would come to me, & would as far as I could, give them all the Instruction I was capable, & did I enjoy better Health, & had a place fit for it, I would have opend a Schole long before now to teach as far as I could any such as would have send their Children, for what I do at night is mostly for Apprentices, who are miserably Ignorant of their Duty, & not able to read them in the Book of God.

I'm now building an House, driven to it by Necessity, for that in which I live in, is so small, that I have not room sufficient to have as many People about me as their Ignorance requires & my Intention could wish. Another Motive that forc'd me to build, is the scarcity of Houses, especially since that so many People resort among us, that has made Houses both scarce & very Dear, & as every Body is endeavouring to make the Best of their old Houses, I found that my Land Lord intended to raise & repair his, in order to make better Rent of it. So that had I not taken the Step which I took, I might in a little Time have found my self without an Hole to put my Head in. Tis true that I have brought my self even by building a little House of four Small Rooms only, into a Distemper the most Grievous of any that I have ever dreaded, I mean in Debt, but as twas not my Choice but Necessity, & with a good Design, in order to have more Room for the Instruction of both White & Black, I am confident that that God who knows my Heart, & who has wonderfully deliver'd me of all the Calamities that have attended my passd Life, that he will now for the sake of my dear Redeemer free me from that great anxiety that I labour under; but will incline the Hearts of pious Christians to afford me some small Assistance.

And now having done troubleing you, I shall conclude by beging of you two Favours, first that you'll Pardon, my None sense & the Slips of Orthography, & the rather because you must not expect better from a Foreigner. The Second is, that you will be so Good to comfort me now & a then with your Lines, Mean While may the God of all Spirits & Comforts, Bless you & all that belong to you, with Temporal Felicity, & an eternal & joyful Eternity. With this my hearty Prayers for you, accept my sincere Respects, & if tis in your Way to converse with my Kind Benefactore Mr. Vernon,[7] pray tender my Duty to him, as well as to the Revd. Mr. Smith, & am Sir Your most Sincere Humble Servant

J. Ottolenghe

Savannah in Georgia November 19th. 1753

P.S. I forgot to tell you that Mr. Lloyd has charg'd the Fraight for the Box of Books to Messrs. Harris & Habersham[8] to whom I am to pay it, but how much, I know not as yet.

ALS. Endorsed "August 30. Accepted a Bill from Mr. Ottolenghe in favour of Rasbury. Sent by Honeywood & Fuller." This letter was read by the Associates at their meeting of 21 June 1754, at which time they "Resolved that the Associates do approve thereof. Resolved that for the Satisfaction of the publick & to excite well disposed persons to contribute to the Enlarging this Branch of the Associates Designs, that a Part of Mr. Ottolenghe's Letter giving an Account of his Method of Instructing the Negros be published in one of the Daily papers. Resolved that whereas Mr. Ottolenghe hath by Mistake drawn upon the Associates for twenty Shillings more than his half Years Salary, the Same be given as a present in Consideration for his Satisfactory Account of his proceedings sent to the Associates." Minutes, 1:91. Waring's reply, dated 22 June 1754, has not been found.

1. Letter not found.

2. In August 1753 the Associates shipped 154 volumes to Ottolenghe. See "Catalog of Books," p. 1. In the Book of Common Prayer the Psalms are presented as they appeared in the Miles Coverdale Bible of 1535, rather than in the King James Version.

3. These books have not been identified.

4. Samuel Lloyd, a London merchant, was elected a Georgia Trustee on 19 March 1746/47. He became a member of the Common Council of the Trustees in May 1749. Lloyd had spent fourteen years in Italy and was greatly concerned in the silk industry. He handled the sale in England of the silk produced in Georgia. On 7 July 1752 Lloyd and Benjamin Martyn attended the Board of Trade and presented two papers concerning the encouragements given by the Georgia Trustees to the growth and culture of silk in Georgia since 1748. Lloyd's letter to Ottolenghe has not been found. *Ga. Col. Recs.* 1:30, 533; *Journals of the Board of Trade* 9:342; Thaddeus Mason Harris, *Biographical Memorials of James Oglethorpe, Founder of the Colony of Georgia in North America* (Boston, 1841), p. 412.

5. Merchants of Port Royal, South Carolina. Ga. Col. Recs., unpub., 31:563–64.

6. Ottolenghe had been underpaid by £5; he therefore should have drawn for £17.10, not £18.10. See bibliographic note to this letter.

7. James Vernon (for whom see Ziegenhagen to [Smith], 3 May 1735, note 6, above) petitioned the secretary of the S.P.G. and the archbishop of Canterbury on Ottolenghe's behalf in January 1750/51. He asked that they support Ottolenghe's request that the S.P.G. supplement the £25 per annum stipend appropriated by the Associates. The S.P.G. voted in February to grant Ottolenghe £15 per annum. S.P.G. MSS., B18, nos. 78, 79. See also Ottolenghe entry in the Biographical Appendix.

8. The firm of Francis Harris (1710–71) and James Habersham (1713–75), established in the mid-1740s, was the leading mercantile house in Savannah. Harris had been clerk and manager of the Trustees' store from his ar-

rival in the Colony about 1740 until it closed in the early 1740s. Then instead of the pay owed him Harris took goods from the store and established himself as a merchant. Harris served on the Council from 1754. Habersham had come to Georgia in 1738 with George Whitefield and cooperated with the evangelist in establishing the Bethesda Orphanage. Habersham was also a planter, secretary of the colony, and a member of the Council. *DAB*; Kenneth Coleman and Charles Stephen Gurr, eds., *Dictionary of Georgia Biography*, 2 vols. (Athens, Ga., 1983), 2:377–78, 398–99.

Joseph Ottolenghe to [Rev. John Waring]

[Savannah, 18 November 1754]

Revd. Sir

I recd. your last dated June 22d. 1754[1] with a great deal of Pleasure, especially when I consider that I never had an answer from the Society of prop: of the Gospel in foreign Parts, of Letters which I sent from Time to Time for Instruction,[2] & but two Letters (& them from you) from the Associates since my Pilgrimage in these Parts. And therefore I shall with alacrity answer your Last orderly as it stands before me. And

First, I am very glad that you seem to approve of my Method towards the Instruction of the Negroes, as I hope that it will meet with the Approbation also of the Associates, but because I am willing to reduce my self into as narrow a Compass as possible & because also my present ill State of Health will not permit me to do otherwise, therefore once for all assure your self that both my Interest but more my Conscience & real Inclination are Motives enough to make me use all the Christian Means to answer those happy Ends for which the Associates & the Society propos'd, but the Event remains in the Hands of a gracious God. It is true the Means are to be used, & his Blessing to be implor'd for the success, but beyond the Means left us we cannt go. The Colony hitherto has been unsettled, & the People in it no way fix'd in their Determinations to settle in Town or Country, but since the news of the Government's being settl'd, & a Governour arrivd,[3] many Families are withdrawn into the Country to their Plantations; & many of those Negroes who had begun to make a tolerable Profisiency, are gone with them. But supposing that these had remain with me, you know Sir how Circumpspect & Cautious the Primitive Christians were with the Catechumens, a Caution worthy of those best of Times, & yet they had none of those many Hindrancies, & great Difficulties which are to be met with in the Instruction of Negroes. The Formers understood the Language of the Instructors, & if not Persons were appointed skill'd in the Language of the Novices, whereas our Negroes are so Ignorant of the English Language, & none can be found to talk in their own, that it is a great while before you can get them to understand what the Meaning of Words is, & yet that without such a knowledge Instructions would prove Vain, & the Ends proposd abortive, for how can a Proposition be believed, without first being understood? And how can it be understood if the Person to whom it is offer'd has no Idea even of the Sound of those Words which expressess the Proposition? Indeed in the Romish Church where their Belief is mostly plac'd in dumb Idols, & Ignorance is the Mother of their Devotion, a convert is compleatly made, when he can repeat an Ave Mary & a Pater Noster & in a Language, that is as little understood by the People, as their Transubstantiation is agreable to Reason & Scripture. But blessed be God, that neither the holy Gosple of our adorable Jesus, nor the Principle of our best of Churches, wants such Parot-like Members, but she is ready to receive into Christ's Flock such as can give a Reason of the Hope that is in them. God knowes that we abound too much every where with ignorant Christians, & to add new ones to their Number, twould be encreasing the Bulk of nominal Christians, but no ways add one Believer to the Household of Faith.

Again, Slavery is certainly a great Depresser of the Mind, which retards their Learning a new Religion, propos'd to them in a new & unknown Language, besides the old Superstition of a false Religion to be combated with, & nothing harder to be remov'd (you know) than Prejudices of Education, riveted by Time, & entrench'd in deep Ignorance, which must be overcom'd by slow Advances, with all the Patience & engaging Means that can be studied, to make them fall in Love with the best of all Religions, & so to Captivate their Minds, as to give all their very little Leisure to the Study of it, & I have so far gain'd this Point, in drawing the Negroes to it, with the Cords of Love; that if their unchristian Masters would but suffer them to come to me, they are willing & ever ready to be with me. But I bless God that there are many in Town who have not bended their Hearts to gain only, but think it highly necessary to have their Slaves instructed, & careful in sending of them, in somuch that at Times a large Room that I have for that Purpose, is as full as it can hold; tho' I must own that it is not the 3d. Part of the Negroes that are about us. However I am in great hope that when every Things are settled amongst us, that Religion will take another Turn for the Best, & I shall have (if God prolong my Life) better pleasure in my Mission than I have eitherto had, & indeed my good & pious Friends here, comfort me with this happy Expectation of better Time. Had all those Negroes which began their Instruction at the Begining of my coming to this Colony, continud with me to this Time, some of them would by this Time have been forward enough for an Admittance into the Church of Christ, by the holy Sacrament of Baptism, but they are most of them removd to remote Plantations, or sent into other Colonies. However I have several now who are gone thro their Catechism, & can repeat it by Heart, together with such Prayers suitable to their Conditions, necessities & Capacities; & am labouring now to make them sensible of the Meaning of what they have been learning. But the Best Harvest which (I through Gods Assistance) expect from [them] is out of the Infants that encrease daily upon us, as these are more susceptible of Instruction, so are they Free from enveterate Prejudices from a bad Education, & from these I hope that Christ's Kingdom will be spread among these poor forlorn unhappy People.

I will therefore conclude what I have said upon this subject, by assuring the Associates with the Pleasure that I should receive if they would get Information from proper Persons of this Town, & when upon just Inquiry they find that I have either been remiss in discharging that high Trust repos'd in me, or wanting Capacity in the Conducting of it, I shall be as willing immediately to resign it, as I was ready to accept it.

I come now to another Pargraph of your Letter which has given me much Uneasiness & that is with regard to my Draught upon you for 20s. more than I ought to have done a Fact which as I acknowledge to be true, so likewise I can with all the Sincerity of my Heart appeal to the searcher of it, that what I did was neither from Design of Fraud, or any sinister View, but from mere Ignorance & a discompos'd Mind, by a languishing Body thro' a long Fit of Sickness, & therefore I am extremely thankful to you for the charitable Construction which you was so good to put upon my said unhappy Action, as also for your Generosity in honouring the Bill which God will reward you for it, & for which I beg with all my Heart your Pardon, & that I may make ammend for what I foolishly committed, I shall make a Restitution in my next Draught by making it 20s. less than usual upon you, that you may be reimburs'd with what you so candidly paid for me.[4]

The circular Letters of Dr. Bray[5] have been wellcome to me & thank you for it. I shall make the best Use that I can of it. At present I want no Books, but if you would be so good to procure for me a good Edition of the Homilies of the Church of England, as also a Vindication of the Liturgy of our best of Churches.[6] Our People have been so poisond by a Parcel of unreform'd Reformers, who from Time to Time have visited & disturbd these Parts, that every Points of our best establish'd Church are canvas'd or ridicul'd, & have found my self often dragg'd into this irkesome Task. Irkesome I say, because it tends to no manner of Edification; as also because that [I] have no Books by me to furnish my self with proper Answers to baffle their Cavils; & therefore if such a Book could by you be provided for me together with the Former, I would thankfully pay the Price of them & the sooner they reach, the greater will be my obligation to you.

And now to conclude but first let me repeat again my sincere Thanks to you for your Favours towards me, as also to beg of you that you would comfort me with your Letters & Advices. Be pleas'd also to present my Humble Respects to the pious Associates & you may assure the Gentlemen which compose that Body, that I have & will through the Grace of God continue to do my uttmost to answer their pious End in sending me here. Accept also my Respect to you & believe me to be in all Christian Duty Revd. Sir Your most Oblig'd & sincere Humble Servant

J. Ottolenghe

Savannah in Georgia
November 18th. 1754

ALS. The bracketed word in the third paragraph is a conjectural reading, the manuscript being torn.

1. Letter not found.

2. The only surviving letter from Ottolenghe to the S.P.G. before this date is dated 9 September 1751. S.P.G. MSS., B19, no. 149. His letter of 4 June 1752 is abstracted in *Abstract of the Proceedings of the S.P.G. for 1752*, appended to Edward Cresset, bishop of Llandaff, *A Sermon Preach'd . . . on Friday, February 16, 1753* (London, 1753), p. 54.

3. Following the surrender of the Georgia charter by the Trustees in June 1752, the colony reverted to royal control. John Reynolds (1713–88) was appointed the first royal governor of the colony in August 1754, and he arrived in Georgia on 29 October 1754. His failure to deal with the problems of the colony and his inability to maintain amicable relations with the Council and the Assembly resulted in his recall in August 1756. Reynolds left the colony in February 1757. *DAB*; William W. Abbot, *The Royal Governors of Georgia, 1754–1775* (Chapel Hill, N.C., 1959), chap. 2.

4. See Ottolenghe to [Waring], 19 November 1753, bibliographic note, above.

5. Thomas Bray, *Several Circular Letters to the Clergy of Mary-Land, Subsequent to Their Late Visitation, to Enforce Such Resolutions as Were Taken Therein* (London, 1701).

6. Ottolenghe's request was honored at the meeting of 10 March 1756, when the Associates "Resolved that a Book of Homilies & Such a Defence of the Church of England as Mr. Waring & Skinner shall approve of be sent to Mr. Ottolenghe . . ." Minutes, 1:96.

Rev. Thomas Pollen to [Rev. John Waring]

Newport July 6. 1755

Revd. Sir,

As I have great reason to think that the Letter I sent You dated November 9th. is miscarried (the Vessel being lost at Sea as is generally supposed)[1] I take this Opportunity to send you a Duplicate of It, having nothing new to acquaint you with.

I hope You will not look upon my deferring to write hitherto as a Neglect. I was willing before I wrote, to acquaint my self thoroughly with the Subject I was to write upon. I am very sensible of the Obligation I am under, even from a principle of Gratitude for your Society's extraordinary kindness to me, (if there were no other reasons) to answer the cheif End propos'd by It.[2] I find upon enquiry there are but few Indians in & about this Town, or indeed in the whole Island; & these few so scatter'd from each other, & mixt with other People that They are hardly to be perceiv'd; & even almost all of them are (as the term is here) of some Christian Society or Another.[3] But here are (as I am credibly inform'd) as many Negroes as in all the rest of the Government beside:[4] who for the most part are unbaptized, & in the same state of Heathen Ignorance, as the Wild Indians. I have ask'd two or three of our Communion, how it comes to pass, that the Masters have taken no more care to see their Negroes baptized. They answer'd that it has been observ'd, They grow worse after Baptism. I have likewise taken occasion to ask as many of the Negroes, who have been baptized, the same question. They said they could not tell, unless The Masters thought that their Servants would by Baptism come too near Themselves: but as for the Negroes growing worse after baptism, tho' it might happen in one or two instances, out of many, yet They were persuaded that in general it was not true. However it be I do not despair of meeting with success in my attempts (thro' God's Grace) of converting & baptizing some of them. I shall begin with persuading those Masters who profess to have a true sense of Religion, at least not to oppose them. And if They will shew the way, 'tis not improbable, but some Others will follow. I shall endeavour by degrees (for it will be no easy matter) to bring the less serious & knowing of them, to attend at certain times to an explanation of the Church-Catechism which I shall direct to their Children. Because there are many grown Persons who come regularly to Church, yet (I presume for want of a due sense of the necessity of Baptism,) never were baptiz'd themselves, & therefore it is no wonder they are unwilling their Negroes should. I have desired the Negroes abovemention'd to tell their Acquaintance that I am ready to instruct any of them, in the Christian Religion: & that if I find them at any time duly qualified, & rightly dispos'd, I shall make no scruple of baptizing them. I have indeed already baptized some few, & have defer'd baptizing One Woman, who offer'd herself, because of the bad Character She bore, till I hear a better account of Her. I shall be glad, Sir to have a Letter from You, & whatever Instructions your Society shall think proper to give me, I shall receive them with all the Deference that is due to them.

I am your most Humble Servant

Tho: Pollen.

P.S. Be pleas'd to direct for me Minister of Trinity Church &c. I return you thanks for your trouble in buying for me Holes Catechism.[5]

ALS. The reading of this letter is not recorded in the Associates' Minute Book, but on 10 March 1756 a letter from Pollen dated 4 September 1755 was read, and an abstract of the letter was copied into the Minute Book. From the abstract it appears that the two letters were almost identical; that of 4 September may have been a duplicate of the present document. Upon reading the 4 September letter it was "Resolved that the Associates do approve of Mr. Pollens Proceedings, & that he be desired to continue his catechetical Instructions, as & that twelve Copies of the Revd. Mr. Bacon's Six Sermons be sent to Mr. Pollen to be disposed of in such manner as he shall Judge most conducive to promote the Conversion of the Negroes." Minutes, 1 : 95–96. These publications were by the Rev. Thomas Bacon (c. 1700–1768): *Two Sermons, Preached to a Congregation of Black Slaves . . .* (London, 1749), and *Four Sermons, upon the Great and Indispensable Duty of All Christian Masters to Bring Up Their Negro Slaves in the Knowledge and Fear of God* (London, 1750), the latter published by the S.P.G.

1. Letter not found.

2. In December 1753 the Associates gave Pollen ten guineas as a present to encourage him "to engage in this his pious Design" of converting and instructing Negroes in Rhode Island. Minutes, 1 : 88–89.

3. In 1755 there were approximately 1,300 Narragansett Indians in Rhode Island. James, *Colonial Rhode Island*, p. 231.

4. In fact only about 800 of the colony's approximately 4,700 blacks resided in Newport in 1755. James, *Colonial Rhode Island*, p. 255n; William D. Johnston, *Slavery in Rhode Island, 1755–1776* (Providence, 1894), p. 18.

5. Matthew Hole (c. 1640–1730), *Practical Exposition of the Catechism* (London, 1708).

[Rev. Mungo Marshall to Rev. John Waring]

[Orange County, Virginia, c. September 1756]

Read a Letter from the Revd. Mr. Mungo Marshall of Orange County in Virginia, who saith that his Parish is very extensive &

abounds with Negroes who are destitute of any Principles of Religion, on whom he hath bestowed great pains in repeated Endeavours to bring them to Baptism & the Lords Supper. He desire the Associates will favour him with Some Books & pious Tracts to enable him more effectualy to promote the Instruction of the Negroes.

Letter not found. Extract from Minutes, 1:99 (meeting of 15 December 1756). After reading this letter the Associates "Resolved that One Copy of each Book in the Store & 25 Copies of the Several Catachetical Tracts, together with 25 of Mr. Bacons Six Sermons on the Conversion of the Negroes be sent to Mr. Marshall." See "Catalog of Books," p. 17.

Rev. John Waring to Benjamin Franklin

[London, 24 January 1757]

Sir

I trouble You with this [*torn*] the Death of a worthy Clergyman the [Reverend Henry] Wheatley, Lecturer of St. Leonard Shoreditch,[1] [*torn*] me the Sole Executor of his last Will, by which [*torn*] a Legacy to some of his Relations now (if alive) at Philadelphia in the following words: "I give and bequeath to Benjamin Franklin Esqr., of Philadelphia in Pensilvania One hundred Pounds Sterling in Trust for John Cole Grandson of my late Brother John Wheatley of the same Place, & the elder Son of James Hunter which he has by the Mother of the said John Cole Daughter of my said Brother John Wheatley to be paid to them for their Use equally at the Discretion and Judgement of the said Mr. Franklin."[2]

Mr. Henry Wheatley died on the Sixth Day of Last may, of which I had sent You earlier Advice, but that being a Clergyman & consequently but little connected with mercantile Affairs, the last Ships saild before I was apprized of it, & I was the less solicitous to write to You About this Legacy till I cou'd be pretty certain that I should be able to honour Your Draught. I am advised to desire the favour of You to send over a Letter of Attorney to Your Correspondent here to impower him to receive this Legacy & to give a proper Discharge for the same.[3] This I am told is the legal & consequently the most safe way, &, if You approve of it shou'd be glad it were observed. Shou'd the Legatee John Cole, or all James Hunters Sons by John Coles Mother, have been dead before Mr. Wheatley, in Such Case I presume that the Legacy lapses and reverts to the Residuary Legatee, whose Name is John Kittermaster:[4] I shall be glad of the favour of a Line from You on this Subject by the first Opportunity, & am Sir Your most humble Servant

Jn. Waring

[*Torn*] pleased with every Opportunity of doing [*torn*] Reason tis needless for me, Worthy Sir, to [*torn*] what follows. I am a Member of a Society [*torn*] by the Name of the Associates of the late [Dr. Bray, a Gen]tleman whose Memory ought to be dear [*torn*]vers of piety in the British Plantations [*torn*]jects of our Attention as a Society are the [Instruct]ion & Conversion of the Negroes in the Plantations to Christianity & founding parochial Libraries for the Use of the Clergy in England & America: We shall be much obliged to You, if You will favour Us with Your Sentiments on the first Design, & let us know how & by what means those poor ignorant people may be most effectualy instructed whether the parochial Clergy *do* take any pains with them & what Helps & Assistances they may want to enable them to diffuse the knowledge of our Religion among them? As the Lately imported Negroes are Strangers to our Language, Little Good I fear can be done with them, but might Not the black Children born in the Province be taught to read & instructed in the Principles of Christian Morality, & if the planters woud permit them, pray What Sum Sterling, per Ann. wou'd be a suitable Salary for a Sober honest Master? Some few Years ago a pious Clergyman in Wales set on foot a Scheme of itinerant Schoolmasters; who after residing three Six or nine Months in one place, & teaching persons of all Ages to read, who came to them, removed to another, & did the Like there, by this means Six or Seven thousand persons (Young & old) for some Years past have been annualy taught to read & instructed in religious knowledge. Might not some Such Scheme be set on foot in Your province for the Service of the blacks?[5] The Associates beg the favour of You to consult with the worthy Commissary[6] & some of the other Clergy in the Neighbourhood & favour Us with the Result of Your Deliberations. One word more Both Planters & Slaves, I am told have mistaken Notions concerning [*seven or eight lines missing*] might have a very good effect upon their [morals?] & make them more faithful & honest in their Masters Service, & Such of them only, from time to time, admitted to baptism as came recommended by their Masters for their good behaviour, or who shewed by the general tenour of their Conduct that they had right Notions of Religion. I fear I have tired Your patience, but when we converse at this Distance, it is necessary to say all that occurs upon the Subject, because there may Not be an Opportunity soon of sending a Supplement.

Our fund at present is but Small, however I hope by the blessing of God we shall be able to furnish those worthy Clergymen who engage with zeal in this truly Christian Design with religious Books & tracts to enable them more effectualy to carry it on & perhaps also with some useful Books towards forming a parochial Library for the

Use of themselves & Successors: We shall be very thankful to You or them for any Informations which may be of Service. Letters upon this Subject directed to mee in Wood Street Spitalfields London shall be duely laid before the Associates & punctualy answered. I am once More Sir Your most humble Servant

Jn. Waring

January 24: 1757.

ALS: American Philosophical Society. Waring wrote this letter in two parts, the second part beginning on the verso of the first folio. The upper right hand corner of the first folio has been torn off, thus removing several words from the first few lines of each part. The top quarter of the second folio has also been torn off, removing seven or eight lines at the place indicated in the text. The entire letter has been given the date of the second part, although it is possible Waring may have written an earlier date in the torn section at the head of the first part.

1. The Rev. Henry Wheatley (c. 1689–1756), A.B. Trinity College, Oxford, 1709. Foster, *Alumni Oxonienses*.

2. The two legatees of this bequest were sons of John Wheatley's daughter Mary. She had married, first, a man named Cole, by whom she had a son, John Cole. She later married James Hunter, by whom she had a son whose name is not given. In his letter to Waring of 17 February 1758, below, Franklin reported that John Cole would be bound as an apprentice and that the Hunter boy would be schooled until he was old enough for apprenticeship. The Hunter boy must have died young without leaving full brothers, for Franklin wrote to James Hunter on 10 February 1773 proposing to pay the boy's £50 share with interest for the benefit of Hunter's daughter, now "arrived at an Age when the Money may be of Use to Her." *Franklin Papers* 7:99n.

3. As this letter reached Philadelphia after Franklin's departure for London, he received the legacy through Henton Brown (c. 1698–1775), his London banker, rather than through an agent. *Franklin Papers* 7:99n, 379n.

4. John Kittermaster, a fishmonger at Billingsgate, annually subscribed one guinea to the Associates from 1757 until at least 1775.

5. The Welsh circulating charity school movement was begun by the Rev. Griffith Jones of Llandowror, Carmarthenshire, in 1737. The schools, which taught adults as well as children, used thousands of Bibles, psalters, catechisms, and other books provided by the S.P.C.K., all in Welsh. It is not surprising that Waring suggested this method to Franklin for use in Pennsylvania, because 1757 was the high-water mark of the movement, with 218 schools serving 9834 pupils. W. K. Lowther Clarke, *Eighteenth Century Piety* (London, 1944), pp. 79–80.

6. The Rev. Robert Jenney, for whom see Sturgeon to Waring, 1 July 1762, note 3, below.

Benjamin Franklin to Rev. John Waring

Craven street [London], January 3. 58.

Revd. Sir,

I send you herewith the Extract of Mr. Sturgeon's[1] Letter, which I mentioned to you. He is, among us, esteemed a good Man, one that makes a Conscience of the Duties of his Office, in which he is very diligent; and has behaved with so much Discretion, as to gain the general Respect & Good-will of the People. If the Associates of Dr. Bray should think fit to make Tryal of a School for Negro Children in Philadelphia, I know no Person under whose Care it would be more likely to succeed. At present few or none give their Negro Children any Schooling, partly from a Prejudice that Reading & Knowledge in a Slave are both useless and dangerous; and partly from an Unwillingness in the Masters & Mistresses of common Schools to take black Scholars, lest the Parents of the white Children should be disgusted & take them away, not chusing to have their Children mix'd with Slaves in Education, Play, &c. But a separate School for Blacks, under the Care of One, of whom People should have an Opinion that he would be careful to imbue the Minds of their young Slaves with good Principles, might probably have a Number of Blacks sent to it; and if on Experience it should be found useful, and not attended with the ill Consequences commonly apprehended, the Example might be followed in the other Colonies, and encouraged by the Inhabitants in general.

I am, sir, Your most humble Servant

B Franklin

ALS: American Philosophical Society. Waring reported the contents of this letter to the Associates at their meeting of 5 April 1758, at which time they "Resolved that a School be opened at Philadelphia for the Instruction of the Negroes under the Care & Superintendency of Mr. Sturgeon & that J. Waring be desired to write to him upon that Subject, & acquaint him that the Associates are willing to make a Trial of a School for three Years & request of him to agree with a proper Master or Mistress upon the Best Terms he can, but not to exceed twenty pounds Sterling a Year." Minutes, 1 : 114. Waring's letter, dated 2 March 1758, has not been found.

1. For the Rev. William Sturgeon see Biographical Appendix.

Enclosure
[Rev. William Sturgeon to Benjamin Franklin]

[Philadelphia, 22 August 1757]

Extract of a Letter from the Revd. Mr. Sturgeon,
dated at Philadelphia, August 22, 1757.

Mrs. Franklin[1] favoured me with the Sight of a Letter wrote to you by one Mr. Waring, in which your Thoughts are desired on the important Subject of instructing the Negroes in the Principles of Christianity. As I have the Honour of being employ'd by the Society, a Catechist to the Negroes in this City, I take the Freedom to make mention of the Affair to you. When I first arrived here, few or none of the Colour were Christians; but by the Blessing of God, several of them, after proper Instruction, have been baptised, and are regular Communicants of our Church; and others who do not communicate, behave orderly, and attend the Service of the Church.

I am forced chiefly to instruct them by the Ear; but if a School could be opened for their Use under the Care and Inspection of the Minister, or some other prudent Person or Persons, the Work would in time become easy, & much Good might be done to them, and several of the lower Rank of White People.

Copy: American Philosophical Society. In Franklin's hand. This extract, except for the first two sentences, was published in *An Account of the Proceedings of the Associates, for the Year 1757* [London, 1758], where the date is given as 4 August 1757.

1. For Deborah (Read) Franklin see Biographical Appendix.

Benjamin Franklin to Rev. John Waring

Craven Street [London], February 17. 1758

Reverend Sir

I beg Pardon for not answering sooner your Favour of the 16th. past.[1] I unluckily mislaid it just after it came to hand, and was in daily Expectation of finding it. It is now before me; and I am of Opinion that for 30£ a Year, Sterling, a good Master might be procur'd that would teach 40 Negro Children to read; I think he could scarce do his Duty to a greater Number without an Assistant. But as the School may not probably be so large for some time, and if they were taught some useful Things besides Reading it might be an Encouragement to Masters and Mistresses to send them. I think a Mistress might be best to begin with, who could teach both Boys & Girls to read, & the Girls to knit, sew & mark;[2] a good One might be had, I believe, for about 20£ Sterling, that would well instruct in this Way about 30 Scholars. And when the School becomes so numerous as to make a Division necessary, then a Master may be procured for the Boys, and the Mistress retained for the Girls; the whole Charge not exceeding 50£ Sterling per Ann. for 60 or 70 Children.

This whole Charge, however, it is not necessary that the Associates should pay. If they set the School on foot and engage for the Salaries, it will be sufficient. Most of the Owners of Negro Children are able to pay for their Schooling, and will be willing if they like the Design, see it well manag'd, and find it useful. The Persons you intrust as Visitors of the School (suppose the Minister, with the Assistance of the Church Wardens and Vestry) may appoint the School-master or Mistress, agree with and pay them, receive what can be obtain'd for the Schooling, and draw on the Associates only for the Deficiency. The Accounts should be fairly stated & laid before you from time to time, perhaps quarterly: A Year or two's Trial will show you what is to be expected from this Undertaking, and I hope it may, at a small Expence, afford you much Satisfaction.

I find by the enclosed, which I lately receiv'd from Philadelphia, that your Letter to me, concerning Mr. Wheatly's Will, being receiv'd in my Absence, was communicated by my Wife to James and Mary Hunter.[3] I do not think it prudent to deliver the Money to the Parents for the Use of the Children, having no Opinion of their Management; but shall apply Part of it to the Binding the Boys Apprentices to Trades, & the Remainder, with the Interest in the mean time arising, towards purchasing Tools & Stock when they come to act for themselves. I believe the eldest Boy may be now fit to go Apprentice, and shall by the next Ship write to a discreet Friend to get him a good Place, and take some Care of the other's Schooling. With great Respect, I am, Revd. Sir, Your most obedient & most humble Servant

B Franklin

P.S. Whenever it is convenient to you, the Legacy may be paid into the Hands of my Banker, Mr. Henton Brown in Lombard Street, and I will give you the proper Discharge.[4]

ALS: American Philosophical Society.

1. Letter not found.

2. To mark: to embroider; to place an identifying mark on linen or other household furniture by means of embroidery or stitching, or with marking-ink. *OED.*

3. The enclosure has not been found. It may have been an extract of a letter to Franklin from his wife.

4. See Waring to Franklin, 24 January 1757, note 3, above.

Joseph Ottolenghe to Rev. John Waring

[Savannah, 12 July 1758]

Revd. Sir

June the 20th, I receivd your Letter,[1] but its Date I cannot remember now for Reason that I shall e'er long acquaint you with. I was extremely touch'd to find my self under so high a Displeasure of the Associates. In your's of January 1757 you inform me that the Associates were surprizd that they heard nothing from me the Year before, and yours now to be answerd, acquaints me that the Associates are very much surpriz'd that they have not heard from me these 3 or 4 Years.[2] I hope Sir that I may be believed when I solemnly declare that not a Year has pass'd since my coming into this Province without writing to you or to the worthy & Revd. Mr. Smith. If my Letters have miscarried since the breaking out of the War, Im not to be charged and punish'd for neglect. Five or six Month's Experience in these Parts of the World, would soon convince you that it is not so easy as imagin'd to write for England. Opportunities from hence are scarce, and those few during the unhappy Times, very precarious, and our Governor[3] can tell that even Duplicates & Triplicates, are not always means sufficient for Correspondence. I would not here be understood to mean that I have wrote Duplicates to all my Letters to you, or any Body else, for I never did, except in the Year 57 to you and to Dr. Bearcroft; the first of Mine to you was in June, on the Juno, Leslie Commander, from Georgia to London, and another a Month after it, by Way of Charlestown.[4] I am in hopes that long before now you're in possession of both, especially the First, since that I have recd. answers for all the Letters sent by that Ship. Tis true as you say that I ought to write Duplicates, but Sir I dare say that any Humane Breast that knew the Distemper which I labour under, would even excuse my Writing at all. I have been for these 16 Years afflicted with a nervous accute Distemper in my Head, and tho' for three Years after my coming to Georgia I found my self greatly relievd, yet a Violent fever which I had between three or four Years since, has renewd the Pain & fiercer than ever it had been, in somuch that I'm obligd to forbare reading and writing for several Days, & when I am under an interval, I am not permitted to use my Pen long at a Time, least I should encrease the Distemper, and if I throw into this Ballance the several Fits of the

Stone that I'm Yearly subject to, would I hope somewhat extenuate my Crime if [I] did not write. However I must again repeat that I never omitted writing as I said before, and if an Affidavit is requir'd I can take it with a safe Conscience that ever since I have been in Georgia I have annually transmitted an Account of my Labour to the Associates either through the Revd. Mr. Smith or through you. As for my not giving an Account of the Negroes that comes to me for Instruction I believe if I mistake not that I have given some Reason why that cann't be done with any certainty at all, but as all the Letters receiv'd from England together with the Answers sent are unhappily burnt, I shall not depend upon my Memory, & therefore shall give here my Reasons why their Number cannot be fixd without imposing, because some Times I have had fifty & more at once, & perhaps in a Month or two after it not half that Number, and at others, not Ten, and so on, more or less alternatly; again some will attend for 6 Months and then disappear for 6 Months or Year, & some two, before I see them again, and as they have no will of their own, their Motions are guided by the Dispotic will of their owners and have no other Leizure but what is allowd them. Tis true that the Public has of late demanded a good Deal of their Time in building of Forts throughout the Province and Cutting of Roads and consequently during that Time few have resorted to me.[5] Upon the Whole from what I have already, and more that might be said, twill appear that my not ascertaining the Number of Negroes was not out of any Designe to impose upon the Associates, but because I could not with any probability and consistent with Truth have fix'd upon the real Number. If the Masters were as willing to send their Slaves as these poor Creatures are desirous to be instructed, twould be some aleviation to my sufferings in this sickley uncomfortable Climate. I came here with pleasure, because I was to enter upon a sphere of Life extremely agreably to my Inclination, and as it became a choice as well as a Duty I resolv'd through God's Assistance to spare no Pains that might prove conducive to the desir'd End; whether I have taken these Steps or not, is what ought to be inquir'd into, & I remember that in my first Letters that I wrote, of having requested that no regard be paid to what I say, but that an Inquiry be made by some upon the Spot, and in this Case I shall fear nothing but Malice. Would to God that I may never have any Thing to answer at that awful Day when the Quick and Dead will be Judged, but my neglect in this Undertaking, & I doubt not to be plac'd at the right Hand of my gracious Judge. Suffer me to boast my self a little, not only because St. Paul encourages me,[6] but also because Im upon my Vindication, & if I'm believ'd in what I say twill be found whether or no I have not even gone somewhat beyond my Duty, and my low Circumstances.

I have built a Large Room with a large Chimeney for the Use of these poor souls the Latter extremely necessary for them who are of a Chill Constitution, ill fed and worse cloathed, that many are not fit to be seen by a modest Eye; and while in Summer we're ready faint with Heat, they solace themselves round a large fire. I have laid my self under the Expence of Candles (which cost ten Pence per Pound and wretched stuff) by teaching them by Night, to cut off their Pharaoh's excuse that they cannot send their Negroes by Day, because of their Labour. I have rais'd and cherish'd by proper Rewards a Spirit of Emulation in them with Success. I never refrain persuations and Exhortations to their Owners to induce them to suffer their Negroes to come to me, & made it Evident beyond Demonstration that even their Temporal Interest would be benefited by having their slaves well instructed in the Principles of our holy Religion. I have (excuse my Boasting once more) the satisfaction to think that many grown white Persons who have neither Leisure to attend a public schoole, nor Money to procure private Instruction, will I hope remember poor Joseph who has allotted some part of his Time that is most convinient for them to instruct such. These will have the Comfort of reading the Book of Life which perhaps might have grown old in Ignorance. But then twill be ask'd what fruits have these Methods produc'd with respect to the Negroes? To this I answer, as much as I could reasonably expect from a set of People naturally stupid; loaded with a Cruel Slavery; Ignorant of our Language and Manners; no Idea of our holy Religion; nurs'd in extravagant Idolatry; loaded with hard Labour & worse Usages; ill fed, ill cloathed; cruelly corrected & barbarously treated, in somuch that a Dog and an Horse are treated like humane Creature when compared with the Usages that these poor unhappy Wretches are dealt with who first have been robb'd of dear Liberty— their Native Country—beriev'd of their Friends, Parents, Relations Wives & Children—and at once reduc'd to a most deplorable & cruel Slavery! How often the present humane Governor and I have commiserate their hard and forlorn Fate; and propose to find out some Relief for them, which would not be difficult, but who must give the Consent to such Regulations? Why the Legislative-Body compos'd mostly of owners of Negroes, who would as soon consent to it as an Assembly of Lawyers would pass a Bill to curtail their Fees or reduce their Practices to an honest & Christian Standart. However I will even hope against Hope especially when I consider that tho I have met with almost unsurmountable Difficulties to have a Church-Bill passd in an Assembly mostly compos'd of Dissenters & in an upper House of all Dissenters save two, & yet I obtaind my Desire tho not so fully as I could wish.[7] But to return, the Negroes which have given constant Attendance are many of them capable of Saying all the Catechism by Heart, the Prayers used in the Schole, Grace before Meat and Thanks after it, prayers at their going to and rising from their Bed; some can read but in general poorly; at Church (such as are suffer'd to go there) behave decently, and devoutly join in our Prayers and singing. But was I a Minister I would not baptize any as yet, because I have reason to believe that they tho ready to repeat every Thing as they are instructed yet have very little Notion or Idea of what they thus repeat, and consequently a Parrot might as well be baptiz'd as any of them, especially as I observ'd before their Ignorance of our Language, to which may be added that their herding among themselves and never hear no other Discourses but what passeth among themselves and no white People will have any thing to say to them but to abuse them with bitter Execrations & cruel Blows. I have got 2 Negroes a young fellow and his Wife which I have had them for these 4 Years. They were very Young when I bought them, forbad them to keep Company with any other Negroes except in Schole, used them rather like Children than Servants, took an infinite Deal of Pains in their Education, yet altho' they are very faithful & very Honest, in point of learning very slow and Defficient, and yet eager in the pursuit of it, notwithstanding which I can not send them an Earrant without putting it in writing. I could expatiate enough upon this Subject, but your Time as a Minister of Christ has been already too much by me taken up, when you can spend it to much more Valuable Purposes, all that I would be willing to be understood by the foregoing is this that the Office of a Catechist uninspired, is not so easy as it may be imagin'd, and that if he does discharge his Duty as he ought to do, will find Difficulties hard enough to combat with. Thus have I done what I had to say upon this Subject, & as I hope that before now you have recd. mine of July 57 wherein you'll find that I have acknowledged the rect. of the Books sent me and as far as I was capable returnd suitable thanks, but in particular for Mr. Hoadly's Reasonableness of Conformity which has given me more satisfaction than any of the Bp. of Winchester's Writings.[8] It remains now that I take notice of one Part more of your Letter and that is (according to the Minutes which I have made of it) that you allow me to draw upon you from Christmas last that is I suppose you mean for half a Year's Sallary, and then you forbid me to draw any more Bills upon you for you say that you'll not accept of any more of my Draughts. As to the Sallary I dare say that there must be some Mistake since that I have not drawn upon you ever since middsummer 57 and consequently at middsummer 58 there must be a Year's Sallary due to me, but if my suppos'd Crime deserves also this Punishment I beg of you that as I had not Notice of this Suspension ob Beneficio[9] till Just at the Time of drawing and had already contracted Debts for the same, that if I must lose the half Year's Sallary, I must entreat you to acquaint my truly worthy & pious friend the Revd. Mr. Broughton to whom I shall God willing write by the first Opportunity to prevent if possible the Disgrace and expence of a Protest.[10] I shall punctually observe your charge in not drawing any more Draught on you, nevertheless shall continue to do my Duty even without a Sallary, and altho' tis the only earthly certainty which I have to depend upon for my support, yet I'm not so mistrustful of a Divine Support as to despond, when his infinite Goodness & Mercies have not forsaken me from my Youth up till now, & hope that I shall not be left destitute now in my infirm and declining State. My Friends to whom I have communicated your Letter among other Reasons which they have offer'd in order to comfort me is that I'm not accused for neglect of Duty here, neither any Complaint for which I am now suspended, has been made before the comencement of the War, and sure am I that they from the highest to the lowest of them in the service of the Government ought to have met with my Fate & for the like Reasons, but I suppose that as the Government at Home know that of 3 ships that went from Georgia for these 2 Years pass'd were all taken, and the public Papers, must have inform'd them how many Ships from Carolina went the same Way. And indeed my self ought to have met with the same fate from the Board of Trade as I met from your Letters, but am only told that my Letters must have been lost which is the real Fact.[11] I have but one Favour more to ask of you, and that is that these poor undigested scrawls of mine may not thro' any unadvert Words be blam'd for it, I have too great a Load of Affliction upon me at present. Know then that on the fourth Instant the whole silk House between 4 & 6 O'Clock in the Morning was entirely consumed by Fire. My loss compar'd to the Public's is a Trifle but when put in Competition with my poor Circumstances tis great or indeed more than I can afford; and if I say that it is more than 20 Pounds Sterling I shall not exceed Truth. As for the Public it is great for besides the buildings there is also consum'd a large Quantity of Silk Balls for as this Year has produc'd the largest Quantity of Cocoons that Georgia ever saw, so the loss of them must be great. Tis true that the Silk reeld, and the Seed for next Year is preserv'd because at my House, but still the Loss is great. There was no possibility of quenching the Fire by Reason of a Powder Magazine that lay just by, and the People expecting every Moment that twould blow up, and had that been the Case the Concil House, the Assembly-Chamber, the Secretary's & Surveyar General's Ofices, where all the Writings of the Colony are, must have been consumed together with greater Part of the Town, and what mischief the Explosion of so great a Body of Powder must have done & how many Lives must have perishd had it taken fire, the perserver of Man alone can tell. The Buildings of this Town as well the Magazine are of Timbmer full of Rozin. Had there been the least breath of air that Morning no Humane Means could have sav'd the Town. The outside Boards of the Magazine were already so scoarch'd that the Razinous Substance began to Melt. At last some resolute People enterd the Magazine, and their Example being follow'd by many, by the Blessing of God the Powder and all the Writings and Stores were remov'd. And then when the fears of being blown up [passed] the Preservation of the Council and other Buildings which through the Goodness of God was happily accomplish'd, but the Silk House entirely consumd. As this was during the Silk Season, the Place of my abode from three in the Morning till Eight in the Evening, I kept by reason of the Distance from my House & the excesive Heat every things there which I thought I should have ocasion for them there. And Consequently severall Books out of my poor Stock, together with all the Letters that I recd. from England from my first coming here, and answers to them, between 50 & 60 Pounds Sterling of Tax paid me there at the Filature as Collector appointed by the Assembly, between eight & Ten Pounds belonging to the Fortifications of Savannah paid to me their Treasurer,[12] besides private People's Money lodged in my Hands by small sums at a Time towards paying their Creditors which together with theirs the Public's and my Account are all irrepareably consumed. Every Day discovers some new Loss either of a Private or public Nature, so that you may conclude that neither my Head Heart and Spirits are in any tolerable degree of Ease, therefore twill not require an uncommon Share of Charity to our look [13] the Errors that I may have committed in these Lines. I do assure you that if I have any that hates me they cann't wish me in a more deplorable situation and Circumstances, but Gods Holy & blessed Will be done, and may he of his infinite Mercies preserve you and yours from all Calamities, and that you and all that are employ'd to serve at the Altar of our gracious Redeemer, may ever be found faithful in his House to the Glory of God and the Salvation of their Souls & those Committed to their Care. I beg that you'll be so good to present my Duty and sincere Respects to the Associates, accept the same from him who in all Christian Duties is Revd. Sir Your most Obedient and Afflicted Humble Servant

J. Ottolenghe

Savannah July 12th. 1758

ALS. This letter was read by the Associates at their meeting of 6 December 1758. Minutes, 1 : 118.

1. Letter not found.

2. Letter not found. Waring's letters to Ottolenghe of 1757 and 1758 were written after the Associates agreed that "it did not answer the Intent & Purpose of Mr. D Allones Bequest to continue Mr. Ottolenghe as their Catechist in Georgia for the Instruction of the Negroes," and informed Ottolenghe that they would not continue his salary past 24 June 1758. Minutes, 1 : 135–36.

3. For Henry Ellis see Biographical Appendix.

4. Ottolenghe's letters of 1757 to Waring and Bearcroft have not been found. The Rev. Philip Bearcroft (1695–1761) was secretary of the S.P.G. from 1739 until his death. He was educated at Oxford (A.B. Magdalen Hall, 1716; A.M. Merton College, 1719) and became B.D. and D.D. in 1730. Bearcroft was ordained deacon in 1718 and priest in 1719, and became chaplain to John, Lord Percival (later first earl of Egmont) in 1719, preacher to the Charterhouse in 1724 (master in 1753), chaplain to King George II in 1738, and rector of Stormonth, Kent, in 1743. *DNB*; Foster, *Alumni Oxonienses*.

5. "An Act to Impower Several Surveyors Hereafter Named to Lay Out Public Roads in the Province of Georgia," passed 7 March 1755, assessed the inhabitants of Georgia according to their estates to raise money for road work, "where the same cannot be performed by Personal labour of themselves or Servants." "An Act for the Security and Defence of the Province of Georgia by Erecting Forts in the Several Parts Thereof, & for Appointing Commissioners to Carry the Same into Execution," passed 19 July 1757, required all male inhabitants, both white and black, to work not more than twelve days on the construction of forts or forfeit a sum not to exceed two shillings per day in lieu of their labor. *Ga. Col. Recs.* 18 : 87–101, 202–11.

6. I say again, Let no man think me a fool; if otherwise, yet as a fool receive me, that I may boast myself a little. 2 Corinthians 11 : 16.

7. Ottolenghe served on the committee of the Assembly which drafted "An Act for Constituting and Dividing the Several Districts and Divisions of this Province into Parishes, and for Establishing of Religious Worship Therein According to the Rites and Ceremonies of the Church of England; and Also for Impowering the Church Wardens and Vestrymen of the Respective Parishes to Assess Rates for the Repair of Churches, the Relief of the Poor, and Other Parochial Services," passed 15 March 1758. This act, although it established the Anglican Church, declared "that no Rector or Minister, is or shall hereby be invested with any Power or Authority to exercise any Ecclesiastical Law or Jurisdiction whatsoever." *Ga. Col. Recs.* 13 : 248, 260–61, 265–66, 274, 298, 18 : 258–72.

8. The Associates shipped a box of books to Ottolenghe in February 1757. See "Catalog of Books," p. 17. Benjamin Hoadley (1676–1761), bishop of Winchester 1734–61, was the author of *A Defence of the Reasonableness of Conformity* (London, 1707).

9. Ottolenghe probably intended *a beneficio*, or "from the service."

10. The Rev. Thomas Broughton (1712–77) was secretary of the S.P.C.K. from 1743 until his death.

11. Ottolenghe corresponded indirectly with the Board of Trade through Benjamin Martyn, the colonial agent of Georgia. Ottolenghe's letters

to Martyn relative to the silk culture were laid before the Board for their consideration, and Martyn's drafts of letters to Ottolenghe were agreed to by the Board before being sent. The last letter from Ottolenghe to Martyn recorded in the journals of the Board was dated 25 November 1754. *Journals of the Board of Trade* 10:9, 10, 123.

12. From 1755 to 1761 Ottolenghe was assessor and collector for Savannah of taxes levied to defray the expenses of the court of oyer and terminer, the militia, and other contingent charges of government. *Ga. Col. Recs.* 18:69, 244, 343, 398.

Ottolenghe was named as one of the fourteen commissioners for Savannah in "An Act for the Security and Defence of the Province of Georgia by Erecting Forts in the Several Parts Thereof, & for Appointing Commissioners to Carry the Same into Execution," passed 19 July 1757. The act does not mention treasurers, but perhaps Ottolenghe was named by the Savannah commissioners to handle funds raised for the construction of the forts. Male inhabitants were required to work not more than twelve days, or they could forfeit a sum not to exceed two shillings per day in lieu of their labor. Money thus raised, as well as money raised by fines levied on the overseers who neglected their duty (five shillings per day) and on commissioners who neglected their duty (forty shillings per day), was used to purchase timber for the forts. *Ga. Col. Recs.* 18:202–11.

13. An obsolete form of overlook. *OED.*

Rev. Bartholomew Zouberbuhler
to Rev. John Waring

Savannah In Georgia July 25th. 1758.

Revd. Sir

Your favour of the 19th. of January[1] last I have received and agreable to your Request now offer my Thoughts on the Method of instructing the poor benighted Negroes in the Principles of Christianity. I have once proposed the erecting of a publick School, But from the Observations I have since made, particularly on the Labours of Mr. Ottolenghe, who whilst he acted in the Capacity of a School-Master & Catechist discharged his Duty with great Care & Diligence, I am now of Opinion that such a Foundation is not only too limited, but also attended with many Inconveniencies. This Province is as yet but thinly inhabited,[2] consequently such a School can only reach to a few adjoining Neighbours, & there are but few Masters who will spare their Negroes capable of any Service to be taught in the Day Time, tho' they may be induced to spare them for such a Purpose after their daily Work. The best & most effectual Method then of delivering these poor Creatures out of their Darkness, & to make them Pertakers of the Light of the Gospel, is, to attend them at their respective Habitations & to embrace all favourable Opportunities of instructing them in the fundamental Truths of Christianity. And if two or three Men properly qualified would undertake to be itenerant Catechists or School Masters, They might be dispersed two or three Months in One District & the same Time in another and thereby compass the whole Colony. Tho' I am noways fond of Itenerants, Yet where People unavoidably live at a vast Distance from each other, & where Negroes are in no shape their own Masters & consequently cannot command One hour of their Time to attend on the Word of God, itenerant Catechists or School Masters appears to me most eligible to effect this pious and worthy Design, is more extensively beneficial, liable to less Expence & more equitable to the Proprietors of Negroes. May God guide, direct & bless You. I am Revd. Sir Your most Obedient Servant

Barthw. Zouberbuhler

ALS. Sent "per the Upton, Capt. Wilson Q.D.C." Another copy of this letter, in the same collection, was sent "per the Princess Carolina, Capt. Rupke Q.D.C."

1. Letter not found.
2. In 1760 there were about 3,600 blacks and 6,000 whites in Georgia. Davis, *Fledgling Province*, p. 32.

Rev. William Sturgeon to Rev. John Waring

Philadelphia November 9 1758

Revd. Sir,

I received your Letter of March 2 1758,[1] and I am greatly obliged for the Honor, you and the other Gentlemen, Associates of Dr. Bray, have been pleased to do me; by impowering me to open a School in this City, for the Instruction of Negro-Children.

As soon as [I] received your Directions, I acquainted our Vestry with the Design, which seemed to give them Pleasure. I agree'd with a Woman, used many Years to teach a School, to undertake the Charge of the Blacks, and the School would have been opened some Time ago, but the Books did not come to Hand till October last.

Every Thing is now ready, and the Mistress will begin in a few Days, and you may depend on my Care, that she shall execute the Trust with Fidelity.

The Terms are, that the Mistress is to teach 30 Children, the Boys to read, the Girls to read, sow, knit, and mark; and to attend at Church with them every Wednesday and Friday; and that all her Endeavours are to be directed towards making them Christians. The lowest Salary she will accept is 20£ Sterling a Year, to be drawn for half yearly, from the Time she opens the School. By the next Opportunity I hope to have the Pleasure of acquainting you with the Success of the pious Undertaking. After my sincere Regards to the Associates of Dr. Bray, I remain Reverend Sir your most obliged humble Servant

Wm. Sturgeon

ALS. This letter was read by the Associates at their meeting of 7 February 1759. Minutes, 1 : 120–21.

1. Letter not found. For its probable contents see Franklin to Waring, 3 January 1758, bibliographic note, above.

Rev. William Sturgeon to Rev. John Waring

Philadelphia june 12 1759

Revd. Sir

In my Letter of November 9 1758 I acquainted you of my employing a Mistress for the Negro-School at 20 Pounds Sterling per Annum. I have now the Pleasure to inform you, that the School was opened the 20th. of the same Month; and with such Encouragement, that 36 Scholars now attend regularly. Many of the Scholars are very young, but I hope they will make good Progress in their Learning. Several of them can already say the Creed and the Lords Prayer, and other Parts of our Catechism. Every Wednesday they come to Church and divine Service being ended, I examine them in the Catechism, and explain such Parts of it as they are capable to comprehend. And as their Minds open, I shall be more large in my Expositions to them. I supply them with Books agreeable to your Directions.

And I hope the School will answer the pious Intentions of the worthy Associates of Dr. Bray, whom I pray God to bless and prosper in all their noble Undertakings for the Glory of God and the Good and Welfare of Mankind.

The first Half-Year was ended the 20th. of May, and I have drawn a Set of Bills of Exchange upon you for 10 Pounds Sterling paiable to Edward Duffield[1] or Order. Please to present my dutiful Regards to the Associates and assure them I will do every Thing in my Power to promote the School and I remain Reverend Sir your most humble Servant

Wm. Sturgeon

ALS. Endorsed by Sturgeon on address leaf: "This by Creighton." This letter was read by the Associates at their meeting of 5 September 1759, at which time they "Agreed that Such part of Mr. Sturgeons Letter as relates to the Church be published in a daily paper & two of the Evening Papers." Minutes, 1:124.

1. For Duffield see Biographical Appendix.

[Deborah Franklin to Benjamin Franklin]

[Philadelphia, 9 August 1759]

Extract of a Letter from Mrs. Franklin in Philadelphia, to B. F. in London, dated August 9. 1759

I went to hear the Negro Children catechised at Church. There were 17 that answered very prettily indeed, and 5 or 6 that were too little, but all behaved very decently. Mr. Sturgeon exhorted them before and after the Catechising. It gave me a great deal of Pleasure, and I shall send Othello to the School.

Copy. In Franklin's hand. At their meeting of December 1759 the Associates agreed to print the extract in the *Daily Advertiser*, the *Gazetteer*, and the *London Chronicle*. Minutes, 1:127–28.

Joseph Ottolenghe to [Rev. John Waring]

Savannah October 4th. 1759

Revd. Sir

'Tis now above a Year since I had the Pleasure to write an Answer to one of yours, but whether it reach'd your Hands or not, am not able to determine.[1] Some little Time before Christmas, I troubled you with another Letter[2] to explain some Passages in my Former, as also to apologize for Expressions perhaps dropt from my Pen, that might have given Offence, tho' I can not charge my Memory with any thing of this Nature, nor having a Copy of that Letter for my perusal, but only surmise, that as I then labour'd under great Afflictions, the Filature just burnt to the Ground, with many Weights of Silk Balls, together with all the Machines and Implements for carrying on the Silk-manufacture—A great Loss to the Public!; My Wife languishing in a Bed of Sickness; my self far from being well; and under the Displeasure both of the Honoble. Society, and the Associates, I concluded therefore that while under such a Pressure of Mind, I might have then wrote what I should not have done at a more calm Season, and therefore I shall only repeat here, what I requested in that Letter, viz. That if any such Thing has slipt from my Pen, that you would be so Good as a Christian, a Gentleman, and a Minister of Christ, to pass it by. I sincerely thank you for honouring the Draught for my Sallary, due to June 1758.

Some Time since, I recd. a kind Letter from the Revd. Dr. Bear-croft, and have in my Answer to it, endevaour'd as far as tis in my Power to give him all possible Satisfaction.[3] I have acquainted him with the Result of my Undertaking, as near as Recollection could serve me, for all my Writings relating to the Instruction of Negroes, together with other Papers of Moments, were unhappily consumd with the Filature, and consequently no exact Account could be transmitted; however upon the Whole, considering the many Impediments that the Instruc-tion of Negroes is clog'd with, arising both from the unhappy Circum-stances of the Negroes, and the ill Disposition of their Owners to-wards their being instructed; many of them nevertheless can repeat the Church Catechism by Heart, and give answer to such Questions as their low Understanding will permit of. Several of them can read tolerably well, and very few of them that can not repeat the Lords Prayer, Creed and Ten Commandments, and such Prayers as are fit-ting for their wretched Conditions & Judgements. I have also pointed out some of those principal Difficulties which create the Impediments in the Instruction of Negroes, and am almost certain, that I have at large given you a particular detail of them, therefore shall just touch on them to prevent Repitition. And first, Possessors of Slaves purchase them for hard Labour, out of which an Annual Profit is propos'd, to obtain which, a daily Task is allotted them, and severely exacted from them. And as the Mahometans look upon their Women to have Souls of an inferiour Nature to those of Men, so our Americans look upon their Slaves, to have no Souls at all, and a favourite Dog or Horse meet with more humane Treatments than they; add to this, that if it be con-sider'd what little Sense of Religion is retain'd by the Inhabitants of these Parts of the World, contrary to the Prediction of good Herbert of Pious Memory,[4] twill be no Wonder that those who have so little Concern for their immortal Souls, should not attempt the Salvation of those whom they believe to have no Souls at all! As for the Negroes of these Parts they are mostly Africans born, and are as Ignorant of our Language, as we are of theirs, and consequently no Impression can be made on them, untill they are capable of understanding what it is that is offer'd to them in order to forsake Paganism and embrace Christianity. It requires Length of Time, great Patience and much In-dustry before they can have a sensible Idea of our Language, and the strong riveted Prejudices of Education can be remov'd. Stupidity the Concomitant of a hard felt everlasting Slavery, the little Time allow'd them for Instruction and the few or no Opportunities to converse with such as might produce an improvement in their Learning, together with other Causes of the like Nature, are great Impediments in their Way of Instruction, and not well Known but to those that experience them. However all these Difficulties on the Part of the Slaves would through God's Assistance be overcom'd with Diligence and Patience, provided that their Owners would suffer them to be instructed. To obtain which, I propos'd in my said Letter to the Doctor, that the Minister of the Place where a Catechist is Stationd, should be desir'd to make it their study both in private and from the Pulpit as Opportunity offers to persuade their Masters to consent the having their Negroes instructed; and the said Minister should also from Time to Time visit the Schools & examine what Progress the Negroes make in their Learning and if any among them are found fit to be admitted to the holy Sacrament of Baptism, to procure their Master's Leave to administer the Same—A Duty which our Planters in General are much avers'd to for Reasons given you in some of my former Letters and now repeated in that of the Doctor. But these too a prudent Minister might with proper Arguments convince at least some into a Compliance, and I am apt to believe that if such or other Methods were put in practice very good Fruits might be reapt from them. I do not know a greater Piece of Charity or a better Offering fit for Heaven than the bringing of these poor Creatures from Darkness and the Shadow of Death to the Light and Knowledge of the Gospel of our Redeemer. Great, very great would be the Blessings procur'd to the poor Slaves once convinc'd of a crucified Saviour and the inestimable Benefits procur'd by it, and that thro Faith, Patience and continuance in well doing they shall inherit the Promisess. Secur'd in this Hope & entrench'd in this Faith, tho twould not undo the heavy afflictive Burden of Slavery! nor break assunder the cruel Yoke of Oppression! yet twould make the thorny Path of Bondage become somewhat smoother, and some Degrees sweeten the bitter Cup of Servitude, so as to afford them Strength to run with Patience the Race that is set before them. Thus taught and thus gently led to the Sanctuary of God, their unworthy Philemons, would entertain many faithful & pious Onesimus in their Service, to the Comfort and Joy to the one and safety and Profit to the Other.[5] And tho' the reasonings drawn from the Principles of self Interest, and self Preservation are the most Cogent and the most predominant in humane Affairs in our present Case of Masters towards Slaves becomes of no Efficacy or Consideration, contrary to dear bought Experience and daily Examples. But to proceed I have had last Year not many Negroes, some few Children have been pretty constant and more I'm promis'd. Would to God that the Number of these were great, because more Fruit can be expected from these tender Plants, than from others. I can but be very unwilling to repeat what I have often declar'd, that I can not charge my self with any Neglect whatever, or the having omitted on my Part any Thing that tended to promote so Laudable and worthy an Undertaking. Malice and Revenge may Injure me, but I defy Truth and Justice to accuse me of any Neglect of Duty whatever. I am never seen abroad except upon very important Business, and that happens but seldom, and I believe that [there is] hardly any man in this Province, that is not confin'd by Sickness or other Accident that leads a more recluse Life than I do. And [I am] therefore ever ready to instruct such as are sufferd to come to me and should I be reduc'd to that uncomfortable Number which compos'd the Congregation of the Dean of St. Patrick with his dearly beloved Roger,[6] tho' twould prove grievous to me, yet I presume that I could not suffer Blame for not performing that which is not in my Power to accomplish untill it appears that omission or neglect of Duty on my Part has been the Cause of it. Annext to the Dr.'s Letter there is a Certificate sign'd by his Excellency the Governour and another from the same Hand will be subjoin'd to this, and hope to the Satisfaction of the Honble. the Associates.[7] I have likewise acquainted Dr. Bearcroft, that I shall draw no more Bills for my Sallary but from June 58 to June 59 except I can transmit such an Account of my Labour as shall be more pleasing to me and more agreable and satisfactory to that Honble. Board, and if I could through your kind Interposition obtain Leave to draw for the last Year's Sallary (as I do not Intend to draw any More but upon the above Condition) as it would be a great Favour done me so I should retain the Memory of the Favour with due Gratitude and thankfullness to the Honble. the Associates, and to you. Having taken up already too much of your Time I shall hasten to a Conclusion by presenting my Respect to the Honble. Board my sincere good Wishes & Respect to you and remain Revd. Sir Your very much Oblig'd Humble Servant

J. Ottolenghe

ALS. This letter was read by the Associates at their meeting of 3 July 1760, "& referred to farther Consideration at the next Meeting. Agreed that Mr. [John] Berriman be requested to enquire what Satisfaction Mr. Ottolenghe hath given to the Society for propagating the Gospel." Minutes, 1 : 141. At the meeting of 4 September 1760 "Mr. Berriman reported from the Society for propagating the Gospel that they payd Mr. Ottolenghe his Salary to Midsummer 1759, from which Time it was entirely to cease, unless he may afterwards perform Some particular Services which may entitle him to further favours from the Society." Minutes, 1 : 141. On 6 November 1760 the Associates "Agreed that the Consideration of Mr. Ottolenghes Request be carried on to the next Meeting." Minutes, 1 : 142. On 4 December 1760 they "Agreed that Mr. Waring be desired to acquaint Mr. Ottolenghe (the Associates Late Catechist in Georgia) that the Associates will present him with half a Years Salary." Minutes, 1 : 145. Waring's letter has not been found.

1. Dated 12 July 1758, above.

2. Letter not found.

3. In 1758 the S.P.G. stopped Ottolenghe's salary as catechist because they had received no letters from him for more than two years. After one of Ottolenghe's English friends wrote on his behalf to the archbishop of Canterbury, the S.P.G. on 19 January 1759 agreed that Ottolenghe should send a detailed account of his work as catechist, attested by the governor. Bearcroft's letter to Ottolenghe conveying the instructions, dated 27 January, has not been found. Ottolenghe's letter to Bearcroft, which has not been found, was read by the S.P.G. on 15 August 1760. The journals of the S.P.G. give its date as 1 August 1760, an error for 1 August 1759. The S.P.G. resolved to pay Ottolenghe's "Salary to Midsummer 1759, from which Time it was entirely to cease, unless he may afterwards perform Some particular Services which may entitle him to further favours from the Society." "An Anonymous Letter to his Grace of Canterbury in favour of Mr. Ottolenghe Catechist to the Negroes in Georgia," n.d., S.P.G. MSS., C, Georgia; S.P.G. Journals, 14 : 122–23, 310–12; Minutes, 1 : 141.

4. Ottolenghe was probably alluding to the Rev. George Herbert (1593–1633), Anglican clergyman and metaphysical poet, whose poem "The Church Militant" includes the following passage (lines 235–48):

> Religion stands on tip-toe in our land,
> Readie to passe to the *American* strand.
> When height of malice, and prodigious lusts,
> Impudent sinning, witchcrafts, and distrusts
> (The marks of future bane) shall fill our cup
> Unto the brimme, and make our measure up;
> When *Sein* shall swallow *Tiber*, and the *Thames*
> By letting in them both, pollutes her streams:
> When *Italie* of us shall have her will,
> And all her calender of sinnes fulfill;
> Whereby one may fortell, what sinnes next yeare
> Shall both in *France* and *England* domineer:
> Then shall Religion to *America* flee:
> They have their times of Gospel, ev'n as we.

C. A. Patrides, ed., *The English Poems of George Herbert* (London, 1974), p. 199.

5. Philemon was the recipient of St. Paul's epistle of that name. Paul converted Philemon's runaway slave Onesimus and persuaded him to return to his master, who was also a converted Christian. In the epistle, which Onesimus carried to Philemon, Paul counseled Philemon to take Onesimus back "Not now as a servant, but above a servant, a brother beloved, specially to me,

but how much more unto thee, both in the flesh, and in the Lord?" Philemon, 1:16.

6. Jonathan Swift (1667–1745) was dean of St. Patrick's 1713–45. "As soon as he had taken possession of his two livings [Laracor and Rathbeggan, Ireland, in 1700], he went to reside at *Laracor*, and gave public notice to his parishioners, that he would read prayers on every Wednesday and Friday. Upon the subsequent Wednesday the bell was rung, and the Rector attended in his desk, when after having sat some time, and finding the congregation to consist only of himself, and his clerk Roger, he began with great composure and gravity, but with a turn peculiar to himself, '*Dearly beloved* **Roger**, *the scripture moveth you and me in sundry places*.' And then proceeded regularly through the whole service." John Boyle, earl of Cork and Orrery, *Remarks on the Life and Writings of Dr. Jonathan Swift* (London, 1752), pp. 31–32.

7. The certificate appended to Ottolenghe's letter to Bearcroft of 1 August 1759 (see note 3, above) is identical to the enclosure to the present document except that it is addressed to the S.P.G. rather than to the Associates and is dated 11 January 1760. S.P.G. Journals, 14:311–12 (meeting of 15 August 1760).

Enclosure
Certificate from Governor Henry Ellis

[Savannah, 11 February 1759]

I do hereby certify the Honourable the Associates of the late Dr. Bray that the several Matters and Things contained in the within Letter so far as relates to my knowledge is true. And that those Matters and Things which are therein set forth and were transacted before my arrival in this Province are to best of my belief true also.

Given under my Hand in Georgia this eleventh day of February

Henry Ellis

DS. The words *eleventh* and *February* were filled in by Ottolenghe.

Rev. William Sturgeon to Rev. John Waring

Philadelphia November 25 1759

Revd. Sir,

Having Notice of a Vessel now under Sail, I embrace the Opportunity to acquaint you that I have drawn upon you for Half a Years Salary due to the Mistress of the Negro School 20th. of this Instant.

The Number of Scholars is 35. 11 Boys: 24 Girls. Of the Girls 15 are learning to sew and work with their Needle. They improve in

Reading, and in the Knowledge of our holy Religion, and I hope will prove good Servants, and true Christians. I use my best Endeavours for carrying your pious Intentions into Execution; but it would be much for the Benefit of the School, if our Churchwardens for the Time being [1] were joined with me in the Care and Government of it, and therefore I request the Favour of you to lay it before the worthy Associates of the late Dr. Bray, and please to impart to me their Resolutions. After my Prayers to God for your Success, and Welfare in Time and Eternity I am Revd. Sir your most humble Servant

Wm. Sturgeon

ALS. Endorsed: "Accept. April 3. 1760. first Bill," and as read 1 May 1760. At that meeting the Associates "Agreed that Mr. Waring be desired to acquaint Mr. Sturgeon that the Associates will consider of the most proper & effectual Means to enable Mr. Sturgeon to promote the School & will transmit their Resolutions by Dr. Franklin." Minutes, 1:137. Waring's letter has not been found, nor has any communication from Franklin to Sturgeon.

1. The churchwardens of Christ Church at the time were Evan Morgan (1709–63), a merchant, member of the Library Company, manager of the Pennsylvania Hospital, and former member of the Pennsylvania Assembly; and Alexander Stedman (1703–94), a merchant who returned to Great Britain in 1776. *Franklin Papers* 2:685n, 7:44n–45n; Dorr, *Historical Account of Christ Church*, p. 297.

Rev. John Waring to Benjamin Franklin

[Russell Street, London, 4 January 1760]

Sir

This is to inform You that the Associates of the Late Dr. Bray unanimously chose You a Member of their Society. The Prospect of Your kind Assistance induced them to accept of the proposal mentioned in their Advertisment, & to resolve upon opening three Schools for Negroes with all convenient Speed: They adjourned to Thursday 17th. Instant with a View to ask Your Advice & Assistance in the establishment of these Schools, & hope to have the pleasure of meeting You on that Day at 10 oClock at Mr. Birds Bookseller in Ave Mary Lane near St. Pauls: [1] to go upon Business at 11 precisely. I am Sir Your most obedient humble Servant

Jn. Waring

Russel Street January 4: 1760

ALS: American Philosophical Society. Endorsed as received 5 January. At the meeting of 17 January

Mr. Franklin declared that in his Opinion New York, Williamsburgh in Virginia, & Newport in Rhode Island are the Most proper Places in the British Plantations for Schools for the Instruction of Negro Children.

Mr. Franklin recommended Dr. S. Johnson President of the College, the Revd. Mr. Barclay Minister of Trinity Church, & the Revd. Mr. Auchmuty at New York.

William Hunter Esq. Postmaster, The Revd. Dr. Dawson President of William & Mary College & the Minister of the Church at Williamsburgh & Also

The Revd. Mr. Pollen Minister of Newport Rhode Island as very proper persons to be requested to take upon them the Care & Management of the several Schools in the places aforesaid.

Agreed that One School for the Instruction of thirty Negroe Children be opend with all Convenient Speed at each of the aforesaid places viz. New York, Williamsburgh Virginia & Newport Rhode Island & that the Salary to the Master or Mistress do not exceed twenty pounds Sterling a Year.

Agreed that Mr. Franklin be desired to write to the aforesaid Gentlemen & request the favour of their kind Assistance in establishing these Schools, that they woud occasionaly & as often as they may Judge convenient visit & inspect them, & from time to time transmit to the Associates an Account of their proceedings & the Progress the Children make & the Reception the Design meets with from the Inhabitants in general. (Minutes, 1 : 130–31)

1. Thomas Bird was a bookbinder and bookseller at the Angel and Bible, Ave Mary Lane. He rented a room to the Associates for their stores and a room for their monthly meetings at £3.10.0 per annum. The Associates first met at Mr. Bird's on 4 April 1759. H. R. Plomer, G. H. Bushell, E. R. Dix, *A Dictionary of the Printers and Booksellers Who Were at Work in England, Scotland and Ireland from 1726 to 1775* (Oxford, 1968), p. 26; Minutes, 1 : 121, 122.

Rev. John Waring to Rev. Thomas Dawson

London. February 29: 1760

Revd. Sir

I am desired by a Society who call themselves The Associates of the Late Dr. Bray (the Objects of whose Attention are the Conversion of the Negroes in the British Plantations, founding Parochial Libraries & other good Purposes) to acquaint You that they lately agreed to open a School at Williamsburgh in Virginia for the Instruction of Negro Children in the Principles of the Christian Religion. They earnestly request that You, Mr. Hunter, Postmaster & the Minister of the Parish will be so kind as to assist them in the Prosecution of this pious Undertaking, & that You will with all convenient Speed open a School for this purpose:[1] & As 'tis probable that Some of Each Sex may be sent for Instruction, The Associates are therefore of opinion that a Mistress will be preferable to a Master, as She may teach the Girls to Sew knit &c. as well as *all* to read & Say their Catechism. They think 30 Children or thereabout will Sufficiently employ one person, & therefore wou'd at present confine their School to about that Number. I need not inform You that it is their Desire, the Expence may be as small as the Nature of the Design & proper Encouragement of it will admit. [They] Hope 15£ or 16£ a Year may Suffice, but desire You will not exceed 20£ Sterling. They are unwilling to Suppose that any persons in Your Province will disapprove of this pious Undertaking, but hope that all Objections will be Silenced by the Schools being put under the Care & Patronage of Such persons & that all prejudices against instructing the Negroes will gradualy die away, as 'tis hoped the good Effects of this School will every day become more & more apparent.

The Associates presuming on Your kind Assistance have Sent a Box of Books for the Use of the School, besides which there is a Folio Volume, a Present from the Associates to Your College Library.[2] There are likewise 5 Copies of Mr. Bacons Sermons on this Subject which may be useful to lend to Such Masters who do not seem Sufficiently apprized how much it is their Duty to take Care that their Slaves especialy those born in their house be instructed in the principles of Christianity.[3]

I am directed to request the favour of a Letter from You as soon as the School is opened, & that You will from time to time Send Us an Account of the State of the School, the number of each Sex admitted, the Progress they make in their Reading & Catechism &c.

About a Year & Quarter ago a School was opened at Philadelphia for 30 black Children on the Associates Account; which met with a very Favourable Reception. The Desire of the Masters to have their black Children instructed, The Progress the Children have made & their decent behaviour give great Satisfaction: That School is under the Care & Inspection of the Revd. Mr. Sturgeon; who requires the Mistress to attend the Children to Church on Weds. & Frid. & after divine Service he charitably catechises & instructs them.

Mr. Franklin of Philadelphia One of the Associates & at present in London intends to write to Mr. Hunter on this Subject, which He probably will receive about the time this comes to Your hands.[4]

Be pleased to draw on Me for the Salary half Yearly or Quarterly as is most convenient: & Acquaint me from time to time What Supply of Books may be wanting for the Use of the Children. Be pleased to direct to Me at Mr. Birds Bookseller at the Angel & Bible in Ave Mary Lane near St. Pauls London. That God may bless & prosper Your Endeavours to the Advancement of his own Glory is the hearty Prayer of Revd. Sir Your most obedient humble Servant

Jn. Waring

Books in the Box

50 Childs first Book
40 English Instructor
25 Catechism broke &c.
10 Easy Method of instructing Youth
3 Indian instructed
2 Preliminary Essays
5 Bacons 4 Sermons
5 Bacons 2 Sermons to Negroes
10 Christians Guide
3 Church Catechism with text of Scrip.
12 friendly Admonitions
70 Sermons before Trustees & Associates

The Box was intrusted to Mr. Franklin's [*torn*] who (I believe) consigned it to Mr. Hunter.

ALS: Bray MSS., McGregor Collection, U.Va.

1. The decision to open a school in Williamsburg was taken by the Associates at their meeting of 17 January 1760. They intended to engage three men to serve as administrators of the school—Dawson, William Hunter (for whom see Biographical Appendix), and the minister of the parish—not realizing that Dawson was the minister. Minutes, 1:130–31.

2. A list of the books sent for the use of the Williamsburg Negro school is appended to this letter. See also "Catalog of Books," p. 61, for comparison with this list. The volume given to William and Mary, which is no longer in the college library and is presumed to have been destroyed in one of several fires which swept the library, comprised (bound together) Bray's *Course of Lectures upon the Church Catechism* (Oxford, 1696 and subsequent eds.); "Allens Discourses" (probably William Allen, *A Discourse of Divine Assistance, and the Method Thereof: Shewing what Assistance Men Receive from God, in Performing the Condition of the Promise of Pardon of Sin and Eternal Life* [London, 1693]); and John Kettlewell's *The Practical Believer; or, The Articles of the Apostles' Creed Drawn Out to Form a True Christian's Heart and Practice* (London, 1688 and subsequent eds.).

3. According to the "Catalog of Books" (p. 61) the Associates sent copies of Bacon's *Four Sermons* (see Pollen to [Waring], 6 July 1755, bibliographic note, above).

4. Franklin's letter to Hunter has not been found.

[William Hunter to Benjamin Franklin]

[Williamsburg, June 1760]

Dr. Franklin reported that he had received a Letter from Mr. Hunter of Williamsburgh Virginia dated June [*blank in MS*] acquainting him that He had received a Packet of Books for the Use of the Negroes, that he was much pleased with the Commission he had received to open a Negroe School, & that he & Dr. Dawson wou'd use their best Endeavours to open a School for Negroes with all convenient Speed.

Letter not found. Extract from Minutes, 1 : 142–43 (meeting of 6 November 1760).

Rev. Samuel Johnson to [Rev. John Waring]

King's Coll. N. York July 28. 1760.

Revd. Sir

I received your's of February 29th.[1] & rejoyce in the excellent Charities in which you are engaged, which I hope may turn to good Account, for which I shall willingly do my utmost. Mr. Barclay[2] & Mr. Auchmuty[3] desire their Complements, & will heartily joyn with me in promoting this good Work. We have not indeed, yet found a good Mistress, but are seeking for one, & will use our utmost endeavours to open a School as soon as possible: And as soon as we have got it going, we will write further & give you an Account of our proceedings. And as Mr. Auchmuty is Catechist of the Negroes he will make it his particular & more immediate Care, that this good Design be faithfully executed, observing all the Rules prescribed in your Letter. I have also received the two Boxes of Books & transmitted to Mr. Pollen of Rhode Island that which was directed to him: & I return you & the Associates, the hearty Thanks of the Governours of this College for the valuable Present you have made of that excellent Book to our Library,[4] & am Revd. Sir, your most obedient humble Servant

Samuel Johnson

ALS. Endorsed as read 6 November 1760. See Minutes, 1 : 143.

1. Letter not found. For its probable contents see Waring's letter to Dawson of the same date, above.
2. The Rev. Henry Barclay (1712–64), a native of Albany, graduated from Yale College (A.B. 1734, A.M. 1740) and received a doctor of divinity

degree from Oxford in 1760. Barclay took up residence among the Mohawks at Fort Hunter, near Albany, immediately upon receiving his A.B., and he was appointed S.P.G. catechist there in 1736. He remained as catechist until leaving for England in 1737 to seek ordination. Barclay was ordained in January 1737/38 and returned to serve at St. Peter's Church, Albany, and Queen Anne's Chapel, Fort Hunter, 1738–46, and at St. George's Church, Schenectady, 1738–45. He then moved to New York City, where he served as rector of Trinity Church 1746–64 and of St. George's Chapel 1752–64. Barclay was also commissary of the bishop of London in New York. Weis, *Colonial Clergy Middle Colonies*, p. 174; Dexter, *Yale Graduates* 1:503–6.

3. For Samuel Auchmuty see Biographical Appendix.

4. The volume given to King's College was the same as that given to the College of William and Mary (for which see Waring to Dawson, 29 February 1760, note 2, above).

William Hunter to Rev. Thomas Dawson

[Williamsburg, c. July 1760]

Sir,

The Bearer is recommended to me, by the inclos'd Letter from Mr. Stevenson.[1] I have been likewise apply'd to in Behalf of Mrs. Wager, who liv'd formerly with Colo. Carter Burwell,[2] and another will apply to Day. I have directed Mrs. Thompson to wait on you; for as we are likely to have many Applications, I imagine you would chuse to examine all that offer'd. I will do myself the Pleasure of waiting on you some Time To Day, and am Sir Your very humble Servant

Wm. Hunter

Monday Morn.

ALS: Bray MSS., McGregor Collection, U.Va.

1. The bearer of this letter was apparently Mrs. Thompson, a Scottish woman, who was later a governess in the home of John Blair, Jr., and in the Page family. The letter from Mr. Stevenson, who has not been identified, has not been found. *WMQ*, 1 ser. 11 (1902): 252.

2. Mrs. Anne Wager (d. 1774) had previously been employed by Col. Carter Burwell to school his children for two years. She may have been the widow of Thomas Wager, who died in Williamsburg in 1725, and/or the mother of Robert Wager, who was appointed doorkeeper of the House of Burgesses in 1752. *JHB, 1752–1758*, pp. 5–6; Goodwin, *Record of Bruton Parish Church*, p. 166; Stephenson, "Negro School in Williamsburg," p. 5.

Rev. James Marye, Jr., to [Rev. John Waring]

[Orange County, Virginia] Duplicate of August 2d. 1760

Revd. & Dear Sir

Some Time after my Arrival in Virginia I came to [a] Resolution of Returning to London, but was prevented by a severe Spell of Sickness. Some Time after my Recovery I wrote to you,[1] but by not receiving an Answer suppose my Letter met with some Accident. However I acknowledge my self highly culpable in not writing many Letters since, but to make Amends for this my Neglect am determined on my Part to keep up the Strictest Correspondence (which upon my Honour you may depend I will do) & will always write Duplicates to prevent the like Accidents. Taking it now for granted that my former Letter miscarried, I will give you a short Detail of my Fortune since my Landing in Virginia. For near a twelve Month after my Arrival there became no Living vacant, the first that happen'd I applyed for & was receiv'd. This was in the Lower Parts of the Country which did not well agree with my Health, for I continued the greatest Part of the Time in a very lingering Way. I was advised to remove in the upper Parts of the Country, which I was determined to do as soon as Occasion should offer. The first Living that became vacant was the one Occasioned by the Death of your Late worthy Correspondent the Revd. Mungo Marshall whose Living I now hold. He left two small Sons, one of which I have taken the Education of. If you could get the other on any Foundation in a good School it would be doing him a great act of Charity. I would be willing to Cloath him and find him in Books. No Person could be more regretted than Mr. Marshall was by every Person in his Parish, & as I was intimately acquainted with him, I can deservedly, for his whole Conduct thro' all Stages of Life, was a truly exemplary Pattern of Virtue & Religion. The Books you sent arrived much about the Time of his Illness.[2] Since his Death I had them conveyed to his Parish, & have distributed about those that were sent for the Purpose to the poorer sort of People that live in the remotest Parts of the Parish. The others I keep by me, & lend out to the Neighbours that desire the Use of them. I shewed those designed for the parochial Library to the Vestry of my Parish (& let them know I expected yearly Additions to them) who promised on the next Addition to build a House entirely for a Library separate from the other Buildings. I have great Quantities of Negroes in my Parish, who all bring their Children to be baptised, & many of the Adults likewise are desirous of Baptism, which I perform after Divine Service. I have four Places of Worship in my Parish three Churches, & one Chapel.[3] The

Chapel I attend 5 or 6 Times in a Year it being very remote. My Parish is near sixty Miles in Length. So that you may Judge any religious Tracts your Society shall think proper to send will be necessary for poor People, that have so seldom Opportunities of attending Divine Service, & whatever you shall be pleased to send you may depend on it shall be disposed of in the properest Manner. I would request you to send especially some dissuasives to Gaming and swearing,[4] which I am sorry to inform you are too common among the Lower Rank of People here. What Additions are sent to the parochial Library I will take the greatest care of during my Residence in the Parish. If possible pray add to the Library Predaux' Connection,[5] Mr. Lock & Dr. Swift's Works. I shall be obliged to you to inform me who are the other Members of the Society. There came to me a cataloge of Books directed to the parochial Library of Orange without any Letter, I suppose from you. I have wrote many Letters to Mr. Lardant[6] your Neighbour, but never have got a Line from him; I should be glad you would be pleas'd to inform me what is become of him. I am Revd. Sir Your affectionate Friend & Brother

Jas. Marye, Jur.

P.S. Direct for me To the Revd. Jas. Marye Jur. St. Thomas Parish Orange County Rappahannock River Virginia. May 30th. 1761

ALS. This letter was first read by the Associates at their meeting of 1 October 1761. Minutes, 1 : 158. At the next meeting, of 5 November 1761, the Associates

> Agreed that Mr. Waring be desired to acquaint Mr. Marye (in answer to his Letter read at the Last Meeting) that the Associates wou'd very readily send him the Books he requests, if their Fund wou'd allow of it; but that at present, in the Choice of Books for parochial Libraries, They must confine themselves to Such as are most immediately useful to the Clergy in the Discharge of their pastoral Function; that their View in presenting Books to Mr. Marye & the Late Mr. Marshal towards parochial Libraries, was to encourage them to promote the Instruction of the Negroes in the Christian Religion. To which Books further Additions will be made as soon as Mr. Marye shall favour the Associates with a particular Account of the progress he hath Made in converting & Instructing the Negroes.
>
> Agreed that eighteen Indian Instructed & Some Tracts against Swearing & Gaming be Sent to Mr. Marye for the Use of the Negroes in his parish. (Minutes, 1 : 159)

The Associates reconsidered Marye's request at their meeting of 4 February 1762 and agreed to send four small collections of books to be placed at his four places of worship. Minutes, 1 : 172. For the books sent, see notes 4 and 5 to this letter and "Catalog of Books," pp. 79–80.

    1. Letter not found.

    2. See [Marshall to Waring, c. September 1756], bibliographic note, above.

3. The three churches in Marye's parish were the Pine Stake Church, the Middle Church, or Brick Church, and Orange Church (fifteen miles northeast, three miles southeast, and eighteen miles west of Orange, Virginia, respectively). Meade, *Old Churches* 2:84–86.

4. Josiah Woodward (1656–1712), *A Disswasive from Gaming* (London, 1726), and Woodward, *A Kind Caution to Prophane Swearers* (London, 1704). don, 1704).

5. Humphrey Prideaux (1648–1724), *The Old and New Testament Connected in the History of the Jews and Neighbouring Nations, from the Declension of the Kingdoms of Israel and Judah to the Time of Christ*, 2 vols. (London, 1716–18).

6. Not identified.

Rev. Thomas Pollen to [Rev. John Waring]

Newport August 12th. 1760.

Revd. Sir,

About six weeks ago I recd. the favour of Yours.[1] Immediately after I call'd a Vestry: & having read your Letter to them they seem'd well-pleas'd with the matter contain'd in it, & express'd their gratitude for it. I then advis'd with them what was best to be done. We agreed, that one half of the Children should be Boys, & the other half Girls; that each Child should be about six or seven years of age at its first entrance, & that It should belong to some Member of our Church; that the Mistress should be a Church-Woman; that She should be allow'd 20£ Sterling per ann.; & that wood should be sent in to her from each Master to keep the School warm in the winter.

After this I sat about to find the Children & a Mistress for them, & to fix the School: when I receiv'd an invitation to Jamaica which I have accepted of. So that upon mature deliberation I think it most advisable for me to drop the undertaking, & to leave it to my Successor. The Members of the Church have desired a Copy of your Letter, which I have allow'd them to take. They intend, it seems, to write themselves, & to obtain from you, if they can, a grant that they may have the management of the School, either with the Minister, or before a Minister comes.[2] But I would by no means have you grant it them: for they are on many accounts unfit to be trusted with the management of it. I am sorry it is out of my power to go on my self with it: since I had so fair an opportunity given me of proving to the Society the grateful sence I retain of their unmerited bounty to me at my departure from London. I beg leave to tender them my humblest respects, & am, Revd. Sir, your most obliged Humble Servant

Thomas Pollen.

P.S. The Box of Books is come to hand:[3] which I shall deliver to the Senior Church Warden[4] taking from him a receipt. Be pleas'd to give my respects to Mr. Berriman[5] & all the rest of your worthy Society.

ALS. This letter was read by the Associates at their meeting of 6 November 1760. Minutes, 1 : 143.

1. Letter not found. For its probable contents see Waring to Dawson, 29 February 1760, above. At their meeting of 17 January 1760 the Associates agreed to open a school at Newport. Benjamin Franklin recommended Pollen to manage the Newport school. Minutes, 1 : 130–31.

2. The congregation voted on 6 August 1760 to take a copy of Waring's letter to Pollen. The copy has not been found, nor has a letter from the congregation to the Associates. "Record of the Transactions of Trinity Parish Church begun 5th. July 1731," p. 85, Newport Historical Society.

3. The Associates shipped a box of 183 books to Pollen about February 1760. See "Catalog of Books," p. 61.

4. Isaac Stelle, a Newport merchant, was elected eldest, or senior, church-warden of Trinity Church on Easter Monday, 7 April 1760. Mason, *Annals of Trinity Church*, pp. 70, 118.

5. For the Rev. John Berriman see Hales to Verelst, 21 June 1749, note 2, above.

[Rev. William Sturgeon to Benjamin Franklin]

[Philadelphia, 1 October 1760]

Dr. Franklin reported that He had received a Letter from Mr. Sturgeon in Philadelphia dated October 1: 1760 wherein He writes— The Negroes School goes on very well & I hope will be attended with Success, and much Benefit to the poor Souls themselves. The Parcell of Books are come to Hand & Shall be distributed to the best Advantage.[1]

Letter not found. Extract from Minutes, 1 : 146 (meeting of 1 January 1761).

1. In October 1759 the Associates shipped 192 books to Sturgeon for the use of the Negro school. At an unspecified time in 1759 they shipped 271 books to Sturgeon for the same purpose. "Catalog of Books," p. 60.

William Hunter to Rev. John Waring

Williamsburg, Virginia February 16: 1761.

Sir.

I receiv'd some Time ago a Letter from Mr. Franklin, informing me that I had been nominated as one of the Mannagers of a School to be erected here, for the Education of Negroes in the Christian Faith, &c. Mr. Dawson, Commissary and Minister of this Parish, receiv'd at the same Time your Letter, on the same Subject.[1] We consulted together and agreed with Mrs. Anne Wager for the opening a School at Michaelmas last, which was accordingly done. We judg'd that the Allowance of £20 Sterling was not Sufficient, we gave the Mistress therefore the whole Sum as a Salary, and Mr. Dawson undertook to raise Ten Pounds Sterling by Subscription for the Payment of the House Rent. But he dying soon after, nothing has been done to that Purpose, neither do I believe did he ever answer your Letter.[2] I should have done it sooner myself, but I could not, 'til lately, procure your Letter of his Executor.

As I did not approve of raising the additional Money, by a petty Subscription, I have not attempted it, but am myself liable for the present Year. I judg'd it more to the Credit of the Associates to pay the whole Expence necessary, than to be aided by a trifling Contribution. I would therefore recommend it to them to increase the Allowance to £30 Sterling, if they would maintain the School in any tolerable Credit. And this I think is as little as it can be done for.

I have the Pleasure of informing the Associates that their Design has been generally well receiv'd.

The School was opened with 24 Scholars, (as many I think as one Woman can well manage). Their Progress and Improvement in so Short a Time, has greatly exceeded my Expectation, and I have Reason to hope that the good Intentions of the Associates will be fully answer'd, by the Care and good Conduct of the Mistress.

At present I stand single in this Undertaking, but Mr. Yates being last Week elected Minister of the Parish in the Room of Mr. Dawson, I shall communicate to him your Letter, and doubt not his Concurrence.[3] As it was the Intention of the Associates to nominate three Trustees, not knowing that Mr. Dawson was Minister of the Parish, I would recommend a Letter to be written to Robt. Carter Nicholas Esqr. to whom I have never mention'd it, imagining that a Letter from the Associates would best secure his Compliance.[4]

The Mistress was paid one Quarter's Salary at Christmas, for which I have given Mr. Tarpley[5] an Order on you, but may probably for the future draw but once a Year, to prevent the Trouble of small Bills.

Be pleas'd to assure the Associates of my hearty Endeavours to further their good Designs, by making this Establishment, at present in its Infancy, as generally beneficial as possible.

I am, respectfully, Sir, Your very humble Servant

Wm. Hunter.

ALS. This letter was read by the Associates at their meeting of 7 May 1761.
See Minutes, 1 : 150–51. Waring's reply is dated 1 June 1761, below.

1. Franklin's letter to Hunter has not been found. Waring's letter to
Dawson is dated 29 February 1760, above.

2. Dawson died on 29 November 1760. The subscription undertaken before his death promised to yield £17, perhaps annually. The following undated document is in the Bray MSS., McGregor Collection, U.Va.:

> All Persons must be sensible, that the Expence of renting an
> House in this Town, and the supporting such a School for 30 Schol-
> ars, the Number proposed by the Associates, will far exceed the
> Fund allotted by them; the Trustees therefore hope, that all pious &
> charitably disposed Christians will co-operate with their Endeavours,
> and that Men of Fortune will contribute towards this good Work.
>
> All such Persons as are disposed to encourage this Design, are
> humbly desired to pay or remit their charitable Contributions to
> Mr. Wm. Hunter, in whose possession there is a Subscription Paper
> in the Following Form.
>
> We the Subscribers promise to pay the several Sums annexed
> to our Names to Mr. Wm. Hunter, in Order to forward the good
> Intentions of the Associates of the late Dr. Bray, and to encourage
> and promote the Instruction of Negroes in the Christian Faith.

In the same collection there are two subscription lists, both undated, headed
by paragraphs similar to the last paragraph of the document quoted above.
One includes only the name of Thomas Dawson, followed by the notation,
"annually, £2." The other includes the following names and amounts: William
Dawson, £5; Thomas Dawson, £2; Thomas Robinson, £1; John Graeme, £1;
John Blair, £5; James Wray, £2; and N. Walthoe, £1. Whether the contributions in the second list were to be annual is not specified, nor is it clear
whether Thomas Dawson intended to subscribe £2 or £4.

3. For the Rev. William Yates see Biographical Appendix.

4. For Nicholas see Biographical Appendix.

5. James Tarpley (d. 1764), a Williamsburg merchant from 1755 until his
death, was the son of John and Elizabeth (Ripping) Tarpley. In 1761 he gave
the steeple bell to Bruton Parish Church. *WMQ*, 1 ser. 3 (1894–95): 177–78,
7 (1898–99): 12, 17 (1908–09): 153.

Rev. Samuel Auchmuty to Rev. John Waring

New York April 4th. 1761

Revd. Sir

At the request of my worthy Brethren, Dr. Johnson, & Mr. Barclay,
I now address you on the subject of your Letter, to the Doctor, concerning the opening of a Negro School in this City, which has already
been carried on with good Success for upwards of Six months.[1]

At first we found a Difficulty in providing a proper mistress, but are now supplied with one Mrs. Lourier,[2] who faithfully discharges her trust. She began with two Scholars, to which thirteen more have since been added, & others dayly coming; so, that I make no doubt, but that the number mentioned in your Letter will soon be compleat. I have hitherto constantly visited the School, & purpose, if blessed with Health, to continue my Visits; &, it's with pleasure, that I now inform you, that the Children already have made a very considerable progress in reading, learning their Prayers, & Catechisms & working.[3] I frequently examine them, & at proper times, give them, & the mistress, such advice & Instructions as are necessary for their future conduct & benefit.

Thus Sir, this best of Charities, will, by the blessing of God, I hope, answer in every respect, the charitable & good Intention of the worthy Associates who support it. No Pains or Care on my part shall be wanting towards it. I should further observe to you that there are about seven of the Scholars that read very well, & are already importuning me for Psalters and Bibles; if the Associates therefore think fit to supply me with a few of each, I think I can dispose of them to good Advantage.

I have but one thing more to add, & that is, that we could not provide a suitable Mistress for the undertaking under twenty pounds Sterling, which considering the great Rents that are paid for Houses, in this City, and the dearness of Provisions, since the War, is reckoned very reasonable; and, as the Mistress has now faithfully discharged her Duty upwards of Six month, Doctor Johnson, agreeable to your Order, has, by this Opportunity drawn for her Salary.

The Doctor & Mr. Barclay desire their Compliments to you & the worthy Associates; & that you & them may succeed in all your charitable Undertakings, & be finally rewarded by our blessed Lord & Redeemer, is, the sincere, & ardent Prayer of Revd. Sir, Your oblig'd Humble servant

Samuel Auchmuty.

P.S. I should be glad to be favoured with a Line from you; & any further Instructions the Associates may think fit, to order.

ALS. Sent "per His Majesty's Ship James, Capt. Lee, Q.D.C." This letter was read by the Associates at their meeting of 13 May 1761, at which time they "Agreed That hearty Thanks be returned to Mr. Auchmuty for his great Care in conducting the Negroe School, & that Mr. Waring be desired to Send some Psalters Testaments Common Prayers & Bibles for the Use of the School." Minutes, 1 : 152–53. Waring's reply, which was dated 1 June 1761, has not been found. For the books sent, see "Catalog of Books," p. 61. There is another copy of this letter in the same collection.

1. The *New-York Mercury* of 15 September 1760 carried the following announcement of the opening of the school:

> This is to inform the Public, that a Free School is opened near the New-Dutch-Church, for the instruction of 30 Negro Children, from 5 years old and upwards, in Reading, and in the Principles of Christianity, and likewise sewing and knitting; which School is entirely under the Inspection and Care of the Clergy of the Church of England in this City: Those Persons therefore that have the present Usefulness, and future Welfare of their young Slaves at Heart (especially those born in their Houses), are desired to apply to any one of the Clergy, who will immediately send them to the aforesaid School, and see that they be faithfully instructed.
>
> N.B. All that is required of their Masters and Mistresses, is that they find them in Wood for the Winter. Proper Books will be provided for them gratis.

The school opened on 22 September. Auchmuty to the Rev. Philip Bearcroft, secretary of the S.P.G., 19 September 1761, S.P.G. MSS., B2, no. 2.

2. Not identified.

3. I.e., sewing and knitting.

James Parker to Rev. John Waring

Woodbridge, [New Jersey] May 18: 1761

Revd. Sir,

By a Letter from my worthy Friend Benjamin Franklin, Esquire I am informed of your kind Intentions to our little Society of the Church in this Place, as also of your benevolent Contribution of a Guinea, to be applied towards building a Press to keep such Books in as may providentially come within our Custody.[1] I yesterday, when the Rev. Mr. Chandler, Missionary from the Society to Elizabeth-Town, was here, and administred the Holy Sacrament amongst us;[2] in the Evening shew'd the Congregation the Contents of Mr. Franklin's Letter, and they gratefully acknowledged the Favour, and desired their Thanks might be given to you. Altho' they would be humbly Thankful, if the Building dedicated to God's Service here, could be rendered more convenient, yet inasmuch, as we are but few, and those not of great Estates, we must be contented since tho' a bare Shell, yet in part sufficient for carrying on the Worship of God. It is true could We proceed to finish it a little more, it might be more becoming. But we trust God in his own good Time, he may raise up some Means to assist and help us. Mean While Rev. Sir, We cordially wish you Happiness, and in the Behalf of the rest of my Brethren remain Your most obliged Servant

James Parker.

ALS.

1. Franklin's letter has not been found. At the Associates' meeting of 6 November 1760 Franklin suggested that a parochial library be sent to Wood-bridge, as the inhabitants "are an industrious well-disposed Set of people & stand in great Need of religious Books." The Associates agreed to establish the library. Minutes, 1:144. At the meeting of 1 January 1761 Waring reported that he had prepared a parcel of books for the Woodbridge library and that at his request the S.P.C.K. had given a packet of books and tracts valued at forty shillings for the library. Minutes, 1:145. For the books sent, see "Catalog of Books," pp. 69–70.

2. The Rev. Thomas Bradbury Chandler (1726–90), S.P.G. missionary to Elizabethtown, New Jersey, and minister of St. John's Church, Elizabethtown, performed missionary work in Woodbridge from 1752 to 1763. Weis, *Colonial Clergy Middle Colonies*, p. 196. For Chandler's involvement in the debate over an American episcopate, see Auchmuty to Waring, 9 May 1768, note 2, below.

Rev. John Waring to William Hunter

[London, 1 June 1761]

Sir

I had the Favour of Yours dated February 4 1761[1] which I laid before the Associates at their last Meeting who expressed great Satisfaction in hearing that the good Work You have undertaken so greatly prospered. They charged me with their most hearty Thanks to You for your ready and vigorous Concurrence in promoting it.

They acknowledge that They are not competent Judges what Salary may be Sufficient for a Mistress, & therefore must refer that Matter entirely to Your Prudence and Discretion; but as they payed no more than 20£ Sterling per Ann. for 30 Children, both at Philadelphia and New York City They hoped the Same Stipend might be Sufficient with You. However that This Undertaking may meet with no Check or Discouragement in its Infancy on this Account, They have directed me to acquaint You that They chearfully increase their Appointment to 30£ Sterling, not doubting but in Time A Proposal for a Subscription towards its Support will be favourably received at Williamsburgh. In the meanwhile They wou'd be glad the Number of Scholars were increased to 30 agreable to their first proposal, & to the Number instructed in their other Schools. And Since Many of the

Children, by this Time, have got over the most tedious and difficult part of Learning, The Associates are of Opinion that the Mistress will now with more Ease teach 30 than She could at first 24 when All of them probably were to be initiated in the first Rudiments. But after all, tho They propose their Opinion, They leave the whole entirely to Your Judgement being perswaded by the favourable Account They have had from Dr. Franklin of your Readiness & Zeal to promote every good Work that nothing will be wanting on your Part to encourage and promote this pious Institution, and to render its good Effects as extensive as may be.

The Associates, for the Satisfaction of their Benefactors, desire to be informed from Time to Time of the Number of Scholars, received into the School, & the Improvement made by those that leave it, & whether Any are baptized in Consequence of their Instruction in the School, & any other Particulars which You may Judge worthy of Notice.

In Order to convince the Masters that the Piety & spiritual Advantage of the Children is principaly intended the Associates earnestly desire that the Mistress be strictly enjoynd to say Morning & Evening Prayer daily with her Scholars at certain stated hours.

I have sent a further Supply of Books for the Use of the School,[2] & hope for Instructions from You when more shall be wanting. I write by this Opportunity to Mr. Neale[3] & Mr. Nicholas to request the Favour of their Concurrence. The Associates have directed me to present their hearty Thanks to You for your charitable Assistance. They pray that God may bless and prosper You in this & all other good Works. I am with the Sincerest Respect & Esteem Your most obedient humble Servant

Jn. Waring

June: 1: 1761 at Mr. Birds Bookseller in Ave Mary Lane
London

A Catalogue of Books in a Box directed to You.
>5 Bibles, 25 Testaments, 25 Psalters, 10 Christian Guide, 10 English Instructor, 10 Burkitts Help & Guide, 40 Childs first Book, 10 Indian Instructed, 2 Scriptural Catechism, 5 Easy Method.

These for the Use of the School.
>20 Common Prayers to be given to the Children when qualified to use them at Church.

The Associates thank You for paying the Freight of the last Parcel, but they will repay You the Expences of Both if You include them in Your next Draft.

ALS: Bray MSS., McGregor Collection, U.Va.

1. Hunter's letter was actually dated 16 February 1761, above.

2. On 13 May 1761 the Associates "Agreed that Mr. Waring be desired to Send a proper Supply of Books for the Use of the Negroe School at Williamsburgh." Minutes, 1 : 153. A list of the books is appended to this letter. See also "Catalog of Books," p. 61.

3. This is an error; Waring meant the Rev. William Yates. His letter to Yates has not been found.

Rev. John Waring to Robert Carter Nicholas

[London, 1 June 1761]

Sir,

The Associates of Dr. Bray having lately opened a School at Williamsburgh for the Instruction of Negroe Children in the Principles of the Christian Religion as professed by the Church of England, & being desirous that this pious Undertaking may be honoured with Your Patronage, have directed me to write to You & in their Name request the Favour of You to Join Your Endeavours to Those of Mr. Hunter and Mr. Yates for the more Effectual prosecution of this good Work. When a Design of this Nature is conducted by Gentlemen of distinguished Integrity Candour & Benevolence, who will take all possible Care to direct it to its proper End; We may reasonably hope that every ill-grounded Prejudice against it, will gradualy Subside & die away. This good Effect The Associates hope for from Your kind Concurrence. And I will not pay You so ill a Compliment as to *doubt* of Your ready Compliance, & therefore beg leave to refer You to Mr. Hunter for further particulars.

I am Sir, Your most humble Servant,

Jn. Waring

June: 1: 1761
at Mr. Birds Bookseller in Ave Mary Lane London

ALS: Bray MSS., McGregor Collection, U.Va.

Joseph Ottolenghe to Rev. John Waring

Savannah Georgia June 5th. 1761

Revd. Sir

This serves to advise you that I have this Day drawn on you a Sett of Bills Exchange payable to the Order of Mr. Thomas Rasberry[1] for

Twelve Pounds ten Shillings sterling which I make no Doubt will be duely honoured.

I am Revd. Sir Your most humble Servant

J. Ottolenghe

LS.

1. Thomas Rasberry (d. 1762) came to Georgia about 1751. He was a vestryman of Christ Church Parish and represented the town and district of Savannah in the Commons House of Assembly 1758–59. S.P.G. MSS., C, Georgia; Greene, *Quest for Power*, p. 494; Lilla M. Hawes, ed., *The Letter Book of Thomas Rasberry, 1758–1761, Collections of the Georgia Historical Society* 13 (1959): i; Kenneth Coleman and Charles Stephen Gurr, eds., *Dictionary of Georgia Biography*, 2 vols. (Athens, Ga., 1983), 2:826.

Rev. Samuel Auchmuty to Rev. John Waring

New York August 8th. 1761

Revd. Sir

I now have the pleasure of acquainting you that the Negro School, in this City, is full; &, would the plan allow of it, as many more might in a few days be added to it. The mistress is very industrious, & the Scholars have already made a considerable progress in their learning. I frequently visit & catechise them, & shall continue so to do; and, acquaint you from time to time with the state of the School. Some of the big Scholars are constantly importuning me for Psalters & Bibles, which are not to be had here, but at an extravagant price, therefore wish that the Associates would indulge them, with a few Coppies of each; I think they would be well disposed of.

I am with due Esteem, Revd. Sir, Your oblig'd humble servant

Samuel Auchmuty.

ALS. This letter was read by the Associates at their meeting of 1 October 1761. Minutes, 1:157–58.

Rev. William Sturgeon to Rev. John Waring

Philadelphia August 21 1761

Revd. Sir,

The Negro-School went on very well under the Care of the first Mistress, till one Mr. Macclanaghan, in the Orders of our Church, left his Mission in New England, and came to this City, and bred much Confusion; the Mistress was one of his Followers, and much neglected her Duty in the School.[1]

Upon receiving sundry Complaints of her bad Management, I was obliged to dismiss her in May last, and put another in her Place, who immediately entered upon her Duty, and is very diligent.[2]

The Institution itself is very humane and good, but it will never meet with the Success desired till it is made more general, and Christians of every Profession admitted to the Inspection and Government of it; which I doubt not will be the Case, when the truly humane and ingenious Dr. Franklin comes over. In the mean Time I shall do my best to promote so good a Design, and am Revd. Sir your most affectionate humble Servant

Wm. Sturgeon

ALS. Sent "per Favour Capt. Hammet." This letter was read by the Associates at their meeting of 5 November 1761. Minutes, 1 : 162.

1. The Rev. William McClenaghan (1714–66), a native of Ireland, graduated from the University of Edinburgh in 1730. He came to America before 1734 and served as a Presbyterian clergyman in several New England towns until 1746. He was ordained a Congregational minister in 1748 and served in Revere, Massachusetts, until his dismissal in December 1754. McClenaghan next went to England, where he was ordained an Anglican priest by the bishop of London in 1755, and he then entered into the service of the S.P.G. as an itinerant missionary to Frankfort and Georgetown, Massachusetts (now in Maine). After spending several years in New England, McClenaghan traveled to Virginia and accepted a vacant parish there. While returning to New England to move his family to Virginia, McClenaghan stopped in Philadelphia in 1758 or early 1759. He was described by the Rev. William Smith in a letter to Archbishop Secker of 27 November 1759 as "an avowed Methodist and follower of Whitfield's plan." Smith also wrote, "The novelty of his manner, his great noise and *extempore* effusions, both in praying and preaching, struck sundry of the lower sort of people." Smith, *Life and Correspondence of Smith* 1 : 225. On 10 May 1759 the vestry of Christ Church read a petition signed by seventy-four members of the congregation asking that McClenaghan be appointed to assist Sturgeon, in view of the rector's (Mr. Jenney's) infirmities. The vestry agreed that McClenaghan could use the pulpit to preach in, as a lecturer only, during Jenney's pleasure. A month later the vestry elected McClenaghan assistant minister to Jenney, to serve in conjunction with Sturgeon. The bishop of London, however, refused to license McClenaghan to officiate in the church. On 25 March 1760 Samuel Nicolls, secretary to the bishop, wrote to Jenney, Sturgeon, Jacob Duché, Jr., and the vestry explaining the refusal: "In respect to Mr. McClenaghan, his lordship has many reasons why he cannot license him in the parts of Pennsylvania. He was ordained and licensed to a mission in the society's service, from which he has withdrawn

himself in a manner that does him no credit." Nicolls went on to say that McClenaghan had committed himself to a parish in Virginia and should go there, "and not . . . give any disturbance in the congregation where ministers are already settled and established." Dorr, *Historical Account of Christ Church*, p. 122. The vestry agreed in June 1760 to have the letter read in the church, after which McClenaghan and his followers broke off from the United Congregations of Christ Church and St. Peter's, and established St. Paul's Episcopal Church. After a dispute with his parishioners, McClenaghan left St. Paul's and became minister of Worcester Parish, Worcester County, Maryland, in October 1765. He served that parish until his death. Fulham Papers, 22 : 138; Perry, *Historical Collections, Pennsylvania*, pp. 307–8, 413; Dorr, *Historical Account of Christ Church*, pp. 118–19, 123; Weis, *Colonial Clergy New England*, p. 131; Rightmyer, *Maryland's Established Church*, p. 199.

2. Elizabeth Harrison (born c. 1715), the new mistress, was appointed on 18 May 1761. She was the wife of Richard Harrison, master of the charity school of the Academy of Philadelphia. S.P.G. MSS., B21, no. 280; Richard I. Shelling, "Benjamin Franklin and the Dr. Bray Associates," *PMHB* 63 (1939): 288n.

Enclosure
List of Negro Children

Began to Keep School November 20th. 1758.

20th.	From Mr. Primer	Ceaser
	ditto Mr. Duff	Jane
	ditto Free Lincoln	John
	ditto Mr. Lyon	Warrick
	ditto Free Emanuel	Mary
23d.	ditto Peter Turner	James
December		
4th.	ditto Mr. Mifflin	William
	ditto Widow McCall	Peggy
9th.	ditto Mr. Jones	James
	ditto Widow Hoot	Jean
18	ditto Mr. Hockley	Rachel
January		
8th. 1759	ditto Mr. Joseph Turner	Hannah, Rachel, & Ceaser
29th.	ditto Spring Garden Free	Joseph
February 5th.	ditto Free John	Caty & Phillis
	ditto Nurse Jones	Rose
March 5th.	ditto Mr. Duche	Silla

April 9	ditto Free Sharper	Mary & Thomas
18	ditto Mr. Bromwich	Phebe
23	ditto Free Benjamin	Sukey
25	ditto Mr. Dupee	Jude
May 7	ditto Mrs. Cliffton	Trombo
14	ditto Jeakle	Caty & Becca
	ditto Mr. Plumstead	Sylpha & Sister
18	ditto Mr. Ludwick	Quash
21	ditto Free Mary Duram	Mary
	ditto Free Coffee Duglass	Septimus & Sukey
	ditto Capt. Mott	Dinah
June 11	ditto Mrs. Sirls	Sarah & Surprize

D. In Sturgeon's hand. On the verso Sturgeon wrote, "Inclos'd is a list of the negro Children which I saw christened."

Benjamin Waller and Thomas Everard to Rev. John Waring

Williamsburg in Virginia, September 1st: 1761.

Sir,

Yours of June the 1st. directed to Mr. Hunter with a Letter to Mr. Yates and another for Mr. Nicholas came to our Hands about ten Days ago, Mr. Hunter being dead.[1] Mr. Yates and Mr. Nicholas will accept of the Trust and write to you and to them we have delivered your Letters and Papers relating to the Negro School and have directed Mrs. Wager the Mistress to apply to them for Instructions and her pay for the future. Mr. Hunter by his Will appointed Mr. James Tarpley (now in London) and Ourselves his Executors. We have duly proved the Will here, and finding by Mr. Hunters Books that £10 Sterling is due to his Estate for two Quarters Salary paid the Mistress inclusive of the first quarter for which he drew on you to Mr. Tarpley we have this day drawn an Order on you to Mr. Tarpley for that Sum which we desire you will be pleased to pay him for the Use of Mr. Hunters Estate. We are Sir Your most humble Servants

Ben: Waller
Thos. Everard

LS. This letter was read by the Associates at their meeting of January 1762. Minutes, 1 : 165–66.

1. Waring's letters to Hunter and Nicholas appear above. His letter to Yates has not been found.

Robert Carter Nicholas to Rev. John Waring

Williamsburg 17th. September 1761

Sir.

I have lately had the Pleasure of receiving your Favour of the first of June under Mr. Hunter's Cover, who died, poor Gentleman, a few Days before it came to Hand. You judged very rightly of my Sentiments, in not allowing yourself to doubt of my ready Compliance with the Society's Request, as I should always be ready most chearfully to concur in any Measures tending to promote Christianity. I took the earliest Opportunity of waiting upon the Revd. Mr. Yates to converse with him upon the Subject of your Letter & found him, as I knew he would be, heartily disposed to cooperate with me in supporting the School to the utmost of his Power. I have also seen the School-Mistress & understand from her that Matters stand pretty much as they did when Mr. Hunter wrote you his last Letter.[1] From what I have already discoverd, for I have not had Time yet to enquire minutely, I find there are several Regulations necessary to be made; and tho' I have no very sanguine Expectations of the School's answering the Design of the pious Founder, you may assure the Society that no Endeavours of mine shall be wanting to procure the wish'd for Success. The Executors of Mr. Hunter inform me that they have drawn for the 3d. Quarter's Salary & I suppose we shall have Occasion to draw soon for the fourth, as I understand the Year is nearly expired. I am, Sir, with great Respect Your most obedient Servant

Ro. C. Nicholas

ALS. Endorsed: "Return Thanks. Refer the Regulations entirely to him & Mr. Yates & hope in time the good Effects of the School may exceed his Expectations." This letter was read by the Associates at their meeting of January 1762. Minutes, 1 : 166–67. Waring's reply is dated 4 April 1762, below.

1. Dated 16 February 1761, above.

Rev. Daniel Earl to Rev. John Waring

No. Carolina Edenton 3 October 1761

Sir

Mr. Hazlewood Merchant in this Town shewed me a Letter from you, wherein you signified to him, that a Society called Dr. Bray's Associates were desirous that a School may be opened here for the Education of Negroe Children; under the Care of him, Mr. Child, and myself;[1] but as Mr. Child, some time ago, moved from here into Virginia, neither Mr. Hazlewood or myself could Learn the Societys Plan 'till very lately, when I waited upon him myself for that Purpose: Since which Time, I have used my utmost Endeavours to recommend their beneficent and charitable Design to the Inhabitants of this Town; and to Represent it in that Light that it ought to Appear to all who Profess our Holy Religion: But am sorry to Acquaint you, that my Exhortations and Remonstrances have not as yet had the desired Effect; but hope they will consider better of it, and not suffer so fair an Opportunity of having their young Slaves instructed in the Principles of Christianity fall to the Ground. They all Allow of the great Expediency of the Design, but say, that as their Circumstances are low and Depressed, (which is generally the Case) they can't spare their Negroes from their Service at the Age that they are susceptible of Erudition: And those that are in Affluent Circumstances are so very few, that the Number of Children sent by them would be so inconsiderable, as not be worth any Person's Acceptance; and as the Teaching of Negroes precludes the taking of white Children, the Parents not Allowing their Children to be Educated among such.

If it should be proposed by your worthy Society to Allow any Sallary for the Education of white Children, it would be readily Embraced, and would be productive of great Utility to this poor and ignorant Colony, as the greatest part of them is brought up in profound Ignorance of every Kind of Literature, occasioned chiefly by the Poverty and Indigence of the Inhabitants.

I sometime ago signified to the Incorporated Society for Propagating the Gospel in foreign Parts, the want of Education in this Province as I have the Honour of being in their Service; but have not as yet received any Answer.[2]

The Society may rest assured, that, as I have hitherto, so I shall hereafter incessantly Endeavour that their Munificent, laudable, and charitable Design may Answer all the good Purposes thereby intended.

I am, Sir, The Society's, and your most Obedient, and Humble Servant,

Danl. Earl

ALS. Endorsed: "Agreed that a Copy of this Letter be delivered to the Secy. of the Society for the propagation, of the Gospel. Agreed that Mr. Earl be thanked for his kind Let. & that he be desired to continue his best Endeavours that the Designs of the Ass. may be carried into Execution." This letter was read by the Associates at their meeting of January 1762. Minutes, 1 : 167–68. Waring's reply, which was dated 1 June 1762, has not been found.

1. At the Associates' meeting of 7 May 1761 Waring reported that he had consulted with Anthony Bacon; who thought it most advisable to open schools in Maryland and at Edenton. Although the Minute Book records that Bacon wrote to his brother, the Rev. Thomas Bacon, in Maryland, and to Child and Hazlewood at Edenton on the subject, the letters, which have not been found, were written by Waring. Thomas Child (b. 1720 or 1721; d. early 1790s) was attorney general of North Carolina 1746–61. He had come to the colony from London, where he had been called to the bar in May 1746, shortly after receiving his appointment. Child successively opposed governors Gabriel Johnston and Arthur Dobbs, and in 1760 he was involved in an unsuccessful attempt to have Bacon appointed agent of the colony. Hazlewood has not been identified. For Bacon, see Lewis to Waring, 31 October 1768, note 1, below. For the books sent to Edenton in 1761 see "Catalog of Books," p. 71. Minutes, 1:150; *N.C. Col. Recs.* 6:13–15, 307–8, 310, 319, 11:109; William S. Powell, ed., *Dictionary of North Carolina Biography*, vol. 1 (Chapel Hill, 1979), pp. 366–68.

Several years earlier the Associates had sent books to Edenton and attempted to encourage the education of blacks. On 7 December 1757 they "Agreed that a Packet of Books from the Store at the Discretion of J. Waring be sent to Mr. [Clement] Hall of Edinton in North Carolina to lay the foundation of a Parochial Library there. And that he be desired to transmit to the Associates an Account of the Success of his Labours among the Negros." Minutes, 1:110. Neither the letter to Hall nor his reply has been found.

2. In a letter to the secretary of the S.P.G. dated 5 May 1760 Earl asked the assistance of the S.P.G. in establishing schools for the children of North Carolina, "as the Depressed, and mean Circumstances of the Inhabitants Render them incapable of Educating their Children." Earl promised to exert himself in establishing and superintending a school in the parish. S.P.G. MSS., B5, no. 99. The S.P.G. read Earl's letter on 19 September 1760 and "Agreed, that Mr. Earl be desired to enquire after a proper Person to teach School, and to consult his Parishioners what they will advance towards his maintenance, and then the Society will be ready to add their assistance to it." S.P.G. Journals, 15:5.

Rev. Samuel Auchmuty to Rev. John Waring

New York October the 7th. 1761.

Revd. Sir

Your very obliging favor of the first of last June,[1] is now before me, & affords me a very sensible pleasure; as, it acquaints me that my proceedings, with regard to the Negro School, in this City, have hitherto met with the Approbation of so worthy a set of Gentlemen, as are the Associates of that late truely Christian Divine, Dr. Bray. It certainly is the indispensable Duty of every Clergyman, to use his utmost endeavors to inlarge the Kingdom of our blessed Redeemer, which is the glorious design of the Associates; and, I have the happiness to think, & say, that it is also the Inclination, & hearty desire, of the American Clergy, sincerely to join with their worthy Brethren, on your side the Water, in every Scheme, that can be offered, towards the promoting so laudable, and glorious an Undertaking.

As the Negro's here are more immediately intrusted to my Care, by that very worthy & charitable Body, the Society for the Propagation of the Gospel in foreign parts; so, the Negro School has a right to demand all the Care & Attention that I can spare it; And, I thank God, my Duty happily co-incides with my Inclination, and pleasure. I could indeed wish, that the Duties of this parish, which are very great, and executed by my very worthy Friend, & Brother, Dr. Barclay, and my self, as his Assistant, would allow me more time, to visit the School, than I now have: however, I take care that few Week's pass without My going to the School, & examining the Scholars. And, I now upon a very late Visit, can with pleasure inform you, that the School is quite full; that several have been refused for want of Room; that the mistress appears to be very diligent & Industrious; that the Children are clean, & orderly, & begin to read, sow,² say their Catechise³ & prayers, as well as I could expect for the time.

In your Letter You observe, that the Associates, are inform'd, that "too many both of Masters & Slaves are possessed with a groundless perswasion that Baptism breaks asunder the bonds of Slavery." If the Information extends to this province, I am very confident it is a very wrong one; for, I am very sure there are very few Negro Children born here but what are baptized; & out of the thirty now in the school, only three are unbaptized, & the Owners of these three have requested me to baptize them, which I shall soon do. For some Years past I have not baptized less than 80, or 90 Negro Children, & often upwards of 100; besides, several Adults. Dr. Barclay has also baptized many, & the Dutch Ministers & the Dissenters dayly do the same, and yet they continue peaceable Slaves.

I have not been unmindful of your further Observations, but have often requested the mistress of the School, to make use of every Opportunity of impressing on the minds of the Children, Sentiments of piety, & a due fear of God; &, have reason to think that my request to her has been comply'd with. I have cautiously avoided requiring too much from the mistress at first, therefore, have not as yet required her Attendance with her Scholars, at Church, on Prayer Days, for, after the School is out, she has her self & Children to take care off, & victuals to prepare, which she can'ot do, while the Scholars are about her; besides some of the Children begin to be useful at Home, are able to lay a Cloth, & wait upon Table; therefore should I detain them till Prayers are over at Church, I fear it would occasion some uneasiness and grumbling, which I would chuse to avoid. Perhaps a favorable Opportunity may present of accomplishing even this desire of the Associates; if it offers, they may assure themselves I shall readily embrace it. I take great Care that they constantly attend divine Service on the Lords Day; & also, that they attend my plain & familiar Lecture to the Blacks, between the two services; they then hear the Adults Catechized, & are also Catechized themselves. By this means, and some others that I shall endeavor to think off, & put in execution, they may, by degrees (by the blessing of God) be led on to happiness here, & glory hereafter. Taking them early before they have imbib'd bad principles, affords me a prospect of a much greater harvest, than I could expect, from the same Number grown up, & used to a wrong way of thinking.

The other reasonable & judicious requests of the Associates shall carefully be comply'd with; & indeed, in part were, before the reception of your kind favor.

The Names, Ages, &c. &c. of the Children & who they belong too, are as follows:

	Names	Owners	Age		Improvement	When admitted
1	Isabella	Mr. Cockcraft	19	Bap.	Reads works &c.	October 29. 1760
2	Flora	Mr. Vanhorne	11	N.B.	Learning to spell &c.	December 1760
3	Mercy	Mr. Romer	11	Bap.	Ditto	February 17. 1761
4	Rosannah	Mr. Roades	10	Bap.	Ditto	February 19. 1761
5	Judah	Mrs. Rinders	9	Bap.	Reads well &c.	February 19. 1761
6	Thomas	Ditto	7	Bap.	Learning to spell &c.	Ditto
7	Flora	Ditto	5	Bap.	Ditto	Ditto
8	Sarah	A free Child	11	Ditto	Ditto	January 1761
9	Rachel	Ditto	8	Ditto	Ditto	Ditto
10	Nancy	Mr. Cockcrafts	7	Ditto	Ditto	February 1761
11	Susannah	J. Cruger Esqr.	6	Ditto	Ditto	October 27. 1760
12	Mary	Mr. Wendelhams	6	Ditto	Ditto	October 29. 1760
13	Hannah	R. Nicholls Esqr.	8	Ditto	Reads very well &c.	
14	Dinah	Mr. Ludlows	6	N.B.	Learning to spell &c.	May 27. 1760
15	Cloe	Dr. Johnsons	7	Bap.	Ditto	May 1761
16	Sally	Mr. Devoot	6	Ditto	Ditto	January 1761
17	Mercy	Mr. Governeur	6	Ditto	Ditto	November 3. 1760
18	Andrew	Ditto	5	Ditto	Ditto	Ditto
19	Elizabeth	Mr. Kittletash	5	Ditto	Ditto	November 3. 1760
20	Mary	Mr. Banckers	5	Ditto	Reads well &c.	September 22. 176

	Names	Owners	Age		Improvement	When admitted
21	Polly	Mrs. Shavers	6	N.B.	Learning to spell &c.	Ditto
22	William	Mr. Fells	9	Bap.	Ditto	May 5. 1761
23	Jack	Mr. Montanies	6	Ditto	Ditto	
24	Jack	Mr. Astines	6	Ditto	Ditto	January 1761
25	Samuel	Dr. Bards	5	Ditto	Ditto	Ditto
26	Aneas	Mrs. Elistons	10	Ditto	Ditto	July 18. 1761
27	Cuffee	Mrs. Moone	6	bap.	Learning to spell &c.	April 8. 1761
28	Richard	Mr. Banckers	5	bap.	Ditto	October 1760
29	Marian	Mr. Schuylers	7	bap.	Ditto	Ditto
30	Sylvia	Free Child	8	bap.	Ditto	May 1761

This Sir, is the present State of the School, and whatever altera-
tions may happen, I shall take care to inform you of them. One Alteration I have made with regard to the Bills drawn for the mistress'es
Salary, by Signing them myself, as I found it ill-convenient waiting
upon Dr. Johnson, who lives at the College, & is at a considerable distance from me, only to put his Name to them. You will please to return
my hearty Thanks to the worthy Associates for their kind & pious
wishes with regard to me; and that you and they may prosper in all
your truely pious designs, may be Instrumental to the saving of many
poor Souls, & may be rewarded hereafter with a Crown of Glory, is
the sincere and ardent prayer, of, Revd. Sir, Your Obliged Friend &
Brother in Christ

Samuel Auchmuty.

P.S. A set of Bills for the last half Years Salary for the Mistress accom-
pany this. Drs. Johnson & Barclay desire you, and the Associates
would accept of their sincere respects. The Box of Books is come to
hand,[4] & the Associates may assure themselves that I shall distribute
them in such a manner, as will be agreeable to them. I believe it would
be agreeable to Dr. Bearcroft was you to favor him with a sight of this
Letter.

ALS. Endorsed: "Bill of £10 accepted July 2d. 1762. Due August 4." This
letter was read by the Associates at their meeting of January 1762, at which
time they "Agreed that Mr. Waring be desired to take the earliest Opportunity
of returning hearty Thanks to Mr. Auchmuty for his great Diligence & Zeal in
superintending the Negroe School, & also for his full & very satisfactory Account of the State of the School, & that he be Acquainted that the Associates
are so well pleased with his judicious Proceedings that They Refer the future
management entirely to his Discretion." Minutes, 1 : 168–71. Waring's reply,
which was dated 8 January 1762, has not been found.

1. Letter not found. See Auchmuty to Waring, 4 April 1761, bibliographic note, above.
2. Obsolete form of sew. *OED*.
3. Obsolete form of catechism. *OED*.
4. See "Catalog of Books," p. 61.

Rev. William Sturgeon to Rev. John Waring

[Philadelphia, 23 November 1761]

Revd. Sir,

I acquainted you in my last[1] that I was obliged to commit the School to a new Mistress; I have now the additional Pleasure to inform you that she conducts herself so well in the School, that the Number of Scholars are increased to 30; the Boys read and the Girls read and work; but the chief Endeavour is to instill the Principles of our holy Religion into their Minds.

The Scheme you mention I leave till Dr. Franklin comes Home.[2] At present I shall do my best to answer the design of the Associates, and please to present my best Regards to them. I have drawn upon you for £10 Sterling the Mistresss Half Years Salary.

After wishing Prosperity to your Undertakings I am Reverend Sir your affectionate Brother and humble Servant

Wm. Sturgeon

Phila. November 23 1761

ALS. Endorsed as answered 10 February 1762. This letter was read by the Associates at their meeting of 4 February 1762. Minutes, 1 : 172. Waring's reply has not been found.

1. Dated 21 August 1761, above.
2. This scheme has not been identified.

Rev. John Waring to Robert Carter Nicholas

[London, 4 April 1762]

Sir

The Rest of the Associates join with me in returning You most sincere & hearty Thanks for your obliging favour of the 17th. of September last, & for the kind Assurance You gave Us that No Endeavours of Yours shall be wanting to procure the wished for Success to the Negroe School. The Associates think themselves obliged to Mr. Yates for his chearful Offer to cooperate with You in supporting the School. You say You have no very sanguine Expectations that the School will answer our Design; I hope good Sir, that in a Little time You will find Reason to alter your Opinion. We have a School at Philadelphia & another at New York, in both which the Success hath exceeded our most Sanguine Expectations; & if You or Mr. Yates will be so good as to visit the School once a week, You will find that it will produce very good Effects as to the Care of the Mistress & the Improvement of the Scholars. But this I ought to retract, because I am perswaded it is what You have already done. The Associates beg leave to refer the Whole Management to You & Mr. Yates, & hope You or He will favour Us with a Line as often as You can to acquaint Us with the State of the School. If it be not too much Trouble we cou'd wish to be favoured with a List of the Childrens Names, their Age, Improvement, baptized or Not, & dates of their Admission. We had one from new York School[1] which gave great pleasure to many of our Benefactors who saw it, & Who expressed a great Desire of seeing the like Account from our other Schools. We are very unwilling to add to the Trouble You have so charitably taken upon Yourselves & therefore this is mentioned only in Compliance with the Request of some of our Benefactors.

I received a Letter from Mr. Hunters Executors,[2] acquainting me that they had sent to Mr. Tarply a Draft for 10£ 2 Quarters Salary, but I have been since Informed that Mr. Tarpley set out for Virginia Some time before. Shall I beg the favour of You to present my Respects to them, & to let them know their Draft for that Sum Shall be duly honoured.

A Supply of Books shall be sent immediately as soon as You let me know they are wanting. I am directed to present the sincere Respects of the Associates to You & Mr. Yates. I am Sir Your most obliged humble Servant

Jn. Waring

at Mr. Birds Bookseller in Ave Mary Lane near St. Pauls
London
April 4: 1762

ALS: Bray MSS., McGregor Collection, U.Va. Sent by the *Desire*, Captain Peterson.

1. See Auchmuty to Waring, 7 October 1761, above.
2. See Waller and Everard to Waring, 1 September 1761, above.

Rev. Samuel Auchmuty to Rev. John Waring

New York May 18th. 1762

Revd. Sir

Your very obliging favour of the 8th. of last January,[1] is now before me, and demands my most sincere Thanks.

Next to the satisfaction I feel from a consciousness of faithfully doing my Duty, and endeavouring, as far as I am able, to enlarge the Kingdom of our glorious Redeemer; the Approbation of my conduct, from so good a Body as the worthy Associates, gives me a real pleasure. They may assure themselves, that as long as it pleases God to bless me with Health, their School shall not be neglected.

Since my last, dated October 7th. 1761, the School has been compleatly full, and so continues. Two or three of the Old ones, being grown up, & well instructed, have left it, & others have supplied their place. Such is the repute the School is now in, that no sooner is there a Vacancy, but immediately, several Candidates offer.

As to the improvement of the Children in reading, Spelling, learning their Catechise, sewing &c. it is as great as can be expected. They all attended me last Sunday, (as indeed they do almost every Sunday) & were, before a considerable Number of Adults examined, & Catechis'd, & performed extremely well. They constantly attend divine Service, on the Lords Day, and are a very pretty, little, decent Flock, which in time I flatter myself, will be exemplary, and an ornament to our most holy Religion.

I readily conceive the real pleasure the worthy Associates feel, at hearing of the progress these poor little Blacks make in their learning; and very great must be their Satisfaction, when they reflect that they are instrumental in promoting the Temporal Welfare, and eternal happiness of a Number of poor Souls, who might, without their benevolent Interposition, have long sat in Darkness, & in the Shadow of Death. In my next, I intend to send you an exact List of the Scholars, their Ages, proficiency &c. I have drawn for the Mistress's Salary in favor of R. Nicholls Esqr.[2] She is really a deserving Woman, & conscientiously discharges her Duty.

This will be delivered to you by Doctor James Jay, a Native of this City, a Gentleman of a liberal Education & of eminence in his profession. His private Affairs calling him to England, he generously offered his Service to the Governors of our Infant College here. They have thought fit to impower him to receive any generous Donations that the Friends of useful Literature, and well wishers to the best of Churches, the Church of England, may be disposed to bestow upon our College, surrounded by Dissenters, who look upon it with an evil Eye.[3] My Brethren, its Governours, have desired me to solicite your kind Assistance; & to beg you (after the Doctor has acquainted you with our Difficulties & present Situation, if you then think us worthy of Notice & Aid) to mention our wants to all your worthy Friends & Brethren, particularly the Body of Associates.

I beg you'll present my sincere Respects to the worthy Associates; & pray the continuance of their, and your Prayers; and that you, and they may enjoy happiness here, & hereafter, is the warm wish, & ardent prayer, of dear Sir, Your much Oblig'd & very humble Servant & Brother

Samuel Auchmuty.

P.S. Doctors Johnson & Barclay desire their Compliments to you & your worthy Brethren.

ALS. Endorsed as answered March 1763. This letter was read by the Associates at their meeting of 7 October 1762. Minutes, 1 : 179–80. Waring's reply has not been found.

1. Letter not found. See Auchmuty to Waring, 7 October 1761, bibliographic note, above.

2. Richard Nicholls was clerk of the vestry of Trinity Church in 1752 and 1753. He became registrar of the court of vice-admiralty in 1763. Nicholls's daughter Mary married Auchmuty in 1749. Schneider and Schneider, *Samuel Johnson* 1 : 172, 4 : 180, 324, 331; Edmund B. O'Callaghan, ed., *Calendar of New York Colonial Commissions, 1680–1770* (New York, 1929), p. 34; Sibley and Shipton, *Harvard Graduates* 11 : 116.

3. Dr. James Jay (1732–1815), New York physician, was an older brother of John Jay. He received an M.D. from the University of Edinburgh in 1753 and returned to New York to establish his medical practice. Upon his arrival in England in 1762 Jay met the Rev. William Smith, provost of the College of Philadelphia, who was in England raising funds for his institution. Together they published *An Humble Representation . . . in Behalf of the Lately Erected Colleges of New York and Philadelphia* (London, 1762) and succeeded in raising £10,000 for each of the colleges. In March 1763 King George III knighted Jay upon his presentation of an address from the governors of King's College. *DAB*. For the early years of King's College, see David C. Humphrey, *From King's College to Columbia, 1746–1800* (New York, 1976).

[Rev. William Sturgeon to Rev. John Waring]

[Philadelphia, May 1762]

The Reverend Mr. Sturgeon, in a Letter dated May, 1762, says, "The Negroe School at Philadelphia goes on very well; the Mistress is very careful and diligent, and the Children make suitable Improvements in Reading, their Catechism, &c."

Letter not found. Extract from *An Account of the Designs of the Associates of the Late Dr. Bray; With an Abstract of Their Proceedings* (London, 1763), p. 29. The letter was read by the Associates at their meeting of 4 November 1762. Minutes, 1 : 181.

Robert Carter Nicholas to Rev. John Waring

Williamsburg in Virginia 23d. June 1762.

Sir.

I have only at present to acquaint you that Mr. Yates & I have this Day drawn upon you for £25 Sterling in Favour of Mr. James Johnson of London[1] on Account of the Negro School under our Care in this City, & we have not the least Doubt but that you'll give due Honour to our Draughts. I have had the Number of Children augmented to thirty as you desired; the Mistress is very diligent & I'm in Hopes we shall be able to give you soon an agreeable Account of the Progress they make under her Care & Tuition. I must own to you that I am afraid the School will not answer the sanguine Expectations its pious Founders may have form'd; but we will endeavour to give it a fair Trial. I am, Sir, Your most obedient Servant

Ro. C. Nicholas

ALS. Endorsed: "Acct. September 27." This letter was read by the Associates at their meeting of 7 October 1762. Minutes, 1 : 180.

1. Not further identified.

Rev. William Sturgeon to Rev. John Waring

[Philadelphia, 1 July 1762]

Revd. Sir

I inclose to you a List of the School,[1] and as Dr. Franklin is daily expected here his Advice and Assistance will enable me to put it on the best Footing of which I shall give you proper Advice. I have drawn upon you for Half a Years Salary due to the Mistress, which I make no doubt you will honor.

I embrace this Opportunity of requesting your Interest with my Lord of London in my Favour.[2] We have lost Dr. Jenney our Minister,[3] and the Vestry have done me the Honor to elect me with the Revd.

Mr. Duche to be their Ministers on an Equality to the united Congregations of Christs Church and St. Peters in this City, and have prepared Addresses in our Favour to my Lord Bishop, for his Approbation and Licence, which go by Mr. Duche.[4]

Last October a Neighbours Daughter of mine was debauched by a young Man on a Promise of Marriage and was going to leave her in that Condition, but being prevailed on to marry her they came to me in the Night, when the Office for granting Marriage Licences was Shut, and had her Parents Consent and a Promise from him that he would obtain a Licence the next Morning. I joined them in Marriage.

The Young Man was from New England and Soon went off from this City. And we have a Report here that his Father had lodged a Complaint with my Lord of London against me and also with the Society Supported by the Quakers in England. At a Time when I must have his Lordships Approbation and Licence for my Settlement here, I beg your good Offices with him in my behalf, as I assure my motive was only Compassion to an injured Woman and a destressed Family.[5]

Please to present my best Regards to the worthy Associates, and assure them of my Endeavours to instruct the Negroes. I am Revd. Sir your most affectionate Brother and Servant

Wm. Sturgeon

July 1 1762

ALS: Fulham Papers, 7:332–33, Lambeth Palace Library, London. Sent "per Favor of the Revd. Mr. Duche." This letter must have been forwarded to the bishop of London, for it is now in the diocesan archives and is endorsed, "Mr. Waring desires to have this Letter returned to him."

1. Enclosure not found.

2. The Rt. Rev. Richard Osbaldeston (1690–1764) was bishop of London from 1762 to 1764. *DNB*.

3. The Rev. Robert Jenney (1687–1762), a native of Ireland, was ordained in 1710. He was a chaplain in the Royal Navy before coming to America in 1714. Jenney served various parishes in Pennsylvania, New York, and Connecticut before becoming rector of Christ Church in 1742. He was also commissary of the bishop of London in Pennsylvania from 1743 until his death on 5 January 1762. Weis, *Colonial Clergy Middle Colonies*, p. 246.

4. Sturgeon and the Rev. Jacob Duché, Jr., (see Biographical Appendix) were elected by the vestry to succeed Jenney on 16 January 1762. Duché had been assistant minister since September 1759, when he returned from England in deacon's orders. He had now to go to England for priest's orders, and he carried with him the addresses of the wardens and vestry of the United Congregations of Christ Church and St. Peter's to Bishop Osbaldeston, dated 8 June 1762, requesting him to license Sturgeon and Duché. The Rev. Richard Peters (for whom see Sturgeon to Waring, 15 May 1765, note 3, below), a for-

mer assistant minister of Christ Church, was chosen to officiate with Sturgeon during Duché's absence. Upon Duché's return in December 1762 Peters was elected rector and Duché and Sturgeon became co-ministers of the United Congregations. Dorr, *Historical Account of Christ Church*, pp. 120, 131–34; Fulham Papers, 7 : 318–19.

5. After Sturgeon had married Charlotte Maus and William Deadman without a license, it was discovered that Deadman was already married. Sturgeon had performed the ceremony because the Maus family and their friends persuaded him that Deadman might leave town if the marriage did not take place immediately, and because Deadman had sworn a solemn oath that he was not previously married. The incident did not prevent Sturgeon from becoming co-minister with Duché of the United Congregations, although the Rev. William Smith reported to the vestry on 4 June 1763 that Sturgeon "has not quite escaped his lordship's censure in the affair." Smith, *Life and Correspondence of Smith* 1 : 323; Fulham Papers, 7 : 316–17.

Rev. Alexander Stewart to Rev. John Waring

Bath N: Carolina August the 12th. 1762

Revd. Sir,

Your Favour of the 20th. of April,[1] Came safe to hand a few days ago, and I shou'd be unworthy of the Honour the Associates have done me in appointing me Superintendent of their Seminary here; Did I not, to the utmost of my Capacity & Station endeavour to promote this their truly pious & Christian Design. To this purpose I have already made known the Associates Intentions at the Church In Bath & the Several Chappels within my Parish, & with pleasure found most People approvers & many that promised to be encouragers of this publick Utility. But, there are many Difficulties which we Labour under in this Province, which other Provinces are Exempt from. For the towns of N: Carolina are all of them very Small, & Bath particularly has the fewest Inhabitants of any of them; so that the Number of Schollars to fill up a School cou'd by no means be had in any of the towns of this Province. Our towns likewise on the Seaboard, (where Negroes are most to be had,) are all of them built on very wide Rivers, often Impracticable to Cross; this Cutts off one half of the Country Children & added to the Expence of boarding Negroe Children, the Loss of their time, & the Prejudices of the Ignorant, are the Difficulties which at present Stand in the Way. However Sir I have advertised for a Mistress according to the Directions of the Associates, & if a Well recommended one can be had will make an Essay on their Plan, & open the School at Bath by Sending two Boyes & two Girls out of my own family, One of which Boyes has already been at school, & will send the rest of my young Negroes, as they grow up & can be spared.

The most probable Method to make the Associates Scheme take footing in this Country till we are somewhat better peopled, Wou'd be to divide their Bounty among three or four Schoolmasters; One in this town & the Others in the Country; & as some of these School Masters that I woud recommend have Wives who wou'd be capable of teaching the Girls to work, these Masters might have Charge of the Girls & the Single Men of the Boys. The Parishes here are vastly Extensive, mine till lately divided was above a hundred Miles long & 40 Miles wide,[2] so that my Attendance is not Confin'd to the Church at Bath, but equally divided between that & Several remote Chappels. In my Attendance therefore of my Parish I will take upon me to Visit the Several Schools at least twice in the Quarter & Catechize the remote Children on the Evenings of those days when I preach at the Chappels, & Every Easter & Christmass day will Oblige the Masters to have their Negro Schollars brought to the Church, to be publickly & alltogether Catechizd; & will take care to keep a publick Register of the ages, Baptisms, & times of Admission of the Different Children.

As this Societies Charity, (I presume) is not bound; I make bold to propose to them this Method of making it as extensive & Beneficial as the Nature of this thin Settel'd Country will admitt of: & will be always reddy with my best endeavours to forward their Laudable, publick Spirited, & truly Christian Intentions.

I have wrote to Governour Dobbs (Who is a Member of the Incorporated Society, to whom likewise I am a Missionary;) & inclosed to him a Coppy of your Letter & the Abstracts of the Associates, & make no doubt but he will be an Encourager of your Design, but he lives at too great a Distance to have any Influence on a School in this or any of the neighbouring Parishes.[3]

Mr. Palmer was gone for England before Your letters & Books arrived;[4] & as he is now in London & knows well the Situation of this Country, I Shall refer you to him for further Information & am Revd. Sir with my best wishes for the Society your most obedient & humble Servant

Alexr: Stewart

P.S. The School Masters that I woud recommend are such as already keep publick schools in this Parish for White Children, to whom it wou'd be great encouragement to have this Small Bounty from your Society.

ALS. Endorsed as answered in March 1763. This letter was read by the Associates at their meeting of 6 January 1763, at which time they "Agreed that

Mr. Waring do return the Thanks of the Associates to Mr. Stewart for his kind Letter & acquaint him that they refer it to him to make choice of the Method of promoting the Instruction of the Negroes, which to him may seem most likely to be attended with Success, only they desire he will not exceed twenty pounds Sterling annualy for teaching thirty Children & so in proportion for a greater or Less Number." Minutes, 1 : 182–83. Waring's reply, actually dated 7 April 1763, according to the acknowledgment in Stewart to Waring, 1 May 1764, below, has not been found.

1. Letter not found. The Associates agreed, on 4 March 1762, to send proposals for opening Negro schools for thirty children each, with a salary not exceeding £20 per annum, to Bath and five other colonial towns. Minutes, 1 : 173.

2. On 1 January 1761 Pitt County was created from the northern portion of Beaufort County. St. Thomas's Parish, which was coextensive with Beaufort County, was thus divided into the two parishes of St. Michael's, Pitt County, and St. Thomas's, Beaufort County. *N.C. State Recs.* 23 : 531–34.

3. Arthur Dobbs (1689–1765) was governor of North Carolina from 1754 until his death. *DAB*. Stewart's letter to Dobbs has not been found. Waring evidently sent Stewart copies of the most recent edition of *An Account of the Designs of the Associates of the Late Dr. Bray; with an Abstract of Their Proceedings.*

4. Robert Palmer was collector of the customs at Bath 1753–72 and a member of the Council 1764–75. He was also a justice of the peace for Beaufort County from 1760. Palmer fought against the Regulators at the Battle of Alamance in 1771. He remained a Loyalist during the Revolution and his considerable property was confiscated. *N.C. Col. Recs.* 5 : 36, 6 : 343, 1076–77, 9 : 323, 10 : 377, 11 : 155–56.

Rev. Charles Smith to Rev. John Waring

[Portsmouth, Virginia, 22 September 1762]

Sir

Your very courteous letter of April 8 relative, to the design of Doctor Bray's Associates I received September 1st. & the package of books, in July;[1] but as they came without a letter, I concluded they had been Sent, by the old Society, & distributed Some of them to poor white Children, & likeways to Negroes, of whom I had a good opinion, to learn & practise Christian dutys; But what remains of the books shall be kept for the purpose you imparted. By the printed Memoirs, of the Associates, & their Correspondents,[2] it appears, they intend to erect, their Schools for young Negroes in the principal Towns of North America, and of which, Norfolk in Virginia promises to become one & whereof I was Minister Almost twenty Years; But the Town & Country About it, being too learge for one Parish, It was divided about 18 moneths ago into three, And I am Now retired into one of them in the Country.[3] After being pretty well worn out, with fatigues of Mind & body, that I cannot be, of any great Service, to the pious design of the Associates, there being but few Negroes in my Neighbourhood, whom I will do my utmost, (as I always did) to instruct, & make them in love with christianity, whose rewards, they of all others, have most reason to aspire After, as finding little or none in their present State. I communicated your letter to the Revd. Mr. Rhonald, My Successor in the Town of Norfolk,[4] whom I Satisfyed, that your letter would have certainly been addressed to, had you known, that he was the Incumbent there. He expressed, (As he could not otherways do) a great esteem for the Associates, but begs Some time till he imparts the Scheme, to his Vestry, & parishioners before he begins the School, & upon your writing to him, it is not to be doubted, but he will undertake its Superintendency, to the Satisfaction of the Associates which is the Sincere prayer of, Reverend Sir, Your most obedient Servant & Brother

Chars. Smith

Portsmouth Parish
in Virginia, September 22d. 1762

P:S: Colo. Ludwells[5] favourable opinion of me, you may be sure was pleasing; which proceeded from his own candour & good Nature, & which all Virginians, are remarkable for, towards their Clergy, that it must be our own faults, if we are not, on a good footing here. Adieu

C: S:

ALS. This letter was read by the Associates at their meeting of 7 April 1763. Minutes, 1:188–89.

1. Waring's letter has not been found. The Associates agreed, on 4 March 1762, to send a proposal for opening a Negro school for thirty children at Norfolk with a salary not exceeding £20 per annum. Minutes, 1:173. A box of seventy-eight books was sent to Smith in April. See "Catalog of Books," p. 81.

2. Waring may have sent Smith a copy of the most recent edition of *An Account of the Designs of the Associates of the Late Dr. Bray; with an Abstract of Their Proceedings*.

3. On 1 May 1761 Elizabeth River Parish was divided into Elizabeth River, St. Bride's, and Portsmouth parishes. Smith became minister of Portsmouth Parish. Hening, *Statutes* 7:416–19.

4. For the Rev. Alexander Rhonnald see Biographical Appendix.

5. Philip Ludwell (1716–67), of Greenspring, James City County, was a burgess for Jamestown 1742–49 and served on the Council 1751–67. Ludwell removed to England some years before his death; he was there in

June 1761, when he donated a guinea to the Associates. Minutes, 1 : 154; *Executive Journals of the Council* 5 : 347, 6 : 153; Greene, *Quest for Power*, p. 471; *VMHB* 19 (1911): 288–89.

Rev. Alexander Rhonnald to Rev. John Waring

Virginia, Norfolk Borough, September 27th. 1762

Revd. Sir

On the 21st. of this current the Revd. Mr. Charles Smith my Predecessor waited on me at my School, where he produced a Letter from You, intending a School for Negroes in Norfolk. I was agreeably surprized at it, but when I had read your Letter, I was likewise heartily sorry that in the Method & manner proposed it will not answer here for many reasons, As

1st. I find that a School Mistress is rather desired than a Master, for which reason it is Obvious, that more Girls are to be benefited than Boys, as they are to be educated in Affairs more proper for that Sex. Which thing will answer exactly the Ladies of this place, who have many Such to send, & will hinder others, So that this Charity must consequently be wrong applied.

2dly. If a Mistress must be had, qualified with such Accomplishments, but especially with the Fear of GOD, the only Principle Qualification, Such a One may be found Superannuated, who might instruct in some Measure about Five or Six, but there is not that Woman in this County Young or Old who could manage Thirty Negro Children, at one & the same Time, however Worthy or Wicked She may be, which I can attest by Experience, who have had but a few under my Care, within these last Twenty Years of my Life.

3dly. Supposing that such a Mistress could be found in this or any other Government with all due Accomplishments, the Salary, if £20, is not much above half the Trouble, or what is paid here for Whites, which is a little more respected Employment as there are 24/ Sterl. paid for each, & proportionably more according as Girls are taught in the Branches of Work, or Boys at Arithmetic, &c., So that the Salary must be equal, at least, with what is given for White Children, otherwise, No Woman, however gracious, would undertake that Charge. I myself would be willing to add £5 of this Currency to the £20 Sterl., which will make it exactly £30 a Year, but I can perceive none willing under £50 & a House found for that purpose which will be about Ten pounds more, So that this must be a great Bar in this pious Proposal.

4. If these Difficulties could be happily Surmounted, There is

one Obstacle which I can plainly foresee, would attend it, And that would be, That the Gentlemen & their Ladies would fill up the Number with their Negroes first, in spite of all Opposition here, otherwise endeavour by Insinuations either to ruin a School in the place, or by Misrepresentations to inform the honourable Society of the Minister of the parish who would be only for promoting all he could the pious & worthy Dr. Bray's Intentions, & that there was no Need for Such a School here, So that at last, finding nothing in his Favour, it would drop of Course, which would exactly be the Case with Me. So that there is a Necessity of adding more Trustees to that School, & in my humble Opinion, appointing Mr. Commissary[1] the chief Trustee, to whom the Minister of this parish is to answer, & account from limited Time to Time, concerning the Number of Scholars, whose they are, & what progress they make, that he may place or remove any as he Sees most convenient, but not to depend on the Minister of the parish as chief Visitor only, as it would occasion him the Ill will of most of his parish, if he insisted on a charity School for poor Negroes, & not for the Great & powerful of this place.

5thly. There are many poor Free Negroes & Mulattoes in this Borough & Parish, who could not be the better of this School, by reason of the Gentlemen insisting that their small Negroes Boys, whom they perhaps design for Domesticks or Livery Men, shall be preferred before them, & So of the Girls who are to be brought up in Needlework or Knitting, fitting them for the House, when at the same time, I can plainly discern, That these Girls will be more instructed for the latter Employment, than in that which may conduce to the Saving of the Soul, if well applied, & for that reason I am not a proper Person to be chief Manager of that School here, because

6thly. If I could act without Offence, I would go through the Borough & parish among Such free Negroes, or poor people who cannot afford to teach them themselves, & if I could find any Young hopeful Lad or Young Woman of that Colour, who, after good Education at School, would open or assist Such a School, I would not only place but promote them all that lay in my power, by boarding some of them, or giving them what I thought might the more encourage them, altho' I am poor & just entring on the World in an Age when many are above Want, having a large Family of Children & Servants in my house, & other Necessities abounding which I would never mention, had I not thought that the Society might conceive that I trifled with them & truckled to Interest here. I have no Ends of my own to Serve, being above all things willing to serve my Master in whose Work I am Now more particularly engaged, but still it is my Endeavour to follow peace with All Men, & to cut off Occasion from them who Seek Occasion.[2]

I observed in the end of Mr. Smith's Letter, a Small List of Books, Sent for that purpose, which he says, he hath distributed almost to such Whites as he pleased, but that he has a few remaining on his hands that he has not yet given away. He might have sent them to my house not being above 30 yards from his house, when he had them, as he does not design to bring the People about his Ears, but he was careful enough not to mention any thing of that kind till he moved out of this place (about 6 Weeks ago) from his dwelling House to his Glebe in Portsmouth parish.

I also assure the honourable Society That if the Great Ones here have the sole property & privilege of the School, no Master nor Mistress will undertake it, for Negro Children in general are very dull & Stupid, & they will always be for telling Tales to the prejudice of the Teacher, to which, I have all along experienced, their Masters or Mistresses will most greedily listen, & then Such Persons are ruin'd for ever from that time, if they stay any longer there, So that in Seven Years space, there possibly may be a Change of a Dozen of Teachers, unless Some barefaced Convict, an old undaunted Soldier, or an impudent Sailor who are all void of Shame or Fear, should happen to have the Charge. Three Sorts of people, I should always be careful not to encourage, tho' I dare to affirm, None could match the People better, but GOD forbid that I should be the Witness of either, as I want Youth instructed only by the Good & praise Worthy, where they may be found.

And now if I may be allowed to add my own Sentiments to the end of this long Epistle, I would not undertake such a Charge, altho' I had nothing else to support Me, for any Consideration of Money, neither, as I have before said, should I be willing to be the chief Trustee of the School, lest I might find it worse than it was, when I had a Charity School in a neighbouring County, where the Gentlemen's Children were many Years educated, & the Objects of Charity disdained, till I was oblig'd to leave the School, & lodge a Complaint in the Assembly, which has prevented the Grandees to reign longer.[3] But from that time, they use Me with the most invidious Terms of Ill nature for my pains, & because I baptise more Negroes than other Brethren here & instruct them, from the Pulpit, out of the common road, & encourage the Good among them to come to the Communion, after a due Sense of the matter, I am vilified & branded by such as a Negro Parson, for which reason & many more might be offered, I do not chuse to throw my Self out of the respect of my Parish altogether for upholding a Thing where I have none to stand by Me, but shall most readily do it, if supported by the honourable Society & the Worthy Revd. Mr. Commissary Robinson.

All I have now to add, is, That considering my Years, & the sorry Circumstance of my Family, the honourable Society will be pleased to pity my Case, who means nothing but the Good & Spiritual Advantage of those poor unhappy illiterate Creatures. And if the honourable Society will insist on Me to be an Inspector, to regulate the School, they would be good enough to find out a proper Expedient to strengthen my hands, that with the Strength of GOD, I may be Instrumental in their eternal Happiness, which is the earnest prayer & hearty Desire of Revd. Sir Your unknown humble Servant

Alexander Rhonnald
Minster of Eliza. River parish Norfolk County

P.S. If such a School was to be settled at Hampton in Eliza. City County about 20 Miles from this place, it might do very well, as I understand that the Revd. Mr. Thos. Warrington is a Member of the honble. Society,[4] & so would have no Occasion of being in pain of disobliging any of his Grandees.

ALS. Addressed: "To the Reverend John Waring, To be forwarded by the Favour of the Revd. Dr. Saml. Nichols Minister of the Temple, London." Endorsed: "This I thought proper to take no Notice of. H. [Owen?]." This letter was read by the Associates at their meeting of 7 April 1763, at which time they "Agreed that the Design of having a Negroe School at Norfolk be laid aside for the present." Minutes, 1 : 189.

    1. The commissary of the bishop of London in Virginia at the time was the Rev. William Robinson (1717–68), who was educated at Oriel College, Oxford (A.B. 1740). He was ordained in 1743 and received the King's Bounty for Virginia in 1746. Robinson served as minister of Stratton-Major Parish, King and Queen County, 1744–68 and as commissary from 1761 until his death. Foster, *Alumni Oxonienses*; Weis, *Colonial Clergy Va., N.C., S.C.*, p. 43.

    2. Occasion: opportunity of attacking, of fault-finding, or of giving or taking offence. *OED*.

    3. Rhonnald encountered the "Grandees" when he was master of Eaton's Charity School in Elizabeth City County. In September 1758 a petition of the inhabitants of the county, in behalf of the poor of the county, was presented to the House of Burgesses. The petition complained of illegal proceedings of the trustees of the school. It was considered by the committee on propositions and grievances, and "An Act for Better Regulating Eaton's Charity-School" became law on 14 April 1759. The act read in part: "And whereas the said foundation hath been abused, by admitting a great number of children into the said school, whose parents are well able to pay for their education: For remedy whereof, *Be it enacted, by the authority aforesaid,* That no person shall enjoy the benefit of the said charity-school without consent of the master, for the time being, except such poor children as the said trustees and governors, and their successors, or the greater part of them, shall from time to

time declare to be the proper objects of the pious founder's charity" (Hening, *Statutes* 7:317–20). *JHB, 1758–1761*, pp. 18, 62, 73, 128.

4. The Rev. Thomas Warrington (d. 1770) was ordained a priest and licensed for Virginia in September 1747, and he received the King's Bounty the following month. He was minister of Charles Parish, York County, 1749–56 and minister of Elizabeth City Parish, Elizabeth City County, 1756–70. Warrington, who was a trustee of Eaton's Charity School in 1760, was active in opposition to the Two-Penny Acts, and he unsuccessfully brought suit against the vestry of his parish in 1763 for salary withheld under the Two-Penny Act of 1758. He does not seem to have been a member of the S.P.G., nor was he an Associate. Weis, *Colonial Clergy Va., N.C., S.C.*, p. 53; *VMHB* 17 (1909–10): 322; Rhys Isaac, "Religion and Authority: Problems of the Anglican Establishment in Virginia in the Era of the Great Awakening and the Parsons' Cause," *WMQ*, 3 ser. 30 (1973): 19, 20; Fulham Papers, 42:16, 33.

Rev. William Yates and Robert Carter Nicholas to [Rev. John Waring]

Virginia Williamsburg 30th. September 1762

Sir,

Agreeable to your Request, we send you inclosed a List of the Negro Children now at the School under our Direction in this City, with an Account of their Ages as nearly as they can be judged of; but it is not in our Power to determine exactly. The Dates of their Admission into the School are various, some of them having been there ever since it was first opened & others admited just as Vacancies have happened. The Mistress has not been so exact as to keep any Account of the Times of their Entrance, so that it is impossible for us to give the desired Satisfaction in this Point. You may from hence easily judge how difficult it must be for us to inform you particularly of the Progress each Child has made. We can only say in general that at a late Visitation of the School we were pretty much pleased with the Scholars' Performances, as they rather exceeded our Expectations. The Children, we believe, have all been regularly baptized; indeed we think it is a pretty general Practice all over Virginia for Negro Parents to have their Children christened, where they live tolerably convenient to the Church or Minister, & some Times a great Number of Adults are baptized together in different Parts of the Country. We would not have you think, from what was wrote to you last Fall, that we had the least Inclination to discourage so good & pious an Institution; we were indeed & still are apprised of many Difficulties, which we shall have to struggle with, & were willing to prepare you for a Disappointment, in Case the Undertaking should not answer your Expectations. From the small View we have had of the Associates' extensive Charity, we flatter ourselves that we see the Situation of our poor Slaves, with Respect to their spiritual Concerns, with the same piteous Eyes that they do, & should think ourselves extremely fortunate if any Endeavours of ours could contribute towards their Happiness. You no Doubt are already apprised that the Slaves in this & the neighbouring Colonies are the chief Instruments of Labour & we fear that they are treated by too many of their Owners as so many Beasts of Burthen, so little do they consider them as entitled to any of the Privileges of human Nature; & indeed many Owners of Slaves, 'tho they may view them in a different Light & treat them with a great Degree of Tenderness, concern themselves very little or not at all with their Morals, much less do they trouble themselves with their religious Concerns, so far from it, that we don't think ourselves the least uncharitable in saying that we fear the Negroes are often corrupted & rendered more abandoned by the ill Examples that are set them by many white People in the Country & no inconsiderable Number of these themselves Masters of Slaves. This Observation may be justified by a Comparison of new Negroes when they are first imported with those who have resided amongst us for some Years; for 'tho' the former, no Doubt, bring with them vicious Inclinations & a Number of ill Customs, yet we may venture to say that they contract new Vices, which they were Strangers to in their native Country. From this cursory View of the Situation of our Slaves, you may easily judge how extremely difficult it would be, if not morally impossible, to work any Thing like a thorough Reformation amongst them, unless some of their Masters & the Generality of white People were first reformed, we had almost said new moulded. We would not have it infered from hence that we intend any particular pointed Reflections upon the People of this Country; on the contrary we believe them as good as their Neighbours & think they are much of the same Complexion as the Inhabitants of other Countries. And 'tho' we almost despair of an entire Reformation, yet we have our Hopes that a Scheme like yours properly conducted, if it could meet with due Encouragement, might have a good Effect. We find that many People in this City, upon the first opening of your School, were well enough inclined towards it &, if the Fund allotted was sufficient, we believe that double the Number of Scholars might easily be procured; but at the same Time we fear that many People who have sent or would send their little Negroes to School, would not do it upon the Principles which they ought; we mean purely with a View to have them instructed in the Principles of Religion, & enabled to instruct their Fellow Slaves at Home. Some People we fear send their Children more to keep them out of Mischief, others to improve them in Hopes by their being made a little more sensible, that they may be more handy & useful in their Families; We form this Opinion from observing that several, who put their Negroes to School, have taken them Home again so soon as they began to read, but before they had received any real Benefit or it could be supposed that they were made acquainted with the Principles of Christianity. This is one great Impediment which we are apprehensive will obstruct the Success of our Endeavours. We shall strive to guard against it, 'tho' 'twill be with great Difficulty that we shall be able to accomplish our Purpose. Few People have more Negroes than they can employ, & 'tho', when they are very young & useless, they may be willing to send them to School, yet when they grow up a little & become able to tend their Owners Children or do any other little Offices in their Families, they chuse & will take them Home. Another Difficulty which arises on the Part of the Owners is that an Opinion prevails amongst many of them, that it might be dangerous & impolitick to enlarge the Understandings of the Negroes, as they would probably by this Means become more impatient of their Slavery & at some future Day be more likely to rebel; they urge farther from Experience, that it is generally observable that the most sensible of our Slaves are the most wicked & ungovernable; these Observations, we think, are illy founded when used as Objections to your Scheme, which is by no Means calculated to instruct the Slaves in dangerous Principles, but on the contrary has a probable & direct Tendency to reform their Manners; & by making them good Christians they would necessarily become better Servants. We shall not fail endeavouring to remove Scruples of this & every other Sort, but finding they have taken deep Root in many Minds, we are apprehensive of great Difficulties in overcoming them. There is still one greater Discouragement which we fear we shall labour under. 'Tho' the Owners of the Negro Children should chearfully close with our Proposals & submit them entirely to our Government; 'tho the Mistress of the School should be ever so diligent in her Duty, & 'tho the Scholars should make as great a Progress as could be wished, yet we fear that, notwithstanding all our Endeavours to prevent it, any good Impressions which may be made on the Children's Minds at School will be easily effaced by their mixing with other Slaves, who are mostly abandoned to every Kind of Wickedness. If evil Communications have a general Tendency to corrupt good Manners, the Observation is never more likely to be verified than in Instances of this Sort, where the very Parents of the Children will probably much oftner, from their Intimacy, set them bad Examples than any others. Notwithstanding these & many other Difficulties, which the narrow Limits of a Letter will not permit us to particularize, stare us fully in the Face, we are resolved not to be discouraged; but hope, by the Blessing of God upon your Charity & our Endeavours, that the Undertaking will greatly prosper. The late Reverend Mr. Dawson & Mr. Hunter, we believe, had it in their Intention to form Rules for the better Government of the School but were prevented by Death; we have hitherto contented ourselves with permiting the Mistress to carry on the School in the Way it was begun; but, being sensible that Nothing of the Sort can be properly conducted without certain uniform Regulations, by which all Parties concerned may know how to govern themselves, we have drawn up such a Set of Rules as appear to us properly adapted & send you a Copy of them inclosed for your & the rest of the Associates' Approbation & should be glad to know your Sentiments; we shall be willing to add or diminish any Thing as you may advise. We probably shall have Occasion for a few Testaments Psalters & spelling Books & perhaps a Number of Mr. Bacon's Sermons, recommending the Instruction of Negroes in the Christian Faith, properly dispersed over the Country might have a good Influence. We would not put you to the Expence of any other Books at present. We will not conclude without offering our best Respects to you & the rest of the worthy Associates; Believe us, Sir, we cannot enough admire a Set of Gentlemen, who at the same Time that they are employed in exercising every Act of Benevolence at Home, have so far enlarged their Charity as to extend it to the most distant Colonies. We are, Sir, with the greatest Esteem Your most obedient humble Servants

William Yates
Ro. C. Nicholas

LS. Another copy of this letter, in the same collection, is endorsed as read 3 March 1763, at which time the Associates

> Agreed That the Sincere & hearty Thanks of the Associates be returned to the Revd. Mr. Yates & Mr. Nicholas for their full and very Satisfactory Account of the present State of the Negroe School, & for their generous Assurances that notwithstanding the manifold Difficulties & Discouragements they have to contend with, They are resolved to persevere in the Prosecution of this pious & charitable Undertaking.
>
> Agreed That hearty Thanks be returned also for their Care in drawing up Rules & Regulations for the Better Government of the School & that They be made acquainted that the Associates do entirely approve thereof as Judiciously calculated to answer the Good End proposed.
>
> Agreed that 25 Spelling Books 25 Psalters 20 Testaments & 25 Bacons Sermons be Sent for the Use of the Negroe School at Williamsburgh. (Minutes, 1:186–88)

Waring's reply has not been found. For the books actually sent see "Catalog of Books," p. 96.

Enclosure
List of Negro Children

[Williamsburg, 30 September 1762]

A List of Negro Children at the School established by the Associates of the late Reverend Doctor Bray in the City of Williamsburg, Mrs. Anne Wager, School Mistress.

Names of the Children	their Ages as nearly as can be judged of	Owners Names
1 John	8 Years	Mrs. Davenport
2 Anne	6	Ditto
3 Dick	3	Mr. George Davenport
4 London	7	Mrs. Campbell
5 Aggy	6	Ditto
6 Shropshire	6	Ditto
7 Aberdeen	5	Mr. Alexr. Craig
8 Mary	7	Mr. Thomas Everard
9 Harry	5	Ditto
10 George	8	Mr. Gilmer
11 Bristol	7	Ditto
12 Mary Anne	7	a free Negro
13 Aggy	7	Peyton Randolph Esqr.
14 Roger	7	Ditto
15 Mary	8	Mr. Thomas Hornsby
16 Rippon	3	Mr. Anthony Hay
17 Robert	6	John Randolph Esqr.
18 Lucy	5	Ditto
19 Elizabeth	10	Mrs. Dawson
20 George	6	Dr. James Carter
21 Locust	8	Mrs. Armistead
22 Sarah	7	Mrs. Page
23 Hannah	7	Ro: C: Nicholas
24 Mary Jones		a free Negro
25 John	7	John Blair Esqr.
26 Jane	9	Ditto
27 Doll	7	Ditto
28 Elisha Jones		free
29 John	3	Mr. Hugh Orr
30 Phoebe	3	Mr. Wm. Trebell

Williamsburgh 30th.   September 1762

D. Another copy was enclosed with the other copy of the covering letter.

Enclosure
Regulations

The Associates of the late Reverend Doctor Bray, residing in England, having established Schools in several of the Northern Colonies for the Education of Negroes in the Principles of the Christian Religion, teaching them to read & at the same Time rendering the Females more useful to their Owners by instructing them in sewing knitting &c; encouraged by the Success of these their pious Endeavours & being sollicitous to make this Kind of Charity as extensive as possible, they some Time ago came to a Resolution of establishing a School in the City of Williamsburg for the same Purpose & have thought fit to recommend it to the immediate Care & Government of the Reverend Mr. William Yates & Mr. Robert Carter Nicholas; who have chearfully undertaken the Trust reposed in them & hope that all good Christians will cooperate with them in their Endeavours to promote the Success of so laudable & pious an Institution.

The Associates having engaged in so many Works of this Kind, which will require a very considerable Sum of Money to defray the Expence of, have limited the Number of Scholars to thirty, but as there may be many more Negro Children in this City, equally objects of such a Charity, The Trustees will thankfully accept of any Contributions, which may be offered, towards augmenting the Number & thereby rendering the Scheme more generally beneficial. If the Scholars should increase, so as to make it necessary, they propose to employ another Mistress; And, for the Satisfaction of their Benefactors, they will be at all Times ready to give an Account of their Proceedings.

The Trustees, for the better Government of the School & to render it more truly beneficial, have thought fit to establish certain Regulations, relating as well to the Owners of Slaves as to the Teacher or Mistress, which they are resolved to have strictly observed & put in Execution, unless they should at any Time hereafter be induced by good Reasons to alter or relax them.

With Respect to the Owners

The School being at present full with the Number of Scholars proposed to be educated at the Expence of the Associates, such Masters or Mistresses, who may incline hereafter to send their Negro Children to the School, are desired to signify the same to the Trustees as they would choose hereafter that all Vacancies should be filled up by an equal Number from each Family as near as may be.

As it will [be] needless & by no Means answer the Design of the

Institution for the Children to be put to School & taken away in a short Time before they have received any real Benefit from it, Every Owner, before a Negro Child is admitted into the School, must consent that such Child shall continue there for the Space of three Years at least, if the School should be so long continued.

A decent Appearance of the Scholars, especially when they go to Church, being very likely to make a favourable Impression, All Owners of Children sent to this School must take Care that they be properly cloathed & kept in a cleanly Manner; & if it should be agreeable, the Trustees would propose that the Children should wear one uniform Dress, by which they might be distinguished & it is conceived that this Method would be attended with very little additional Expence.

The Owners must send their Negro Children regularly, & constantly at the Hours of Schooling; must comply with all Orders relating to them & freely submit them to be chastized for their Faults without quarrelling or coming to School on such Occasions; must by no Means encourage or wink at the Children's Faults nor discourage the Teacher in the Performance of her Duty; But if there be any just Grounds of Complaint, they must lay them before the Trustees & Acquiesce in their Determination; the Trustees engaging on their Part to act with the strictest Justice & Impartiality & that they will, to the utmost of their Power, endeavour to redress every just Grievance.

It is not doubted but that the Owners themselves will give the Children, when at Home, good Examples of a sober & religious Behaviour, but they must moreover take Care, as much as in them lies, that they are not corrupted by the Wickedness & ill Examples of their Servants & other Slaves, must frequently catechize the Children at Home & second the Endeavours of the Teacher by inculcating in them the most useful & salutary Principles of Christianity.

Rules to be observed by the Tutoress or Mistress,
(who is preferred to a Master, as the Scholars
will consist of Children of both Sexes.)

She shall take no Scholars but what are approved of by the Trustees & She shall attend the School at seven O Clock in the Winter half Year & at six in the Summer half Year in the Morning & keep her Scholars diligently to their Business during the Hours of schooling, suffering none to be absent at any Time, but when they are sick or have some other reasonable Excuse.

2. She shall teach her Scholars the true Spelling of Words, make them mind their Stops & endeavour to bring them to pronounce & read distinctly.

3. She shall make it her principal Care to teach them to read the Bible, to instruct them in the Principles of the Christian Religion according to the Doctrine of the Church of England, shall explain the Church Catechism to them by some good Exposition, which, together with the Catechism, they shall publicly repeat in Church, or elsewhere, so often as the Trustees shall require & shall be frequently examined in School as to their Improvements of every Sort.

4. She shall teach them those Doctrines & Principles of Religion, which are in their Nature most useful in the Course of private Life, especially such as concern Faith & good Manners.

5. She shall conduct them from her School House, where they are all to be first assembled, in a decent & orderly Manner to Church, so often as divine Service is there performed & before it begins, & instruct & oblige them to behave in a proper Manner, kneeling or standing as the Rubrick directs, & to join in the public Service with & regularly to repeat after the Minister in all Places where the People are so directed & in such a Manner as not to disturb the rest of the Congregation. She shall take Care that the Scholars, so soon as they are able to use them, do carry their Bibles & Prayer Books to Church with them, &, that they may be prevented from spending the Lord's Day profanely or idly, she shall give her Scholars some Task out of the most useful Parts of Scripture, to be learnt on each Lord's Day, according to their Capacities, & shall require a strict Performance of it every Monday Morning.

6. She shall use proper Prayers in her School every Morning & Evening & teach the Scholars to do the same at Home, devoutly on their Knees, & also teach them to say Grace before & after their Victuals, explaining to them the Design & Meaning of it.

7. She shall take particular Care of the Manners & Behaviour of her Scholars & by all proper Methods discourage Idleness & suppress the Beginnings of Vice, such as lying, cursing, swearing, profaning the Lord's Day, obscene Discourse, stealing &c., putting them often in Mind & obliging them to get by Heart such Parts of the Holy Scriptures, where these Things are forbid & where Christians are commanded to be faithful & obedient to their Masters, to be diligent in their Business, & quiet & peaceable to all Men.

8. She shall teach her female Scholars knitting sewing & such other Things as may be useful to their Owners & she shall be particularly watchful that her Scholars, between the School Hours, do not commit any Irregularities nor fall into any indecent Diversions.

Lastly. She shall take Care that her Scholars keep themselves clean & neat in their Cloaths & that they in all Things set a good Example to other Negroes.

D. Another copy was enclosed with the other copy of the covering letter. A draft is in the Bray MSS., McGregor Collection, U.Va.

Rev. Samuel Auchmuty to Rev. John Waring

New York October 18th. 1762

Revd. Sir

The fifth of last April, I had the pleasure of writing to you, which Letter I hope you received.[1] I have not been favoured with a Line in answer to it.

The Mistress of the School having applied for her half years Salary, due the 22th. of last month, I have paid her, and now draw for it in favor of Richard Nicholls Esqr. or Order.

You will please to present my Compliments to the Associates, and inform them, that their School, comitted to my Care is in a very flourishing Condition. The Mistress is very diligent & careful, and the Children improve, in their sewing, knitting, reading, and learning their Prayers, Catechise &c. as fast as can be expected. Since my last Seven have left the School, & seven new ones have been received: But for the future I intend to insist upon it, that none are admitted until I am assured by their Masters [or] Mistresses, that they shall continue in the School, till [they] are perfectly instructed, in the principles of our most holy Religion; which, was not the Case with some that have left it, being wanted to tend Children &c. The whole little Flock constantly attend divine service on the Lords Day, and some of the bigest among them attend also on prayer Days. Between the services on Sunday, I examine & catechise them all, & enjoy great pleasure, and satisfaction, in hearing them perform their several Tasks. Most of them are perfect in their Prayers, & Catechise: I purpose therefore this Winter, begining Lewis's proof Catechism with some of them, not doubting but that they will with ease learn it. I have also prevail'd upon the Master of our Charity School to instruct them, and the black Adults, in Psalmody, in which they will soon become Proficients.[2] Thus Sir, I endeavor all in my power, that the Associates intentions may be fully answered, and their generous Charity well bestowed; and, I have the satisfaction, & pleasure to think, that these ends are fully answered, & that the School committed to my Care is in as flourishing a Condition as the most sanguine Friend to it, could expect for the time. Both Duty, and Inclination, will oblige me to continue my Care of it, and to do every thing in my power to promote the Interest and increase of our blessed Redeemers Kingdom.

I flatter myself the above Account of the School will be agreeable to the worthy Associates, and to you; which will afford me great pleasure. Please to accept of my sincere prayers for your Health, and happiness, and believe me to be, Your Obliged Friend & Brother

Samuel Auchmuty

P.S. My Brethren here desire their Compliments to you & the Associates.

ALS. Endorsed as answered March 1763. The bracketed words are supplied from the text of this letter as quoted in the Minute Book, the manuscript being torn. This letter was read by the Associates at their meeting of 3 February 1763, at which time they "Agreed that Mr. Waring be desired to return the hearty Thanks of the Associates to the Revd. Mr. Auchmuty for his very Satisfactory Account of the Negroe School, & for the kind Assurances he gives of continuing his Care of the School." Minutes, 1:184–85. Waring's reply has not been found.

1. Auchmuty's last letter to Waring was actually dated 18 May 1762, above.
2. Joseph Hildreth (d. 1777) was S.P.G. schoolmaster in New York City from 1743 until the Revolution. He was appointed catechist to the Negroes in 1770. Hildreth was also clerk of Trinity Church from 1744 until his death. S.P.G. Journals, 18:431–32 (meeting of 19 October 1770); William Webb Kemp, *The Support of Schools in Colonial New York by the Society for the Propagation of the Gospel in Foreign Parts* (New York, 1913), pp. 102, 115.

Rev. Marmaduke Browne to Rev. John Waring

[Newport, 29 November 1762]

Revd. Sir.

Your Letters dated February 25th. & June 1st. came to hand much about the same time in October last.[1] This did not surprise me, as I am well acquainted with the Obstructions that attend the Conveyance of Letters in the course of a War: yet I must confess it has given me some uneasiness, lest you should apprehend any neglect or remissness on my Part, from their remaining unanswered. Immediately upon the Receipt of them, I sat about the good work therein recommended to me. I endeavoured to fix upon a Person to undertake the Charge of the School upon the most frugal Terms, but after making all imaginable Enquiry, was obliged to make choice of the Person with whom Mr. Pollen had partly agreed before his Departure, & upon the same Terms he had offered it to her, that is, twenty Pounds per Annum. She is a sober Well disposed Woman, sufficiently qualified for the business she undertakes, And will I hope acquit Herself in a manner answerable to the Pious & Charitable Views of the worthy Associates.[2]

The unaccountable Prejudice, entertained by many in the Plantations, that Learning & Instruction has only a tendency to render Negroes greater Rogues than they otherwise would be, is not without its Adherents in this Place; which I am sorry to inform you renders it somewhat difficult to collect, even the small Number of which the School is to consist; however, I am not without a Prospect of shortly effecting it, as I have already admitted to the Number of twenty one. The short Time the School has been opened does not allow of any considerable progress being made by the Scholars; but this I can say, that the Instructions of the Associates are strictly adhered to, which do even now begin to discover some good Effects in the manners & Behavior of the Children. You may depend upon my readiness to comply with every thing requested of me by the Associates, And I do really consider it as a happy Circumstance, that by their Means I may become more useful in enlightening the poor Negroes than I otherwise could be. That their pious Endeavours to promote Gods Glory, & the happiness of his Creatures, may be attended with Success, shall be the Endeavour, as it is the earnest desire, of Revd. Sir your most humble Servant & Brother.

Marmaduke Browne

Newport Rhode Island
November 29th. 1762.

P.S. The Books which Mr. Pollen left with the Church Warden I have received, & have distributed such as were necessary.

ALS. This letter was read by the Associates at their meeting of 12 May 1763. Minutes, 1 : 191.

    1. Letters not found.
    2. The mistress of the school was Mary (Howland) Brett (c. 1715–1800), wife of Dr. John Brett. She conducted the school in her house on High Street. Mason, *Annals of Trinity Church*, p. 225.

Rev. Jonathan Boucher to Rev. John Waring

King George County, Rappahannock River Virginia,
December the 31st. 1762.

Revd. Sir

I wrote to You in October last, by Way of Liverpool: this comes by a Vessel bound to Glasgow. In that Letter I requested You to return my sincerest Thanks to the Associates of Dr. Bray, for the obliging Present which They have made to this Parish.[1] The Box was safe in Virginia long before I was: & I hope Every Thing was safe in it that You had pack'd up, tho' I receiv'd no Letter, nor Invoice of Contents along with it.

I spoke so largely before of the many Causes which I apprehended would prevent my Hopes of instituting a Negro School in this Parish, that it must be superfluous to repeat Them. I have therefore only to request your Opinion of Them, whether with these Difficulties in my Way it can be possible for Me to erect a School that may in any Degree answer the Designs & the Expectations of the Founders. But possibly my Letter may have miscarried, & You may still be ignorant of the Acceptance your Proposals are likely to meet with in This Neighbourhood.

Very Early after my Arrival, I mention'd the Scheme You had recommended to Me to the principal Inhabitants of my Parish; who in general started such a Train of Objections, which if They did not totally discourage my Hopes, shew'd Me however how reluctantly They would come into any Measures for the forwarding of so desirable a Work.

I was too much a Stranger amongst Them, & consequently had too little Influence with Them, at this Time to press it too eagerly: & there also appear'd to Me a more immediate Necessity for endeavouring to establish amongst Them some other, perhaps more essential, Reformations. I am griev'd to be oblig'd to make such Reports to You, but it is a melancholy Truth that several Whites, of respectable Characters, think Themselves at Liberty to live totally negligent of either of the Sacraments. I have had several white Adults to baptize, alas! some of Them seem to think it rather a Matter of Form than of Important Consequence. I wish & shall labour to set Them right, & may then hope that any Endeavours to civilize their unhappy Servants will be more successful.

I also told You before how much at a Loss I was to pitch upon a Situation for a School where it could be at all convenient to assemble a competent Number of Children. Except in a few little Towns, the People in Virginia Generally live dispers'd in scatter'd Plantations. And I know not a Place in my Parish where I could fix a Mistress within 5 or 6 Miles of 30 or even 20 Children of a proper Age to be admitted. If my Neighbours wou'd heartily concur in the Scheme (and I will pray & hope that They some Time may) many of these Difficulties could be obviated. Till Then, it must be improper for Me to sollicit Contributions from your Society, who, I trust, will find Means more usefully to dispose of those Charities so commendably delegated to Them. Believe Me, I am distress'd to find myself oblig'd to resign that share which I flatter Myself I should have had in those Christian Services You are Engag'd in: Let Me hope, from the Partiality You have already shewn Me, that You will continue to look upon Me as a Well-Wisher to your Designs, that You will continue to direct Me, & if possible, still make Me subservient to the pious Purposes of your Institution.

Could I have succeeded in erecting the School I had in View, I was under Obligation to contribute £5 annually: I am concern'd that it is not in my Power to leave to You the Disposal of this stipulated Sum, but I have no Money in England & my Circumstances here will not allow Me to make any Remittances hence. I have Hopes that I may ere long be remov'd to a better Situation for This as well as other Purposes: if You would be so obliging as to continue a Correspondence with Me, I would still hope that in some Part of my Life I may be enabled to lend a helping Hand to This so desirable a Work.

Your Books will be of great Service to Me in some public Catechetical Lectures which I purpose soon to commence. I have baptiz'd upwards of 100 Negro Children, & betwixt 30 & 40 Adults in less than 6 months that I have been here. May God continue to grant a Blessing on all your Endeavours, & make all of You greatly Instrumental to the Advancement of his Glory. These are the constant Prayers, of yours and the Associates most humble Servant

Jonan. Boucher.

ALS. This letter was read by the Associates at their meeting of 7 April 1763. Minutes, 1 : 189.

1. Boucher's letter has not been found. At the meeting of 1 April 1762 Waring reported to the Associates that Boucher "had assured him that on his Return to Virginia he wou'd use his best Endeavours to instruct the Negroes in his Parish in the Principles of Religion, & requested the Associates to favour him with a few Books to found a Parochial Library in his Parish." Minutes, 1 : 174. The Associates agreed and later that month shipped a box of fifty-seven books to Boucher. See "Catalog of Books," p. 81. A memorandum among the Associates' papers indicating shipping instructions reads: "To the Revd. Mr. Boucher to be left with Mr. John Orr Merchant at Leeds, Rappahannock River, Virga. Above this To Captn. Wm. Fox of the Carlyle at East Lane."

Rev. Daniel Earl to Rev. John Waring

No. Carolina Edenton 1st. March 1763

Sir,

Your favour of June 1st.[1] I some time ago Received, to which I should have Wrote an Answer before now, only waited to See if my

Persuasions Seconded by your very Cogent and Affecting Letter, could Remove the Objections the Inhabitants of this Town made to your Society's pious and laudable Institution, to all which, I am sorry to Acquaint you, they Give a deaf Ear; so that I have no Expectation of having it established here.

I have repeatedly Wrote to the Society for propagating the Gospel concerning a School for the Education of white Children, but never was favoured with their Sentiments upon it, which I impute to my Letters being miscarried, thro the Casualties of war. I have not as yet Received the Books sent to Mr. Child, but when they come to hand shall Take Care of them, untill I am favoured with your Orders concerning the Disposal of them. I am Sir, The Society's, and your most Obedient and Humble Servant

Danl. Earl

ALS.

1. Letter not found. See Earl to Waring, 3 October 1761, bibliographic note, above.

Rev. Samuel Auchmuty to Rev. John Waring

New York April 19th. 1763.

Revd. Sir

At the request of the Mistress of the Negro School in this City, I now draw upon you for half a Years Salary due to her the 22th. of last month.

You will please to present my best respects to the worthy Associates, & acquaint them, that their School intrusted to my Care continues full, & that the Mistress steadily pursues her Duty, & faithfully discharges the trust reposed in her. The Scholars improve every day in their reading, Spelling, & working. They now constantly attend Divine Service not only on the Lords Day, but also on week Days. I seldom miss hearing them read, & say their Catechise once a week, & can with great pleasure assure you, that they dayly improve. I have put several of them to learn Lewis's Catechism, and propose the rest shall begin with it, as soon as they are perfect in the Church Catechism.

I have only to add that the Associates may assure themselves, that their pious, & generous Donation is well bestowed; & that I shall continue my Care of the School with great pleasure, & faithfulness; And, that I am their's, & Your, Much Oblig'd & very humble servant

Samuel Auchmuty

ALS. This letter was read by the Associates at their meeting of 6 October 1763. Minutes, 1 : 193.

Robert Carter Nicholas to Rev. John Waring

Williamsburg in Virginia 23d. June 1763.

Sir.

I wrote pretty fully to you in the Fall,[1] & since being favour'd with no Letter from you, I have nothing material to add relating to the School founded by the Associates of the late Revd. Dr. Bray in this City. This is only to advise that Mr. Yates & I have drawn on you for £25 Sterling, which we are persuaded you will pay very readily. I shall expect to hear from you by some of the Ships, daily expected & am, Sir, with great Regard Your most obedient Servant

Ro. C. Nicholas.

ALS.

1. Nicholas and Yates to [Waring], 30 September 1762, above.

Benjamin Franklin to Rev. John Waring

New York, June 27. 1763

Revd. and dear Sir,

Being here on my Journey to New-England, I received your Favour of April 5.[1] You will easily conceive that after an Absence of near Six Years from my Family & Affairs, my Attention must be much engross'd on my Arrival by many Things that requir'd it; not to mention a Multiplicity of Visits, &c. that devour abundance of Time. I enquir'd however of Mr. Sturgeon concerning the Negro School tho' I could not visit it, and had the Satisfaction to hear it was full & went on in general well, tho' he had met with some Difficulties during the late Dissensions in the Church; but they were pretty well over.[2] He gave me the enclos'd List of the Scholars. As soon as I return to Philadelphia, which I hope to do by the Beginning of September, I shall inspect the School very particularly, and afford every Assistance in my Power to Mr. Sturgeon, in promoting the laudable Views of the Associates, to whom please to present my best Respects. Since my Arrival in America, I made a Journey too to Williamsburgh, near 350 Miles, which took me 5 Weeks; on Business of the Post Office. I there had a long Conversation with Mr. Nicholus concerning the School in that

Place, of which I need not give you any Account, as you have receiv'd his Letter which he told me he had written to you.[3] He appears a very sensible & a very conscientious Man, and will do his best in the Affair, but is sometimes a little diffident as to the final Success, in making sincere good Christians of the Scholars; their Continuance at the School being short. I think to visit the School here, which Mr. Auchmuty tells me is in a good way. And as I expect to be at Newport in Rhodeisland next Week, I shall speak to Mr. Brown concerning the Letters you have wrote him, and promote a School there if practicable. I thank you for your kind Congratulations on the Marriage & Preferment of my Son,[4] and am with great Esteem, and Respect, Revd. Sir, Your most obedient humble Servant

B Franklin

P.S. At my Return I shall pay my Subscription as you desire to Mr. Sturgeon.[5]

ALS: American Philosophical Society. This letter was read by the Associates at their meeting of 6 October 1763. Minutes, 1 : 193.

1. Letter not found.

2. See Sturgeon to Waring, 15 August 1764, note 2, below.

3. Franklin left Philadelphia about 17 or 18 April and returned by 17 May 1763. He had gone to Virginia to settle accounts with Benjamin Waller and Thomas Everard, executors of William Hunter (see Waller and Everard to Waring, 1 September 1761, above). Franklin to Anthony Todd, 14 April 1763, *Franklin Papers* 10:252 and n. The letter Franklin refers to may have been Nicholas and Yates to [Waring], 30 September 1762, above.

4. William Franklin (1731–1813) married Elizabeth Downes of the West Indies and was appointed governor of New Jersey in September 1762. *DAB*.

5. Franklin paid his annual subscription of two guineas to Sturgeon on 26 November 1763. *Franklin Papers* 10:396n.

Enclosure
List of Negro Children

Philadelphia November the 20th. 1762

A List of Schollars belonging to Christ-Church Charity
by Order of the Revd. William Sturgeon Director

	Boy's Names &c.	
John Dixon ⎫ Wm. Dixon ⎭	Reading	Center House
Thos. Sharper	Ditto	Spring Garden
Jerim[ia]h & Daniel	Ditto	Mrs. Jervise

	Boy's Names &c.	
Tom	Ditto	Mr. Turner
Scires	Ditto	Mrs. Dillworth
Exeter	Ditto	Mr. Reynoalds
Schamony	Ditto	Mrs. Turner
Joseph	Ditto	Mr. King
Tom	Ditto	Mr. Jones
Bash	Ditto	Mr. Turner
	No. 12	

	Girls Names &c.	
Hannah Hellon ⎫ Jane Hellon ⎭	Reading & Sewing	from Water Street
Rebecca	Ditto	Mr. Turner Water Street
Rachel	Ditto	Mr. Loyd front Street
Easther	Ditto	Mr. North in Ditto
Dianna ⎫ Kate ⎭	Ditto	Mr. Mifflins Market Street
Mary King	Ditto	in 5th. Street
Malch	Ditto	in Race Street
Mary Sharper		Spring Gardens
Mary Walder		3d. Street
Pheby		Mrs. Soward Market Street
Pheby		Mr. Bromage 3d. Street
Lavina		Mrs. Williams
Naney		Mr. Barns Moravian ally
Susannah		Mr. Kidwallet Church ally
Pegg		Mr. Mackols 3d. Street
Moll		Mr. Olfords front Street
Rachell		Mrs. Suky Loyds Water Street
Nancy Grime		Chesnut Street
	No. 20	

By Richd. & Elizabeth Harrison

ADS. The list and signatures are in the same hand, presumably either Richard or Elizabeth Harrison's.

Rev. Samuel Auchmuty to Rev. John Waring

New York September 24th. 1763

Revd. Sir

I take the liberty to recommend to your Notice and Countenance, the Bearer of this, Mr. Cuting, a Gentleman that has been for several

Years a Tutor of Kings College, in this City; which important trust he has executed with great fidelity and Reputation. We are very sorry to part with so able a person; but, knowing his Abilities, we make no doubt but that he will equally shine in a higher Sphere of Life. He proposes to enter into the Societys service, and will, I think, approve himself worthy their Employment and bounty.[1]

Pardon the freedom I now take, & be so kind as to give Mr. Cuting such advice & assistance as may be necessary and useful to him. Your known goodness emboldens me to make this request, which will be ever gratefully acknowledged by, Revd. Sir, Your Affectionate Brother & most Oblig'd Humble servant

Samuel Auchmuty.

P.S. We return you many thanks for your kind interposition in favour of our infant Seminary. The Negro School continues to go on extremely well. You shall very soon have a particular Account concerning It.

ALS. Endorsed: "Answered by Mr. Cuting February 1764." This letter was read by the Associates at their meeting of December 1763. Minutes, 1 : 195. Waring's reply, which was dated 13 February 1764, has not been found.

1. The Rev. Leonard Cutting (1724–94), a native of England, was educated at Pembroke College, Cambridge (A.B. 1748), and King's College, New York (A.M. 1758). Cutting served as a tutor at King's College from 1756 until 1763, when he went to England for ordination. He was licensed for New Jersey in December 1763 and served as S.P.G. missionary at New Brunswick and Piscataway 1764–66 and at Hempstead, New York, 1766–82. After the Revolution Cutting was rector of Snow Hill, Maryland, 1784–85 and rector of Christ Church, New Bern, North Carolina, 1785–93. Weis, *Colonial Clergy Middle Colonies*, p. 203.

Rev. Samuel Auchmuty to Rev. John Waring

New York October 20th. 1763

Revd. Sir

The twenty second of last March I had the pleasure of acquainting you with the state of the Negro School in this City, intrusted to my Care. From that time, to this, it has been my bussiness to see that the Children are educated agreeable to the Instructions I received from you. Many of them are now very notable at their work, and read extremely well. They constantly attend Divine Service both on the Lords day, and on Week Days, and behave with great Decency. I examine them almost every Sunday in their Catechism in which they are very perfect; and then give them such Advice & instruction as I find further necessary. I have set Six of them to learn Lewis's proof Catechism, & shall soon employ more the same way. I find most of them apt to learn; and the pains that are bestowed upon them, will not be lost. As my bussiness permits I visit the School, and incourage the Mistress & Scholars to do their duty. I must do the Mistress the Justice to say that she is faithful and diligent. She takes a great deall of pains, and employs her whole time to her bussiness. A few days ago four of the bigest, being wanted by their Masters, left the School, being well instructed for their future conduct. Their births I hope will soon be filled.

I have only to add, that the worthy Associates may assure themselves that their Charity is at present well bestowed, and will, by the blessing of God, be productive of much good. With great esteem and respect, I am, Revd. Sir Your much Oblig'd & most Obedient humble servant

Samuel Auchmuty.

P.S. I have drawn a set of Bills on you, in favor of R. Nicholls Esqr. for half a Years Salary due to the Mistress last Month.

ALS. This letter is endorsed as read 3 February 1764, although the Associates' Minute Book records its reading on 5 January 1764. Minutes, 1 : 198.

Rev. James Marye, Jr., to Rev. John Waring

Virginia Orange County Rappahannock River
October 24th. 1763

Revd. & Dear Sir

Yours dated April 7th. 1762 came to Hand the August following, which I answered in a few Days after,[1] as a convenient Opportunity then offered, but have never since heard from you, the daily Expectation of which has deferred my writing till now. In my former Letter, I gave you my Reasons for not Judging it proper to set up a School in my Parish for the Erudition of young Negroes, which were, that the Planters live so remote from each other, that I could not place a School so that more than five or six perhaps would attend, & they but very small, the Owners of them having various Employments for them as soon as they are able to go about; to remedy which Misfortune I can't recommend any better Method than the distributing proper Books for their Education to the Owners, who for the much greater Part are quite without such necessary Books, should they be ever so much disposed to instruct them. There is a Town on the River to which all in these Parts trade,[2] which makes it very flourishing & populous, where a negro-School might be placed (I think) to great Advantage, which is about hundred & ten Miles distant from Williamsburg, as the Town contains great Number of Negroes & their Owners have not those many Employments for them that they have in the Country. I have a convenient Room now fitted adjoining the Glebe House for the Reception of what Books you will be pleased to send. Those that would best suit my present Necessity I mentioned to you in my last. The Books of the two lending Libraries as they were very slight are much worsted by Use, the Pamphlets in Particular, most of which were of that Kind, so that I am of Opinion to have them well bound would in the End prove the cheapest Way. Be pleased to present my best Respects to the Associates & assure them I will chearfully Execute any Orders they will be pleased to send me. I remain Your Most Obedient Humble Servant

Jas. Marye

ALS. This letter was read by the Associates at their meeting of 2 February 1764. Minutes, 1:200.

1. Neither Waring's letter nor Marye's answer has been found. For the probable contents of Waring's letter see the minutes of the 5 November 1761 meeting of the Associates, cited in Marye to Waring, 2 August 1760, bibliographic note, above.

2. Fredericksburg, Virginia.

Benjamin Franklin to Rev. John Waring

Philada. December 17. 1763

Revd. & dear Sir,

Being but just return'd home from a Tour thro' the northern Colonies, that has employ'd the whole Summer, my Time at present is so taken up that I cannot now write fully in answer to the Letters I have receiv'd from you,[1] but purpose to do it shortly. This is chiefly to acquaint you, that I have visited the Negro School here in Company with the Revd. Mr. Sturgeon & some others; and had the Children thoroughly examin'd. They appear'd all to have made considerable Progress in Reading for the Time they had respectively been in the School, and most of them answer'd readily and well the Questions of the Catechism; they behav'd very orderly, show'd a proper Respect & ready Obedience to the Mistress, and seem'd very attentive to, and a good deal affected by, a serious Exhortation with which Mr. Sturgeon concluded our Visit. I was on the whole much pleas'd, and from what I then saw, have conceiv'd a higher Opinion of the natural Capacities of the black Race, than I had ever before entertained. Their Apprehension seems as quick, their Memory as strong, and their Docility in every Respect equal to that of white Children. You will wonder perhaps that I should ever doubt it, and I will not undertake to justify all my Prejudices, nor to account for them. I immediately advanc'd the two Guineas you mention'd, for the Mistress, & Mr. Sturgeon will therefore draw on you for £7 : 18 only, which makes up the half Year's Salary of Ten Pounds. Be pleased to present my best Respects to the Associates, and believe me, with sincere Esteem Dear Sir, Your most obedient Servant

B Franklin

ALS: American Philosophical Society. The letter is endorsed as read 1 March 1764, but the Associates' Minute Book records its reading on 2 February 1764. Minutes, 1 : 200–201.

1. Letters not found.

Rev. John Waring to Robert Carter Nicholas

[London, March 1764]

Sir

Last April I wrote to You by the Direction of the Associates, who charged me with their most Sincere & hearty Thanks for Your obliging Favour dated September 1762 accompanied with a Copy of Your most judicious and excellent Rules drawn up for the good Government & direction of the Negroe School under the charitable Patronage of Yourself & Mr. Yates.[1] It gives Us uncommon pleasure to find ourselves assisted by Gentlemen who seem animated with a truly christian zeal for advancing the Glory of our gracious Redeemer and enlarging his Kingdom. The Best & indeed only Return We can make to You is to offer up our Prayers to our heavenly Father, that he wou'd bestow upon You abundant Blessings both Spiritual & temporal, that He wou'd grant You long to enjoy Health and Peace in this world, & that in the Next You may share in the Triumphs and Glories of those who turn many to Righteousness.

By Your last Two Drafts I perceive the Salary of the Mistress is advanced to 25£,[2] which Solves the Riddle that puzled me, for as I never had been informed thereof I was much at a Loss to Account for 5£; which I spoke of in my last; but now the Matter is clear.

The Associates humbly request They may be favourd once a Year at least if not oftner with some Account of the State of the School, viz. how Many Children have left it, & how improved, the Number admitted, how many of each Sex their progress in Reading & in the Catechism & Such particulars as You may Judge worthy of Notice. It is with Regret we request this Trouble of You, but Necessity compels Us to it, for as these Schools are in a great Measure supported by voluntary Subscriptions and Benefactions, It is expected that we Shou'd give Some Account of their Success, for the Satisfaction of our present & to invite future Benefactors. And tho the State of the School Shou'd be much the Same it was the preceding Year, yet it will be new to most Persons who read our printed annual Accounts. The Success of this Design, depends, I may say wholly on the Reports transmitted to us by Correspondents, and their kind Letters will probably prove the Source of many future Benefactions, whilst They themselves are justly to be esteemed the greatest Benefactors. We wou'd give as little Trouble as may be. What may be comprized in ten or twelves[3] may in general be Sufficient, unless You See Special Reasons for being more particular. Be pleased to let me know in time what Books may be wanting & They shall be Sent with all Speed.

The Associates join with me in repeated Thanks to Yourself & Mr. Yates, for Your charitable Concurrence. I am with great Esteem Sir Your most obliged humble Servant

Jn. Waring

at Mr. Birds, Bookseller in Ave Mary Lane London.
March

ALS: Bray MSS., McGregor Collection, U.Va.

1. See Yates and Nicholas to [Waring], 30 September 1762, bibliographic note, above.
2. See Nicholas to Waring, 23 June 1762 and 23 June 1763, above.
3. Waring probably meant ten or twelve lines.

Rev. Jonathan Boucher to Rev. John Waring

[King George County, Virginia, 28 April 1764]

Revd. Sir

Notwithstanding that I have already forwarded two Letters to You, since my Residing in this Place, and since the Receipt of Yours,[1] yet, I think, Gratitude to You & to the Gentlemen Associates oblige Me, whenever a favourable Opportunity offers, to give You repeated

Informations of the Success of my Endeavours in Instructing the Negro Slaves that live near my Neighbourhood. For, tho' on my Return to Virginia, I found it not in my Power to raise a Negro School in any Such manner as I think the Associates have a Right to expect, yet I have endeavour'd to dispose of the few Books You and They so obligingly put into my Hands to such Persons and Purposes as, I hope, will meet with the Approbation of The Society. I have before given You the Reasons why it was impracticable to raise a School in such a Parish as This is; but to remedy this Inconvenience as much as I could, I have employ'd a very sensible, well-dispos'd Negro belonging to a Gentleman who lives about a Mile from Me, to endeavour at instructing his poor fellow Slaves in Reading & some of the first Principles of Religion, with which, I have taken Care, that He should not be totally unacquainted. Saturday's & Sunday's Afternoons He employs to this Purpose; and He has, I believe, at this Time betwixt Twenty & Thirty who constantly attend Him. And that He may be the better qualified for his Office, I oblige Him to visit me two or three Times every Week, when either Myself or Some young Gentlemen who live with Me, as Pupils, give Him Lessons:[2] and Once at least in every month He brings his Scholars before Me that I may examine what Progress They have made; which to Persons who properly know the incorrigible Stupidity of the Majority of these wretched Creatures I must own, I think, is not inconsiderable. I find Them in Books, & endeavour too to encourage the Industrious by allotting Them some small Rewards for extraordinary Diligence, as well as to their Master.

Thus, Sir, tho' I have been obliged so greatly to deviate from the Plans of The Associates, yet as it appears that by this means I best answer their Designs, I hope They will not think the few Books They sent to Hanover Parish very improperly bestowed. I am not a little concern'd that all the first Books are gone, and tho', as the Plan I have fallen upon is rather my own than Yours, I could not consistently ask You for a Supply, yet as They are cheap, I should be far from begrudging an Expence of 30/ or 40 Shillings to purchase Them. But, as I am now in a little Time to leave this Place, having lately been selected to St. Mary's which is about some twenty Miles higher up the River, and as I know not who may be my Successor here,[3] I am afraid my little Seminary will dwindle away for Want of Some Person to encourage its President Aaron. Should I find an Opportunity for introducing such a Scheme in St. Mary's Parish, I hope I shall not be thought troublesome in mentioning it to You, or in sollicing from The Associates any such Assistance as my Circumstances & Situation may render necessary for the Accomplishment of my Schemes. In the mean Time I request that You will be so obliging to Me as to present my most respectful Compliments to the Gentlemen of the Society, who, I persuade myself, will not be displeased to hear that their Favours to Me have not been entirely thrown away.

I am, Revd. Sir, Your most obedient & most humble Servant & Brother

Jonan. Boucher

Hanover Parish, in King George County, Rappahannock River, Virginia this 28th. April 1764

P:S: If you again have Occasion to write, Please still to direct to Me as usual.

ALS. Endorsed as read 6 September 1764. See Minutes, 1:213. Also endorsed as answered November 1764 and February 1765. Waring's replies have not been found.

1. One of Boucher's letters was dated 31 December 1762, above; the other has not been found. Waring's letter has not been found.

2. Boucher conducted a small boarding school in Hanover Parish. He wrote in his autobiography, "In the autumn [of 1762] I took a good and pleasant house near Leeds, called Smith's Mount, furnished it, and commenced housekeeper, along with my sister Jinny. I also now resumed my former employment, and soon had half a dozen boys boarded in my house" (Boucher, *Reminiscences of an American Loyalist*, pp. 38–39).

3. Boucher's successor was the Rev. Thomas Landrum (or Lendrum) (d. 1771), a native of Scotland and a graduate of Aberdeen. He was a lawyer in King George County after 1758. Landrum went to England for ordination in 1764 and was licensed for Virginia in 1765. He was minister of Hanover Parish 1765–71 and was a justice of the peace for King George County from 1767. Gundersen, "Anglican Ministry in Virginia," p. 282.

Rev. Alexander Stewart to Rev. John Waring

Bath N: Carolina May the 1st. 1764

Revd. Sir,

I recd. your favour of the 7th. of April 1763,[1] which I shou'd have answered much Sooner; had I not waited to return a more Satisfactory one, than that I am at present Obliged for to give.

Upon Shewing your Letters, to some of the Inhabitants, I was fed up with Hopes of erecting three Schools in this & the neighbouring Counties in a Short time; but after I had distributed parts of your Books among the School masters & encourag'd them all I could, I found at length that it was but Labour & Sorrow, owing to the mean, low Prejudices of the People of North America. I made one Short lived Effort, you may see by the Inclosed to erect a School (not altogether on the Societies plan) for the Instruction of ten Indian & Negro Children at Attamuskeet in Hyde County;[2] The Master in the Letter signd Jas: Francis[3] shews you the Objections of the people, & the Expectations we are to have. He instructed six Indian Boys & Girls whom I baptized in October 1763, their ages & names you may see by the Inclos'd rect. for his Quarters Sallary which I have paid, but Whither He continues or not, I am uncertain of, having not since heard from him, It being above 70 Miles by Water from this place.

The other Letter from Anthony Kinnin[4] who lives about 30 miles to the Westward of this town, I likewise inclose to you, that your Society may see that I have not been regardless of their good & pious Design, and tho' it has not been in my power hitherto to carry it on to any Purpose, yet that my best Wishes attend it, & that I shall always be reddy upon the least dawn of Success, again to renew my endeavours.

The 1st. Box of Books directed to Mr. Palmer I have never had in possession but remains in his Stores unopened; the 2d. Box I almost distributed and am Sorry to no better purpose. The remainder may be orderd to any place where they will be more useful but they can be carried to no place where they are more wanted among the poor & Ignorant Whites.

I am Revd. Sir your obedient & humble Servant

Alexr: Stewart

It wou'd give me great pleasure to correspond with the Society, & to know whether an Indian School in the Manner I have begun, comes within their Scheme.

Ballance due to me is 33s. 9d. Sterling.

ALS. Endorsed as read 6 September 1764. See Minutes, 1:214. Also endorsed as answered 20 February 1765. Waring's reply has not been found.

1. Letter not found. See Stewart to Waring, 12 August 1762, bibliographic note, above.

2. Stewart wrote to the Rev. Daniel Burton, secretary of the S.P.G., on 23 November 1763 concerning the school at Attamuskeet:

> The Remains of the Attamuskeet Roanoke & Hatteras Indians live mostly along that Coast mixd with the White, they attended at the place of Publick worship while I was there & behaved with decency, seemd desirous of Instruction & Offerd themselves & their Children to me for Baptism and I accordingly baptized the above mentiond Infants [six adults, four girls, six boys, five infants]—and for their further Instruction (at the Expence of a Society called Dr. Brays Associates who have done me the Honor to appoint me Superintendent of their Schools here) I have a fix'd a School Mistress

among them to teach four Indian & 2 Negroe Boys & four Indian Girls to work & to read, & have supplied them with Books for that purpose, and hope that the Lord will forward this their pious design. (S.P.G. MSS., B5, no. 89)

3. Not further identified.
4. Not identified.

Enclosure
James Francis to Rev. Alexander Stewart

Attamaskeet, [North Carolina] February 22d. 1764.

Sir,

Having so good an Opportunity by Capt. Goddard,[1] I have made bold to trouble You with this, and allso a List of what Indian Children hath been with Me to be School'd for this first Quarter just expired. As for Negroes, tho' their Masters might possibly give You some Promise to send, more, or less, and tho' some of them, made Professions of sending, both to Mr. Lockhart,[2] and my self, Yet did they neglect the same. Neither have there been any More than Six Indians; But I assure You Sir those People are not able to continue their Children, for if I had not fed them, three fourths of the time they did come, they must have gon with many a hungry Belly, those that are able to work must do something to prevent it, or they wou'd infallibly be naked as well as starvd for their friends are unable to maintain them, and those that cannot work are not Cloathed sufficiently to withstand the Cold. This is realy the Case with them. As for their Capacities, there is no Objection more than Common with the White Children.

And as I have a Call to Core sound which Promises much more to my Advantage than here, I expect to move there, Early next month. I have therefore made bold, at the Bottom of the List, sent by Capt. Goddard, to request You will please to Pay him forty five Shillings for this Quarter which is Due on Acct. of these Six Indians, that have been with Me; and if Sir it was in my Power to serve You in any shape, at Core sound, where I am design'd next Month, I shou'd think it an Honour to have Your Commands. In the mean time, hoping You will please to favour my Request, By Capt. Goddard, I Beg leave to Remain Sir Your most Obedient humble Servant

Jams: Francis.

ALS.

1. Capt. John Stoddard, not further identified.
2. Not identified.

Enclosure
Account of James Francis and List of Children

Aramaskeet February 20th., 1764.

Doctr. Alexander Stewart, To James Francis   Dr.

To the Schooling Six Indian Children ⎫   £ s d
Three Months, as per Agreement at 7/6 ⎬   2 5
Each, per Quarter ⎭

A List of the above Six Indians, With their Entrance &c.

1763	Then Entered for the Schooling, Two Indian
November 7th.	Boys, Vizt. Solomon Russel, about 17 Years of Age and John Squires about 16 Ditto. The same Day Entered, Two Indian Girls, Vizt. Bet Squires about 13 Years of Age and Poll: Mackey about 13 Ditto.
November 18	Then Entered Two Indian Boys, Vizt. Joshua Squires about 9 Years of Age and Bob; Mackey at 7 Ditto.
	All Which made out their Quarter.

Jams; Francis.

Sir,

Please to pay Capt. John Goddard the above Sum of Two Pds. five Shillings, and his Receipt Shall be a Discharge in full for the same, from February 20th., 1764.

Sir, Your very humble servant,

Jams: Francis.

To The Revd. Doctr. Alexr. Stewart.

ADS. Endorsed: "Jas: Francis, Rect. for Attamuskeet School. February 4th. 1764, 45s. proclamation money, 33s. 9d. Sterling." Also endorsed, in Goddard's hand, "Received Contents In full. John Goddard."

Enclosure
Anthony Kinnin to Rev. Alexander Stewart

[North Carolina] January the 21, 1764

Reverend Sir

I have discoursed with some of the Masters of the Slaves in this Countrey about their cooperating with the Charitable Society with regard to puting their Negro Children to School. Some of said Masters who seems to have the Salvation of their Negroes Souls at heart (but Olas they are but few!) has told me they could mighty well approve of the Charitable design of the Society were the Parents of the Negro Children them selves first instructed in the Principles of the Christian Religion for say they it is to little purpose to send the Children to School while[1] this is done, and it is the oppinion of some of the most knowing here that if the Society would apply their Charity for a few years towards paying Sober Qualified Catechists that by the blessing of God in a few years the masters them selves would ease the Society of that Charge and if the Society pleasd to apply it then towards paying for Schooling their Negro Children would by the owners be gratefully and thankfully accepted of. For my part I purpose God willing to use my utmost endeavours according to my Capacity to Instruct what Negroes comes to my School House on Sunday in the Afternoon and if you are so kind to mention me to the Society I doubt not as my Circumstances are but low but that they will by your earnest application to them consider my Circumstance Especially if you write to them that you have incouraged me in Expectation that the Society would consider me which if they do they may depend upon my attending more places and consequently of devoting more of time to that Service but if they should not yet I have this to incourage me that what I do in this way I hope will be acceptable to God through Christ our Lord as indeed if it was not for this for what I have of the World it would not hardly be worth my while to attend Reading every Sunday. I hope I am sincerely Reverend Sir your very much obliged humble Servant

Anthony Kinnin

ALS.

1. An obsolete use of "while," meaning "until." *OED*.

Rev. Samuel Auchmuty to Rev. John Waring

New York May the 2d. 1764

Revd. & Worthy Sir,

Your most Friendly favour of the 13th. of last February, by Mr. Cuting, demands my most sincere Thanks, which I beg you will be pleased now to accept.[1] Your information of Mr. Sturgeons omission of Duty, & discharge from the Venerable Societys Service, greatly surprized me.[2] That Gentleman I have been informed has conscientiously discharged his Duty for many Years, & has been instrumental under God, in promoting our blessed Redeemers Kingdom among a set of poor unfortunate Blacks, whose Masters in general, all over America, care very little what becomes of their poor Souls. Was not his Dismission rather too precipitate? Ought he not to have been previously acquainted with the Complaint against him? Will not his dismission give the Enemies of the Society an opportunity to say, that their whole Care is to establish Missionaries, where there are already sound Orthodox Clergy, neglecting at the same time the Native Indians, and the poor Negroes?[3] However I submit my Judgment to the venerable Boards, and doubt not but they had sufficient reasons for what they have done.

As for myself I can, and do declare, that I have never omitted any Duty that was ever done by those employed before me, but have Conscientiously exerted my small Abilities in the service of the poor Slaves; Besides attending them on the Lords day, explaining the Catechise to them, & hearing them their several tasks, I frequently have some of them, at my House on the Week days, especially those that are preparing for Baptism, or the Sacrament of the Lords Supper, and devote a considerable part of my time to their service: And I have the unspeak'able satisfaction to find, that my labour & trouble (thanks be to God) are not lost. I have now more Communicants than ever were here before, many more preparing themselves, and an increasing Flock both of Old & Young Blacks. I wrote a few Weekes ago to the Secretary of the Society, (which duty I never omit twice, or thrice a Year, and should readily write oftener, was I not apprehensive that the charge of portage would run too high) acquainting him with the above Information, which Letter I hope he has received.[4] I have only to observe further, that sure, I am, the Societys bounty can never be better employed than in providing for those, that do their duty, and instruct, and bring to the knowledge of the true God, and his blessed Son, Christ Jesus, our Lord, the poor unfortunate Blacks; which Duty as a Christian Minister, I shall never omit, while blessed with Health, tho' I should receive no recompense for it in this World.

I greatly rejoice to find that my accounts hitherto concerning the Negro School, have afforded you, and the worthy Associates, any Satisfaction.

Since my last we have had a considerable large number that have left the School, no less than fourteen. Their Masters, as they grew handy, and were pretty well instructed in reading &c. could not as they say, do any longer without them: Though they have left the School, yet they constantly attend me on Sundays, & are now learning Lewis's Catechism, & have made considerable progress in it. I could wish their Masters in general could be prevailed upon to let them stay a little longer at School; but alass! such is their eagerness for their Service, and such the prejudice in favour of keeping their Slaves in Ignorance, for fear of their being rendered by Instruction too knowing, that I have a hard Task to persuade some that it is certainly their Duty to have them instructed, and that their poor Souls are as precious in the sight of God, as theirs. With many worthy Christians I have the pleasure to succeed, & their Blacks constantly attend me, and their Numbers increase. At present there are nine Vacancys in the School, which I conclude will soon be filled up, when known. The reason of there being so many at once, was owing to the Number already mentioned, leaving the School lately. I visited it Yesterday, and still find the Mistress very careful, & industrious; the Children which she now has, are but small, but very orderly & for their standing pretily taught. They say their prayers twice a day, & attend Divine Service at Church, on Wednesdays Fridays, and Holy days. To behold a Number of poor little Slaves upon their Knees, lisping out their prayers to their All bountiful Creator often fills my heart with raptures, & forces the Tears of Joy to flow from my Eyes.

The Number that have left the School, is, Twenty two, The greatest part of which were taught to read, to say their Prayers, the Church Catechism by heart, and those that were Girls to sew &c.

Thus Revd. Sir, I have given you as particular an account as I can at present. It is not upon the whole so good a one as I could wish, but hope, and expect that my next will be better. You may assure the worthy Associates (to whom please to present my best respects) that I have their charitable design much at heart, and have and will do all that lays in my power to promote it, and bring it to perfection. God grant that it may succeed.

I have only to add repeated Thanks for your kind & Friendly Letters, & to beg a continuance of your Corrispondence. If any thing in the former part of this long Letter, should by you, be thought of consequence enough to mention to the Societys worthy Secretary, Dr. Burton,[5] you have my consent so to do. With most sincere prayers for your Health and Happiness, I am, with great respect, Revd. Sir Your much oblig'd & most Obedient Humble Servant

Samuel Auchmuty

ALS. Endorsed as read 6 September 1764. See Minutes, 1:215.

1. Letter not found.

2. See Sturgeon to Waring, 15 August 1764, note 2, below.

3. The "Enemies of the Society" were led by Jonathan Mayhew (1720–66), Congregational minister of Boston's West Church and the author of *Observations on the Charter and Conduct of the Society for the Propagation of the Gospel in Foreign Parts; Designed to Shew Their Non-conformity to Each Other . . .* (Boston, 1763). In this work, and in two subsequent defenses of the *Observations* (Bos-

ton, 1763, 1764), Mayhew accused the S.P.G. of violating its charter by sending missionaries to convert New England dissenters to Anglicanism rather than to minister to the spiritual needs of Indians, Negroes, and unchurched whites.

4. Auchmuty to the Rev. Daniel Burton, secretary of the S.P.G., 29 March 1764, S.P.G. MSS., B2, no. 7. The letter was read by the S.P.G. at their meeting of 20 July 1764. S.P.G. Journals, 16:156.

5. The Rev. Daniel Burton (d. 1775), rector of St. Peter-le-Poer, London 1751–75, was secretary of the S.P.G. 1761–73. S.P.G. Journals, 15:149, 19: 357 (meetings of 12 November 1761, 19 February 1773); *Gentleman's Magazine* 45 (1775): 207; Venn, *Alumni Cantabrigienses*.

[Benjamin Franklin to Rev. John Waring]

[Philadelphia, 25 June 1764]

Dr. Franklin in a Letter dated Philadelphia June 25 1764 says the Negroe School there is not near So full as it used to be the Reason of which He will enquire into, & inform in his next what it appears to be.

By a List inclosed it appears that there were only fifteen Negroe Children at School at that Time.[1]

Letter not found. Extract from Minutes, 1:214 (meeting of 6 September 1764).

1. Enclosure not found.

Rev. William Sturgeon to Rev. John Waring

[Philadelphia, 15 August 1764]

Revd. Sir

The Receipt of your Letter[1] gave me great Pleasure, and I am much obliged to the worthy Associates for their Approbation of my Conduct towards their School here. I should before now have been able to give you a much better Account of the Success of that Institution, had it not been for that unfortunate Affair, the Complaints made by one Mr. Ross to the Society against me, and their Dismission of me from their Service.[2] This made my Influence amongst the Congregation less, and gave even the Negroes a bad Impression. The Complaint was without any Foundation except that of Malice as Dr. Smith[3] informed you, but the Consequences have been very injurious to me both as a Minister and the Father of seven small Children, who have no Support but my Income and Character. The known Wisdom and Goodness of the Society makes me hope they will take my Case into Consideration, and make me Satisfaction. My Labor for more than 17 Years has been very great with the Congregation and the Negroes, and for six Years while Mr. Jenney lay in a Palsy I had the whole Weight of the Parish on me, and I attended several Winters his Majesties Troops in Quarters here without any Chaplin. I would not have mentioned these Things to you but your Goodness emboldens me, that you may lay it before the Honble. Society. I think I have still a Right to my Salary, as I have always done every thing that could be expected from a Catechist circumstanced in the Church as I have been for so many Years, and this makes me expect that even in justice the Society will continue to allow me to draw as usual, and make such other Satisfaction as they in their Prudence may think proper. I have not been able this Summer to do as much as heretofore, having been thrown into a bad Habit of Body, by the Hard Returns my many and long Services have met with; but your kind Letter and Dr. Smiths Account[4] have been some Help to me, and I hope God will restore me my Health, and make me as useful as ever. The worthy Dr. Franklin is Well and does every Thing to promote the School, and hope we shall be able to give a good Account of it. Some Books, especially Bibles and Prayer-Books are much wanted.[5] You will please to let me know the Determinations of the Honble. Society by the first Opportunity. After my best Regards to the worthy Associates and sincere Thanks to you I am Revd. Sir your most affectionate Brother and humble Servant

Wm. Sturgeon

Philadelphia
August 15 1764

ALS. Endorsed as read 1 November 1764. See Minutes, 1:216–17.

    1. Letter not found.

    2. Sturgeon's dismissal by the S.P.G. as catechist to the Negroes resulted from accusations made by John Ross (1714–76), a lawyer and the son of an Anglican clergyman. Ross complained to the S.P.G. in a letter of 2 July 1762, "The Society, I am told, allow Mr. Sturgeon, of this City, £50 sterling per annum as Catechist to the negroes. I presume he has omitted to draw for that Salary the last two years. If he has drawn for it, he has done very unfairly (to say no worse) by the Society." S.P.G. MSS., B21, no. 219. Ross was a leader in the movement in favor of McClenaghan and the founding of St. Paul's Church and was described by the Rev. William Smith in a letter to the S.P.G. of 26 August 1760 as "the chief Fomenter of all this Trouble [the McClenaghan controversy] in Order to be at the Head of a Party." S.P.G. MSS., B21, no. 248. A committee consisting of the Rev. Richard Peters and four vestrymen of the United Congregations investigated the charges of neglect of duty and completely exonerated Sturgeon on 23 April 1763. Nevertheless, the S.P.G. on 15 July 1763 agreed "that although Mr. Sturgeon has cleared himself of the total neglect of his Duty as Catechist, yet his attention to it has been very Superficial, and unequal to the nature of that Duty, and therefore since Mr. Stur-

geon is elected one of the Ministers of Christ Church in Philadelphia, and to have the same Appointment as Mr. Duche, there seems no occasion for the Society to continue their Allowance." S.P.G. Journals, 15:399. On 20 November 1763, after being informed of the Society's decision, Sturgeon replied to the Rev. Daniel Burton, the S.P.G. secretary, that he had been dismissed "by the Means of one who has been the chief Instrument of dividing our Church. He is and has long been my Enemy, and I glory to have him as Such till God is pleased to touch his Heart." S.P.G. MSS., B21, no. 281. Sturgeon wrote to the Society on 25 March 1765 to inform them that he had resumed the instruction of black adults and children, but apparently not under the auspices of the Society. S.P.G. Journals, 15:281, 16:106–8, 422 (meetings of 19 November 1762, 16 March 1764, 20 September 1765); Perry, *Historical Collections, Pennsylvania*, p. 325; *Franklin Papers* 6:384n, 10:299n, 15:130n; Dorr, *Historical Account of Christ Church*, pp. 137–38.

3. The Rev. William Smith (1727–1803), a native of Aberdeen, Scotland, emigrated to New York in 1751, where he worked as a tutor. He settled in Philadelphia in 1754 and taught logic, rhetoric, and natural and moral philosophy at the new Philadelphia Academy (after 1755 the College of Philadelphia). Smith was provost of the college from 1755 and was active in efforts to provide schooling for Pennsylvania Germans. He was in England from 1762 to 1764, raising funds for the college. See Auchmuty to Waring, 18 May 1762, note 3, above. After the Revolution Smith was influential in the organization of the Protestant Episcopal Church but failed in his ambition to become a bishop. *DAB*.

4. Waring's letter has not been found. Smith's "Account" was probably given to Sturgeon orally upon Smith's return to Philadelphia in June 1764.

5. At the Associates' meeting of 3 January 1765 Waring reported sending some Bibles and prayer books to Sturgeon pursuant to his request. Minutes, 1:218.

Rev. Samuel Auchmuty to Rev. John Waring

New York September 10th. 1764.

Revd. Sir

Though I have wrote to the Secretary of the Society at large, yet I take the liberty of just mentioning to you, the Death of the late worthy Dr. Barclay and my succeeding that good man, as Rector of this Parish. I have acquainted the Society, that I shall no longer than the 29th. of this Month act as their Catechist, but shall employ one Mr. Charles Inglis, who is chosen my Assistant, to discharge the Catechists Duty.[1] I am a little apprehensive that there will be an attempt to drop the Catechists Salary, therefore I beg leave to assure you that it will be both impolitic, & attended with bad Consequences so to do. It will be impossible for me, considering the extensiveness of my parochial Duties to attend the concerns of the poor Slaves, & I do not suppose that my Assistants will trouble themselves much about them, unless they have some gratuity for their Trouble: Indeed as part of my Congregation I must, & will do for them, all that I possibly can: but to administer to all their spiritual wants will not be in my power. There are Numbers of them now that have a very serious sense of Religion, but if they are not incouraged in it, & constantly Catechised, I fear there will be great fallings off. I would also beg leave to observe to you, that the Negro School, now in a flourishing way, will greatly suffer, if there is no Catechist; for though I shall always continue to visit it, yet, considering my extensive Duty, it will be impossible for me to inspect it as much as I have hitherto done: besides, Sir, It can'ot be expected, that I should now, after Sixteen Years faithful Service, to the poor Negro's, attended, I bless my God, with success, continue any longer to spend a great part of my time, in attending a Duty, which must naturally greatly interfere with the duty that I now owe to my large, numerous and extensive parish. My sole Ambition is, to do all the good that lays in my power, but some ease, some respite is necessary, after a life of fatigue, pains, & trouble. I am far from dictating to the Venerable Society, not doubting, but that they will do what is right; but, my sentiments, knowing your good Disposition, and Christian Attachment to the poor Slaves, I have ventured to communicate to you, to make what use of them, you please. Should the Society determine to continue the Catechist, I believe it would be best for them to leave it to me to recommend the person, that I shall think, will execute the important trust, Conscientiously & with success. This I venture to mention to you, but not to them. I have no other Motive, in what I have mentioned than to discharge my Conscience, & if possible promote the eternal welfare of the poor, & much to be pitied Slaves. Your goodness will readily excuse the Freedom I now take; & your sentiments upon the Subject will be highly acceptable, & with me, will have great weight.

The Negro School is full, & in a very thriving way. I have only to add, that I beg you will excuse this hasty Scrawl, having at present my hands full of bussiness, and the Vessell sails to morrow Morning. A Continuance of your obliging Corrispondence, will, Revd. Sir, be ever esteemed as an honor, & favor conferred on, Your much Oblig'd & Affectionate Friend & Brother

S. Auchmuty

P.S. I most sincerely thank you for your kindness to Mr. Cuting.

ALS. Endorsed as read 1 November 1764. See Minutes, 1:216.

1. Auchmuty to the Rev. Daniel Burton, secretary of the S.P.G., 10 September 1764, S.P.G. MSS., B2, no. 8. Barclay died on 20 August 1764.

The Rev. Charles Inglis (1734–1816), a native of Ireland, emigrated to America about 1755. He returned to England for ordination three years later and served as S.P.G. missionary at Dover, Delaware, 1759–65. He was assistant to Auchmuty from 1765 to Auchmuty's death in 1777, after which Inglis was chosen rector of Trinity Church. Inglis was a staunch Loyalist. He left America for England in 1783, and four years later he was consecrated bishop of Nova Scotia, becoming the first colonial Anglican bishop. *DAB*.

In his letter to Burton, Auchmuty informed the S.P.G. that the vestry and churchwardens had chosen Inglis to succeed him as assistant and that they intended to write to the Society to request that Inglis also be appointed catechist to the Negroes. Auchmuty also informed the S.P.G. that Inglis would have charge of the Negroes until the Society's directions were known. The Society read Auchmuty's letter, as well as the letter from the vestry and churchwardens (dated 22 September 1764), on 16 November 1764 and postponed consideration of the appointment of a successor to Auchmuty. S.P.G. Journals, 16:219–21. Inglis was never appointed catechist. See Auchmuty to Waring, 3 May 1765, note 1, below.

Rev. James Marye, Jr., to Rev. John Waring

[Orange County, Virginia, 25 September 1764]

Revd. Sir

I have now before me yours dated 6 March 1764,[1] wherein you complain I had not informed you of the Receipt of a Box of Books, which I now tell you did come to Hand, or one at least is come to Hand, if that is all you have sent. I likewise now inform you, as I did in my last, that I divided the Books in two Libraries.

I mentioned something in my last relative to a School for the Instruction of Negroes, & told you I did not think one in the Country would answer on Account of the Remoteness of the Inhabitants from each other, which Opinion I still continue in, but mentioned a Possibility of it's succeeding in a growing Town, to which all in these Parts trade, & you seem much disturbed that I neglected mentioning the Name of that Town; had I been certain that Evin's Map of Virginia, or Jefferson's & Fry's[2] never fell in your Hands, where you might have seen that all that live in Orange County might be reasonably supposed to trade to the Town nearest to them, which said Town is 45 Miles from where I live, & is called Fredericksburg. However I acknowledge it was an Omission in me not to have mentioned the Name in my last. But I now inform you the Name of the Town I meant, was Fredericksburg on Rappahanock River. I likewise inform you that being in the said Town since I wrote you, I made Inquiry what Number of small Negroes would be sent, should a School be set up there for the Purpose, & could not learn it would be possible to get above four or five or thereabouts, & they not to go constantly, but only at spare Times when it suited their Owners.

You desire an Account of the Number of Negroes in my Parish, which I cant, with any Certainty, inform you but guess there is a thousand grown ones or thereabouts, & at least the like Quantity of young ones. As to the Number that attend Divine Service on Sundays it is greater at some Churches than others, as they are placed nearer to where Quantities of the Negroes live, but in general there is about 30 or 40 and on some Sundays I have seen 60 or more.

You must understand there are great Quantities of those Negroes imported here yearly from Africa, who have Languages peculiar to themselves, who are here many years before they understand English; & great Numbers there are that never do understand it, well Enough to reap any Benefit from what is said in Church which was my Reason for mentioning, as I did in some former Letter, that the distributing religious Tracts to the Owners would be a more probable Way of Success, as those being wrote in the most plain intelligible Style, they might by their Owners be made in Time to understand what was said to them.

But you must suppose it to be impossible for me to go from House to House, to instruct a thousand Negroes perhaps or more, some of which would take me a Week to make them understand one single Sentence.

The Number of Negroe Communicants is very small not exceeding half a Dozen in the Parish or thereabouts. All that understand English, & that are but tolerably convenient to Church, bring their Children to be baptised. The Name of the Minister of the Parish in which the said Town of Fredericksburg lies, is my Father the Revd. James Marye who is now very aged being upwards of 70 years of Age.[3] I have now given you Every Information that I can recollect, if I have omitted any please to inform me in your next, and will Endeavour to satisfie you in any thing in my Power, pray present my best Respects to the Associates I am, Your Most Obedient Humble Servant

Jas. Marye Junior

Virginia Orange County Rappahanock River
September 25th. 1764

ALS. Endorsed as read 4 April 1765. See Minutes, 1:222–23.

1. Letter not found.

2. Lewis Evans, *Geographical, Historical, Political, Philosophical and Mechanical Essays. The First, Containing an Analysis of a General Map of the Middle British Colonies in America* . . . (Philadelphia, 1755). For a facsimile see Lawrence Henry Gipson, *Lewis Evans* (Philadelphia, 1939).

A Map of the Inhabited Part of Virginia Containing the Whole Province of

Maryland, with Part of Pensilvania, New Jersey and North Carolina, Drawn by Joshua Fry & Peter Jefferson in 1751 (London, [1754?]). For a facsimile see Dumas Malone, ed., *The Fry & Jefferson Map of Virginia and Maryland: Facsimiles of the 1754 and 1794 Printings, with an Index* (Charlottesville, Va., 1966).

3. The Rev. James Marye, Sr., (d. 1767) was a native of Rouen, France, and a former Roman Catholic priest. In 1726 he abjured Catholicism, fled to England, and was ordained in the Church of England. Marye was licensed for Virginia in December 1729. He was minister of St. James's Parish, Goochland County, and minister of the Huguenot settlement at Manakintown, King William Parish, from 1730 to 1735. He was minister of St. George's Parish, Spotsylvania County, from 1735 until his death. Brock, *Huguenot Emigration to Virginia*, pp. 183–84; Fulham Papers, 42:32.

Rev. Marmaduke Browne to Rev. John Waring

Newport Rhode Island November 6th. 1764

Revd. Sir,

Your letter of March the sixth sixty four,[1] came to hand in August last, during the confinement of a slow fever, which rendered me unable to officiate for thirteen weeks, & is the true cause of that letters not being answered sooner. With regard to your not receiving a line of advice with the bills, it was partly owing to the expectation I had of receiving a letter, with information, whether my conduct respecting the salary to the Mistress, which I was under the necessity of fixing rather beyond what the associates seemed to think necessary, was satisfactory to them, or not: And partly to the chagrin I suffered in observing the pious & charitable designs of worthy Persons less regarded than they evidently deserved, by which means I could not transmit so favourable an account of the school, as upon its first opening I had sanguinely promised myself. The Church Wardens & Vestry of this place upon the first proposal for opening a school in Mr. Pollens time appeared extremely well pleased with the offer, & engaged to assist in procuring a school Mistress, & the number of Children required, they declared themselves in the same manner upon my communicating to them the contents of your letter, but I am sorry to say, they have not fulfilled their engagement, the school never has been full, notwithstanding some of them had Children which they might have sent if thereto disposed. This neglect I conceive to be in some measure owing to the contempt incident to the colour & slavery of the Blacks, which renders their Masters for the most part extremely negligent of their future interest. They consider them as living purely for their service, & if their instruction interferes in the least with their Servitude, it must be intirely neglected. I have not been wanting I assure you to touch them both publickly & privately upon their mistakes with regard to the treatment of their slaves; which they for the present will acknowledge to be wrong, but are not so easily brought to apply the remedy. I am sensible there are complaints made of the negligence of the school mistress, & I am also sensible that they are not altogether ill-founded. She was of their own chusing, & I thought at first would have done well, but I since find her too much disposed to earn her money without exertion. I therefore would propose your writing a smart letter of complaint; That the school does by no means answer the expectations of the worthy founders; That it appears never to have been full, which must be the fault of the Minister, Church Wardens, & Vestry; That it does not appear the Children make any proficiency; which must be the fault of the Mistress; & consequently that there must be a reform in both these respects, or the school must be removed. This I am in great hopes will cause [an] alteration, will rouse the Mistress, & put the Vestry [on] filling the school; & if it does not, I promise to give speedy information, that so good a charity may not be abused but may elsewhere be applied, among more deserving people. I do assure you it is matter of grief to me that this school has not answered our expectations; yet some good it has done; there have generally been in it from twenty to five & twenty Children, eight or ten of which, said their Catechism in Church last Lent without missing a word, & several of them have made some proficiency in reading & the Girls in sewing. I am not without hopes much good may be done, but what I have hinted above I think necessary to assist in it. I am Revd. Sir, with much respect your affectionate Brother & humble servant

Marmaduke Browne

ALS. Endorsed as read 4 February and answered 25 February 1765. The bracketed words are supplied from the text of this letter quoted in the Minute Book, the manuscript being torn. The Associates actually read this letter at their meeting of 7 February 1765, at which time they "Agreed that Thanks be returned to Mr. Brown for his Information of the State of the School at Newport, and that, agreable to his Intimation, a Letter of Complaint be addressed to the Minister Church Wardens & Vestry, acquainting that unless more Satisfactory Accounts of the School Shall for the future be transmitted, the Associates will think themselves obliged to withdraw their Salary." Minutes, 1 : 220–21. Waring's letters have not been found.

1. Letter not found.

Rev. William Sturgeon to Rev. John Waring

[Philadelphia, 6 November 1764]

Revd. Sir

I wrote to you some Time ago, which I hope came safe to Hand,[1] and that you have been so good as to state my Case to the Honble. Society; our worthy Friend Dr. Franklin goes Home once more on the Affairs of this Province and I hope you will receive this from him.[2]

The Negro-School is in much the same Condition as I acquainted you by my last Letter, but as a new Mistress must be put in the 20th. Instant I hope it will very soon be in a flourishing Condition.[3]

It would give me great Pleasure to hear often from you, especially how the Honble. Society determines my Case; what they have already done has been of great Disservice to me, and when I shall be able to repair the Damage Time alone will tell, but at the same Time I have not the least doubt but they will do me ample justice. Please to present my Duty to the honble. Society, and assure the worthy Associates that no Care shall be wanting to forward the Negro School. In the mean Time I take the Liberty to assure you Revd. Sir that I am your most obliged Friend and affectionate Brother

Wm. Sturgeon

Philadelphia November 6 1764

ALS. Sent "per Favor Dr. Franklin." This letter was read by the Associates at their meeting of 3 January 1765. Minutes, 1 : 218.

1. Dated 15 August 1764, above.
2. On 7 November 1764 Franklin embarked for England as the Pennsylvania Assembly's agent. *Franklin Papers* 11 : 447.
3. The new mistress was Mrs. Ayres (or Ayers), who served the school until about May 1768.

Robert Carter Nicholas to Rev. John Waring

Williamsburg 21st. December 1764.

Revd. Sir.

I have been too long indebted to you for your two last Favours, which duly came to Hand, tho' I assure you that I have not been unmindful of them. I have defer'd writing to you hitherto in Hopes that I should have been able to make some few Alterations in favour of the School, which I have not yet been able to accomplish. It gives me great Pleasure to find that my former Letter had met with so thorough an

Approbation; the Rules transmitted to you, were rather what I would wish to have comply'd with, than what I expected would be given into at once; however I must endeavour to enforce them by Degrees; I assure you, Sir, however strange it may appear, 'tis a very difficult Business I am engaged in. I find it necessary to manage it with great Delicacy. The School is much in the same State, as when I wrote last, except in the Change of a few Scholars. The Mistress I believe is very diligent, but I am very much puzled to furnish her with a convenient House for the Purpose. I am sorry to acquaint you that poor Mr. Yates is dead; he left us about the Middle of September last; so that I am left alone in this Business. He is succeeded, as President of our College & Minister of this Parish by the Revd. Mr. James Horrocks; who I dare say would chearfully give me his Assistance, if it were asked; I would therefore recommend it to you to write to this Gentleman on the Subject;[1] I have not yet drawn upon you for any more Money since June 1763, tho' I have punctually paid the Mistress her Wages; perhaps I may trouble you with a Draught in a few Days for £25 Sterling, & don't doubt but it will meet with due Honour. I am almost ashamed to send you this Scroll, but I am hurried at present with a great Variety of Business & my Clerk is also closely engaged. I shall be more full in my next & therefore must hasten to assure you that I am with the greatest Esteem & Regard, Revd. Sir, Your most obedient Servant

Ro. C. Nicholas

ALS. Endorsed as read 4 April and answered 23 April 1765, and "Agreed that Mr. W[aring] be desired to request Mr. Horrocks to Join with Mr. Nicolas in conducting the Negroe [School]." See Minutes, 1:222. Waring's letter to Horrocks has not been found.

1. The Rev. James Horrocks (c. 1734–72), a native of England, was educated at Trinity College, Cambridge (A.B. 1755, A.M. 1758). He was ordained in September 1757 and was licensed for Virginia in November 1761. Horrocks was rector of Bruton Parish 1764–71, president of the College of William and Mary 1764–71, commissary of the bishop of London 1768–71, and a member of the Council 1770–71. He died in Oporto, Portugal, in March 1772 on his way to England, to which he was returning because of ill health. *Executive Journals of the Council* 6:344; Venn, *Alumni Cantabrigienses*; Weis, *Colonial Clergy Va., N.C., S.C.*, p. 26.

Robert Carter Nicholas to [Rev. John Waring]

Williamsburg in Virginia 27th. December 1764.

Revd. Sir.

I did myself the Pleasure of writing to you a few Days since,[1] & then advised that I should soon draw upon you for £25 Sterling on

Acct. of the Negro School in this City; I at the same Time acquainted you of the Death of poor Mr. Yates & that the Bill would therefore be drawn in my Name only. The Design of my troubling you with these few Lines is merely that you may in Time & properly be again advised of my Draught to Mr. John Norton[2] for the Sum of £25. I am very respectfully, Sir, Your most obedient Servant

Ro. C. Nicholas

ALS.

    1. Dated 21 December 1764, above.

    2. John Norton (1719–77), head of the firm of John Norton & Sons, was Virginia agent of the firm before 1764, when he moved to London. Norton was a justice of the peace for King William County in 1744 and for York County in 1747, and he was sheriff of York in 1748. He served as a burgess for York County 1749–55. Norton and Nicholas were friends and business associates, and were joined familially in 1772 when Nicholas's daughter Sarah married Norton's son John Hatley Norton (1745–97), the Yorktown representative of the Norton firm. Samuel M. Rosenblatt, "Merchant-Planter Relations in the Tobacco Consignment Trade: John Norton and Robert Carter Nicholas," *VMHB* 72 (1964): 454–55; *John Norton & Sons.*

Rev. Jonathan Boucher to Rev. John Waring

[Caroline County, Virginia] January the 22d. 1765.

Revd. Sir

I am much obliged to You for your Letter bearing Date October 17, 1764,[1] which came to Hand about the Middle of last Month: And I beg You will be pleased to make all suitable Acknowledgements, in my Name, to the Gentlemen Associates for the Marks of Attention with which They have been pleas'd to honour my poor Opinion's & Endeavours. How truly Christian is that generous Benevolence & pious Zeal of Their's for the Preservation of the Souls of so many poor, bewilder'd human Creatures! And who can forbear being grieved, (if it be true what Dr. Mayhew, with so much Appearance of Reason on his Side, has asserted) if all these amiable Designs & religious Purposes produce no suitable Effects?[2] For my own Part, I confess myself almost totally unacquainted with the State of these Institutions; but from what has occurr'd to my own Observation, I have Ever been of Opinion that all the good Effect of these Charities entirely depends on those Persons who are employ'd in the immediate Direction & Management of Them. Had it been in my Power to have erected a School, agreeable to the Expectations of the Associates, how chearfully wou'd I have attempted it? But, I again repeat it, I think it impracticable. Yet many important Services may still be done amongst the poor Negros; & I hope I have been the Means of doing some. At present I know no Way so likely as That which You have happily taken. Proper Books, distributed amongst Them, & proper Enquiries into their Improvements seems to be all, that is in the Power of the Best of us to do, in Parishes like Ours. A great Deal however this is of itself: & I might surprise You were I to relate to You some of the Conversations I have had with Negros to whom I had given Books. It must be a Comfort to the Associates, if any Applause upon Earth can be a Comfort, to have the Prayers & Blessings of many of these unfortunate People, which I have so often heard xpress'd with Tears of Gratitude.

It is a great Grief & Loss to Me that the Box so kindly sent Me by the Associates is not come to Hand, and I fear never will. It was a Pity You had not mention'd the Ship's & Captain's Name by which it was sent; as I am at a Loss where or how to enquire about it. I hope You will inform Me in your Next, tho' I'm afraid it may be too late. For the future, Give Me Leave to recommend it of You always to prefer a Ship for Rappahannock River; as most of these Captns. are personally acquainted with Me, & would be careful of Things entrusted to Them. In the present Case, cou'd I even find out the Captn., by whom the Box was sent, it is in his Power either to produce it or not, as I have no Bill of Lading to shew for it, as is usual in such Cases, & necessary, where the Captn. is a Stranger. The Letter came by Post, which is now regularly established thro' This & all the Northern Colonies.[3]

I am now to inform You that at Christmas last, I left the Parish of Hanover. This which I now hold is higher up the River, & is esteem'd easier & healthier; a Circumstance which render'd a Change greatly desirable, as in August last, I was taken with one of the severest & most violent Fits of Sickness I have ever been try'd with, the Effects of which I yet feel, & fear I shall continue to feel thro' the Rem[ainde]r of my Life. I shall be equally desirous, & hope equally able, to xert my Endeavours in promoting the spiritual Interests of the Slaves, who, in every Parish, make so considerable a Part of the Souls under our Care. And if You will still be pleased to continue your Friendship & Correspondence, assure yourself I will always chearfully concur in any Schemes which may propose to [torn] to any Part, how inconsiderable or despicable soever, of [the] human Race. I am, Sir, Yours & the Gentlemen Associates' most obedient & most humble Servant

Jonan. Boucher

Direct for Me Rector of St. Mary's, in Caroline County
Rappahannock River Virginia

ALS. Endorsed as read 3 October 1765 and "Answered July. 20: 65. Bill of Lading inclosed to Mr. Orr. Box & Lett. sent by the same Ship. If Box lost, another shall be sent. Inquiries of State of Religion among the Slaves." See Minutes, 1:227–28. Also endorsed as answered again on 23 October 1766 and 25 March 1767. For the books sent, see "Catalog of Books," p. 115. Waring's replies have not been found.

    1. Letter not found.

    2. See Auchmuty to Waring, 2 May 1764, note 3, above.

    3. The addition of so much territory to Britain's colonial empire, which resulted from the Treaty of Paris of 1763, made necessary the creation of two separate postal districts in 1764. The line separating the two districts was the Virginia–North Carolina border, so that Virginia was thereafter linked more closely with the northern colonies than it had been under the previous postal arrangements. Ross Allan McReynolds, "History of the United States Post Office, 1607–1931" (Ph.D. diss., University of Chicago, 1935), p. 35.

Lewis De Rosset to Rev. John Waring

[Wilmington, North Carolina, 22 April 1765]

Revd. Sir,

    I am to acknowledge the Rect. of your Esteemed favour which together with the Box of books you sent came to my hands last Year.[1] I should have Answered your Letter before now, but I thought it would be best to deferr writing untill I had tryed all Methods to carry into Execution the Laudable Designs of the Society, But am very sorry to say that all my endeavours for that purpose have proved Innefectual as I can find no Person here properly qualified to Instruct the black Children in the manner you propose. And If such a one could be found yet in this Country Twenty Pounds Sterling is by far too little to Support them and Am much afraid that nothing more can be got here, for I have spoke to several Gentlemen here who I thought might send black children to School and proposed to them to give the Master or Mistress something out of their own pocketts to encourage the undertaking, but have not found them willing to doe that. I thought that the same Master or Mistress might teach white Children as well as black their Parents paying for it, but there seems in this a repugnancy in them to have their children instructed with their Slaves, which though in my Opinion a very trifling reason, yet their prejudices are very deeply Rooted.

    I think upon every thing that I can Judge of there is but one way to carry here into execution the charitable designs of the Society, which is by sending over here a proper person themselves, who perhaps with the Salary and taking in sewing work may make a shift to get a Living. As for my part I shall doe every thing in my Power to promote the Designs of the Society, and for whatever black Children of my own that I shall put to School I will give A reasonable allowance to the Mistress besides the Salary the Society allows, and I hope others may follow the same example, but this is by no means very certain and is Rather what I wish for than any certainty. You will therefore determine whether it will be worth while sending a person over from England.

I am ashamed to Inform you that in this Parish we have no Clergyman, for though We have a Law that makes a handsome allowance for a Minister of the Church of England we have been so unhappy as not yet to have obtained one; many representations have been made to the Society for propogating the Gospell In Foreign parts which have been either neglected or totally disregarded and sectarys of different denominations are daily increasing.[2]

I salute You And Am with due Respect Revd. Sir Your most Obedient Humble Servant

Lewis De Rosset

Wilmington Cape Fear April 22d. 1765

ALS. Endorsed as read 3 October 1765. See Minutes, 1:228–29.

1. Waring's letter has not been found. It was probably written after the Associates' meeting of 7 April 1763, at which they "Agreed That proposals be sent to Wilmington in N. Carolina for opening a School for 30 negroe Children at a Salary not exceeding 20£ Sterling a Year, & that a Box of Books be sent for the immediate Use of the School." Minutes, 1:190.

2. "An Act for Making Provision for an Orthodox Clergy," passed in 1762, provided for a salary to every parish minister of £133.6.8 proclamation money, as well as a glebe of at least two hundred acres. N.C. State Recs. 23:583–85.

St. James's Parish, New Hanover County, had not had a minster since the Rev. Michael Smith (b. 1698), who served the parish 1759–60. Governor Arthur Dobbs wrote to the S.P.G. on 29 March 1764 asking the Society to send a clergyman as missionary to the parish, but the Society did not comply with the request. The parish was served from 1766 by the Rev. John Wills, who had come from England on his own and without a license or missionary appointment (see Barnett to Waring, 11 June 1768, note 3, below). Although St. James's Parish sought the services of a clergyman, the vestry was apparently unwilling to have a minister formally inducted; Wills served on a year-to-year basis. In a return of information on counties and parishes submitted to the S.P.G. in 1767, the St. James's Parish entry reads, "Able to support, tho' expressed no desire to receive an inducted Minister." N.C. Col. Recs. 6:58–59, 1041, 7:541; Weis, Colonial Clergy Va., N.C., S.C., p. 90.

Rev. Samuel Auchmuty to Rev. John Waring

New York May the 3d. 1765

Revd. Sir

I hope you will attribute my late Silence to my many and repeated Duties, which fell very hard upon me after the Death of Doctor Barclay, my late very worthy Predecessor. I am now more at leisure, as I have an Assistant that saves me a great deall of trouble. In my last I believe I hinted to you that I should not continue much longer in the Service of the Venerable Society, and therefore was not much concerned whether the Negro Catechist's were continued or not; *only* on account of the poor Slaves. Since my appointment to the Rectory, I have taken the Liberty to mention the Affair to the Society, in the light, I conceive it; And, after thanking that Venerable, and good Body, for their many and repeated kindnesses to me, which I shall ever gratefully acknowledge; I beg'd my dismission, and took the Liberty to recommend to them, the Revd. Mr. Ogilvie my Assistant, as a very proper person to succeed me.[1] I am very confident that unless the Society take the poor Slaves under their immediate Care, and appoint them a Catechist, with a Salary of only thirty pounds Sterling per Annum, they will be neglected and suffer greatly in their Spiritual Concerns; which, considering their present good Disposition, and their Numbers (upwards of thirty Communicants) will be a great pity.

Your School I have not neglected, but have not been at it quite so often as I used to visit it; having many things to settle and regulate upon my coming to the Rectory of this City, which naturally engaged my Attention: however I find, that the Mistress continues faithfully to discharge her Duty, that the Children make a considerable proficiency in their learning, and, that the worthy Associates bounty is extremely well disposed off. I intend (God willing) to bend my Attention and thoughts to it as usual. I have drawn upon you for the Mistresses half Years Salary, due the 22th. of last March.

If you have sufficient leisure, you will particularly oblige me, with your sentiments about the appointment of a Bishop for America. One is extremely wanted, & much wished for, by many, but feared and dreaded by those, who ever have been, & ever will be Enemies to Order and Decency.

The Continuance of your Correspondence will afford me a high Satisfaction; and be esteemed an honor conferred upon, Revd. Sir Your Much Obliged Brother & very humble servant

Samuel Auchmuty

P.S. I flatter myself you will excuse haste, as I really h[ave no time to] Copy a Letter.

ALS. Sent "Per favor of Capt. Davis Q.D.C." Endorsed as read 3 October 1765. See Minutes, 1:229. Also endorsed as answered October 1765. The bracketed portion of the P.S. is a conjectural reading, an ink blot having obscured the manuscript. Waring's reply has not been found.

1. Auchmuty to the Rev. Daniel Burton, secretary of the S.P.G., 13 April 1765, S.P.G. MSS., B2, no. 9.
The Rev. John Ogilvie (1724–74), of New York City, was educated at Yale College (A.B. 1748) and received degrees from Columbia College (A.M. 1767, D.D. 1770) and Aberdeen (D.D. 1770). Ogilvie was ordained by the bishop of London in June 1749 and received the King's Bounty for New York the following month. He was S.P.G. missionary to the Mohawks and minister of St. Peter's Church, Albany, and of St. George's Church, Schenectady, 1750–60. During the French and Indian War he was chaplain to the Royal American Regiment. Ogilvie was assistant to Auchmuty from 1764 until his death. Dexter, *Yale Graduates* 2:174–77.
Late in 1764 Auchmuty wrote to the S.P.G. that Ogilvie was settled as one of his assistants and that he had for the present delivered the charge of the Negroes to Ogilvie. After reading Auchmuty's letter of 13 April 1765, which expressed his wish that Ogilvie be appointed catechist, the Society resolved that "the People of New York be acquainted, that it is expected they should support the Catechist to the Negroes themselves, without any assistance from the Society, they being well able to do it." S.P.G. Journals, 16:384–86 (meeting of 19 July 1765). Ogilvie was never appointed catechist, although his correspondence with the S.P.G. indicates that for a time he instructed New York's blacks. The S.P.G. did not appoint a new catechist until 1770. Auchmuty to S.P.G., n.d., read 15 February 1765, S.P.G. Journals, 16:297–98; S.P.G. Journals, 18:431–32 (meeting of 19 October 1770); Ogilvie to S.P.G., 23 April, 29 September 1765, S.P.G. MSS., B2, nos. 116[a], 116[b].

Rev. William Sturgeon to Rev. John Waring

[Philadelphia, 15 May 1765]

Revd. Sir,

I have received a Letter from you,[1] and I take it very kind that you are so plain with me. When first the Honble. Society by their Secretary informed me that a Complaint was lodged against me for totally neglecting my Duty for two Years,[2] I was much provoaked, that my neighbour, nay, a Member of the Church, and a Member of the Society should be capable of such a Design, without letting me know the least of it, and that the Honble. Society should dismiss me their Service in such a Manner, after having spent the prime of Life therein.

I never neglected my Duty to the Negroes, till I was advised by Dr. Smith, and even then I catechized and instructed their Youth not on Sunday Nights but on every Wednesday and Friday immediately after Prayers. Indeed I endeavoured to spend the whole of my Time in such a Manner as might answer the good Designs of the Honble. Society. I have again reassumed the catecatical Lecturs for the Adult Negroes and I have from thirty to forty that attend regularly every Sunday Evening at the Church School-House. If I have been too warm your Goodness of Heart will plead my Excuse with the Honble. Society. As to any Certificates in my Favour seems to me needless as Mr. Peters and Dr. Franklin are both in London and my good Friends and Lovers of justice and therefore I would freely risk my Character and Diligence in my Office to their Testimoney.[3] I have the Pleasure to let you and the other Associates know that the Negro School begins to flourish under the new Mistress. Of which I shall give you the Particulars in my next. Please to present my Duty to the Honble. Society, and best Regards to the Associates and Revd. Sir believe to be your most affectionate Brother

Wm. Sturgeon

Philadelphia May 15 1765

ALS. Sent "per Favor Capt. Budden." Endorsed as read 3 October 1765. See Minutes, 1:229.

1. Letter not found.

2. Sturgeon received such a letter from the Rev. Daniel Burton, secretary of the S.P.G., early in 1763. The text of the letter is given in the Christ Church vestry minutes of March 1763. S.P.G. MSS., B21, no. 280.

3. The Rev. Richard Peters (1704–76), a native of England, was ordained in 1731 and arrived in Pennsylvania in 1735. He was an assistant at Christ Church from 1735 until July 1737, when dissension in the congregation resulted in his resignation. He then held various secular offices (secretary of the land office, clerk of the provincial Council, trustee of the Academy and College of Philadelphia, manager of the Pennsylvania Hospital, Pennsylvania representative at the Albany Congress of 1754, and member of the Council) until being called to officiate at the United Congregations during the absence of Duché in England in 1762. On 6 December 1762, upon Duchés return, Peters was elected rector of the United Congregations. Sturgeon and Duché joined with the vestry in requesting Bishop Osbaldeston to license Peters by letter, as "his absence would be very detrimental to our churches." Dorr, *Historical Account of Christ Church*, p. 135. Osbaldeston replied in May 1763 that he approved the appointment of Peters but that he expected Peters "will embrace the first convenient opportunity of coming to England, and he will find me disposed to grant him a license in due form." Ibid., p. 143. Peters was absent from Philadelphia on his voyage to England from the summer of 1764

until December 1765. He served as rector of the United Congregations until September 1775, when he resigned because of his age and infirmities. Dorr, *Historical Account of Christ Church*, pp. 67–69, 131, 134–36, 142–43, 147, 157, 177; Charles P. Keith, *The Provincial Councillors of Pennsylvania Who Held the Office between 1733 and 1776* (Philadelphia, 1883), pp. 235–41; Weis, *Colonial Clergy Middle Colonies*, p. 289.

Rev. Samuel Auchmuty to Rev. John Waring

[New York, 31 May 1765]

Revd. & very worthy Sir

Your very obliging favor of the 18th. of last March, was delivered me a few days ago, by my Friend, the Revd. Mr. Munro;[1] your Civilities to him will ever be gratefully remembered by both him, and myself. Being just ready to set out upon a Journey to Boston my Native City, I have not time to execute any part of the Scheme you mention to me, but hope to put it in execution upon my return Home; which will not be, till near the Fall.[2] It is now nine Years that I have been confined to this Parish, having, in that time, not been absent one week. My close application to parochial Duties, without any Avocation, I perceive has a little impaired my Constitution; my intended Jaunt, I hope will be the best Physician. The Scheme I have shown to a few of my Brethren, but as they are Missionaries from the Venerable Society they think, that they should have their Approbation of it, under the hand of their Secretary to me. This I suppose may easily be obtain'd. This prudence in the Missionaries I can'ot blame. Upon my return from Boston you shall hear from me, further on the Subject.

I Yesterday spent My Afternoon in the Negro School; and find, that every thing in regard to their Education goes on as well as I could wish. There are now no less than thirty Seven Scholars. The reason of exceeding the Number is, that some of the Oldest will leave the School this fall; and the Mistress has interceeded with me to permit her to take all that at present offer, which will more than fill up their places. Those that are to leave the School are well instructed in reading, & sewing &c. and say their Catechise & prayers perfectly well; & what is very Commendable, & pleasing, are very sober & orderly Children. The whole Flock attend Church on the Lords Day, and on Week Days. In my absence I shall get Mr. Ogilvie to visit the School; tho' really the Mistress is so good a Woman that she may very well be trusted. My haste is such, (which I beg you will excuse) that, at present, I can only add, that you have my most sincere prayers for your Health and happiness, and that I am, Revd. & worthy Sir, with great Esteem & Respect, Your much Oblig'd, affectionate Brother & Friend

Saml. Auchmuty

N. York May 31st. 1765

ALS. This letter was read by the Associates at their meeting of 3 October 1765. Minutes, 1 : 230.

1. Waring's letter has not been found. For the Rev. Harry Munro see Biographical Appendix.
2. The scheme has not been identified, but may have been that mentioned in Munro to Waring, 9 September 1765, below.

Rev. William Sturgeon to Rev. John Waring

[Philadelphia, 24 June 1765]

Revd. Sir

I have drawn upon you a Set of Bills of Exchange for ten Pounds Sterling being Half a Years Salary due to Mrs. Ayers for keeping the Negro-School. She takes great Care in their Instruction, and the Number you will see by the inclosed List under the Hand of the Mistress and her Husband.[1] I spare no Trouble to promote the pious Designs of the worthy Associates, and I assure you Numbers of Negroes who have been educated in the School make Profession of our holy Religion and attend regularly at Church.

In your last[2] you intimate that my Letters to the Honble. Society are expressed in Terms too warm, very like it was the Case, for I was very much affected, with the Affair, both as it injured my Character as a Minister of the Gospel, and narrowed my Support, having a large Family of Children to bring up and educate. I would therefore request the Favour of you to make my Appoligy to the Board and assure them that I always had, and still have a Heart flowing with Love and Gratitude towards them, and should think [it] a peculiar Honor if I should be so happy as to be taken into their Service.

I have always catechised the Negro-Children, and explain'd its several Parts as their Capacities would admit; I have assumed the Instruction of the Adults, more than Half a Year, more than 30 attend every Sunday Evening. As to the Particulars of my Conduct from the Time that I was taken into the Societies Service I refer to Dr. Franklin and the Revd. Mr. Peters both in London. Any other Recommendation from this Place would be giving the Honble. Society needless Trouble. Mr. Hughes and I joined a Petition to the Honble. Society thro Dr. Burton acquainting them of several Islands lying in the River and Bay of Delaware that are as yet seized in the Crown, and praying them to obtain a Grant, which would be in Time a very considerable Addition to the Incomes, of that Honble. Body. Please to let us know by a Line the Fate of it.[3] After my warmest Regards to the worthy Associates, and most fervent Prayer to Almighty God for Success on their pious Endeavours I am Revd. Sir your most affectionate Brother and humble Servant

Wm. Sturgeon

Philadelphia
june 24 1765

ALS. Sent "per Mr. Evans." Endorsed as read 3 October and answered in the same month. Also endorsed: "No List inclosed. Lett. to 3d. Person little regarded. Had Dr. F[ranklin] & Mr. Pet[ers] signd a Memorial it might have had its use; desired him to apply to Dr. Smith for his Annual Subscription." See Minutes, 1 : 231. Waring's reply has not been found.

    1. Enclosure not found.

    2. Letter not found.

    3. John Hughes (c. 1712–1772) was a Philadelphia merchant, farmer, and distributor of stamps for Pennsylvania under the Stamp Act. He served in the Pennsylvania Assembly from 1755 to 1764 and moved to Portsmouth, New Hampshire, in 1769, where he had been appointed collector of customs. *PMHB* 35 (1911): 442n; *Franklin Papers* 6: 284n–85n; Morgan and Morgan, *Stamp Act Crisis*, chap. 14.

    Hughes and Sturgeon wrote to the Rev. Daniel Burton, secretary of the S.P.G., on 23 March 1765 advising him of the availability of many islands in the Delaware River between New Jersey and Delaware. They claimed that "these Islands are not the Property, nor yet subject, to the Laws of either Province, but in many Cases are, Assylums for Dishonest Men to screen themselves from paying their just Debts," and if acquired from the crown by the S.P.G. would provide revenue for the support of the Church in the colonies. S.P.G. MSS., B21, no. 283. Their advice was apparently never heeded.

Rev. Marmaduke Browne to Rev. John Waring

[Newport, 1 August 1765]

Revd. Sir,

Your favour of February 25th. came to hand July the fourteenth.[1] Immediately upon the receipt of it I called a Vestry, & laid your letter before them; with the contents of which I had the satisfaction to observe them duly affected. They appeared roused with the alarming &

233

affecting consideration it contained, & promised to exert themselves for the future, in procuring the number of children required, & in affording me such other assistance, as might tend to promote the religious instruction of the poor Blacks. You will perceive by the date of this, that I have scarcely had time to determine whether they will comply with their engagement or not; I must therefore beg your patience 'till October next, when upon the receipt of another draught, you shall also receive a full & circumstantial account of the school, & of the Mistress, & whether it is in our power to continue the school upon such a footing, as that the charity of the worthy Associates may not be misapplied, & others more deserving deprived of it. It is matter of real concern to me, to observe, the difficulty which has hitherto attended the carrying this charitable scheme into execution; but I am encouraged to further perseverance, from the information Mr. Auchmuty of [New] York has given me, of the difficultys & obstructions he had to contend with, in settling the Associates School at that place; all which he at length subdued, & is now satisfied that it answers the purposes intended. That this may be the case here, is the hearty desire, & I assure you shall be the earnest endeavour of him who is with much esteem your affectionate Brother & humble Servant

Marmaduke Browne

Newport August 1st. 1765.

ALS. Initially endorsed as read in November 1765, subsequently corrected to 5 December 1765. See Minutes, 1:234.

1. Letter not found. See Browne to Waring, 6 November 1764, bibliographic note, above.

Rev. Harry Munro to Rev. John Waring

[Philipsburg, New York, 9 September 1765]

Revd. & Dear Sir,

Soon after my arrival in New york I had an Opportunity of seeing Several of my Brethren of the Clergy, both of this & the Neighbouring Provinces. Mr. Auchmuty & I finding so favourable an Opportunity, laid before them your Scheme, or laudable proposal for forming a charitable Society in America; particularly in New-york, & the adjacent provinces.[1] Mr. Auchmuty & I did all in our power to explain the Nature of it, & make them Understand it; Also informing them of your generous Benefaction towards laying a foundation for such a Society. Our worthy friend Mr. Auchmuty highly Approved of it, & did all he could to promote it; But will you believe it my dear Sir? I dare say, you'll be surprized; neither Mr. Auchmuty nor I could prevail on our Revd. Brethren. They all disapproved of the Scheme, or at least did not chuse to favour it. Their Reasons for so doing I can not tell. The only Reason they gave was, that no Society or Corporation should be formed here, till we get a Bishop sent over to us. If this be a sufficient Reason, I leave you to judge. With all due submission to my Revd. Brethren, I must beg leave to be of a different Opinion. I am as desirous of having a Bishop in America, as they are; but can not conceive, that our forming a Society on your plan, could have the least tendency to hinder or prevent a Bishop's Coming over. As we have no such happy prospect at present, I humbly think, we ought to do all the good we can, till we get a Bishop; & I am still of the Opinion, that a Society formed on your plan, would be of great Service. But what shall we say? To my great surprize & astonishment, it was carried in the Negative, by a great Majority of Voices. Pray let me hear from you by first Opportunity, and let me know what to do with your Books, I should rather say Pamphlets, whether you will have me to sell them on your account, or send them back to London. I must now tell you something Concerning myself. My mission is like to do well. My Church daily increases, and I have now a pretty decent Congregation. I think, I can say without Vanity, that my Preaching & other Services give entire Satisfaction to my people; but yet I can not help thinking, they might do more for me & the Church, than they really do. My Encouragement as to money matters, is very Small. If the Society should think proper to appoint me for Some other Mission, & leave it in my own Option to Stay here, or to move to Some vacant parish, I have great Reason to think, I could put this Mission on a more respectable Footing, than it is at present; for I know, my Congregation, rather than part with me, would augment my Salary, & do Something extraordinary for the Parsonage-house & Glebe.

This my dear Sir, I only mention to you as my Friend; and as you are well acquainted with several members of the Society, I am fully persuaded, you have Interest enough to obtain such a favour, & I hope you will make a proper use of it, not only on my account, but also for the good of the Church. You may easily guess my Reasons for asking this favour, tho' I can not fully explain them. I must only say in general, that it is here, as in other parts of the world, Ready to make fair promises, but slow to perform. They require a Spur, and this is the only Spur I can think of.[2]

Please to give my kind Compliments to Mr. Bird the Bookseller. His Letter & the little money sent in it is still in my hands; which is owing to my not finding a proper person going to that place; But Mr.

Bird may depend upon it, I will not forget to send it by the first sure opportunity. It is a remote place & people of Credit do not often go that way.

I offer you my best Respects, & am with great Esteem Reverend & Dear Sir Your most affectionate Brother & Servant

Harry Munro

Philipseburgh. 9 September 1765.

ALS.

1. Waring's scheme has not been further identified. Munro must have met his colleagues informally, for the annual convention of the clergy of New Jersey, attended by several New York clergymen, including Auchmuty, was not held until October 1765. The Rev. George Morgan, D.D., *History of the Church in Burlington, New Jersey* (Trenton, 1876), pp. 281–85.

2. In a letter to the S.P.G. of 23 October 1764 asking that Munro be appointed missionary to Philipsburg, Col. Frederick Philipse III stated that he had erected a stone church at his own expense and had laid out a 250-acre glebe for a clergyman; that a good house would be provided; and that the parishioners would contribute £81 currency, or £48 sterling, as an annual salary for Munro. S.P.G. MSS., B3, no. 255. Because these commitments were not fulfilled Philipse had difficulty several years later in obtaining a successor to Munro. For Philipse and his later correspondence with the S.P.G. see Auchmuty to [Waring], 30 March 1769, note 2, below.

Robert Carter Nicholas to [Rev. John Waring]

Williamsburg 13th. September 1765.

Sir.

I fully intended by some of the Ships this Fall to have given you a distinct & circumstantial Account of the Negro School under my Care in this City; but my Indisposition for several Months past has almost interrupted my Attention to Business of every Kind. The Number of Scholars continues pretty much the same, about thirty; the Mistress is pretty much advanced in Years & I fear the Labours of the School will shortly be too much for her; if I find this is really the Case, I will endeavour to procure another, tho' I am apprehensive of great Difficulties in fixing upon a proper Person. I have tried to enforce some of the Rules, which you were pleased to approve, but find they are not well relish'd; however I will persevere. I find it extremely difficult to procure a proper House for the Mistress & her Scholars, Rents are so very high in this Place. I will make it my Business very soon to visit my Charge & by some future Opportunity you shall hear more particularly from me. I am much obliged to you & the Associates for your kind & friendly Wishes; be pleased to pay my Respects to them, & believe me, on all Occasions, to be very sincerely, Sir, Your Friend & Servant

Ro. C. Nicholas

ALS. The letter is endorsed as read November 1765, although the Associates' Minute Book records its reading on 5 December 1765. Minutes, 1:234–35.

Fielding Lewis to [Rev. John Waring]

[Fredericksburg, Virginia, 14 September 1765]

Sir

Your Favour with a Box of Books I received by Capt. Steel,[1] and shall with pleasure do everything I can to promote the pious design of the Society. I had some difficulty in procuring a proper Person to undertake the School for the Education of Negroe Children the allowance being so small, that the greatest part of it will be paid for House rent & Fireing; Mr. Nicholas has furnish'd me with the Rules establish'd at the School in Williamsburg which are so well calculated for the well Government of it, that I have establish'd the same in Fredericksburg; The School was opened the [*blank in MS.*] of April and there are now Sixteen Children who constantly attend who have improv'd beyond my expectation. The Revd. Mr. James Marye the Minister of the Parish has given me all the assistance he could, and has promised to call frequently and examine the Children; As they begin allready to Read prittily there will be occasion for a few Testaments and Prayer Books, for I propose introducing them into Church as soon as they are capable of joyning in the Service; I shall in my next send you a Copy of the School Register werein is enter'd the Ages of the Children and the time of their admittance, and at the same time draw on you for the first Half Years Salary. I am with the greatest Respect, Sir Your most Obedient Humble Servant

Fielding Lewis

September the 14th. 1765

ALS. Endorsed as read November 1765 and answered 16 March 1766 "by Russia Merchant Capt. Carnaby by which a Box of Books was sent freight paid." The Minute Book records the reading of this letter on 5 December 1765, at which time the Associates "Agreed that Thanks be returned to Mr. Lewis for his kind and charitable Concurrence in promoting the Charitable Designs of the Associates and that Mr. Waring do send by the first Opportunity a Packet of Books." Minutes, 1:235–36. For the books sent, see "Catalog of Books," p. 128. Waring's reply has not been found.

1. At their meeting of 3 May 1764 the Associates "Agreed that Proposals be sent to Fredericksburgh in Virginia for opening a School there for thirty Negroe Children, & that a Packet of Books be sent for the Use of the School." Minutes, 1:211. Later that month a box of 110 books was sent. See "Catalog of Books," p. 115.

Rev. Samuel Auchmuty to Rev. John Waring

New York October 26th. 1765

Revd. Sir

I have once more the pleasure to acquaint you that the Negro School in this City, intrusted to my Care is more than full. There have been all the Summer Seven above the Complement, and there are now three. The Mistress performs her part intirely to my satisfaction, and the School is in as flourishing a Condition as I could wish. The Children constantly attend divine Service, on Sundays, and on week Days; and are frequently Catechised by me. The few that have left the School turn out sober industrious, honest Slaves; constantly attend Mr. Ogilvie's Catechetical Lecture; and will, I have great reason to expect, be a Credit to our most holy Religion.

I have, in a former Letter, acquainted you, that the Children besides being taught to read, and to learn their Catechise and prayers, are also taught to sew & knit; at both which employments several of them are considerable Proficients.

This little Nursery of Christians will, by the blessing of God, be the means of inlarging our glorious Redeemer's Kingdom; and spreading the true knowledge of Jesus Christ among the poor unfortunate Blacks; whose Masters & Mistresses have not their eternal Welfare as much at heart, as Christians ought: tho' I must do them the Justice to say that they mend of late.

I must beg of you to supply me with a few more Spelling Books, as I gave the last I had to the Mistress some time ago. She is as careful of their Books as possible: but, still Children will destroy them.

As I have no time to Copy my Letter, I must beg you will excuse Inaccuracies &c.: And assure yourself that I am Revd. Sir, the worthy Associates' & your, much Obliged & very humble Servant

S: Auchmuty.

P.S. I have drawn for ½ Years Salary due the 22th. last month. Are we never to be blessed with a Bishop in America?

ALS. Endorsed as read 7 February 1766 and "Answered March 16 & sent a Box of Books by the Amalia Cap. Richards." This letter was actually read by the Associates at their meeting of 6 February 1766, at which time they "Agreed that Some Spelling Books & suitable catechetical ones be Sent to Dr. Auchmuty." Minutes, 1:239. For the books sent, see "Catalog of Books," p. 129. Waring's reply has not been found, but an indication of its partial contents is given in a letter from Auchmuty to the Rev. Samuel Johnson of 12 June 1766: ". . . in a letter from my worthy and pious friend and brother, Dr. Waring, there are the following words: 'As to a bishop for America, which you enquire about, I am extremely doubtful whether such a desirable event will soon take place. The King is very anxious about it, and hath more than once assured the Archbishop of his cheerful concurrence to forward so desirable an event!'" Schneider and Schneider, *Samuel Johnson* 1:362. According to the acknowledgment in Auchmuty to Waring, 21 June 1766, Waring's letter was dated 28 February.

Rev. Marmaduke Browne to Rev. John Waring

[Newport, 20 November 1765]

Rev. Sir,

In my letter of august the first, I promised shortly to give you a full & circumstantial account of the success of our scheme for rousing the vestry & school-mistress, with whose conduct in regard to the school there was not altogether reason to be satisfied. I have now the pleasure to inform you, that a considerable alteration for the better has taken place in consequence of your letter, the mistress has been more careful & diligent in her duty, & the gentlemen of the vestry have discovered a becoming zeal for filling the school, & to that end have chosen a committee of three out of their body to see it effected. 'Tis true all is not done that might be wished, the school has never yet had the full number required, six & twenty are the most that have been collected, & this I am now so well convinced to be owing to disregard in the Masters for the future welfare of their slaves, that I fear it will not be otherwise, until they can be brought to a more just way of thinking in this respect: It is really lamentable to observe, that whilst worthy & charitable persons in England are disposed to exert themselves in behalf of the poor blacks, from whose slavery they reap not the least advantage, those planters whose property they are, & who reap considerable temporal advantages from them, should in return give themselves no trouble or concern about their future & eternal interest, but rather frequently to obstruct & impede it; this is something so much unlike the christian as almost to exceed belief, tis however absolute matter of fact, & many instances can be produced in confirmation of it. I shall not trouble you for any more books until I stand more in need of them than is the case at present. Being determined to put the associates to no other expence than what is absolutely unavoidable, I have endeavoured to make the books I have been already favoured with go as far as possible, so that some remain. Whenever you shall think it proper to give me advice or directions relative to this school I shall endeavour to the utmost of my power to comply therewith, & am Revd. Sir with much respect, Your most obedient humble Servant

Marmaduke Browne

Newport Rhode Island
November 20. 1765.

ALS. Endorsed as read 6 March 1766. See Minutes, 1 : 240. Also endorsed as answered May 1766. Waring's reply, which was dated 30 May 1766, has not been found.

Robert Carter Nicholas to Rev. John Waring

Williamsburg in Virginia 27th. December 1765.

Revd. Sir.

I send you inclosed a List of the Negro Children who belong to the Charity School in this City. It is impossible for me to fix their Ages, but I suppose them to be from about four to ten Years; the Times of their Standing at School, from the Mistress's Acct. which she has not kept with any scrupulous Exactness, are from about six Months to two or two & an half Years. The Rules which I formerly drew up for the better Government of this School & which you & the other Associates were pleased to approve, I would gladly have executed, but soon found that the Masters & Mistresses were so averse to every Thing that lookt like Compulsion, that I thought it most adviseable to relax a little in hopes that Things might be put upon a more agreeable Footing. You'll observe there are thirty four Children in the List, which exceeds the Number, which the Mistress engaged to teach; it is not in her Power to oblige them to give a constant Attendance & therefore, I believe, she is willing to instruct all such as offer themselves; The Owners of Negroes as soon as they are old enough to do little Offices about their Houses, either take them away entirely from the School, or keep them from it at Times, so that they only attend, when there is no Employment for them at Home. The Term, which I proposed for the Children to continue at School was three Years at least; few are allow'd to stay so long, but those, who do, generally learn to read pretty well, & learn their Prayers & Catechism, tho' I fear that most of the good

Principles, which they are taught at School, are soon effaced, when they get Home, by the bad Examples set them there & for want of the Instructions necessary to confirm them in those Principles. I have a Negro Girl in my Family, who was taught at this School upwards of three Years & made as good a Progress as most, but she turns out a sad Jade, notwithstanding all we can do to reform her. I am heartily glad to hear of the Success of your charitable Endeavours in the Northern Provinces; they have but few Negroes in those Places compared with the Number in Virginia & therefore I suppose they are not so much abandon'd. I have lately visited the School here & examin'd the Children, who seem to have made a reasonable Progress; the Mistress is pretty far advanced in Years & I am afraid that the Business will soon be too laborious for her; & how to supply the School better I don't know. I am satisfied that she takes a great deal of Pains with the Children & I shall not fail to encourage her & do every Thing in my Power to promote the Success of so pious an Institution. I shall take the Liberty of making my annual Draught on you for £25 payable to my Merchant Mr. John Norton. Wishing you & the rest of the worthy Associates a long Series of happy Years I remain very respectfully, Sir, Your most obedient humble Servant

Ro. C. Nicholas

ALS. The letter is endorsed as read March 1766, although the Associates' Minute Book records its reading on 3 April 1766. Minutes, 1:243.

Enclosure
List of Negro Children

[Williamsburg, November 1765]

A List of Negro Children who are at the Charity School in Williamsburg November 1765

Mrs. Campbell's young & Mary	2
Mrs. Davenports' William	1
Mr. Hay's Jerry	1
Doctor Carter's Nanny	1
Mr. Blair's John, Dolly, Elizabeth, Catherine, Fanny, Isaac & Johanna	7
Mrs. Burwell's Joseph & Davy	2
Mrs. Prentis's Molly	1
Colo. Johnson's Squire	1
Colo. Chiswell's Edmund & Johnny	2
Mr. Charlton's Nancy & Davy	2
Mrs. Grymes's Phillis	1

Mrs. Orr's Pat & Jack, James & Sal	4
Mr. Thompson's Charles	1
Mr. Brown's Elizabeth	1
Mr. Thompson's Betty	1
Matt. Ashby's Harry & John	2
Mrs. Vobe's Sal	1
Mr. Waters's Sylvia	1
Mr. Randolph's Roger & Sam	2
	in all 34

D. In Nicholas's hand.

Rev. John Barnett to Rev. John Waring

Castle Tryon near Brunswick North Carolina
1st. February [1766] 10 o'Clock at night

Revd. Sir

Since my arrival in Carolina I have heard from no one friend; nor any of my friends (but once) from me; our ports as well as Courts of Justice are shut up and all business at a stand, and this ever since the first of November, and God knows how long it may continue so.[1]

Two Vessels are about to sail, one tomorrow for Portsmouth with Dispatches for the Government, and the other for London with Naval Stores on Thursday next. This comes by the former; by the Latter I write Dr. Burton.[2]

My Situation at present is no farther agreable than as his Excellency our worthy Governor and the most amiable of Women his Lady endeavor to render it so.[3]

At present I have no other *certain* Income than what I receive from the Society: our publick disturbances are risen to such an height, and the Consequences of them are such as you can form but little conception of.

The Vestry have voted me £133:6:8 per Annum Currency (a guinea is 42s.) but I have no other Security for the payment of that Salary than *their honor* as no agreement ent'red into can now be Legal without *stamp'd papers*, and the honor of this Country is but a poor Basis to build any great hopes on.

I cannot have the Cure of Wilmington tho' join'd in the Mission, as that Town is the Capital of another County and pluralities are not known in these parts.

Our Governor writes by this opportunity to the Society & incloses an handsome sum in a bill on Messrs. Drummonds at Charing Cross:

And desires to be admitted a Member of the Society. He is one of the worthiest of Men and has the Interest of Religion much at heart. He has lately procur'd an Act of Assembly for the better Encouragement of the Clergy; he has rais'd their Salaries to the sum within nam'd, and has happily got the right of Induction *vested in the Crown*.[4]

I have genteel Apartments assigned me in the Governor's house and I thank God live extremely happy in the family.

I judge it proper to acquaint you that one Stevens a Scotch presbyterian teacher, comes in this vessel to get Orders; I did purpose to have given you some very particular account of him, but the Captain waits for the Letter and will not give me time to say more than that this Stevens has ill used the Governor, affronted all the Kings Council (but one *Scotch* Gentleman), most villianously abus'd me, and now comes to apply to the Bishop of London for Orders without any recommendation to his Lordship. You'll be able to form some Judgment of the Man when I tell you he has several times preach'd here in a Lawyers old Gown given him at Wilmington to make some waistcoats of. He has I assure you Sir Baptis'd several Children in the Character of a Clergyman of the Church of England, which before I came he had the Impudence to assume, and upon my detecting him he said in public Company he wou'd go home to London, wou'd make a genteel present to the Bishop and knew he cou'd get an Order from his Lordship to supersede me in my Mission. This he afterwards told me himself. And he told some of the King's Council here Any one might get Orders on making a Bishop a present of the price of a good Beaver hatt which he intended doing.

He came here a distress'd Stranger; the Govr. took pity on him and promis'd to recommend him to the Society if he behav'd well for some time, and also give him 50 guineas to bear his Expences, but his Excellency soon saw into the man, forbid him his presence, and will never suffer him to take a living here if he shou'd get ordain'd.[5]

The times are so distracted, that I cannot possibly propose a Negroe School. I beg my best respects may be given to good Mr. Skinner and family[6] and my good friend Mr. Hopkins and his very amiable family.[7]

With the most Extraordinary haste I subscribe Your most humble Servant

John Barnett Missionary

I must write you a[gain] by the other ship as [this one c]annot wait one Moment longer.

ALS: Fulham Papers, 6:312−13, Lambeth Palace Library, London. Sent "per Heron Capt. Parker Q.D.C." Endorsed as read 21 April [1766]. The bracketed portions of the text are conjectural readings, the manuscript being torn.

1. The Stamp Act, which went into effect on 1 November 1765, required the use of stamps on clearance papers issued by customs officers and on documents used in legal proceedings. Thus the colonial boycott of the use of stamps effectively closed the ports and courts. In most colonies, customs officials began issuing clearances without stamps within two months of the effective date of the act. In North Carolina all ports except Cape Fear were open by 12 February 1766. Most North Carolina courts remained closed until news of the repeal of the Stamp Act reached the colony in April 1766. Morgan and Morgan, *Stamp Act Crisis*, pp. 158, 212–14, 228; Donna J. Spindel, "Law and Disorder: The North Carolina Stamp Act Crisis," *North Carolina Historical Review* 57 (1980): 1–16.

2. Barnett to the Rev. Daniel Burton, secretary of the S.P.G., 3 February 1766, S.P.G. MSS., B5, no. 36.

3. William Tryon (1729–88) was governor of North Carolina 1765–71. He married Margaret Wake of London in 1757. *DAB*.

4. Tryon's letter to Burton was dated 29 January 1766. *N.C. Col. Recs.* 7:158. "An Act for Establishing an Orthodox Clergy," passed in May 1765, provided for a salary of £133.6.8 proclamation money, or about £70 sterling, and a glebe of at least two hundred acres. *N.C. State Recs.* 23:660–62. The act was silent on the question of the right of presentation, but since previous acts had explicitly vested the right in the vestries, the silence of the new act was interpreted as giving the right to the crown by implication. See Tryon to Richard Terrick, bishop of London, 6 October 1766, quoted in the following note.

5. Stevens appeared before Richard Terrick, bishop of London, seeking ordination, but was refused. Governor Tryon wrote to Terrick on 6 October 1766:

> By the honor of your Lordships letter bearing date the first of May last I am informed Mr. Stevens came before your Lordship for ordination and brought him an appointment to the parish of Wilmington, which I believe to be a forgery: In the first place the patronage to livings is by the last Clergy Bill implied to be in the Crown, which patronage is reserved to the Governor for the time being by his Majesty's instructions; and secondly I cannot find any person who acknowledges to have given Mr. Stevens such appointment. He was a short time in this province during which time he behaved himself so indiscreetly that I refused to give him letters recommendatory to your Lordship. (*N.C. Col. Recs.* 7:261–62)

Tryon later wrote Terrick, on 20 March 1769, "It is reported that Mr. Stevens has obtained ordination orders and is at present Chaplain to a Man of War." Fulham Papers, 6:330–31.

6. This is probably the Rev. Thomas Skinner, M.A., who was elected an Associate on 16 March 1748/49. Minutes, 1:68.

7. Not identified.

Rev. John Waring to Robert Carter Nicholas

[London, 30 May 1766]

Sir

I am charged with the hearty Thanks of the Associates for your two very obliging Favours One of September 13th. the other December 27th., and more particularly for the latter, wherein You gave a very minute Account of the State of the Negroe School under your Inspection, together with a List of the Children then in the School; The whole, I assure You, was extremely Satisfactory, and gave most Sincere pleasure. The Mistress's Diligence and Fidelity will meet with an ample Recompence from the Hands of our gracious Master, whose Merciful Designs she so assiduously endeavours to promote, and I trust the same good providence which hath hitherto blessed your pious Endeavours in carrying on this benevolent Design, will continue to assist You, and enable You to find out a proper person to undertake the Charge, whenever it shall please him to take the good Woman to himself, or to disable her from performing the Duties of the School. Mr. Lewis of Fredericksburgh, I find, hath acquainted You with the good Success his Endeavours to establish a School there have been blessed with. I am sure we have abundant Reason to be thankful to almighty God for raising up to Us Such able and zealous Coadjutors; and I hope nothing will be wanting on our part according to our Abilities to assist You in promoting this good Work. That God may bless You and Yours with Health and Peace in this world and eternal Glory in the next is the hearty prayer of Sir Your most affectionate humble Servant

Jn. Waring

May. 30: 1766
at Mr. Birds Ave Mary Lane London

ALS: Bray MSS., McGregor Collection, U.Va.

Rev. Samuel Auchmuty to Rev. John Waring

New York June 21th. 1766

Revd. & Worthy Sir,

Your sensible & obliging favor of the 28th. of last February I received but a few days ago.[1]

In General what Mr. Munro has mentioned to you, is too true;

but yet, the Scheme was not drop't; and the reason that nothing has since been done in the Affair, was partly owing to my Absence, and partly to Mr. Munro's being in the Country; & consequently my having but little Conversation with him, since my return from Boston. The Spirit & Success with which you have conducted the Original Intention of the late worthy, Dr. Bray, is astonishing. Divine Providence has remarkably blessed your endeavours, as it ever will all those that are so humanely & piously disposed as you have been. I intend to write to Mr. Munro, and request his coming to me, that He and I may review the Plan, you have proposed, & if possible fall upon some way to put it in Execution. When I went to Boston he was but just returned from England; and what with the bussiness of my Parish, which wanted some new Church Regulations and just then, want of Health, it was not in my power to advert to what he had to say, with the Attention that the Subject required. Assure yourself, it shall be revived, and I hope 'ere long carried on with Success.

You will be pleased to assure the worthy Associates that their School here, continues under the same flourishing Circumstances that it was when I wrote last. It is quite full, and the Scholars are a set of orderly Children, and advance in Spelling, reading, & Sowing & knitting as well as can be expected. They are constant in their Attendance upon Divine service, both on the Lords Day, & on week Days; are in general, perfect in their Catechism & prayers. The Mistress still performs the Duty to great acceptation; and I believe I may venture to say, That the School is in as thriving a way as you could wish; and I flatter myself that, by the blessing of God, it will continue so. The Mistress had half a Years Salary due to her last March, for which I have now drawn, in favor of Richard Nicholls Esqr.

I return you my sincere Thanks for your Congratulation, & good wishes, upon the honor the Illustrious University of Oxford has been pleased to Confer upon me.[2] It came quite unexpected. I shall ever retain a grateful sense of the Condescension & Goodness of the University, and it shall be my future Study to render myself worthy of the Esteem, & Regard of that Ancient, Loyal, & Learned Body, the Chancellor, Masters, and Fellows of the University of Oxford. I wish I was more deserving of their distinguished favor.

I find we must give over even the pleasing hope, of seeing a Bishop among us. I submit to the Judgment of my Superiors, & am convinced that they have adopted the wise & prudent part: But alass! My own Experience and knowledge of the Americans, and the present situation of the Established Church here is such, as makes me dread the Consequence of postponing the sending of Spiritual Fathers among us. In this City the Church increases surprizingly; but assure yourself that in the province, & indeed on the Continent it does not gain Ground in general, nor never will while it is deprived of a perfect & Constitutional Government. These are my sentiments, and I believe they will be found to be well grounded.

I have only to add at present that, I am with great respect & esteem, Worthy Sir, Your Affectionate Brother, & much Obliged humble Servant

Samuel Auchmuty.

P.S. The Box of Books you mention; the unfortunate Mrs. Giles sends me word she has just received, with some Books of her late Husband.[3]

ALS. Endorsed as read 4 October 1766 and answered March 1767. This letter was actually read by the Associates at their meeting of 2 October 1766. Minutes, 1:247–48. Waring's reply has not been found.

    1. Letter not found. See Auchmuty to Waring, 26 October 1765, bibliographic note, above.

    2. Oxford conferred an honorary doctor of divinity degree on Auchmuty on 23 January 1766. The degree was procured for Auchmuty through the recommendation of the Rev. Samuel Johnson. See Johnson to Thomas Secker, archbishop of Canterbury, 20 September 1764, in Schneider and Schneider, *Samuel Johnson* 4:345–48.

    3. For the Rev. Samuel Giles see Biographical Appendix. For the books sent to Giles see "Catalog of Books," p. 128.

Rev. Marmaduke Browne to Rev. John Waring

[Newport, 1 July 1766]

Revd. Sir,

As I have drawn a bill upon you in favour of one Mr. Channing,[1] I do agreeable to your request send a letter of advice therewith. I have at the same time the satisfaction to inform you, that we have at length compleated the number required to fill the school, & that the affairs of it in general are much more agreeably circumstanced than has hitherto been the case. The Mistress I think is more diligent & industrious, & notwithstanding the difficulty that attends the instruction of the blacks, whom I really think to have in general faculties much inferiour to the whites, several of them read tolerably, & the girls have made proficiency in knitting & sewing, & many of both sexes answered in Church the last Lent to general acceptation. None have as yet been presented for baptism, the reason of which you will perceive when you are let into the state of this Colony. Rhode Island Colony has ever been remarkable for an unbounded licentiousness both in principles

& practice, to which no doubt the numberless jarring sectaries it was at first composed of, & at present in a great measure consisteth, have not a little contributed: You will be surprised to hear that not one third of its present inhabitants, which are rated at forty thousand, have been admitted into the church by baptism. I need not observe to you the difficulty that attends conquering the prejudices of education more especially in narrow minds; but hence it is that the principles in which numbers who profess themselves Churchmen were educated, are not so thoroughly eradicated, as to leave them convinced of the necessity of the Sacraments. Judge then whether such Persons who are unbaptised themselves, & who have frequented the service of the Church for many years without submitting to the ordinances, can be very solicitous to have them administered to others, more especially the blacks, whom they are disposed to consider as an inferiour or rather despicable race. This I can assure you is a great impediment in the way of christianizing the blacks; from which I trust time & better information may at length free us. I do not recollect that I have any thing further of moment to communicate at present; You must however give me leave to express my satisfaction at observing your election into the venerable Society for propagating the Gospel;[2] which I do from a conviction of your good & charitable disposition; & give me leave to add that a line from you when at leisure will be esteemed a favour by him who is with much respect, your affectionate Brother & humble Servant

Marmaduke Browne

Newport Rhode Island
July 1st. 1766.

ALS. Endorsed as read 4 October 1766 and answered March 1767. The Associates actually read this letter at their meeting of 2 October 1766. Minutes, 1:248. Waring's reply, which was dated 25 March 1767, has not been found.

    1. Probably John Channing (c. 1715–1771), a native of Boston, a prominent merchant of Newport, and the grandfather of William Ellery Channing. Stiles, *Literary Diary* 1:91–92.

    2. Waring was elected a member of the S.P.G. on 22 September 1763. S.P.G. Journals, 15:405.

Benjamin Franklin to [Rev. Abbot Upcher]

Craven Street London, October 4. 1766

Revd. Sir,

    Since my Return from abroad I have been inform'd of your good Purpose to purchase a land[ed] Estate in America of the Value of One

Thousand Pounds & to apply the Rents and Profits thereof to the Support of Schools for the Instruction of Negro Children. And I have been desired by the Associates to consider the Matter, and give my Opinion where, & in what Manner the Purchase may best be made.[1] I do accordingly acquaint you, that I think the best Province to make the Purchase in is Pennsylvania, where Titles are generally clear, and that it would be well to impower three Persons in Philadelphia to purchase Ground Rents within that City and other safe & profitable Estate in or near the same, as Bargains may offer, in Trust for the Purposes you mention; drawing for the Money here from time to time as the Purchases are made; the Money remaining at Interest here till so drawn for. And the Rents as receiv'd by such Trustees to be applied as you direct. Any farther Advice or Assistance that I can give in the Choice of Trustees or otherwise, shall not be wanting: being respectfully, Revd. Sir, Your most obedient humble Servant

B F.

Draft: American Philosophical Society.

1. In a letter dated 28 June 1766 Upcher desired "the Associates to inform Him how he may lay out One Thousand Pounds by the Purchase of an Estate in America or otherwise that They may receive the clear Rents and Profits thereof for the purposes of educating Negroe Children till Episcopacy is settled in America when He designs settling the said Estate or Money for ever." In a second letter, dated 14 July 1766, Upcher notified the Associates that he had deposited the money at 3 percent interest "till an Estate can be bought in America worth the Money." Minutes, 1:245–46 (meeting of 24 July 1766).

At their meeting of 2 October 1766 the Associates "Agreed that Dr. Franklin be desired to write to . . . Upcher . . . to acquaint him with the Circumstances of purchasing Lands in America." Minutes, 1:248.

[Fielding Lewis to Rev. John Waring]

[Fredericksburg, 12 December 1766]

Fielding Lewis Esqr. of Fredericksburgh, Virginia, says in a Letter dated December 12th. 1766 that He had received a Second Box of Books for the Negroe School,[1] that the Children when admitted into the School were very young, which woud be no disadvantage to them, provided they cou'd be kept at School a Sufficient Time, which he fears the proprietors will not consent to, & therefore He is apprehensive this Undertaking will not Succeed so well as He at first hoped. He will admit none herafter, unless the Masters will engage to continue them at School at least five Years, which Term He thinks necessary for their attaining a proper Degree of Instruction, for unless there is some Regulation of this kind, few will be kept longer than two or three Years which, considering how Young they are admitted, is too short a time for them to make any great progress, & therefore He recommends it to the Associates to discontinue the School after this Year unless the proprietors will agree for the time proposed. Otherwise he thinks the money will be expended, & no good purpose obtain'd. He desires the direction of the Associates. In his Letter was inclosed a List of Seventeen Children then in the School with their respective Ages at Admission, by which it appears they were from five to Eight Years old.[2]

Letter not found. Extract from Minutes, 1:258 (meeting of 2 April 1767). The enclosure has not been found. After reading this letter the Associates "Agreed that Thanks be returnd to Mr. Lewis for his charitable Inspection of the Negroe School, & that He be requested to continue the School on the best terms He can, & endeavour that the Number may be compleated as soon as may be, & that He be acquainted that the Associates are desirous of keeping the School on foot Some time longer, in hopes that much good may result from it." The reply has not been found.

1. For the books sent see "Catalog of Books," p. 128.
2. Enclosure not found.

Rev. Samuel Auchmuty to Rev. John Waring

New York December 22th. 1766

Revd. Sir,

This will be delivered to you by Doctor Johnson Junr., Son of the worthy Clergyman of that Name.[1] He visits you in a public Capacity, and is well qualified to give you any information you may want, concerning Church or State Affairs, in this part of the World.

A Multiplicity of Bussiness of one kind or another has prevented me for some time past, from writing to you, and acquainting you of the present situation of the School. In the Winter season there are not so many Scholars that attend constant as there are in the Summer: however tho' the Weather is severe there are now twenty Eight. By the Spring new one's enough will present. I fully determined to have sent you the complete Number that have entered, and an exact account of those that have left the School since it was opened, but have not time to make the proper enquiry as the Doctor is to Sail to Morrow, and I have many Letters to write. The Children improve as well as can be expected under the Care and Instruction of an able and industrious Mistress. They attend Divine Service every Sunday, and every prayer Day, and behave decent and orderly. After Prayers I sometimes Catechise them, without any previous Notice, and they generally acquit themselves very well. At School they are kept close to their bussiness, and several of them read and work very well. I think upon the whole that the School succeeds beyond my Expectations, and is a great blessing to the poor Slaves.

Mr. Munro, and myself, have not been wanting in making known your Proposal, but as yet with little Success. Better times may offer. One Obstacle is, our Clergy have bent all their thoughts towards the obtaining a Bishop and will hear of nothing else at present. I must confess they have been too importunate, and have dictated rather too much to their Superiors. The Church in America certainly suffers greatly for want of a Spiritual Father to protect and encourage it, and great is our hardship in being deprived of one. But in this, as well as in other Affairs, we must wait with patience till divine Providence is pleased to bless us with an Episcopate. In the interim, for the well governing of the Churches among us, Commissaries should be appointed [and] the Governors of every Province should be ordered to a[id] and assist them, and to countenance the established Church of the Nation more than they now do. But to return.

I hope the account I have given you of the School will be satisfactory to the worthy Associates; and I could wish that It was in my power to bring to perfection your pious & charitable Scheme. Perhaps something further may be done in it before long.

With the most sincere wishes for your health and happiness, I am, Revd. Sir, Your Affectionate Brother and Obliged Servant

Samuel Auchmuty.

P.S. Not long since I drew upon you for the Mistresses Salary; but was just then going out of Town which prevented my writing.

ALS. Sent "Per favor of Dr. Johnson Junr. Q.D.C." Endorsed as answered March 1767. The bracketed portions of the text are conjectural readings, the manuscript being torn. This letter was read by the Associates at their meeting of 5 March 1767. Minutes, 1:256. Waring's reply has not been found.

1. William Samuel Johnson (1727–1819) was the eldest son of the Rev. Samuel Johnson. He graduated from Yale College in 1744 and received an A.M. from Harvard in 1747. Johnson was awarded an honorary doctor of laws degree by Oxford in 1766, at the same time Auchmuty received his D.D. Johnson entered the study of law after graduation from Harvard and began a long career as a statesman and jurist, during which he served in the Connecticut legislature, in the Stamp Act Congress, as Connecticut's colonial agent in London (the occasion of this voyage to England), in the Continental Congress, in the United States Senate, and as president of Columbia College. *DAB*.

Robert Carter Nicholas to Rev. John Waring

Williamsburg in Virginia 27th. December 1766.

Sir.

I wrote to you last June,[1] but I have not been favour'd with your Answer; indeed I'm sorry I troubled you & my other Friends with the Business I have wrote upon, as our General Assembly has confirm'd me in the Treasury & thereby gratified every Wish for Promotion.[2] However you & the rest of my Friends will be pleased to accept my grateful Acknowledgments for whatever Instances of Regard you may have shewn me on the other Occasion. I have Nothing material to say on the Subject of the Charity School more than I mention'd in a former Letter, Things continue pretty nearly Statu quo. That you may be acquainted with the State of our Accounts, I send you a Copy of it from my Book; if any Errors they shall immediately [be] rectified, upon being pointed out. That we may not be confused, I propose begining a new Acct. & have therefore drawn on you for £37.10.8 Sterling the exact Balance which will be due to me the first Proximo. You may perhaps be surprised at the Difference of the Value of our Current Money; it is owing to the fluctuating State of our Exchange, which is now at 25 per cent & I suppose will soon be considerably lower. Be pleased to make my respectful Compliments to your worthy Associates & accept the most cordial Wishes for your own Prosperity & Happiness of, Revd. Sir, Your most obedient humble Servant

Ro. C. Nicholas

ALS. Sent "per Capt. Lilly." The letter is endorsed as read January 1767, although the Associates' Minute Book records its reading on 5 March 1767. Minutes, 1:257.

1. Letter not found.
2. Nicholas was appointed interim treasurer of the colony by Governor Francis Fauquier following the death in May 1766 of Treasurer John Robinson, Jr. Nicholas was confirmed in the post by "An Act for Appointing a Treasurer," signed by Fauquier on 16 December 1766. Hening, *Statutes* 8:211–14; *JHB, 1766–1769*, pp. xiii–xv, 75.

Enclosure
Account

[Williamsburg, 27 December 1766]

The Associates of the late Revd. Doctor Bray in Acct. with Ro. C. Nicholas for the Negro School in Williamsburg

Dr.

1761	December	To Cash paid Mrs. Anne Wager the Mistress ½ years Salary	£ 14.	.
1762	April	To ditto paid her a quarter's Salary	7.	.
	1 July	To ditto . . . . ditto	7.	.
	5 October	To ditto . . . . ditto	7.	.
1763	24 March	To ditto . . . . ditto to 1st. January	7.	.
	7 May	To ditto . . . . ditto to 1st. April	7.	.
	June	To Cash paid Colo. Dudley Digges for a Years Rent[1]	8.	.
	1 July	To ditto paid the Mistress another Quarter	7.	.
	1 October	To ditto . . . . ditto	7.	.
1764	January	To ditto . . . . ditto	7.	.
	1 April	To ditto . . . . ditto	7.	.
	28 April	To Cash paid Colo. Digges for Rent	8.	.
	1 July	To ditto paid the Mistress another Quarter	7.	.
	1 October	To ditto . . . . ditto	7.	.
1765	1 January	To ditto . . . . ditto	7.	.
	1 April	To ditto . . . . ditto	7.	.
	8 May	To ditto paid Colo. Digges for Balance Rent to the Time the Mistress moved from his House in December	6.13.4	
	1 July	To ditto paid the Mistress another Quarter	7.	.
	1 October	To ditto . . . . ditto	7.	.
1766	1 January	To ditto . . . . ditto	7.	.
		To Cash paid Mr. President Blair for Rent[2]	12.	.
	1 April	To ditto paid another Quarter	7.	.
	8 July	To ditto . . . . ditto due the first Instant	7.	.
	1 October	To ditto . . . . ditto	7.	.
	27 December	To a years Salary due 1st. of next Month	7.	.
		To Cash paid Mr. President Blair for Rent due 25th. Instant	12.	.
			£200.13.4	

N.B. the Years Rent paid Colo. Digges in June 1763 was due the April before.

1762	23 June	By Mr. Yates's & my Exchange on the Revd. Mr. Waring	£25 Sterling	
		Exchange at 55 per cent	13.15.0	
				£38.1
1763	23 June	By ditto to Mr. Ch's Steuart[3]	25	
		Exchange at 60 per cent	15	
				40.
1764	December	By my Exchange to Mr. Norton	25	
		Exchange at 60 per cent	15	
				40.
1765	December	By ditto . . . . ditto	25	
		Exchange at 40 per cent	10	
				35.
1766	December	By ditto . . . . ditto	37.10.8	
		Exchange at 25 per cent	9. 7.8	
				46.
				£200.

Virginia Errors Excepted 27th. December 1766.

Ro. C. Nicholas

ADS.

1. Col. Dudley Digges (1718–90) was a burgess for York County 1752–76, a member of the Virginia Conventions and of the Committee of Safety 1775–76, and a member of the state Council 1776–80. The house he rented for the Associates' Negro school was on the northeast corner of Henry and Ireland streets, Williamsburg. *Mason Papers* 1:xlviii; Stephenson, "Negro School in Williamsburg," p. 4.

2. John Blair, Sr., (1687–1771) was a burgess for Jamestown in 1734 and for Williamsburg 1736–40. He was deputy auditor general of the colony from 1728 until his death and was a member of the Council from 1745 (president from 1757) until his resignation in October 1770. *Executive Journals of the Council* 4:182, 5:185, 6:52, 366–67; Greene, *Quest for Power*, p. 467.

3. Charles Steuart (1725–97) was a merchant in Norfolk and served as receiver general of customs for the eastern-middle district of North America. Marylee G. McGregor, comp., *Guide to the Manuscript Collections of Colonial Williamsburg*, 2d ed. (Williamsburg, 1969), entry 56.

Rev. Jonathan Boucher to Rev. John Waring

[Caroline County, Virginia, 9 March 1767]

Dear Sir

I think myself infinitely obliged to You for the respectful Attention which You are pleased to pay to my Correspondence; and I can hardly forbear reproaching myself for having suffered any Cares or Businesses whatever to prevent my making this Acknowledgement earlier. Were it possible for Me to give You an adequate Idea of the thousand disagreeable Concerns & Engagements, Clergymen in Virginia must necessarily be subject to, I am pursuaded You are too candid & benevolent a Man to expect of Us that Exactness & Punctuality, which We acknowledge it is our Duty, as well as Inclination, to observe.

The Box of Books You shipp'd for Me in 1765,[1] came into Potomac, & by that Means were difficultly heard of or come at. Yet, at length, I received Them all safe, & agreeable to your List: for which I again return You & The Associates my sincerest Thanks. I have already distributed many of Them amongst the poor Slaves who are very numerous in this Parish. In many of my former Letters I have told You of the Difficulties Ministers are under to reconcile the Owners of Slaves to their being instructed: and, besides This, They generally are so dispersed, that I cannot see how a School could well be established; unless in Towns, consistent with the Designs of The Associates. And I shou'd never forgive myself were I to be the Means, in ever so small a Degree, of persuading Them to misapply so well-meant a Charity. The Method I take I hope They will think is not misapplying it: I generally find out an old Negro, or a conscientious Overseer, able to read, to whom I give Books, with an Injunction to Them to instruct such & such Slaves in their respective Neighbourhoods. This, I own, coincides not exactly with your Plans; but as I am convinc'd it is the only practicable Method of accomplishing the End You have in View, in Parishes where there are no Towns, I hope You will excuse Me for presuming to judge for You.

Last Summer, in one Day, I baptised 315 Negro Adults, & delivered a Lecture of about an Hour's Length, after reading Prayers to Them, to above 3000. It was the hardest Day's Service I ever had in my Life: yet I know not that I ever before felt such a pleasing Exultation of Heart as I then did: for I cou'd not but think my Employment then truly primitive & Apostolical. It was on Whitsun Monday, which is a general Holiday for Slaves throughout the Colony: & as I had given Notice, that I wou'd on that Day preach to Them in particular, They eagerly flock'd to Me from all Quarters, in greater Numbers than my Churchyard could contain.[2] Delighted as I was, I must confess I was seriously grieved to observe that, having but a weak Voice, but a Few cou'd hear Me, & Fewer still cou'd understand Me. And This reminds Me to ask You whether in such Cases, You think a Man may be allowed, in a few not absolutely essential Particulars, to differ from the Forms directed by the Rubric. Of the three hundred & odd Negroes I that Day baptised, perhaps it wou'd hardly have been possible to have found Three capable of understanding, in the manner required, either the Nature or End of the Sacrament. Was I not then excusable in using Words more level to their Capacities, & exacting Promises from Them better adapted to their Circumstances, than if I had confined myself to the Form prescribed?

It wou'd be difficult to ascertain with Exactness the No. of Slaves in any Parish: I dare say, however, We have in This upwards of 1000. Many of Them attend Church duly, & behave decently: In Summer They are frequently so numerous, as not to be able to find Room. There are five or Six who have Prayer Books, & make the Responses with great Regularity & Propriety. And on Christmas Day last, I believe there were 15 of Them Communicants, &, I am persuaded, very worthy Ones.

I wou'd not willingly be too importunate with the Associates, who have already been very liberal to Me: indeed I do not much want any more assistance, unless They wou'd be pleased to spare Me a few more Prayer Books, Bibles & Testaments. But, as These may be too costly, I shall chearfully submit to whatever They think proper.

One or Two of my Brethren, who live in remoter Parishes, to whom I have mentioned your Contributions to Me, have interceded so strongly with Me for a few of the Books that I could not refuse Them. And might I dare to hope that the Associates wou'd regard a Recommendation from Me, I should take the Liberty of naming these Gentlemen to Them as Persons, I think, very proper to assist Them in the good Work They are Engaged in.

Captn. Fox of The Matty who brings This, is my very particular Acquaintance, & one whom I dare [to] recommend to You for his Care & Diligence.[3] I am, with much Respect, Dear Sir, Yours & The Associates most obedient humble Servant

Jonan. Boucher

St. Mary's, Caroline 9th. March, 1767

ALS. Sent "per The Matty, Captn. Fox." Endorsed as read 4 June 1767. See Minutes, 1:263. The bracketed word in the last paragraph is a conjectural reading, the manuscript being torn.

1. The Associates shipped 233 books to Boucher. See "Catalog of Books," p. 115.

2. Many years later Boucher recalled the event somewhat differently. In his autobiography he wrote, "on the 31st of March, 1766 (being Easter Monday) I baptized 313 Negro adults, and lectured extempore to upwards of one thousand." Boucher, *Reminiscences of an American Loyalist*, p. 57.

3. William Fox (d. 1773), a businessman and tavern operator of Port Royal, Virginia, was the owner and captain of ships in the transatlantic trade

from about 1755 to 1771. T. E. Campbell, *Colonial Caroline: A History of Caroline County, Virginia* (Richmond, 1954), pp. 174, 398, 412, 468, 484.

Rev. Samuel Auchmuty to Rev. John Waring

New York May the 1st. 1767.

Revd. & dear Sir,

It is now some time since I had the pleasure of addressing you; tho', if I mistake not, you are one or two Letters in my Debt. I have nothing very particular to mention to you. The School is still full, and the Young blacks are very constant in their attendance, and improve in their learning. I yesterday visited it, Catechised the Children, heard them their prayers & examined their work—All which gave me pleasure. The Mistress attends her Duty with great faithfulness, and is very clever at her bussiness. Those that have left the School, after proper Instruction, attend every Sunday Evening on Mr. Ogilvie's, with the Adult blacks, & are Catechised. And, I have the pleasure to inform you, that I have not heard of one among them, that has turned out bad. I some time ago drew for the Mistresses Salary, but had not time then to write, as my hands are generally loaded with bussiness of one kind or other.

Our Application for American Bishops, I mean the Clergy's, I suppose is not unknown to you.[1] We are greatly distressed for want of them. The Church can never thrive in America in the manner we could wish, till we are blessed with an Episcopate. It is very hard, hard indeed! that the Roman Catholicks, and Moravians in America are indulged with Bishops, and the established Church denied One.[2]

Quis talia fando
Temperet a Lachrymis[3]

If it would not be a disagreeable Task, I should be obliged to you, if you would let me know your sentiments upon the Subject; and the sentiments of our very worthy Brethren the Clergy of London & Westminster; at least, as many of them as you are acquainted with. Besides being deprived of a Head (which is productive of too many bad Consequences) the dangers of the Seas, the risque of life by the small pox, or other Disorders, the expense attending going to England and back again, are such insurmountable Difficulties, that we ca'not get Clergy to supply our vacant Churches, nor never shall, till we are blessed with an American Bishop. Pardon me my dear Sir, for troubling you with our present distresses, & assure yourself, that your sentiments on the subject will be highly agreeable to, Revd. Sir Your Much Oblig'd & Affectionate Brother

S: Auchmuty.

ALS. Endorsed as read 2 July 1767. See Minutes, 1:264.

1. Colonial clergymen of the Church of England had been petitioning for a resident American bishop at least since the first years of the eighteenth century. Their most recent appeal, and the one to which Auchmuty is probably referring, came from the annual convention of Anglican clergy held in Shrewsbury, New Jersey, in October 1766. Representatives from five colonies attended and drafted a plan which was submitted to the bishop of London, Richard Terrick. Bridenbaugh, *Mitre and Sceptre*, pp. 266–67.

2. The Moravian bishop resident in America was Peter Boehler, who had been consecrated in 1748. See [Smith to Beaufain, c. 5 March 1739/40], note 1, above. The only Roman Catholic bishop in British North America was Jean-Olivier Briand (1715–94), bishop of Quebec from 1766 to 1784. *New Catholic Encyclopedia*, 15 vols. (New York, 1967), 2:794.

Shortly after Briand's arrival, Auchmuty's assistant, the Rev. Charles Inglis, voiced a similar complaint. He noted that Briand "was recieved with universal Joy & Congratulations, as well by Protestants as Papists. This I hope is a Prelude to the like Indulgence to the best Friends that England has in America—the Members of the Church of England. Surely it would sound very strange, & the Politics must be preposterous, that denied *them* an Indulgence which is granted to Moravians & Papists, when equally necessary & as earnestly desired; yet no Way more injurious to other Denominations." Inglis to the Rev. Daniel Burton, secretary of the S.P.G., 10 July 1766, S.P.G. MSS., B2, no. 59.

3. "Who while relating such calamities could restrain his tears." Virgil, *Aeneid*, Book 2, lines 6, 8.

Rev. Marmaduke Browne to Rev. John Waring

[Newport, 4 June 1767]

Revd. Sir,

My letter dated sometime in December last with a bill drawn in favour of Mr. Channing for half a years salary due to the school mistress, was unfortunately lost by the vessels being shipwrecked on the coast of England. This I think proper to advertise you of, as the second bill of the same tenor & date remains still to be presented. Your favours of may the 30th. sixty six & of March 25th. sixty seven came safe to hand:[1] And have afforded me much pleasure as my conduct appears from them to be very satisfactory to the worthy associates. I can assure both you & them, that no future endeavours of mine shall be wanting to further this charitable work of theirs, that it may have the desired effect to bring the neglected blacks to the knowledge of our holy religion, & in some measure to recompence them for the servitude [in] which uncivilized paganism, & I fear not the most justifiable traffick on the part of christians has involved them. It is certainly an exalted pleasure which arises in the mind upon the performance of acts of charity & benevolence, but this is small when compared with the reward in view, the continuous prospect of a glorious futurity, which is such encouragement & support as no man in his senses one would think would grudge some time & labour to secure; & is moreover such a lawful spur & incentive to duty as notwithstanding the refinements of some speculative men, will I hope never fail to excite christians & more especially us of the ministry to the faithful & laborious discharge of the great trust committed to us. I have the satisfaction to inform you that the school continues in a promising way; the number of scholars is compleat 'tho some few have been discharged; their improvement satisfactory, some of them reading tolerably, & the girls acquit themselves well both in sewing & knitting; neither are they deficient as to their prayers & catechism many of them having answered in Church during the last Lent in a manner that sufficiently demonstrated them to be capable of instruction. I visit them frequently, & am I believe a very proper check upon the mistress, who I fear without constant inspection would not so conscientiously discharge her duty as she ought. With regard to books for the school; I shall be obliged to you for a small supply, as soon as conveniently may be, of such as were formerly sent, viz. childs first book, the english instructor in the art of spelling &c.[2] I remain Revd. Sir with much esteem & respect your affectionate Brother & most obedient humble Servant,

Marmaduke Browne

Newport Rhode Island
June 4th. 1767.

ALS. Endorsed as read 1 October 1767. At that meeting the Associates "Agreed that Thanks be returned to the Revd. Mr. Browne for His Attention to the Negroe School under his Inspection, & that a packet of Books for the School be sent immediately." Minutes, 1:265. Waring's reply has not been found. For the books sent, see "Catalog of Books," p. 141.

1. Letters not found.
2. The first work has not been identified. The second was Henry Dixon, *The English Instructor; or, The Art of Spelling Improved. Being a More Plain, Easy, and Regular Method of Teaching Young Children, Than Any Extant*, various eds.

Rev. Jonathan Boucher to Rev. John Waring

[Caroline County, Virginia, c. June 1767]

Dear Sir

I well remember already to have answered all your Enquiries contained in this last Letter of the 25th. March 1767;[1] tho', as I seldom keep Copies, I do not exactly recollect in what Month I wrote. I hope however, my Letter came safe to Hand. From the whole Spirit & Tenor of my Letters, ever since the Commencement of our Correspondence, I dare say You would easily collect that it has always been my Opinion, that no very considerable Services can be done amidst the Slaves any where in America. Yet, some little Instructions it is in our Power to give Them, & in Theirs to receive; & that little every conscientious Minister will doubtless think it his Duty to do, & gratefully acknowledge the Assistances derived from your Society. The Negroes in my Parish are too numerous for my Church to contain, were They all constantly to attend Divine Service: I believe, however, I have always more than any other Man, at least, their Numbers are complain'd of by The Whites, during the hot weather Months, when They really are very offensive. They are regularly & universally baptis'd in St. Mary's: and the Number of Communicants amongst Them constantly encreases. No longer ago than Yesterday, I am pretty certain I distributed upwards of two dozen Books; so that at this Time the Stock You sent Me, tho' pretty considerable, is almost entirely out. The Gentleman who succeeded Me in Hanover, is so very infirm & valetudinary, that He is by no means able to discharge his other Parochial Duties, without charging Himself with the additional Burthen of The Negroes. The Society has a School here in Fredericksburg, which is not above 7 Miles from hence, which, I am told, does much Service.[2]

I think myself particularly obliged to You for your kind & constant Enquiries after my Health, which, I am sorry to inform You, becomes every Day more & more precarious. In the Winter I am generally pretty happy, but no sooner does the hot Season come on than it brings along with it, to Me, its never-failing Attendants, Slow, wasting Fevers. So that after a resolute Struggle of now almost 8 Years, I believe I shall at last be obliged to submit, & endeavour to seek my Safety by Flight. But where shall I fly to? In England, alas! I have no Friends able to assist Me: & it is terrible to think of spending one's Life in perpetual Pain & Sickness. Cou'd You, & wou'd You, my dear Sir, venture to recommend Me to an Easy Curacy, in any healthy Part of England, that would just maintain Me with Decency? Thankfully would I resign my Rectory here, & joyfully fly to Health & Ease even in the remotest Corner of the Island. Yet This may be too much for Me to ask of You, or impracticable for You to do for Me: if it be, only be kind enough to say so, &, if You can, obligingly point out to Me a Way to obtain what I want, without the Expence of much Sollicitation.

I am, Dear & Revd. Sir, Your most affectionate Friend & Brother

Jonan. Boucher

ALS. Endorsed as received in August 1767, read 1 October 1767. See Minutes, 1:266. Also endorsed as "Answered October 16: 1767 by the Good Intent." Waring's reply has not been found.

1. Letter not found.
2. The Fredericksburg Negro school was of course supported by the Associates of Dr. Bray, not the S.P.G.

Rev. John Barnett to Rev. John Waring

[Brunswick, North Carolina, 17 August 1767]

Dear Sir

About a month since I reciev'd your letter dated 25th. March last in Answer to one I wrote you November 24th. 1765.[1]

My letter I intended only for your own perusal; that, on making yourself acquainted with the Man, you might be able to form an opinion of him, and represent him accordingly to Dr. Burton: therefore it was I did not write the Dr., to whom I know all letters on business *immediately relative* to the Society shou'd be address'd. The Bishop last Year wrote to our Govr., and therein mention'd his having seen my letter to you and was satisfy'd with the contents.[2]

I find his Lordship had refus'd Mr. Stevens Orders before he saw that letter; and if I remember right you shew'd it him on the very day of Ordination, (Trinity Sunday).

I fear I shall be no more successful in my endeavors for the establishment of a Negroe School than Mr. Lewis De Rosset.

Allow me to say no one is more earnestly desirous [of] such an institution than myself; nor has any struggled with more difficulties, solely arising from the unhappy prejudices of the people. I had agreed with a Widow Woman here, of good Character, some months since, and had propos'd opening School With so small a number as fifteen but I cannot make up more than 8 or 9, therefore must for a time drop the design.

I had agreed with the Mistress to teach the girls to Sew, knit and Mark, thinking that wou'd excite people to send young Negroe Girls, but I find they wou'd rather their Slaves shou'd remain Ignorant as brutes.

In the course of the year I ride near fourteen hundred miles to visit the out parts of my Parish. In one place thirty miles from Town where I officiate nine times in the Year a great number of Negroes always attend with great seeming devotion. Of them I have baptised twelve Adults and eighteen of their Children. Several among them can read and having promised me to take pains to instruct such of their fellow Slaves as are desirous to learn I have given them many of the Associates books.[3]

I write to the Society to beg leave of Absence from my Mission for six months from Easter next on some business of real importance.[4]

I am too bashful publickly to own the business but to you will confess, I want to follow the Example you have set me, and take unto myself a Wife. Let me beg you to contribute your aid in the Affair; which you can facilitate by speaking to the Bishop of London or good Dr. Burton.

I have had a long and dangerous Illness; and my health yet is in so poor a State, that I am assur'd by every body I cannot perfectly recover till I have taken a Voyage at Sea, to England or the Northern Colonies or Bermudas.

The latter place my Physicians advise me to sail to immediately, but I am determined to run the hazard of a stay here this Summer; in hopes of the Society's Indulgence in leave for me to visit London next Spring. By my errand to England then (if please God I live) I shall avoid the heats of the next Summer, get my health perfectly reestablishd and get a good Wife to return with me. Let Mr. Laurence (one of your Lecturers) know that I have found the right Magnolia or Laurel Tree.[5] If he will immediately write me how to propagate [it I will] bring it over with me; no one here can give me any instruction. My Father[6] the Corner of little Queen Street High Holborn will take [care] of and forward any letters for me.

If you will favor me with a letter (which I very much desire) pray write immediately.

But pray use your interest for my leave of absence. I am glad to hear Mr. Skinner and family are well, beg my complements to them, and Mr. Hopkins & family.

I am Dear Sir Your most affectionate Brother and humble Servant

John Barnett

Brunswick Cape Fear
August 17th. 1767

ALS. Sent "per The Caesar Captn. Hume Q.D.C." This letter was read by the Associates at their meeting of 5 November 1767. Minutes, 1:267. The bracketed words in the eleventh paragraph are conjectural, the manuscript being torn.

1. Neither of these letters has been found.

2. The man referred to was Stevens. See Barnett to Waring, 1 February [1766], above.

3. The Associates gave Barnett ninety-four books before he sailed for North Carolina for a parochial library and the use of a Negro school. See "Catalog of Books," p. 116.

4. Barnett wrote to the Rev. Daniel Burton, secretary of the S.P.G., on 22 August 1767, begging "leave of the Board to return to London next Spring on some very earnest business. I ask so short a stay there as only while the Ship I come in is ready to return which is commonly about seven weeks I believe." S.P.G. MSS., B5, no. 37. It does not appear that Barnett ever made the journey to England.

5. This may have been the Rev. John Laurence (1705–91), lecturer at St. Peter-le-Poer, Broad Street, and minister of St. Mary Aldermanbury, London. Laurence was the son of the Rev. John Laurence (1668–1732), an author on theology and agriculture whose obituary noted that he was "fam'd for his Writings on Gardening." *Gentleman's Magazine* 2 (1732): 775. Venn, *Alumni Cantabrigienses*.

6. Not identified.

Robert Carter Nicholas to Rev. John Waring

Williamsburg in Virginia 1st. December 1767.

Sir.

Having so repeatedly advised you of the State of the Negro School in this City, I have nothing material to add upon that Subject. The Mistress, I believe, is as diligent as usual & the Children are managed in the Manner I formerly mention'd. I have taken the Liberty of drawing upon you in favour of Mr. Norton for £30 Sterling, which will not quite defray the Expences of the present Year, the Balance will be brought to an after Account. I am very respectfully, Sir, Your most obedient Servant

Ro. C. Nicholas

ALS. Endorsed as read March 1768. See Minutes, 1:271 (meeting of 3 March). Also endorsed as answered 20 April 1768.

Benjamin Franklin to Francis Hopkinson

London, December 16. 1767

Dear Sir

I received yours of November 6 with the Account of your safe Arrival, which gave me and your Friends here great Pleasure.[1]

I have sent your Letter to Mr. Morgann, & by some Discourse I have had with him I am inclin'd to think you will find it no great Difficulty to agree for the Office when you see him on the Spot; and he is now preparing for the Voyage, intending for Maryland or Virginia in the first Ship.[2]

The Associates of Dr. Bray have lately a 1000£ promis'd them for the Support of Negro Schools in America, the Money to be laid out in Ground Rents or other safe Estate in or near Philadelphia; and they have appointed you, Mr. E. Duffield & myself to make & hold the Purchase for that Use. 200£ of the Money is already in their Hands, and they desire that we may immediately proceed to purchase as far as that Money will go.[3] I wish therefore that you and Mr. Duffield would look out for such kind of Purchases, and make them, drawing on the Revd. Mr. John Waring, at Mr. Bird's in Ave Mary Lane for the Sum you lay out. You will draw a Deed of Trust and execute it for your selves, if any thing is done in the Affair before I come over.

Mr. Sturgeon had the Care of the Negro School; but the Associates having had no Line from him, nor any Account of the School these two years past, they pray that you two would visit it, enquire into the State of it, and send them some Account of it, directed as above, by the first Opportunity. Mr. Waring is Secretary to the Associates.

I hope to be at home pretty early in the Summer, and to have the Pleasure of finding you and your good Mother well.[4] My best Wishes attend you, being with sincere Regard Your affectionate Friend & humble Servant

B. Franklin

Mrs. Stephenson & Miss present their Compliments.[5] I shall remember the Telemachus.[6]

ALS.

1. Hopkinson's letter has not been found. He arrived in Philadelphia from London on 23 October 1767. Hopkinson had sailed to England in the summer of 1766 to seek political preferment through the influence of friends and relatives, including James Johnson (1705–74), bishop of Worcester and the cousin of his mother, but was unsuccessful. *Pennsylvania Gazette*, 29 October 1767; Carl and Jessica Bridenbaugh, *Rebels and Gentlemen: Philadelphia in the Age of Franklin* (New York, 1942), p. 105; *DAB*.

2. Maurice Morgann (1726–1802) was private secretary to Lord Shelburne and undersecretary of state for the southern department. Earlier in 1767 he had been appointed secretary of New Jersey, and in July he appointed Joseph Reed as his deputy. Perhaps Hopkinson hoped to replace Reed as Morgann's deputy. Morgann was in Canada on business for Shelburne in 1768 and 1769 and returned to England via New York. Hopkinson

apparently never obtained office from Morgann. *Franklin Papers* 13:430n, 14:339n.

3. At their meeting of 5 March 1767 the Associates "Agreed that Dr. Franklin be desired to look out for a Purchase of Lands in N. America pursuant to the Design of Mr. Upchers Benefaction." Minutes, 1:257. On 7 May 1767 Franklin was desired to invest the £200 already received in improvable land in Pennsylvania. In addition to Franklin, Hopkinson, and Duffield, the Associates also named as trustees of the property the Rev. Jacob Duché and David Hall (for whom see Hopkinson and Duffield to [Waring], 30 June 1769, note 2, below). Minutes, 1:260.

4. Hopkinson's mother was Mary (Johnson) Hopkinson, daughter of Baldwin Johnson of England. *DAB.*

5. Margaret Stevenson (c. 1706–1783), the widow of Addinell Stevenson, was Franklin's landlady during his stay in England. Her daughter was Mary (Polly) Stevenson (1739–95). *Franklin Papers* 7:273n, 8:122n.

6. Hopkinson apparently requested Franklin to procure a copy of *Les Aventures de Télémaque, fils d'Ulysse,* by François de Salignac de la Mothe Fénelon (1651–1715).

Benjamin Franklin to Francis Hopkinson

London, January 24. 1768

Dear Sir,

I acquainted you in a late Letter[1] that the Associates of Dr. Bray requested that you and Mr. E. Duffield, with my self, would purchase some Estate for them, the Profits of which might hereafter be apply'd to the Support of the Negro School; and I desir'd you would as soon as possible make such Purchase to the Amount of 200£ Sterling Value, so much being already in their Hands for that purpose. I am now to acquaint you farther, that their Request is, that a Square of Ground may be purchased, one of those within the Plan of the Town, and likely in Time to be built upon, if such a one can be had, at any rate tolerably reasonable; this will be paid for immediately without waiting for the remainder of the 1000£ I mention'd, as the Associates have other Money in Bank. I am, my dear Friend, Yours affectionately

B. Franklin

ALS. Sent "per Capt. Duncan."

1. Dated 16 December 1767, above.

[Francis Hopkinson and Edward Duffield to Rev. John Waring]

[Philadelphia, c. March 1768]

Read a Letter from Messrs. Hopkinson and Duffield of Philadelphia, who have charitably undertaken to Superintend the Negroe School in that City, upon Mr. Sturgeons retiring to the Country, with an Acct. of the State of the School as given to them by Mrs. Ayers the Mistress. Who says, that from the Time of her Appointment to that Office, November 20th. 1764 to March 24: 1768 Fifty nine Negroe Children had been admitted, that at that Time twenty seven attended, whereof Three are in the Bible, One in the Testament, Two in the Fables[1] Nineteen in Spelling and Two learning the Alphabet. That of these 27 Nineteen are Slaves, & Eight free, & that Ten of them can say their Catechism pretty well.

Letter not found. Extract from Minutes, 2:9 (meeting of 5 May 1768).

1. Fable books were used for the initiation of children in reading. *OED.*

Rev. John Waring to Robert Carter Nicholas

[London] April 20, 1768

Sir

I had your Favour dated 1st. December last, which I laid before the Associates, & also have honoured your Draft for 30£ which You say is not the whole Expence of the School for the last Year, & that You will draw for Remainder per Next. The Associates are thankful to You for the Care You take in superintending the Negroe School, but when they first began this charitable work at Williamsburgh They did not intend to allow more than 20£ Sterling a year for its Support, & were in hopes that if that Salary were not sufficient, what was further wanting wou'd have been supplied by the charitable Contribution of the Inhabitants for whose Benefit this Institution was intended: They now find, by an Increase of Salary, & the Addition of Rent, your School stands them in more than 30£ Sterling whereas no other School costs us more than 20£ Sterling, Books excepted.

I am therefore directed to acquaint You, that the Associates have resolved to allow no more than 25£ Sterling to your School from Midsummer next, & hope that if any thing more be wanting, it will be supplied by Contributions at Williamsburgh. Indeed considering the Nature & tendency of this Institution, it might have been reasonably

expected that such a Scheme woud have met with liberal Encouragement on the Spot, without being indebted to Strangers for its Support; for I cannot but be of Opinion, & herein I am not Singular, it
was the Opinion of the Father of the Faithful, that a master is as much
bound to have his Slaves instructed in the way of Salvation, as his own
Children; & that if he doth not use his best Endeavours herein, he will
have a dreadful Account to give at the last Day. I further think that in
point of worldly Wisdom, every Master woud wish to have his Slaves to
be good Christians, for certainly persons who have lively Impressions
of the tremendous Sanctions of our Religion are more likely to make
honest faithful & industrious Slaves, than those who have no fear of
God, & act only as Eye Servants,[1] aw'd only by fear of corporal punishment. Moreover, how can Gentlemen on Your Side the Water expect
that We on this shou'd Subscribe two, three, or four Guineas a Year
apiece, as I have for many Years, to promote the Instruction of the
Slaves of those Masters, who themselves will contribute Nothing to it.
This Conduct of the Masters appears unaccountable, & I wish our
Brethren in America woud consult their own Honour a little more in
this respect, & join their Contributions to ours in that most divine Imployment, viz., instructing the Ignorant in the way of Salvation. I am
perswaded that if one or two Gentlemen wou'd begin a Subscription
many others woud follow the Example. The Salary was raised from
20£ to 25£ & the Rent allowed without our Consent previously obtained, unless I forgot myself, & we acquiesced, in hopes that the Masters of the Slaves woud in a little time find it to be their Interest as well
as Duty to ease us of a part if not the whole of the Expence, that we
might be At Liberty to extend the like Benefit to some other place. As
You have given Us Credit for Rent, we shall repay You up to 24th. of
June next, before which time I hope this will come to your hands. And
Be pleased to draw on me for the Arrears due & half a Years Salary.
And afterwards I am ordered to pay no more than at the Rate of 25£
Sterling by the Year.

I wrote to Mr. Yates,[2] when you first Joined him with yourself, to
request him occasionally to visit the School & examine what progress
the Children make in Christian Knowledge, & to favour Us with a
particular Account of it, but never have received a Line from Him. For
our Subscribers have a right to know whether their good Intentions
are in any measure answered, which is the chief motive they can have
to continue their Subscriptions. And therefore I am directed to request that either You or He will indulge Us once, if not twice a Year
with an exact Account in general of the Childrens Progress in reading, Saying their Catechism & Prayers, of their attendance at publick
worship & behaviour there: Such an Account wou'd do honour to the

worthy Inspectors as well as be satisfactory to the Subscribers, & tho' the School may be much in the Same State from time to time, yet it may be very proper to repeat the same particulars, which will always appear new to the Readers. The Associates have charged me with their affectionate Respects to yourself & Mr. Yates. I am Sir Your most humble Servant

Jn. Waring

April. 20. 1768
at Mr. Birds Ave Mary Lane London

ALS: Bray MSS., McGregor Collection, U.Va. Another copy of this letter, in Waring's hand and in the same collection as the present document, included the following addition: "Copy. June. 1. 1768. If the Original shall not have come to Hand before the 24th. Inst. The Associates, I am perswaded, will not scruple to continue the Salary for another Quarter on the old Terms, because as You have generously given them Credit for it, they must think it but reasonable to repay You, & they hope that before Michaelmas A Subscription (if necessary) will be entered into by the Gentlemen at Williamsburgh to defray the Extra Expences." A draft of this letter is among the Associates' manuscripts, U.S.P.G. Archives.

1. Eye servant: one who does his duty only when under the eye of his master or employer. *OED.*
2. Letter not found.

Rev. Samuel Auchmuty to Rev. John Waring

New York May 9th. 1768.

Revd. & dear Sir,

A few days ago I had the pleasure of receiving your favor of the Eleventh of last February.[1] It gives me a singular pleasure to find that your worthy Associates are pleased with the little Care I bestow upon the Negro School; I should be very happy if I could, consistent with my extensive Duty, of various kinds, pay more attention to it than I do; though there would not be that necessity for it, as the Mistress is extremely careful and honest in the discharge of her trust, that there would otherwise be. At present the School is full and the poor little Things are very orderly, and attend the School and Church punctually. The Mistress seems to be very happy with her employment, and I am convinced Conscientiously discharges her Duty. I will order her to give me a particular List of the Boys and Girls with their Ages, &c. which I will send you by the first private hand.

I am not a little pleased to find that we are so happy as to have you for an Advocate in favor of an American Episcopate. We labor under peculiar hardships for want of one; and the Church greatly suffers for want of a Head. We are much indebted to our most gracious Sovereign for the Notice he has paid to our request; & can'ot sufficiently lament that he is opposed in his pious intention by a set of Men who wish not well to our Zion. Dr. Chandler's piece has engaged us in a paper war. All that Hell or Malice can produce against the Church is spewed out every week from the American presses. We take care to answer them as well as we can.[2]

I must differ from you concerning the place for the residence of a Bishop (would to God we had one!). New York certainly should be the Spot; it is the most central of any of the Colonies. And the Church here is so far established that by an Act of the Legislature, this City is but one parish, and the Inhabitants of every Denomination are taxed for my support.[3]

I have only time at present to add, (as I am now sent to for this Letter), that I am, Revd. Sir, with most hearty prayers for your temporal & spiritual happiness, Your much obliged & most Affectionate Brother

Samuel Auchmuty

P.S. Pray excuse great haste. I hope soon to address you when I shall have more leisure. Mr. Munro has left a parcell of small Tracts with me which he received from you. Pray what is to be done with them? He is removed to Albany.

ALS. Endorsed as read 1 December 1768. See Minutes, 2:13. Also endorsed as answered 1 March 1769. Waring's reply has not been found.

1. Letter not found.

2. The Rev. Thomas Bradbury Chandler published *Appeal to the Public in Behalf of the Church of England in America* (New York, 1767) in support of the establishment of an American episcopate. Chandler's pamphlet engendered a bitter exchange of pseudonymous newspaper articles between proponents of the episcopate and dissenters who opposed the plan. His *Appeal* was attacked in a series of sixty-four articles written by the "American Whig" (William Livingston, John Morin Scott, William Smith, Jr., Noah Welles, Charles Chauncy, and perhaps three Presbyterian ministers—John Rodgers, Joseph Treat, and Archibald Laidlie) and published weekly in the *New York Gazette; or, The Weekly Post Boy* between 14 March 1768 and 24 July 1769. Chandler and his colleagues in the ministry Myles Cooper, Samuel Seabury, Jr., and Charles Inglis responded with a series of sixty-four articles under the title "'A Whip for the American Whig,' by Timothy Tickle, Esq.," published in the *New-York Mercury* between 4 April 1768 and 10 July 1769. See Bridenbaugh, *Mitre and Sceptre*, pp. 296–99.

3. This is a reference to "An Act for Settling a Ministry and Raising a

Maintenance for Them in the City of New York, County of Richmond, West-chester and Queen's County," the so-called Ministry Act of 1693. Auchmuty favored an expansion of the Anglican establishment, and he proposed in a letter to the Rev. Samuel Johnson of October 1764 that Parliament pass an act for New York "to erect every County at least thro'-out the Government into a parish, and make the Inhabitants pay Taxes, toward the support of a minister of the Established Church." Bridenbaugh, *Mitre and Sceptre*, pp. 246–47. *Ecclesiastical Records of the State of New York*, 7 vols. (Albany, 1901–16), 2:1076–79; R. Townsend Henshaw, "The New York Ministry Act of 1693," *HMPEC* 2(1933): 199–204.

Francis Hopkinson and Edward Duffield to Rev. John Waring

Philada. May 28th. 1768

Sir,

This is to advise you of our having drawn upon you for Ten Pounds Sterling by Bills of Exchange dated the 20th. Inst. in Favour of Mrs. Ayres the late School-Mistress; which Bill we doubt not will be duly accepted & paid. Mrs. Ayres, having removed into the Country hath resign'd her Care of the School; and we have put Mrs. Sarah Wilson[1] in her Place, a Person whom we think well qualified for the Purpose; our next Bill therefore for the usual Salary will be drawn in her Behalf. We have as yet done nothing determinate respecting the Purchase of any Lots or Ground Rents, as it is a Matter of Consequence & requires Circumspection; but we are making proper Enquiries for that Purpose, & shall not neglect the first good Opportunity of laying out the Associate's Money to Advantage. In the mean Time we are Sir Your Friends & humble Servants

Edwd. Duffield
Fras. Hopkinson

Direct to Mr. Francis Hopkinson in Philadelphia.

ALS. This letter is in Hopkinson's hand; both signatures are in autograph. Endorsed as read 1 December 1768. See Minutes, 2:14.

1. Not identified.

Rev. Marmaduke Browne to [Rev. John Waring]

[Newport, 10 June 1768]

Revd. Sir,

I wrote you sometime ago[1] relative to the school of the associates in this place, when I particularly mentioned my being in want of a few books for the supply of the children to be admitted; & as I have not since heard from you, I am a little suspicious that my letter has not come to hand. The school still I think is in a prosperous way; it has been constantly kept full, & notwithstanding I am not altogether satis-fied with the Mistress in all her conduct, as I do not, nor ever did think her, so conscientiously industrious as she ought to be, yet by frequent visiting & repremanding her, for negligence & remissness, I keep her with a good deal of trouble to myself, in a great measure to her duty. I believe I should be induced to make application to the Associates for her dismission could I find any person that would answer their pious intentions better, but as I have not at present the least prospect of meeting with such a one, I shall be under the necessity of doing the best I can with the person already imployed, tho I have much reason to be dissatisfied with her. Several children have been taught to read tolerably well, & many of the girls have made proficiency in sewing & knitting, whilst at the same time they have been well instructed in their prayers & catechism; & yet melancholy to relate I am not without fears that the good seed sown, will through the contempt & negligence of those whose property they are bring forth little fruit unto perfection. Could people be brought to consider their slaves as of the same spe-cies with themselves, it is probable they would pay more regard to their temporal & eternal welfare than the planters of America in gen-eral do: But being accustomed to buy & sell them as they do herds of Cattle for their own particular use or conveniency, they treat them nearly upon the same level; that is, scarcely with any other attention than feeding & cloathing them for their service. As to Christianizing them, they for the most part give themselves little or no concern about it; & with regard to instruction they think it has no better tendency than to render them more acutely vicious. I shudder when I reflect on the load of guilt that numbers are involved in, who without due reflec-tion or consideration engage in, or are accessory to that savage & I think unlawful traffick, of enslaving the blacks; I could wish they would either leave them in a state of liberty, or at least make them some sort of amends for the loss of it by treating them with humanity, & instructing them in the truths of Christianity.

I am Revd. Sir with much respect your affectionate Brother &
humble Servant

Marmaduke Browne

Newport June 10th. 1768
I have drawn on you this day in favour of Mr. Channing.

ALS. This letter was read by the Associates at their meeting of 1 December
1768. Minutes, 2:14–15.

1. Dated 4 June 1767, above.

Rev. John Barnett to Rev. John Waring

[Brunswick, North Carolina, 11 June 1768]

Dear Sir

Your kind favor came safe to hand and I am greatly obliged by
your remembrance of me.[1]

His Excellency has not yet recd. any Letter from the Society relative to my leave of Absence; but yours to me has been so far sufficient that the Govr. is willing to give me permission for visiting you
in October; however I have lain aside all tho'ts of leaving the Continent this Year.

It is not yet determined whether I settle in this Parish.

The right of Presentation to all the Livings in this Province being
Vested in the Crown, our worthy Govr. is desirous of presenting me to
Brunswick; but the opposition is so Violent and General that I believe
I shall be under a necessity of removing to some Parish more obedient
to Acts of Government.

Two such now present themselves, Granville and Northampton,
the latter of which I give the preference to.

Let me add here, the people of this Parish are desirous of my stay
among them on the Old Terms (an Annual reElection) but this both
my Duty and Inclination forbid.

You will very much oblige me in writing me by first opportunity
your opinion whether the Venerable Society will please to permit me
to carry the Mission to Granville or Northampton, if the people of
Brunswick shou'd remain refractory.[2]

Be pleased to write directly and give it to my Father who will send
it by first opportunity.

I am Dear Sir Your much obliged humble Servant

John Barnett

Brunswick 11th. June 1768

The Revd. Mr. Wills comes to England for the recovery of his health; you will see him as he waits upon the Society.[3] Give me Leave to recommend him to your Acquaintance and Notice as a very deserving and worthy Man.

If Our Associates wou'd please to send me a parcel of Books for the use of the poor Slaves they will be of great Service especially prayer Books, Directions for prayer, easy Spelling Books, and such little Tracts as may be most easily understood. Upwards of 150 Slaves have applied to me for books; therefore shou'd be glad to have them by the return of Captn. Loreing[4] who will arrive here about the last of November.

ALS. Endorsed as read 1 December 1768 and answered 27 March 1769, "& sent the Books by the Neptune, Watts." At the meeting of 1 December the Associates "Agreed that 12 Com. Prayers, 12 Spellings & some other Tracts be sent to Mr. Barnett." Minutes, 2:13. See "Catalog of Books," p. 151. Waring's reply has not been found.

    1. Letter not found.

    2. Barnett also wrote to the Rev. Daniel Burton, secretary of the S.P.G., on 11 June 1768 requesting permission of the Society to remove to Northampton or Granville county. S.P.G. MSS., B5, no. 38.

    3. The Rev. John Wills arrived in North Carolina about 1766, but as he did not have the required license from the bishop of London, he could not be inducted into a parish. He ministered informally to the parish in Wilmington until the summer of 1768, when he returned to England to restore his health and secure a license from the bishop and a missionary appointment from the S.P.G. He was licensed on 30 January 1769 and returned to Wilmington, where he served as S.P.G. missionary until the Revolution. He was apparently suspended from his ministry for loyalty to the crown and received £50 from the archbishop of Canterbury's fund for "distressed American clergymen." Malone, "North Carolina Anglican Clergy," pt. 2, pp. 410–12.

    4. Josiah Loring, captain of the *Peace & Plenty*.

Fielding Lewis to Rev. John Waring

[Fredericksburg, Virginia, 31 October 1768]

Revd. Sir

I am greatly concern'd that the Negro School Establish'd at Fredericksburg has not answer'd the expectations of the Associates, for at this time there remains only Nine Young Negro's at School who constantly attend, and Four in the Summer season only. And I have the greatest reason to think that there will not soon be any greater Number, for I observe that several have left the School as soon as they could read tolerably to attend in the Houses of the Proprietors, or to take care of the Younger Negros in the Familys to which they belong. Yet I am in hopes the little time these have remaining may be of service as great care is taken by the Mistress to impress on their Minds the Dutys of our Holy Religion, and I shall continue to call frequently at the School to see that the Mistress does her Duty so long as the Associates think proper to continue it. I have regularly paid the Twenty Pounds Sterling per An. which please to repay Antho. Bacon Esqr.[1] & Company for my Account and you'l Oblige Your most Obedient Humble Servant

Fielding Lewis

October the 31st. 1768.

ALS. Sent "per Capt. Cuzzins." Endorsed as read 6 April 1769. See Minutes, 2:22. Also endorsed as answered the same month. Waring's reply is printed below.

1. Anthony Bacon (c. 1717–1786), of Maryland, settled as a merchant in London about 1748, dealing in tobacco, coal, and slaves. He held government contracts during the Seven Years' War for victualling and paying the troops in West Africa, and from 1764 onwards in the West Indies. Bacon was M.P. for Aylesbury 1764–84 and during the Revolution was one of the chief contractors for provisioning British troops in America. Bacon was the younger brother of the Rev. Thomas Bacon of Maryland (see Biographical Appendix) and was elected an Associate in April 1761. He often attended meetings and advised the Associates regarding the establishment of Negro schools in America. Bacon was also elected a member of the S.P.G. in November 1770. Sir Lewis Namier and John Brooke, *The House of Commons, 1754–1790*, 3 vols. (Oxford, 1964), 2:35–36; Minutes, 1:148; S.P.G. Journals, 18:448.

Francis Hopkinson and Edward Duffield to [Rev. John Waring]

Philada. November 26th. 1768

Sir,

We wrote to you long ago about several Matters respecting the Negroe School under our Care,[1] but have not as yet been favour'd with any Answer. We hope we shall hear from you soon. The School is at present full, & several applying who cannot be admitted. We flatter ourselves it is as well taken Care of as it hath ever been, as the Mistress we have employed does her Duty to our Satisfaction. The half Year being compleated the 20th. Inst. we have drawn upon you for her Salary, for £10 Sterling which Bill we hope you will honour. It is endorsed to Francis Hopkinson & by him again to Mr. James Warren of Craven Street London.[2] If the Draught should not be according to Form, we hope you will not protest it upon that Account, but accept this, & give us proper Instructions for our future Government. We are, Sir, Your very humble Servants

Fras. Hopkinson
Edwd. Duffield

ALS. This letter is in Hopkinson's hand; both signatures are in autograph. It was read by the Associates at their meeting of 2 March 1769. Minutes, 2:21.

1. Dated 28 May 1768, above.
2. Not identified.

Robert Carter Nicholas to Rev. John Waring

Williamsburg in Virginia 16th. February 1769.

Revd. Sir.

I have received both your late Letters[1] & am sorry to find you expressing the least Dissatisfaction at my Conduct with Respect to the Negro School in this City, the Success of which I have done every Thing in my Power to promote. When I first engaged in this Business, tho' I could not but very cordially commend the pious Designs of its' Authors, yet I was aware of the many Difficulties it might meet with & therefore communicated them to you freely & without Reserve. I formerly sent you a List of the Negro Children at School & could only in general observe that I thought they were properly attended to & had made as good a Progress as I expected, all Things consider'd. I don't know what farther Information I can give; the Children are so often shifted, that it would be almost endless to attempt giving you the Dates of their Entries & Times of leaving the School. The Regulations which I formerly drew up & transmitted to you, I was in hopes of carrying into Execution, but have been disappointed in several Respects. I send you a List of the Children now at School & another of those who have left it. The Books you sent I have taken Care of;[2] the Mistress has such as she wants from Time to Time, & I have occasionally lent & given others of them to grown Negroes in different Parts, who I thought would make a good Use of them; this Measure I consider'd as cooperating with your principal Design, & hope you will approve of it. It gives me Pain that you should suppose I had exceeded your Limits so far as you mention. You may Remember that I succeeded Mr. Hunter in this Business & of Course must have conform'd to your Directions to him, when not alter'd by subsequent Instructions to me. Give me Leave to quote a Passage or two from your Letter to him of the 1st. of June 1761 viz.; "They (meaning the Associates) acknowledge that they are not competent Judges what Salary may be sufficient for a Mistress & therefore must refer that Matter entirely to your Prudence & Discretion, but as they paid no more than £20 Sterling for 30 Children both at Philadelphia & New York City, they hoped the same Stipend might be sufficient with you, however that this Undertaking may meet with no Check or Discouragement in its Infancy on this Account, they have directed me to acquaint you that they chearfully increase their Appointment to £30 Sterling, not doubting, but in Time a Proposal for a Subscription towards its Support will be favourably received at Williamsburg, in the meanwhile they would be glad the Number of Scholars were increased to 30 agreeable to their first Proposal & to the Number instructed in their other Schools &c." The Number of Scholars was at first, as I understood, only 24; this Letter coming to my Hands, soon after Mr. Hunter's Death I had the Number increased to 30 & obliged the Mistress that there might be no partiality shewn to white Scholars, of which she then had about a dozen, to discharge them all & this at the Risque of the Displeasure of their Parents, with whom she was in high Repute for her Care & Method of teaching. Having this Letter for my guide & Direction, you may easily Judge at my Surprize to find you complaining that I had advanced the Salary to £25 sterling without proper Authority. Mr. Hunter had fix'd the Mistress's Salary at £7 a Quarter, a Sum, for 30 Scholars, much less than is paid for Schooling in this City to other Mistresses; but, as Mrs. Wager had no House of her own, she was at first allow'd £8 Current Money[3] more to pay for the Rent of a House, which was much too small for such a Number of Children; however she continued in it, as long as it was tenantable; I was then obliged to rent the House, where she now resides, of Mr. President Blair, for twelve Pounds Current Money. My first Bills were only for £25 Sterling; this did pretty well with my advancing, generally, a Years Salary before I drew the Bills & when our Exchange was at 55, 60 & 40 per Cent but, when Exchange fell to 25 per Cent, you see that £30 Sterling yielded not enough to pay the Salary & Rent; if you'll be pleased to calculate, you will find that my Draughts upon an Average are considerably under £30 Sterling, besides that I have generally been considerably in Advance, a Circumstance, which I never regarded & should not mention it, but upon this Occasion. As to raising Money by Subscription, I have sounded many of the Inhabitants, but never had the least Encouragement to hope for Success in such a Scheme. I have still ventured to continue the School upon the old Footing, till I know the Associates' farther Pleasure, after they have been made thoroughly acquainted with the whole Matter & reconsider'd it. I have my hopes that they will think there is some Consideration due to the Mistress, who has actually thrown herself out of other Business by engaging in theirs. I could not at any Rate discontinue any Part of the Allowance before the first of January last, as both she & her House were engaged for the Year certain. I think, that I before sent you my Acct. to December 1766, when I drew for £37.10 Sterling the exact Balance then due to me;[4] I send you now my farther Acct. by which it will appear that there is now due to me £42.10 Current Money, for which I have drawn on you to my Friend Mr. Norton, & can have no Doubt of its' meeting with due Honour.[5] If there should be any Mistake in the Acct., it shall be immediately rectified upon being pointed out. You have forgot another Thing, I mean the Death of my very worthy Friend the Revd. Mr. Yates, who left us several Years ago, of which I [ver]y soon after advised you. I am very resp[ectfully, Rev]d. Sir, Your most obedient Servant

Ro. C. Nicholas

ALS. Endorsed as read 4 May 1769 and answered 24 May 1769. Waring's reply was dated 25 May 1769, below. The bracketed portions of the text are conjectural readings, the manuscript being torn.

    1. One of these is Waring's letter of 20 April 1768, above. The other, possibly an answer to Nicholas's letter of 27 December 1766, has not been found.

    2. The Associates sent 182 books to Williamsburg in 1760, 164 books in 1761, and 103 books in 1763. See "Catalog of Books," pp. 61, 96.

    3. Virginia currency.

    4. Nicholas actually drew for £37.10.8. See Nicholas to Waring, 27 December 1766, Enclosure, above.

    5. Enclosure not found. Nicholas drew a bill for £34 sterling on Waring to Norton on 13 January 1769. *John Norton & Sons*, p. 84.

Enclosure
List of Negro Children

Negroes now at School.

Mrs. Prisca. Dawson's Grace	1
Mr. R. C. Nicholas's Sarah	1

Mr. President Blair's Catherine, Nancy, Johanna & Clara Bee	4
Mr. Hay's Jerry, Joseph, Dick	3
Mrs. Chiswell's Jack	1
Mrs. Campbell's Mary, Sally, Sukey	3
Mrs. Speaker's Sam	1
Mrs. Vobe's Jack	1
John & Mary Ashby . . free	2
Mr. Ayscough's Sally	1
The College. Adam, Fanny	2
The Commissary's Charlotte	1
Mrs. Blaikley's Jenny, Jack	2
Hon. Robt. Carter's Dennis	1
Mr. Hornsby's Nancy, Judy, Ratchel	3
Mr. Cocke's Mourning	1
Mr. Davenport's Matt, Harry	2

D. In Nicholas's hand.

Rev. Samuel Auchmuty to [Rev. John Waring]

New York March the 30th. 1769

Revd. Sir,

This will be delivered to you, by Abraham Mortier Esqr.,[1] who is impowered by a worthy Friend of mine, to procure him a Tutor for his Children: I therefore, knowing your goodness, take the liberty of requesting you to assist Mr. Mortier in procuring a fit and proper Person for such an Employment.[2]

As your acquaintance with the Clergy must be considerable, I flatter myself that with their assistance, a Gentleman of a fair and unblemished Character may be found; and you may be assured Sir, whatever pains you take in the Affair will be most gratefully acknowledged by my Friend, Colonel Phillipse, and myself.

The Colonel lives about twenty miles from this City, has five Boys. He chuses to have them educated under his own Eye, and is willing to give any Gentleman qualified to teach them the Languages &c. whose Character is fair and good £50 Sterling, or £60, rather than be disappointed, besides his Board & washing. He must be a Person of a serious Disposition, fond of retirement and his Employment. For further particulars I must refer you to Mr. Mortier who is fully impowered to treat and agree with any Gentleman, and to get him a Passage here at the Colonels expence, that you recommend. Pardon me for giving you this trouble.[3]

The Negro School is in a very good way. The Children improve very fast, and are a decent pritty Flock. They constantly attend divine Service both on Sundays & week days; and the Mistress, continues to be very industrious and careful of her School. She has half a Years Salary due which I shall draw for in a few days.

I find that we are not to be indulged with an American Bishop, and consequently our poor Church is left destitute of a head. I do assure you, that we suffer greatly for want of a worthy Bishop among us: but we must submit to the determination of our Superiors, and wait with patience till Almighty God shall be pleased to open their Eyes, and have pity upon us.

I have only to add, that you have my most sincere prayers for your Health and Happiness; and that I am with great esteem; Your Affectionate Brother & Obliged servant.

Samuel Auchmuty

ALS. Endorsed as read 7 September 1769. See Minutes, 2:24. Also endorsed as "Answered September 1770. Hinted to him to set on foot a Subscription toward the Support of the School at N. York." Waring's reply has not been found.

1. Abraham Mortier (d. 1771) was deputy paymaster general for the northern district of North America. He built Richmond Hill, a house in the present Greenwich Village section of Manhattan, later occupied by George Washington and Aaron Burr. His daughter Elizabeth married Goldsbrow Banyar (1724–1815), secretary of the colony, in 1767. *The Papers of Sir William Johnson*, 14 vols. (Albany, 1921–65), 1:334n, 8:316, 347, 12:934.

2. Auchmuty's worthy friend was Col. Frederick Philipse III (1720–85), who was a member of the New York Assembly from 1750 and who inherited the Manor of Philipsburg in 1751. During the Revolution Philipse remained loyal to the crown and took refuge with his family behind British lines in New York City. His estate was confiscated, and he went to England at the end of hostilities. He died while his claim for £40,216.18 was being processed. Philipse had been elected a member of the S.P.G. in March 1765.

3. It is not known whether Mortier hired a tutor for Philipse's children, but the Rev. Luke Babcock (1738–77), minister at Philipsburg 1770–77, was also a tutor in the Philipse family. Babcock was a graduate of Yale College (A.B. 1755) and was postmaster at New Haven from 1767 until the fall of 1769, when he traveled to England as a candidate for holy orders. He was ordained and licensed early in 1770 and then returned to Philipsburg, where he began officiating in December 1770. Babcock wrote to the S.P.G. in January 1771 asking to be admitted to their service, but the Society postponed his appointment until they received assurances that Philipse would fulfill the engagements he made to the Society regarding Munro in 1764 (see Munro to

Waring, 9 September 1765, note 2, above). After the receipt of such a letter from Philipse, dated 12 October 1771, the S.P.G. resolved on 20 December 1771 to appoint Babcock missionary to Philipsburg with a salary of £30 per annum. S.P.G. Journals, 16:323, 19:42–43, 160–62 (meetings of March 1765, 17 May, 20 December 1771); Dexter, *Yale Graduates* 2:362–64; Robert A. East and Jacob Judd, eds., *The Loyalist Americans: A Focus on Greater New York* (Tarrytown, N.Y., 1975), pp. 27–43, 98.

Rev. Jacob Duché to Rev. John Waring

Philadelphia, April 15th. 1769

Revd. Sir

I should have answered your Letter much sooner,[1] had not my Brother-in-Law Mr. Hopkinson undertaken to communicate my Sentiments to the Associates of Dr. Bray, at a Time when I was much engaged in the Duties of a large Parish, which, from Mr. Peters's Indisposition, devolved entirely upon me.[2]

I would chearfully comply with the Requisition of the Associates to take the Negro School under my particular Inspection, did it not interfere with the extensive Charge, which at present takes up the whole of my Time & Attention. I will, nevertheless, do all in my Power to promote the pious Designs of the Associates. We are now endeavouring to get another Assistant-Minister for our Churches.[3] If we should succeed in this, I shall have more Leisure, & will readily employ Part of that Leisure in visiting & instructing the Negroe Children: And of this I should be glad you would inform the Gentlemen concerned in that Trust. I am, Sir, Your most obedient Servant & Brother

Jacob Duché

ALS.

1. Letter not found.

2. Since Sturgeon's resignation, the duties of the United Congregations were performed by Peters and Duché.

3. It was to be several years before Peters and Duché obtained any relief. In June 1772 Peters informed the vestry that "the duty was too heavy to be performed by any two persons" and urged the hiring of two assistant ministers. On 30 November 1772 the vestry hired the Rev. Thomas Coombe, who later administered the Associates' Philadelphia Negro school (see Biographical Appendix), and the Rev. William White, later the first Episcopal bishop in the United States, as assistant ministers. Dorr, *Historical Account of Christ Church*, pp. 167, 170–71.

[Rev. John Waring to Fielding Lewis]

[London, April 1769]

[Sir,]

We were grieved & astonished. Grieved to find our good Endeavours so Unavailing & fruitless & astonished at the amazing Inattention of persons who call themselves Christian to the Spiritual Welfare of those of their own household. Do the Masters ever consider that their Slaves have Souls as well as themselves? Pray Do they ever consider that [their] own Souls are immortal & will be happy or Miserable forever according as they treat their poor Slaves? Are They so weak as to imagine divine providence sends the Blacks among them merely to cultivate their Lands & do the severest Drudgery for their Masters worldly profit only without any regard to the Spiritual Welfare of the poor Slaves? If the Masters reap temporal Riches from the Labour of the Slaves Doth not gratitude as well as duty loudly call on the Masters to let the Slaves partake of their Spiritual good Things in return: & how will the Masters be able to stand before the Son of Man at the Last Day, when all rich & poor bond & free will [be] on a level, when a strict account will be demanded for refusing to have his Slave instructed in the word of Life, when the involuntary Ignorance of the Slave will be pardoned but the hard hearted Master will be severly punished? And must Not I & others who annualy subscribe towards their Instruction be swift witnesses against such Masters? Our Willingness to instruct the Negroes at our own Expence not only leaves the Masters who refuse to have 'em instructed without Excuse but must involve 'em in very great Guilt, which I wish for their own Sakes they did but seriously attend to: but if Masters will not attend to their own eternal Interest why will they [not] consider their own worldly Interest, for As the design of the School is to teach the young Slaves the principles of Religion & to imprint the great Duties of it on their minds under a lively sense of those tremendous Sanctions by which they are inforced, This must tend to make 'em more dutiful obedient diligent honest & faithful in their Masters Service, & of course it must be of great Advantage & Satisfaction to Masters to have Slaves conscientious in doing their Duty not as eye Servants & Men pleasers but as to [the] Lord in Simplicity & godly Sincerity. But if neither a regard to the Temporal Nor eternal Welfare can prevail on Masters to send their Children to be instructed in such Numbers as to answer our pious Intentions in Supporting the School at [Fredericksburg] we must & shall withdraw it & then let 'em consider what Reproach & Infamy must attend 'em when it shall [be] said that some pious people in England chearfully at their own Expence woud have Supported a School for the Religious Instruction of young Negroes & the Masters refused to send 'em. It may justly be asked where was their wisdom Christianity or even humanity.

As You Sir have generously & piously espoused this Charitable Undertaking I have spoke my Mind to You freely on this Subject, & now I must acquaint You with the Resolution of the Associates. In the first place they have charged me with their hearty Thanks for your benevolent Assistance & may the divine Goodness reward You & Yours with temporal & spiritual [blessings], in the next place they have directed me to request You to give immediate Notice to the Inhabitants of Frederickburgh that if the Number of Scholars is not immediately encreased to Twenty at least that then You are desired to discontinue the School from the next Quarter Day ensuing, without further Advice.

You will draw on me for what may be due to You on Acct. of the School & Your Bill shall meet with due honour.

P.S. Pray hath the Minister of the parish at all interested himself in this Affair? I wrote to him to request he wou'd favour You with his Assistance & Influence.[1] I am Sure 'tis what he ought to have done with all his Might for the Souls of the Blacks are as essential a part of his Charge as the Souls of the Whites & if he is negligent in promoting their spiritual welfare, to the Great Shepherd & Bishop of Souls must he be accountable at the Last Day.

To the forgoing Effect woud I expostulate with my Christian Brethren at Fredericksburgh were I there & let me beg of You to present my best Respects, Let me conjure only the Mercies of God & the Love of J. C. & their own everlasting happiness to consider the Sin & Danger of denying religious Knowledge to their Slaves. Can they expect [*illegible*] a blessing on themselves or families, Let me intreat 'em to have some regard to a future as well as to this present world, & let 'em remember that wilfully to hinder & obstruct the Spiritual Welfare of their poor Slaves here will be a sure means to exclude themselves from the Church triumphant in heaven. I pray God to give 'em a right Understanding in all Things.

Draft. In Waring's hand.

1. Waring's letter to the Rev. James Marye, Sr., has not been found.

Rev. John Waring to Robert Carter Nicholas

[London, 25 May 1769]

Sir

I received your Favour of February 16: 1769, which I laid before the Associates at their last Meeting.

I am very sorry that any Misapprehension shoud arise between Us in the conducting a Design set on foot purely to promote the Glory of God, and the Interests of true Religion, and from which neither of Us expect any Recompence in this world more than what flows from the Consciousness of well-doing. I am sorry also that any thing I said in my last shou'd give You pain; I freely confess, and beg pardon that I did not recollect what I wrote to Mr. Hunter June 1. 1761 as quoted by You: But You will please to observe that the Reason there assigned for allowing 30£ Sterling per An. to your School was that the good Design might not be checked in its Infancy. Mr. Hunter had informed Us that Dr. Dawson had proposed a Subscription in aid of our 20£ a Year, but was prevented by Death from carrying it into Execution: We flatterd ourselves that his pious Design woud soon be revived & executed, & therefore agreed in the mean while to allow 30£ a Year in hopes that we shou'd soon be eased of the additional part of it at least, by the liberal Contribution of the Inhabitants of Williamsburgh. For four Years Your Drafts were only 25£ per An. from whence we very reasonably concluded that this was the settled Salary, so far as concernd Us, and it was chearfully acquiesced in. You mentioned indeed in one or Two of Your Letters that You might be under some Difficulty in meeting with a House for the Mistress, but we did not in the least imagine that we shou'd be charged any thing extra on that Account, but that if our 25£ sterling was not Sufficient the Deficiencies woud have been made good by those who had the Benefit of the School; being under this perswasion You must allow Us in turn to be a little Surprized when You told Us 1 December 1767 You had drawn for 30£ Sterling which will not quite defray the Expences of the present Year. Must it not greatly Surprize Us to find that Gentlemen possessed of opulent Fortunes, as many of the Inhabitants of Williamsburgh are, have so little Generosity and publick Spirit as to refuse to contribute even in a small Degree to the Support of an Institution calculated purely for their benefit? And that they will rather choose to be beholden to the Benevolence of Strangers to instruct their Children, the young Negroes than to do it at their own Expence? Indeed I am much astonished that any persons descended from Britons, whose Characteristicks are Humanity & Benevolence shou'd so far deviate from the Principles & Practice of their Progenitors.

Don't think I mean to include You in this Charge. No Sir, Your persevering Zeal to carry on this pious Design amidst manifold Impediments is a proof of your piety as well as Your humanity & Benevolence; & our heavenly father whose Glory you so chearfully promote will abundantly reward this Labour of Love. I am sorry, extremely sorry, to hear that your good Endeavours to promote a Subscription have proved fruitless. We cannot help concluding, from the Backwardness of our American Brethren to join with Us, that our good Works are unacceptable to them, that like the Israelites of old, They loath the Manna, this Gift of a School sent to them by providence: if so, we don't desire to obtrude our favours where they are unwelcome: We don't wish to force a negroe School upon them against their Inclination. If They have no Desire to have their Negroes instructed; why Shou'd We? The Blacks are intrusted to their Masters Care, at whose Hands Their Souls will be required. There has been time enough for the Masters to get the better of old prejudices, which might at first disincline 'em to have their Slaves instructed, & this was our chief View in establishing those Schools. Long Experience shows that true Religion must make the Blacks as well as whites (notwithstanding some few exceptions) better Servants: and the former have as just a claim to the Knowledge of Christianity as the latter; & Wo be unto Them who wilfully keep 'em ignorant of it.

According to my computation we have Supported your School about nine Years & have paid on this Acct. £216:10.0 Sterling, Your last Draft included, besides Books and the greatest part of this Sum was raised by our own Subscriptions. This I shou'd think were enough to make our Brethren at Williamsburgh blush at their own contracted Selfishness. Let 'em compare their own Conduct with ours that they may be ashamed. Shou'd You out of Compassion to our unhappy Prejudices, support at your own Expence an Institution purely with a View to remove those prejudices, & shoud we after having acknowledged the Utility of the Design refuse to contribute of our Abundance a very small matter towards the continuance of it, What wou'd You think of Us? I appeal to every mans own breast what his Sentiments wou'd be. Woud You not think You had been very generous to have continued Your kindness to us eight or nine Years? And if the Expence exceeded your original Allotment, woud You not think we ought to do something to ease You of a Share of the Burden, of which we alone reaped the Benefit, more especialy if the Exchange during that time shou'd alter greatly in our favour? Wou'd you not think a person employed here for our Benefit tho paid by You was realy employ'd in our Ser-

vice? And Shou'd You, on Account of our refusal to contribute any-
thing, withdraw your Bounty from Us, Woud You not think it but Just
that We, not You shoud indemnify Such a one for the Loss of Salary?

I fear, Sir, I have tired your Patience, but to the foregoing Purpose shou'd I talk to Your Neighbours were I at Williamsburgh but
whether it would have any Effect God only knows, perhaps their
hearts might remain unaffected. I pray God give them a right Understanding in all Things,[1] in those especialy which relate to their everlasting peace.

If the Gentlemen at Williamsburgh are willing to have the Negroe
School continued they may: but then They must engage to defray all
Expences above 25£ Sterling a Year. If these Terms, very easy to them,
& on our parts very generous are *refused*, You are desired to put an
End to the School at the End of this present Year 1769.

The Associates have charged me with their most hearty Thanks
to You for your charitable Aid in conducting this good work. They
cannot recompense You but You will be recompenced at the Resurrection of the Just. As You have kindly given them Credit from time to
time, They will reimburse You the Expences of the present Year, even
tho the School hath been continued on terms more expensive than
they expected. I hope your Neighbours will be wise enough not to refuse our charitable Offer: if they do, they must answer for it to the
great Judge of the World. With hearty Prayers for Your Health and
prosperity in this Life and Your eternal Happiness in the next.

I am Sir, Your very affectionate humble Servant

John Waring

at Mr. Birds Ave Mary Lane London
May 25: 1769.
On the Death of Mr. Yates I wrote to Mr. Horrocks[2] but have not been
favour'd with an Answer. Please to favour me with a speedy Answer.

ALS: Bray MSS., McGregor Collection, U.Va. A draft of this letter is among
the Associates' manuscripts, U.S.P.G. Archives.

1. Consider what I say; and the Lord give thee understanding in all
things. 2 Timothy 2:7.
2. Letter not found.

Francis Hopkinson and Edward Duffield to [Rev. John Waring]

Philada. June 30th. 1769

Sir,

We have drawn upon you a Bill in favour of Mr. James Warren [1] for £10 Sterling, being the half Year's Salary due the 20th. of May last to the Mistress of the Negroe School, which we hope you will honour. We will only add at present that the School is full, & well attended & we flatter ourselves that the good Designs of it's Institutor, are as fully answer'd as ever they have been. Mr. David Hall insists on another Person's being appointed in his Room, as it does not suit him to undertake the Charge you have put upon him. [2]

We are Your Friends & humble Servants

Fras. Hopkinson
Edwd. Duffield

ALS. This letter is in Hopkinson's hand; both signatures are in autograph. It was read by the Associates at their meeting of September 1769. Minutes, 2:26.

1. Not identified.
2. David Hall (1714–72), printer and bookseller, was a native of Scotland. He came to Philadelphia in 1743 to work as a journeyman in Franklin's printing house, and in 1748 he became Franklin's partner. Hall bought Franklin's interest in the partnership in 1766. *DAB*. Hall had been appointed a trustee of the Associates' Philadelphia property in 1767. See Franklin to Hopkinson, 16 December 1767, note 3, above. A new trustee was not appointed in his place until 1773. See [Hopkinson and Duffield to Waring, 3 July 1773], bibliographic note, below.

Rev. William Sturgeon to [Rev. John Waring]

[Philadelphia, 3 August 1769]

Revd. Sir,

I received your kind Letter [1] in which you return me the Thanks of the Board of the Worthy Associates of Dr. Bray for my Servicies in the Inspection of the free Negro-School in this City; this Sir is more than sufficient to recompence me for any Labour that was necessary for conducting that pious Design, and a proper Sense of the Compliment will remain in my Breast, always ready to make me imbrace any Opportunity of serving or seconding the piously intended Scheme so truly christian.

Please to present my best Regards to that Body and Thanks for thier Approbation of my Services.

I should rejoice to give Messrs. Hopkinson and Duffield any Information necessary for the Benefit of the School, but have been prevented by my private Affairs. When I retired from a publick to almost a private Station, and began to examine into my worldly Concerns, they were found very perplexed, and heavy Debts contracted, chiefly occasioned by the Smallness of my Salary, and the great Increase of my Family, for the Discharge of these I am selling what little real Estate I possessed.

But as if Poverty had been Nothing, the wise Providence of God has afflicted me greatly, without doubt justly; for Jehovah ever acts by unerring Wisdom; in the Space of fifteen Months, I lost, my Wife a worthy Woman, four Children, my eldest Son by the Fall of a Tree, a very valuable Negro Man, and my House by Fire; in which were consumed my Library, Forniture, and Clothing, except a few Beds, and the Cloths on our Backs; so that I am now much troubled how I shall support myself and three Sons, the eldest nine Years of Age.

But I will not despond, since it is the Will of Heaven, the Lord gave, and the same divine Arm hath taken a Way, Oh! that I may ever be enabled to praise his holy Name.

I know your Goodness of Heart will readily find an Excuse for giving you this sad Detail, as Griefs seem to lessen by being imparted to the friendly and pious. I intend, God willing, to return to the Discharge of my Duty, as soon as I find a Door open, all being at present shut as if an afflicted distressed Man, was a Mark of the divine Displeasure. The Want of Books in my Retirement is an uneasy Sensation, wherefore I should look upon a small Supply as a Gift bestowed under the Influence of Heaven.

I will not trouble you with any further narration at present, but after my most sincere Prayers for your Welfare temporal and eternal I am with the greatest Gratitude Revd. and dear Sir your most obliged humble Servant

Wm. Sturgeon

Philadelphia
August 3 1769

ALS. Endorsed as read 31 May 1770. The Associates' meeting that month actually took place on 3 May. Minutes, 2:37.

1. Letter not found.

Francis Hopkinson and Edward Duffield to Rev. John Waring

Philada. November 20th. 1769

Sir,

We have drawn upon you for £10 Sterling in favour of Mr. James Warren by Bills bearing even Date herewith being the half Year's Salaray due to the Mistress of the Charity Negroe School in this City; which Draught, we doubt not, you will honour. The School keeps continually full & is well attended. Twice a Week, those Children whose Masters or Mistresses are of our Communion, are taken to Church & catechised; & every thing goes on (as we believe) according to the pious Intention of the Founders of this Charity.

We are Sir, Your very humble Servants

Fras. Hopkinson
Edwd. Duffield

ALS. This letter is in Hopkinson's hand; both signatures are in autograph. Sent "per Capt. Sparks." Endorsed as read 1 March 1770. See Minutes, 2:34.

Robert Carter Nicholas to Rev. John Waring

Williamsburg 1st. January 1770.

Revd. Sir.

I have received your last Favour of the 25th. of May; &, tho' our Sentiments are pretty much alike, with Regard to the poor Slaves in this Colony, I see very little Prospect of our Wishes being accomplish'd.

I had for many Years before our Correspondence commenced, view'd them with a piteous Eye; I often reflected with myself upon the most likely Means of working a Reformation in their Manners & instilling into them the Principles of Christianity; but the same Difficulties, which I, at first, suggested to you, constantly stared me in the face & checked my Zeal.

When I wrote my last Letter,[1] I determin'd to wait your Answer, before I made any Alteration in the Terms, on which the School had subsisted, & upon being inform'd by your late Letter that the Associates were willing to defray the whole Expences of the current Year, but that they would not allow more than £25 per Ann. in future; I made the Mistress acquainted with this their Resolution; the last Year ends this Day; the Expence accrued is, as formerly, £40 Current Money, which is now equal to £34.15.7 ¾ Sterling our Exchange having fallen to 15 per Cent. For this Sum I have drawn on you in favour of Messrs. Norton & Son; this Sum included with my former Drafts, you'll find does not, upon an Average, exceed £30 per Annum, since I have had to do with the School. I have acquainted the Mistress that she is to expect no more than £25 Sterling per Ann. from you for Rent & every other Expence, & will endeavour to have the Surplus made up here.

My best Wishes always attend you & the rest of the worthy Associates & I remain very respectfully, Revd. Sir, Your most obedient Servant

Ro. C. Nicholas

ALS. Endorsed as read 5 April 1770. See Minutes, 2:37. Also endorsed as answered 4 March 1771 per the *Randolph*, Capt. Walker, and "sent 40 Letters to an American planter." See Waring to Nicholas, 25 March 1773, note 1, below. Waring's letter of 4 March 1771 has not been found.

1. Dated 16 February 1769, above.

Rev. Thomas Baker to Rev. John Waring

April 23d. 1770.
Kingston Glebe in Gloucester County, Virginia

Revd. Sir

According to your Desire I send this to inform You That after a tedious Passage of Eleven Weeks & 3 Day I arriv'd safe at York Town in Virginia, & have been endeavoring, as far as Opportunity would permit to promote the Good your Society intends towards the Negroes here. I wish I could send you an Acct. agreeable to my own Wishes, but I have not that Happiness at present. Many Masters are not only averse to learning their Slaves to read, but did not the Law oblige them, would not have them baptiz'd;[1] for I've heard some of them say (& blessed be God convinced some of them of their Error) That since we got to baptizing them they are become insolent & Idle, Runaways &c.; that they were never so till Baptism came in Fashion amongst 'em. However never a Sunday passes, but I have many at both my Churches, Infant & adult Negroes too. I've baptiz'd some upwards of 60 Years old, who have with Tears runing down their Cheeks, repeated the Lord's Prayer & Creed, & behav'd in such a Manner as would have pleas'd you & every good Christian. They come a great many Miles to me almost every Sunday Morning and I wish I could be of Service to them, but as I observ'd to you, when at London, No Good is to be done if we can't bring the Masters too first. I have disposed of some of

289

the Books I had of you to the best advantage I could,[2] but hope when I get a Parish of my own to have a better Opportunity; for now as I am a Candidate for this I am in, I am forced to be very careful not to give Offence by offering any Favor to their Slaves, even Baptism without their Leave, except at Church. There were 3 Candidates for [this] Parish when I came over & I made the 4th. Two have given up & one says he'll see me out; but as the Vestry have chosen me to do the Duty of the Parish till the Time of Election (October next) I hope I shall see *him* out; especially as the parishoners in general have sign'd and presented a Petition to the Vestry to chuse me; but how it will be is yet uncertain. I've wrote to the Revd. Mr. Howard at Rendlesham in Suff:,[3] but for fear he should not receive my Letter, beg you'll mention this to him when you see him or write to him By doing which you'll again oblige Revd. Sir Your most obedient humble Servant

Thos. Baker

ALS. The letter is endorsed as read 1 November 1770, although the Associates' Minute Book records its reading in October 1770. Minutes, 2:40.

    1. There does not seem to have been a Virginia statute requiring the baptism of slaves. An act of 1667 declaring that baptism does not alter the condition of a slave concerns slaves "by the charity and piety of their owners made pertakers of the blessed sacrament of baptisme." Hening, *Statutes* 2:260.

    2. In November 1769 the Associates gave 182 books to Baker, "going to settle in Charles City County Virginia to be applyed to the Instruction of the Negroes." See "Catalog of Books," p. 151.

    3. The Rev. Eden Howard (c. 1705–1781) was ordained in 1729 and graduated from Cambridge University in 1731. He was chaplain to the East India Company 1732–45 and was minister of Rendlesham, Suffolk. Venn, *Alumni Cantabrigienses.*

Francis Hopkinson and Edward Duffield to [Rev. John Waring]

Philada. May 20th. 1770

Sir,

    We have only now to inform you that we have drawn upon you for £10 Sterling the half Year's Salary due the 20th. of May to the Mistress of the Negroe School. Our Draught, as formerly, is in Favour of Mr. James Warren, which we doubt not you will honour. The School continues entirely full, and many Applications for the first Vacancies, made. We have not done any thing yet with Respect to the Purchase

290

of Lots in Philadelphia for Want of fuller Directions. We are Your Friends & humble Servants

Fras. Hopkinson
Edwd. Duffield

Mr. Duffield being out of Town I am obliged to sign for him.

ALS. This letter was read by the Associates at their meeting of October 1770. Minutes, 2:40.

Rev. John Barnett to Rev. John Waring

[Northampton, North Carolina, 9 June 1770]

Revd. Sir

I reciev'd your favor of March 1769 in February last, which informs me of the Box of Books being sent to Cape Fear for the use of the Negroes.[1]

I being distant thence upwards of two hundred miles, and hardly any Communication thence to this part of the Province; have given directions to a Friend there to distribute them among those Negroes who can read a little; always giving the preference to those who formerly composed part of my Black Congregations.

In September last I inform'd the Associates of the endeavors I was using to establish two Negroe Schools in these parts and of the prospects of Success I had.[2]

About Sixty Adult Slaves have Joyfully accepted the offer of Instruction; and to the honor of their Owners let me add, they are willing to Indulge them with opportunities for learning to read on Sundays and all Evenings.

For Six months past, I have employd two men to teach in different parts of my Neighborhood and the good progress many of the Negroes have made sufficiently evidences *their* diligence and the *teachers* faithfulness.

I last winter purchased of a Merchant here about three dozen Spelling and some other Books proper for the use of the Negroes, who with a view of furthering the Charitable design let me have them at something about prime Cost.

The Notice of this Opportunity being short I have not time to send the Associates further particulars but shall not fail to transmit them by the next.

Be pleas'd Sir to name me as an Annual Subscriber of one Guinea, as I now see such a prospect of forwarding the worthy Associates designs.

I by this opportunity draw on you for ten guineas, not knowing who is at present Treasurer.

The Associates may depend on my utmost Care in point of frugality in the disposition of the Money I draw for; and I do believe the above Sum will be sufficient to defray the Expences of one Year.

I shall solicitt two worthy Clergymen near me to Join the Associates, and shall be glad if they may be Join'd with me in the trust. However I must refer you to my next for further particulars. In the mean time [I] shou'd be glad to recieve a supply of Books by way of Williamsburgh, James River, to the Care of Sir Peyton Skipwith Baronet at Petersburgh Virginia.[3]

After many enquiries I have heard of several Books belonging to Parochial Libraries founded in Virginia by Dr. Bray in the hands of private persons and are shamefully abused. I beg directions how to act in the Case.

I am Revd., Your very humble Servt.

John Barnett

Northampton 9th. June 1770

ALS. Endorsed as read 1 November 1770, answered 5 March 1771 per the *Randolph*, Capt. Walker, and "sent a Box of Books." The Associates actually read this letter at their meeting in October 1770, when they "Agreed that Mr. Barnett's Draft for £10.10.0 be paid that a packet of Books be sent, with Thanks for his zealous Endeavours to promote the Instruction of the Negroes." Minutes, 2:40−41. Waring's reply has not been found.

1. Letter not found. On 25 March 1769 the Associates sent 215 books to Barnett. See "Catalog of Books," p. 151.

2. Letter not found.

3. Sir Peyton Skipwith (1740−1805), seventh baronet. Since Northampton County, North Carolina, was on the Virginia border and, as Barnett noted in the second paragraph of this letter, communication with the North Carolina tidewater was so poor, it was more practicable to correspond through Virginia. Probably because of this reference to Petersburg, the Associates mistakenly believed that Barnett was at Northampton County, Virginia, although that county is on Virginia's Eastern Shore and far from Petersburg. The Associates shipped 377 books to Barnett on 4 March 1771, but he probably never received them, for they were addressed to Northampton, Virginia. See "Catalog of Books," p. 151. Herbert A. Elliott, "Sir Peyton Skipwith and the Byrd Land," *VMHB* 80 (1972): 52−59.

[Rev. John Waring], *A Letter to an American Planter from his Friend in London*

[London, 10 October 1770]

Dear Sir,

The News of your safe Arrival at _____, where you found all your Family in perfect Health, afforded me a Pleasure little inferior to that I felt, when you favoured me with the interesting Detail of your several Adventures, since you first left England, till your final Settlement in what you call your *Land of Promise*; which, like that of old, you say, abounds with all the Conveniencies as well as Necessaries of Life; and where Divine Providence hath blessed you with a comfortable Habitation, an extensive and fruitful Estate, amply stocked with what constitutes the principal Riches of your Province, *viz.* a large Number of healthful robust *Negroes*—These you may remember were the Subject of Conversation one Evening, which we spent *tête à tête*. You sympathized with me in a generous Compassion for the hard and severe Lot of this unhappy Part of the human Species: But when I proposed to you to endeavour to mitigate the Rigour of their Situation, by introducing them to the Knowledge of the Gospel of CHRIST, and of those glorious Rewards, which our Religion promiseth to ALL, Slaves, as well as Masters, who faithfully embrace it, and with humble Resignation submit to the Divine Appointments; I say, when I proposed that you should have your Slaves instructed in the Christian Religion, as the best Mean to reconcile them to their state of Servitude, and support them under it; you started several Objections, and urged them in such a manner as to discover, that how much soever you might approve of the Piety and Benevolence of the Proposal, you seemed to think it almost impossible to carry it into Execution. Since your Departure, I have employed my Thoughts on this Subject, and I hope with dispassionate Candour: and as I am persuaded of the Uprightness and Integrity of your Intentions, and that it is your earnest Desire to behave yourself in every Relation you bear to others, as a good Christian ought to do, I need make no Apology for communicating to you my Sentiments. I shall state the REASONS you then urged against attempting the Conversion of the *Negroes*; and hope you will not be displeased if I expostulate with you on the Subject, with the Freedom of one who sincerely wisheth your Welfare and Happiness in both Worlds.

THE FIRST, and principal Difficulty, which you alledged against attempting to instruct ADULT *Negroes* imported, was their strong Attachment to the idolatrous Rites and Practices of their own Country. Now, deep-rooted Impressions, and long contracted Habits, of whatever kind, are, I grant, hard to be effaced; but not so hard as should make us presume, that it is to no Purpose to attempt it. By diligent and prudent Application, much, we know, hath been done this Way; and, by the same Means, much, I am sure, may be done again. And with regard to the Point you particularly mentioned, permit me to ask you a few Questions:

Were not all Nations, except the Jews, very great Idolaters, at the Time the Apostles were sent to propagate the Gospel among them?

Did the Idolatry of the Heathens hinder the Apostles from endeavouring to convert them to Christianity?

Have not many Heathens, accustomed to Pagan Rites, and to such vicious and licentious Practices as Christianity forbids, been converted to our holy Religion from time to time, without any other help than *the sincere* WORD OF GOD, and the good Example of those who recommended it?

And may not you reasonably hope, if you are as zealous in using the proper Means as you ought to be, that your Endeavours to convert the *Negroes* may be proportionably successful; since you have no Reason to doubt, but that the Divine Grace will be equally assisting to you, as it was to your Predecessors in the same good Work?

But perhaps you will say, "the *Negroes* are utter Strangers to our Language, and we to theirs." But,

Do not many of the *Negroes*, who are grown Persons when imported, even of themselves attain so much of our Language, as to enable them to understand, and be understood in Things which concern the ordinary Business of Life? And if so,

May they not with a little Instruction, easily attain so much further Knowledge of it, as to enable them to understand the Things which concern the Welfare of their Souls? At least,

Might not some *few*, who are more capable and serious than the rest, having first learnt our Language, be taught the Principles of our Religion by themselves; and then be appointed to convey Instruction to their Fellow-Slaves of lower Capacities, in their own Language?

Would you not pursue this Method, if you found it necessary to your own worldly Advantage?

Is there then not greater Reason for doing so, in order to promote the Glory of GOD, and the Salvation of Souls?

Do you take Care of the Bodies of the *Negroes* for your own Sake, and ought you not to take Care of their Souls for CHRIST his Sake?

What Sentence do you think CHRIST will pass upon you at the last Day, should you be not only remiss in forwarding, but even active in obstructing, the Salvation of those Souls for whom He shed his precious Blood?

What, alas! would have become of us, through all Eternity, if CHRIST had discovered no greater Compassion for *our* Souls than we do for those of *others*?

Though our Bodies are distinguished by a Diversity of Colour from the *Negroes*; Doth this Diversity make any real Abatement to the Worth of their Souls? Are they not Transcripts of the same Divine Original? Have they not the same Capacities for Immortality with our own? And did not the same Redeemer who died for us, die for them also?

"Who made you to differ from them?"[1] Might not the same GOD who made you White, and them Black, if it had seemed good unto him, have made you Black, and them White? Have made them Masters, and you their Slave? Why then do you usurp a Superiority which by Nature you have no Right to? Why do you glory over your poor Brother, because the common Father of you both hath given to him a different Complexion? Why do you withhold, and even deny his Right to those Privileges and Blessings, which the Father hath given in common to both?

For what Reason was it that GOD in his Providence, made you Master of so many Slaves! Was it merely that you might employ their Bodies in doing your Drudgery? Surely you cannot think so: You cannot conceive so unworthily of the common Father of All, who is "just and righteous in all his Ways, and no respecter of Persons."[2] GOD intended Mercy to them as well as Kindness to you; that both you and they might be instrumental in promoting each other's Felicity: that whilst they, by the Labour of the Body, promote your temporal Interest, you in Return, might promote the spiritual and eternal Welfare of their precious and immortal Souls.

Do you correct your Slave if he is negligent, or idle in doing his daily Task? And will not the great Lover of Souls severely punish you, if you suffer any whom he hath intrusted to your Care, to perish through your Negligence?[3]

The Advantage at present, Sir, is greatly in your favour: You are now their Lord, and may treat them with Kindness and Gentleness, or with Rigour and Severity: You may teach them "the good and the right Way,"[4] or you may let them continue in their original Ignorance and Idolatry: O, be persuaded, my dear Friend, to let your Slaves reap that Benefit from their Situation, which GOD intended they should reap; if you do not, the Difference will be fatally inverted hereafter, when "they shall be comforted, and you tormented."[5]

That you may escape this Reverse, which if once it takes place, will last for ever, be always attentive to your Duty.—Be careful, extremely careful, to administer to your Slaves the Comfort of knowing what good Things God hath laid up in Store for them, if they act a right Part in that trying State of Labour, in which he hath placed them under you. Here you may inform them, that in the early Ages of Christianity, many Slaves, when converted from Heathenism, were destined to undergo, and patiently endured the most severe Usage and cruel Treatment from their unbelieving Masters, who often persecuted them even to Death, on account of the Religion they professed. And then you may observe how happily different their Situation is at present, when they are kindly invited by their Masters, to believe in Christ; and, provided they behave suitably to their Profession, may reasonably hope to be treated with Tenderness and Humanity by them in this World; and to be rewarded by Christ, the Saviour of all that believe, with Glory and Happiness in the World to come. By thus alleviating their hard Lot, and rendering it more easy and supportable to them, by the chearing Prospect of a better Life, you will gain great Advantage to yourself; for it is the natural Effect of such Instruction, to turn the Eye-service of Slaves into the conscientious Diligence of Servants.[6] And it is likewise worthy of your Consideration, that by this Means, a Branch of Commerce, which carries with it a Reflection upon Human Nature, and is founded on the Misery and Wretchedness of a large Part of Mankind, will become subservient to the Purposes of Benevolence and the Cause of Religion, from which it will derive the Blessings of Providence in Return.

But the Difficulties you alledge against instructing the ADULT Negroes imported, cannot be urged against the religious instruction of the Negroe Children, who are born and bred among you. They certainly may easily be trained up, like all other Children, to learn any Language, and particularly our own; and may with the same Ease and Facility that other Children are, be instructed in the Principles of our holy Religion. And must not their Owners and Governors be absolutely inexcusable, if they do not sincerely endeavour to "bring them up in the Nurture and Admonition of the Lord."[7]

But perhaps you will farther say, that no Time can be spared from the daily Labour of the Negroes, to instruct them in the Christian Religion. But is not this in effect, to say, that you value a little worldly Advantage, more than the Glory of God, and the Salvation of Souls? But sure I am, a little Time may be found for this pious purpose, without much Abatement of their daily Labour. Might not the Slaves be called together in an Evening, two or three Times a Week, on the Lord's Day in particular, to be instructed in the Principles of Religion, by a Person, duly qualified for the Purpose? Suppose you, Sir, whose Slaves are numerous, were at some small Expence for this Purpose. Would this be any more than a just Return to the poor Slaves, for the ample Profits you derive from their Labours? If they make you Partakers of their temporal Things, (of their Strength and Spirits, and even of their Offspring) ought not you to make them Partakers of your spiritual Things, though it should abate somewhat of your Profit from their Labours?[8] And is it not very probable that the Slaves would abundantly repay your Christian Compassion and Kindness to them, by a greater degree of Honesty, Fidelity, and Diligence in your Service? Not to mention that GOD may then, in an especial manner "bless your Basket and your Store, the Increase of your Kine and of your Flocks, and prosper you in all that you set your Hands unto."[9]

But should the Difficulties you mention, or any others, discourage you from attempting to have your *Negroes* instructed in this or any other Way, yet I trust you will give them all possible Encouragement to attend public Worship at Church on the LORD's Day, because this may be a Mean, thro' the Blessing of GOD, of instilling serious Thoughts into their Minds, and of exciting in them an earnest Desire to know what they must do to be saved.

You know very well that GOD hath given one Day in Seven to be a Day of Rest, not only to Man, but to Beasts; that it is a Day appointed by him for the Improvement of the Soul, as well as the Refreshment of the Body; and that it is the Duty of Masters to take care that all Persons under their Authority keep this Day holy, and employ it to the pious and wise Purposes for which GOD, our great Lord and Master, intended it; and therefore I cannot suppose that you will even permit, or connive at your *Negroes* spending this Day in an improper manner; either in the ridiculous Recreations usual with them in their own Country, or in labouring on that Day to provide themselves with any Necessaries or Conveniencies of Life: much less can I suppose that you will lay them under the disagreeable Necessity of doing the latter; which I am told is the Practice of some cruel hard-hearted Owners of Slaves: But where is the Religion of these Men? Do they call themselves Christians? Let them be called Infidels, Heathens, Barbarians, or any thing but Christians: for such Persons are a Disgrace to the Christian Name: I had almost said to Human Nature.

And now, Sir, I can think of no other Objection to the Instruction of the *Negroes* in the Christian Faith, unless you will plead further, that this Instruction being in order to Baptism, you cannot approve of it, because as some of the Planters have said, "Since we have got to baptizing them, they are become insolent, idle, Runaways; and what not? And that they never were so 'till Baptism came in Fashion amongst them."[10]

But, Sir, you may as well suppose *Darkness* to spring from *Light*, and Evil to be the necessary Effect of Good, as say that the Misconduct of some of the baptized *Negroes* is the Consequence of Baptism, or of the Instruction previous to it. Good Instructions and good Principles may produce good Effects, but cannot produce bad ones: If some Blacks misbehave after Baptism, do not you see many Whites no less guilty? You may as truly say that all the Robberies, Burglaries, and other Crimes committed within the Bills of Mortality, are the Consequences of Baptism, as say that Baptism, with the Instruction previous to it, renders the *Negroes* in the Plantations insolent, idle, Runaways, &c.

That some baptized *Negroes* have misbehaved, I will not deny; but this is not to be charged to the Account of Baptism, but to the bad Policy, Imprudence, perhaps Irreligion, of their Masters. The Unwillingness of the Planters in general to permit their *Negroes* to be baptized, hath led these poor ignorant Creatures to imagine that some very great civil Privileges or Immunities are annexed to Baptism; that after it, either they are no longer Slaves, or that their Master's Property in them wholly ceases, or at least that his Authority to punish their Faults is greatly lessened: Under the Influence of some such Mistake, the *Negroes* are very solicitous to be baptized; and after they are baptized, is it any wonder that some of them should prove idle, insolent, and Runaways? In so doing they only act agreeably to the false Principles and wrong Notions their Masters imprudent and impolitic Conduct hath infused into them. Let the Planters reverse their Conduct in this Particular, and make it a constant Rule to have all their *Negroes* duly instructed in the Christian Faith, and afterwards baptized; and I will venture to prophesy, that the Sentiments of the *Negroes* with regard to Baptism will soon be rectified: The Forwardness of Masters to bring them to this Solemnity will soon effectually convince them, that no civil Privileges or Immunities are annexed to it, and their Baptism will not be attended with those bad Consequences which have been hitherto complained of.

It is now very well understood by the Planters in general, that neither Christianity nor the Laws of our Country have annexed any civil Privileges or Immunities to Christian Baptism; and therefore it will be entirely the Planters Fault if they encourage in their Slaves the contrary Opinion, by discovering any Unwillingness to have them instructed and baptized. If they are idle or disorderly afterwards, Christianity doth not deprive you of any Degrees of Strictness and Severity that fairly appear to be necessary for the preserving Subjection and good Government. But still you are to remember that the general Law, both of Humanity and of the Gospel, is Kindness, Gentleness, and Compassion to all Mankind, of what Nation or Condition soever they be; and we are to make the Exercise of these amiable Virtues our Choice and Desire, and to have recourse to Severity only when Necessity requires. Of this Necessity you yourselves remain the Judges as much after they receive Baptism as before: So that You can be in no Danger by the Change; and as to Them, the greatest Hardships which the most severe Master can inflict upon them, are not to be compared to the Cruelty of keeping them in a State of Heathenism, and thereby depriving them of the means of Salvation, as [p]reached forth to *them* as well as to *you*, in the Gospel of CHRIST. Besides, is it not the Want of Religion in the governed, that makes Severity at all necessary to keep Mankind in due Order and Subjection to Government? Were the Minds of the Blacks duly impressed with a lively Apprehension of the great and tremendous Sanctions of the Gospel, everlasting Happiness and eternal Misery;[11] the Hope and Fear of these would, no Doubt, much contribute to make them tractable, orderly and submissive, and in a great measure save the Masters the Trouble as well as Pain of inflicting corporal Punishment.

But perhaps after all you may say, that some of the Blacks imported seem to be so entirely corrupted and depraved, and to have so much inbred Malice and Wickedness of Heart in their very Nature, to be so much sunk into Ignorance, Ferocity and Brutality, that every Attempt to humanize, soften and instruct them, is full as absurd as it is impracticable. But is it possible to suppose that any of the Blacks can be more corrupt and degenerate than some of the Nations we read of in History; who, notwithstanding, were converted to Christianity, and became eminent for their Virtues and good Qualities? I need not mention Particulars; your own Reading will suggest to you Variety of Instances; which may shew that the Conversion of the most vicious and abandoned is not impossible. What hath been done may be done again; and therefore it is your Duty to make the Attempt; "what is impossible with Men, is possible with GOD;"[12] and you are sure of the Divine Assistance co-operating with your pious Endeavours. Our blessed LORD hath promised to be with all those, even to the End of the World, who sincerely endeavour to propagate his Religion. If the Task is difficult, was it not *dangerous* as well as difficult to the first Preachers of Christianity? Yet they were not discouraged from attempting the Conversion of the World, either by Difficulty or Danger, but resolutely persevered, and wonderfully succeeded. You, Sir, run no Hazard by such an Attempt; your Slaves are in Subjection, and can offer no Violence to you for endeavouring to reform them.

You must not think to excuse yourself from this Business by saying, the Propagation of Religion and the Salvation of Souls is the peculiar Duty of the Clergy only. Every private Christian is bound in Gratitude and Duty to communicate to others the Way of Salvation, which GOD hath made known to him; what would you say of a Person who was possessed of an infallible Cure of an epidemic Disorder, should he keep it intirely to himself, when Numbers of his own Family and Neighbourhood were sorely afflicted; and say, that it was not his, but the Physician's Business to cure such Disorders? What would you say farther, if this Remedy was made known to him on this express Condition, that he should freely communicate it to all who were afflicted? Would you not call him ungrateful, hard-hearted, cruel, and what not? Now such a Disorder is human Corruption, and such a Remedy is the Gospel.

What a Reproach, what an Infamy and Disgrace is it to Christians to suffer Thousands of Heathens and Idolaters to dwell among them, and even to make a Part of their Household and Family, without attempting their Conversion?[13] But how aggravated must the Guilt of Englishmen be in this Respect, who, through the Blessing of GOD, have the Light of the Gospel shining in Purity and Splendor among them. Our Rivals the *French* are, I am told, extremely attentive to the religious Instruction of their *Negroes*. As we are fond of copying their Follies, let us not be ashamed of imitating their Virtues; rather let our Zeal in propogating the true Knowledge of the Gospel among our *Negroes* as much exceed theirs, in Proportion as the Blessings spiritual and temporal bestowed upon us by our gracious GOD, are superior to those given to them.

If you rightly consider Things, you will be so far from looking upon the religious Instruction of your *Negroes* as a burdensome Task, that you will acknowledge it as a great and happy Opportunity put into your Hands by Almighty GOD, for promoting and advancing his Glory. The Authority which he hath given you over such a Number of heathen Idolaters, carries in it a manifest Obligation on your Part to endeavour, by all the Weight of your Influence, to convert them from their Errors, and bring them into the Kingdom of his dear SON. This Authority is a Talent committed to your Trust, and a very weighty and important one it is. Do not then, I beseech you, wrap it up in a Napkin, but study to improve it to its utmost Extent, agreeably to the Intention of your great Lord and Master.

You are to consider yourself as a Steward; "whom the LORD hath made Ruler over his Household." Be therefore "wise and faithful." Be attentive to their Wants, "and give them Meat," spiritual as well as carnal, "in due and proper Season." If the Labour is great, the Reward will be proportionable. For "blessed, eternally blessed, will be that Steward whom his LORD when he cometh shall find so doing."[14]

To shew us the Importance and Necessity of doing it, and to keep on our Minds a constant Sense of that Importance and Necessity, our Saviour hath inserted a kind of Remembrance of it in that Form of Prayer which he hath graciously taught us. This Form, I presume you repeat daily. But with what Consistency can you pretend to pray to

GOD that "his Kingdom may come;"[15] that the Gospel may be propogated, unbelieving Nations converted, and the Number of Saints augmented, whilst you yourself wilfully suffer the greatest Part of your own Family and Household to continue Strangers to this blessed Kingdom, in profound Ignorance of the Means of Grace here, and of Glory hereafter? Doth not your Practice fully contradict your Prayers? Again, Do you not pray that "his Will may be done on Earth as it is in Heaven?"[16] But how is it possible for your Slaves to do the Will of GOD, unless they know it? And how can they know it, unless you will take Care that they be duly and properly instructed in it?

Your Neglect to do this, is a plain Indication that you are insincere in your Devotions; and you may as easily reconcile Contradictions, make Light and Darkness dwell together, as you can shew that such a Neglect of the spiritual Welfare of your *Negroes*, is consistent with the Meaning and Purport of your Prayers.

My Zeal for your temporal and eternal Welfare, hath carried me much farther than I at first intended. If I have trespassed on your Patience, you must impute it to my earnest Desire that you may, in the great Day of Account, be numbered among those "who have turned many to Righteousness,"[17] and be honoured with that distinguishing Reward which shall be allotted to all such,—a Crown of Glory eternal in the Heavens.

Believe me to be, Dear SIR, *Your affectionate Wellwisher, And sincere Friend.*

Oct. 10, 1770.

Printed copy. The title page of this rare, anonymous pamphlet indicates that it was published in London by H. Reynell in 1781, but the date is certainly erroneous. The *Letter* is dated 10 October 1770, and in that month an anonymous donor gave 1,000 copies of the pamphlet to the Associates, who agreed that 500 copies should be stitched in blue covers and sent to their American correspondents. Minutes, 2:41–42. Many copies were sent to America in 1771. See Waring to Nicholas, 25 March 1773, below; "Catalog of Books," pp. 60, 96, 151. This pamphlet is here attributed to Waring on the basis of textual and circumstantial evidence. The textual evidence is to be found in striking similarities of phrasing between the pamphlet and the few surviving letters by Waring. Notes 3, 6, 8, 11, and 13 to the pamphlet unite the relevant passages. The circumstantial evidence is provided by the quotation in the twenty-seventh paragraph (n. 10). The quotation is from Baker to Waring, 23 April 1770, above. The letter was not read by the Associates until their meeting of October 1770, by which time Waring had read the letter, extracted the quoted passage, and had his pamphlet printed.

1. 1 Corinthians 4:7.
2. Acts 10:34.
3. See Waring to Nicholas, 25 May 1769, paragraph 3, above.

4. 1 Samuel 12:23.
5. Luke 16:25.
6. See [Waring to Lewis, April 1769], paragraph 1, above.
7. Ephesians 6:4.
8. See [Waring to Lewis, April 1769], paragraph 1, above.
9. Deuteronomy 28:4, 5, 8.
10. See Baker to Waring, 23 April 1770, above.
11. See [Waring to Lewis, April 1769], paragraph 1, above.
12. Matthew 19:26; Mark 10:27; Luke 18:27.
13. See [Waring to Lewis, April 1769], paragraph 1, above.
14. Matthew 24:45–46; Luke 12:42–43.
15. Matthew 6:10; Luke 11:2.
16. Ibid.
17. Daniel 12:3.

Francis Hopkinson and Edward Duffield
to [Rev. John Waring]

Philada. November 20th. 1770

Sir,

We [have] drawn upon you for Ten Pounds Sterling, in Favour of
Mr. James Warren, being the half Year's Salary due to the Mistress of
the Negroe Charity School in this City, which Draught we doubt not
you will duly honour.
We are Your Friends & humble Servants

Fras. Hopkinson
Edwd. Duffield

ALS. This letter is in Hopkinson's hand; both signatures are in autograph.

Rev. Marmaduke Brown to Rev. John Waring

[Newport, 14 December 1770]

Dear Sir,

I am at this present so much indisposed that it is with some difficulty I can forward this letter of advice, of my having drawn a bill in
favour of Mr. Channing, due the eighth of October last. My disorder
is a slow or lingering fever, which has greatly reduced me, & was I
think brought on by the fatigue of a long & most disagreeable voyage
of eleven weeks. How it will terminate, I willingly submit to the divine
dispensation; 'tho I am not without hope of recovering in some degree my former health & strength. Should this be the case you will

hear further & more fully from me. In the mean time I am to inform you that the school of the Associates has its full compliment of children & is in as flourishing a condition as I have at any time known it. I beg you will present my best respects to Mrs. Waring, & I also desire you will both except my grateful acknowledgments for the many civilities shewn me when in London;[1] & believe me dear Sir with the utmost respect & affection to be your much obliged friend & brother

Marmaduke Browne

Newport Rhode Island
December 14. 1770

ALS. This letter is endorsed as read 4 April 1771, although the Associates' Minute Book records its reading on 7 March and 4 April 1771. Minutes, 2:45.

1. In 1769 Browne went to Dublin to secure an estate left him by his wife. He then traveled to London and Antwerp before returning to Newport in August or September 1770. While in London on 5 October 1769 Browne attended a meeting of the Associates "& reported that the Negroe School under his Inspection was full, that the Scholars make a good Progress in Learning but that the Mistress is not so diligent & attentive in doing her Duty as he cou'd wish." The Associates "Agreed that Thanks be given to Mr. Browne for his great Attention to the Negroe School & that he be desired on his Return to appoint another Mistress, unless the present One shall be more diligent & attentive to the Discharge of her Duty." Minutes, 2:29–30. Browne died of his illness in March 1771. The Associates learned of his death in December of that year and asked Waring to request Browne's successor to super-intend the Newport Negro school. Waring apparently did not write to the Rev. George Bisset until 15 May 1772. See Bisset to Waring, 17 October 1772, below. Minutes, 2:47 (meeting of 5 December 1771); Stiles, *Literary Diary* 1:95–96.

Robert Carter Nicholas to Rev. John Waring

Williamsburg in Virginia 22d. January 1771.

Sir.

I have this Day drawn on you in favour of Messrs. Norton & Son for £25 Sterling, the sum to which you restricted me, towards sup-porting the Negro School in this City. There have no material Altera-tions happen'd since my last, so that I have nothing new to offer. With my Compliments to the Gentlemen, your Fellow Associates, I remain very respectfully, Revd. Sir, Your most obedient Servant

Ro. C. Nicholas

ALS. Endorsed as read 4 April 1771. See Minutes, 2:45.

Francis Hopkinson and Edward Duffield to [Rev. John Waring]

Philada. May 20th. 1771

Sir,

We have drawn upon you as usual in favour of Mr. James Warren for £10 Sterling being the half Years Salary due this Day to the Mistress of the Negroe Charity School in this City, which Draught we doubt not will be duly accepted. We have only to add that the School is nearly full, & duly attended & that we are Your Friends & humble Servants

Fras. Hopkinson
Edwd. Duffield

ALS. This letter is in Hopkinson's hand; both signatures are in autograph.

[Francis Hopkinson and Edward Duffield to Rev. John Waring]

[Philadelphia, 20 November 1771]

Messrs. Hopkinson & Duffield in a Letter dated November 20: 1771 say that the School there goes on well as usual.

Letter not found. Extract from Minutes, 2:49 (meeting of 6 February 1772).

Rev. George Bisset to Rev. John Waring

Newport November 23d. 1771

Revd. Sir

This is to advise that I have this day drawn on you for ten Pounds Sterling in favor of Mrs. Mary Brett for her half years salary, as mistress of the negro-school in this town, due the 8th. of October last which I doubt not will be punctually paid. Inclosed you have a List of the negro-children who now attend this School, & I beg leave to assure you that I shall on every occasion be ready to cooperate with you in every thing that may make this charitable donation as useful as possible.

I am with respect Revd. Sir Your very humble & obedient Servant

Geo: Bisset minister of
Trinity-Church Newport

304

ALS. Endorsed as read February 1772 and answered May 1772. At the meeting of 6 February 1772 the Associates "Agreed that Thanks be returnd to Mr. Bisset." Minutes, 2:48. Waring's reply, which was dated 15 May 1772, has not been found.

Enclosure
List of Negro Children

A List of the Negro Children

Mr. Ayrantt sends	1
Mr. Dickenson	1
Mr. Honyman	2
Mr. Thurston	2
Mr. Johnston	2
Mr. Hunter	1
Mr. Whitehorne	1
Capt. Wilkinson	1
Capt. Duncan	3
Capt. Cooke	1
Capt. Shearman	3
Capt. Freebody	1
Mrs. Chaloners	1
Mrs. Honyman	1
Mrs. Cahoone	1
Miss Scott	2
Mrs. Thurston	3
Free Negro's	3
Total	30

D.

Robert Carter Nicholas to Rev. John Waring

Williamsburg in Virginia 17th. December 1771.

Revd. Sir.

I have to advise of my having drawn on you this Day in favour of Messrs. Norton & Son for £25 sterling the Associate's annual Allowance to the Negro School in this City. I would by this same Opportunity, send you a List of the Scholars with proper Remarks on their Progress, but the Mistress has been sick for some time & I myself am at present very much indisposed. You may expect to have this Satisfaction by some future Conveyance; I can only say in general that I believe the Affairs of the school go on much as formerly.

I am very respectfully, Revd. Sir, Your most obedient Servant

Ro. C. Nicholas

ALS. Endorsed as read 7 May 1772. See Minutes, 2:50.

Fielding Lewis to Rev. John Waring

[Fredericksburg,] Virginia February the 1st. 1772

Revd. Sir

Your last favour I received by the Betsy Capt. Cuzzins in the Summer 1769[1] and agreeable to directions there given I endeavour'd all in my power to procure the Number of Negro Children to be educated [as] You directed, but without effect; The Revd. Mr. James Marye gave an excellent discourse in our Church on the occasion yet the purpose was not answer'd. I therefore at the expiration of the year discontinued the School which had subsisted five years, the expence One Hundred pounds Sterling which leaves a Ballance due to me of Thirty Pounds, which please to pay to Anthy. Bacon Esqr. for my Acct. having sent him an Order for it. It gives me the greatest concern that so much Money should have been expended to so little purpose, and am of Opinion that a School will never succeed in a small Town with us, as the Numbers of Negro's are few and many believe that the learning them to read is rather a disadvantage to the owners, we having had some examples of that sort. I have many Books remaining which were sent for the use of the School, please to direct me in what manner you will have them disposed off.[2]

I am Revd. Sir with the greatest respect Your most Obedient Humble Servant

Fielding Lewis

ALS. Endorsed as read 7 May 1772. See Minutes, 2:50–51.

1. See [Waring to Lewis, April 1769], above.
2. The Associates sent 110 books to Fredericksburg in 1764 and 162 books in 1766. See "Catalog of Books," pp. 115, 128.

Rev. George Bisset to Rev. John Waring

Newport April 30th. 1772

Revd. Sir

This is to advise that I have this day drawn on you for ten Pounds Sterling in favor of Mrs. Mary Brett for her half years Salary as Mistress of the Negro-school in this Town due the 8th. Instant which I doubt not will be punctually paid. Inclòsed you have a list of the Negro Children who now attend said school. Whatever you may think necessary in order to promote the ends of this charitable institution shall be readily complied with by Revd. Sir Your very humble & obedient Servant

Geo: Bisset minister of
Trinity Church Newport

ALS. This letter was read by the Associates at their meeting of 3 December 1772. Minutes, 2:52.

Enclosure
List of Negro Children

A List of Negroe Children

Mr. Hunter	1
Capt. Duncan	3
Mr. Honyman	3
Mrs. Cahoone	1
Capt. Buckmaster	1
Capt. Shearman	3
Capt. Freebody	1
Mrs. Thurston	2
Mr. Thurston	3
Mrs. Honyman	1
Mrs. Lyndon	1
Capt. Sneel	1
Mr. Johnston	2
Mrs. Mumford	1
Free Negroes	3
Capt. Wickham	1
Capt. Dupee	2
Capt. Wanton	1
	31

D.

Francis Hopkinson and Edward Duffield
to Rev. John Waring

Philada. 20th. May 1772

Sir,

We have drawn upon you for Ten Pounds Sterling in Favour of Mr. James Warren; being half Year's Salary due to the Mistress of the Negroe Charity School in this City.
We are Your Friends & humble Servants

Fras. Hopkinson
Edwd. Duffield

ALS. This letter is in Hopkinson's hand; both signatures are in autograph. Sent "Via Bristol." Endorsed as read 3 December 1772.

Rev. Samuel Auchmuty to [Rev. John Waring]

[New York, 28 September 1772]

Revd. Sir,

I am this moment seting of for Philadelphia to be present at the Annual Meeting of the Corporation for erecting a Fund for the Relief of Widows & Children of American Clergymen,[1] therefore cannot be particular in the State of the Negro School. In general it is full and thriving. It could not succe'd better. The mistress is diligent, & the Scholars regular in their Attendance upon their Duty.

I propose doing myself the pleasure of writing a long letter to you upon my return from Philadelphia.

I have drawn for a Year's Salary in favor of Mr. Henry Boomer[2] due to the Mistress the 22 Inst. I am Revd. Sir Your Affectionate Brother

Saml. Auchmuty

N. York September the 28. 1772

ALS. This letter was read by the Associates at their meeting of 3 December 1772. Minutes, 2:53.

1. The Corporation was founded in Philadelphia in 1769. Auchmuty delivered a sermon at the second annual meeting, held in Trinity Church, New York, on 2 October 1770. See Auchmuty, *A Sermon Preached before the Corporation for the Relief of the Widows and Children of Clergymen, in the Communion of the Church of England in America . . . to Which Is Prefixed, a Brief Account of the Chari-*

table *Corporation* (New York, 1771); John William Wallace, *A Century of Benefi-cence, 1769–1869* (Philadelphia, 1870).

2. Not identified.

Rev. George Bisset to Rev. John Waring

Newport October 17th. 1772

Revd. Sir

I have had the honor of yours of the 15th. of May last[1] & as I owe you my sincere thanks for the great confidence you have placed in me with regard to the Negro-school so it shall be my constant study to en-deavor to deserve it. I communicated the Contents of your letter to many of the Principal Gentlemen of the Church who very readily promised me their assistance in supporting such an excellent & useful institution. Upon my first visiting the school I found every thing out of order the woman had been sick & there were not more than two or three young negroes who regularly attended but as she was then re-covered I represented to her in the strongest terms the absolute ne-cessity of doing her duty & that if I found her deficient I had particu-lar orders to appoint another. This I believe had its due effect for I have reason to think that since that time she has taken more pains than she usually did before. I shall not however trust to that but shall very often visit the school to examine their progress & shall particu-larly attend to what you particularly recommend their improvement in the Knowledge of the truths of religion. I am sorry to inform you that notwithstanding all my endeavors both by public advertisements & private recommendations yet the Number is not as yet complete.[2] There are not at present more than seventeen or eighteen who con-stantly attend & I am apprehensive the number will not be much increased during the winter many who have negro-children rather chusing to keep them at home than to incur the small expence of al-lowing Fire wood. This is the reason which the woman gives for her school being thinner during the winter & I believe it has considerable weight especially among the poorer sort. I shall do myself the honor to write you again some months hence & hope I shall be able to write you more favorable accounts of the state of the school & the progress of the Negro-children in the mean time if any thing occurs to you which may be of service to it I beg you'l honor me with your com-mands. I have this day drawn upon you for ten Pounds sterling the last half years salary due the 9th. Inst. I do not hear that any Books are wanted at present when they are I will let you know. I sincerely wish you much success & satisfaction in all your public endeavors for the glory of God & the good of mankind & much private health & happiness & am with great respect Revd. Sir Your affectionate brother & very humble Servant

Geo: Bisset

ALS. Endorsed as read 4 February 1773. See Minutes, 2:55. Also endorsed as "Answered in March, recommending either to dismiss the Mistress or put the School on some other plan, viz. either to pay in proportion to the Number of Children, or to have a great Number during the Summer & to discontinue the School three or four Month during the Winter." Waring's reply has not been found.

    1. Letter not found.
    2. Bisset advertised the school in the Newport *Mercury* of 3 August 1772. He acquainted the public "that a SCHOOL will be opened on Monday the 10th inst. by Mrs. Mary Brett, at her house in the High street, . . . for the instruction of thirty negro children, gratis, in reading, sewing, &c. agreeable to a benevolent institution of a company of gentlemen, in London. N.B. The said school is now under such regulations, that it is not doubted but satisfaction will be given to those who may send their young blacks."

Robert Carter Nicholas to Rev. John Waring

Williamsburg in Virginia 1st. December 1772

Revd. Sir.

I have this Day drawn my annual Bill on you in favour of Messrs. Norton & Son for £25 sterling on Account of the Associates' Negro School in this City. I intended to have sent you a List of the Children with some Account of their Progress, but the Mistress's Indisposition for some time past & the great Variety of public Business, in which I am engaged, have prevented my visiting the School, as I design'd. I can, however, venture to tell you that Matters are conducted much as I formerly mention'd; the Number of Scholars is fluctuating & some few of the Inhabitants do join me in contributing towards supporting the School, tho there is far from being a general Disposition to promote its' Success; the Reasons, which I at first foresaw & mention'd to you, will forever work an Indifference in the Generality of the Owners of Negroes as to the Education & Instruction of their Children. I should be glad if you would be pleased to write to the Revd. Josiah Johnson, the present Rector of our Parish & desire his Countenance & Assistance in furthering your charitable Views;[1] I mean that he would join them with my own, for I still am as cordially as ever inclined to do all in my Power to promote them. My respectful Compliments wait on the Associates & I am Revd. Sir, with much Esteem, Your most obedient Servant

Ro. C. Nicholas

ALS. Endorsed as read 4 February 1773 and answered March 1773. See Minutes, 2:56. Waring's letter to Nicholas is dated 25 March 1773, below.

1. For Johnson see Biographical Appendix. Waring's letter to Johnson is dated 25 March 1773, below.

Rev. John Waring to Rev. Josiah Johnson

[London] 25 March: 1773

Revd. Sir

At the Desire of the Associates of the late Dr. Bray I trouble You with This, to request the Favour of your charitable Concurrence with your worthy Parishoner Mr. Nicholas in inspecting their Negroe School at Williamsburgh. We have been much indebted to his Benevolence for superintending this Labour of Love many Years alone since the Death of the Late Revd. Mr. Yates, & we are confident he will continue to patronize & promote it to the utmost of his power; nevertheless we cannot but suppose it will be extremely agreable to him to be favoured with the Assistance of the Minister of his Parish: & we flatter ourselves that You will very chearfully concur with him in promoting a Design which manifestly tends to promote the Glory of God & the Advancement of Religion. I shall acquaint Mr. Nicholas with this Request to You, & doubt not but your kind compliance will afford real pleasure to him as well as to the Associates, & particularly to, Revd. Sir, Your affectionate Brother & obedient Servant

John Waring

from Mr. Birds No. 5 Ave Mary Lane London

ALS: Bray MSS., McGregor Collection, U.Va.

Rev. John Waring to Robert Carter Nicholas

[London] 25 March. 1773.

Sir

I receivd Your Favour dated 1st. December 1772. Your Draft will be duly honoured; We are sorry to understand that the Owners of Negroes continue to be still so unconcerned about, if not averse to their Instruction; with a view to remedy this, about two Years ago I sent 40 Copies of a Letter to an American Planter from his Friend in London on this Subject, wherein various weighty Reasons are offered for their Instruction & the principal Objections against it are answerd, but as You never took any Notice of the Receipt of this Packet I suppose it was not deliverd.[1] When the School was first established at Williamsburgh I flattered myself that, e'er now, the Inhabitants in general, from a trial of its good Effects, woud most heartily have encouraged it, and for their sakes am much concern'd to find they do not. By this conveyance I write to Mr. Johnson to request he will unite his Endeavours to yours, the better to promote this good work: I shall think myself much obliged to You or Him for the Favour of a Line by the first Opportunity. The Associates present thanks for all your good Offices.

I am, Sir Your most obedient Servant

John Waring

Mr. Birds. No. 5 Ave Mary Lane London

ALS: Bray MSS., McGregor Collection, U.Va.

1. Forty copies of [Waring], *A Letter to an American Planter, from His Friend in London* of 10 October 1770, above, were sent to Williamsburg in March 1771 but apparently never arrived. Minutes, 2:41–42; "Catalog of Books," p. 96.

Rev. George Bisset to Rev. John Waring

Newport April 8th. 1773

Revd. Sir

This is to acquaint you that I have this day drawn upon you for ten Pounds sterling in favor of Mrs. Mary Brett for her last half years Salary as Mistress of the Negroe-School. I beg leave to assure you that nothing has been wanting on my part to make it answer the pious design of the founders & that I was much discouraged by the declining state of it during the winter yet I have now the pleasure to inform you that it is [pre]tty full & do not question but it will continue so as I have [receive]d the strongest assurance from some persons of consequence [that they] will warmly interest themselves in its support. Tho it [may] seem hardly credible yet it is really very difficult to perswade [the] generality of the obligation they are under to instruct their young blacks. I have endeavored as much as possible to call up their attention to that duty both in public & private, & some time ago published an advertisement setting forth the absolute necessity of making a better improvement of that charitable institution other ways they must be deprived of the benefit of it which I found had a very considerable effect.[1] The Mistress of it I believe is as diligent as ever she has been at any time. If she fails in her duty I assure you I shall take proper notice of it as I have nothing more at heart than that I may hereby serve the interests of religion & deserve the confidence which you have placed in me. I am with respect Revd. Sir Your affectionate Brother & very humble Servant

Geo: Bisset

ALS. Endorsed as read 2 September 1773. See Minutes, 2:59. The bracketed portions of the text are conjectural readings, the manuscript being torn.

1. The Newport *Mercury* of 29 March 1773 carried Bisset's announcement that the school would be discontinued in six months if more students were not enrolled.

Francis Hopkinson to Rev. John Waring

Philada. 21st. May 1773

Dear Sir,

I have drawn upon you for £10 Sterling One half Year's Salary due yesterday to the Mistress of the Charity Negroe School in this City.

I am Your Friend & humble Servant

Fras. Hopkinson

The Bill is in Favour of Mr. James Warren.

ALS. Sent "per Capt. Sutton." Endorsed as read 2 September 1773.

[Francis Hopkinson and Edward Duffield to Rev. John Waring]

[Philadelphia, 3 July 1773]

Read a Letter from Messrs. Hopkinson & Duffield, of Philadelphia, dated July 3d. 1773 wherein they Say: We have now to inform You that we have made careful Enquiry for a Suitable Lot of Ground for the Purpose, & have fixt our Attention upon one in the principal Street of the City called Market Street, very near the Buildings & Improvements in that Street, & which in all probability will soon become very valuable. It stands in the Corner of a Square, & of course has two Fronts, which is a material Circumstance.

This Lot contains 136 Feet front on Market Str. & 360 feet on ninth Street. The Owner[1] will not take less than 1000£ this Currency which is about equal to £600 Sterling. Should the Associates think proper to purchase the above, they desire further Instructions how to proceed &c.

Letter not found. Extract from Minutes, 2:61–62 (meeting of 2 September 1773). After reading the letter the Associates

> Agreed that Messrs. Hopkinson & Duffield be requested to purchase the above named Lot of Land on the most advantageous terms they can, but not to give more for it than Six hundred pounds.
>
> Agreed that whatever Money the above Purchase may cost more than Mr. Upchers Benefaction, the Same shall be paid out of the general Fund, & that the Treasurer be directed to sell so much of the Associates Stock in the 3 per Cent consol. as may be sufficient to compleat the purchase and defray all other Charges attending it.
>
> Agreed that the Revd. John Waring M.A. John Spiller Esqr. Mr. Samuel Waring Edmund Pepys Esqr. and Mr. Thomas Nixon be appointed Trustees for Lands to be purchased with Mr. Upchers Benefactions The last Two in the Room of Revd. Juckes Egerton & Peter LeKeux Esq. appointed June 16: 1768.
>
> Agreed that the Revd. Mr. Thomas Coom of Philadelphia be added to the Surviving Attorneys nominated June 16: 1768 in the Room of Mr. David Hall deceased.
>
> Agreed that Mr. Pepys be desired to prepare a proper Letter of Attorney under the direction of [Richard] Jackson Esqr. to be sent to Philadelphia to empower the Gentlemen who are appointed Attorneys to transact all Business relative to the intended purchase of Land and the future Management of it. (Minutes, 2:62–63)

The letter to Hopkinson and Duffield has not been found, nor has the letter of attorney.

1. Thomas Lawrence II (1720–75), sometime mayor of Philadelphia. *PMHB* 25 (1901): 449.

Rev. George Bisset to Rev. John Waring

[Newport, 13 November 1773]

Revd. Sir

I am very much obliged to the venerable Associates for their kind acceptance of my weak endeavors to promote their charitable institution in this place. I know the best return I can make them, is, to be always able to inform them that their benevolent views are fully answered, to which therefore I shall on all occasions heartily contribute. In consequence of a hint in your letter,[1] by the assistance of my friends I got the number increased to forty (as large a number as can be properly taken care of) who have attended pretty regularly for nearly six months past but now they are dropping off very fast. And indeed, as I formerly observed to you, such is the general inattention to the instruction of young negroes, that it has hitherto been found impracticable to keep up a full School during winter when it would necessarily be attended with more trouble & expence on the part of the masters. We still however endeavor to keep together as many as we can till next Spring when I doubt not we shall be able again to collect as many as the woman can well manage. I may with truth observe to you that the woman has been more diligent & attentive than heretofore. She has not perhaps that inclination to do her duty which one could wish but she has lately been pretty well watched & has had strong representations made to her of the danger she incured by negligence of losing her imployment; indeed as the teaching of blacks is not here reputed very creditable I believe I should find it difficult to get a better. Upon the whole I may conclude that during Summer the School will be well attended; & I am very sensible of the inconveniencies attending the discontinuing of it (or at least the absence of the greater part) during the winter, but I cannot think of any proper remedy. If you have any thing else to propose I will execute it with great fidelity. This at least you may always depend upon that twice a year you shall know the true state of your school in a plain narration of facts & I should be very happy if I could truly represent it to you as always flourishing without interruption. Tho your charitable benefaction here has not all the good effects I could wish yet I am far from thinking that it is misapplied & I doubt not but the more these negroe children are neglected in the most important points by their inconsiderate masters, so much the more God & the world will approve your labor of love in taking care of their immortal Souls which that it may prosper in your hands is the hearty prayer of Revd. Sir Your affectionate Brother & very humble Servant

Geo: Bisset

Newport November 13th. 1773

ALS. Endorsed as read 19 May 1774. See Minutes, 2:65.

1. Letter not found. See Bisset to Waring, 17 October 1772, bibliographic note, above.

[Francis Hopkinson and Edward Duffield to Rev. John Waring]

[Philadelphia, 22 November 1773]

Read a Letter from Messrs. Hopkinson & Duffield dated 22 November 1773 Who say "We have little doubt but that in the course of 28 or 30 Years This Lot must very considerably improve in Value & will we hope answer the Purposes intended; We have agreed with the Owner for 950 Currency. £1000 Cur[rency] which is nearly equal to 600£ Sterling was the price He long insisted on but we have prevailed on him to strike off 50. The Lot is 132 Feet Front on Market Street & 306 on Ninth Street.

"The School is full & goes on as usual.

"Mr. Hopkinson intends early in the Spring to remove with his Family to another Province and desires Some Other Person may be nominated by the Associates in his Room."

Letter not found. Extract from Minutes, 2:65 (meeting of 19 May 1774).

Robert Carter Nicholas to Rev. John Waring

Williamsburg in Virginia 5th. January 1774.

Revd. Sir.

I have given Messrs. Norton & Son my annual Bill on you for £25 sterling on Acct. of the Negro School in this City, which you, no doubt, will duly honor. The Situation of the School is much as it was when I wrote you last; the Number of Scholars between 20 & 30 & I believe the Mistress gives them proper Attention. Your Letter to the Revd. Mr. Josiah Johnson, our late Minister, did not arrive till his last Illness, of which he died. He is succeeded in the Parish by the Revd. Jno. Bracken, a very worthy Gentleman; it might be of Service to the School, if you, by Letter, would engage his Patronage to it.[1]

I sincerely wish you & the other Associates a Series of happy Years & am very respectfully, Revd. Sir, Your most obedient Servant

Ro. C. Nicholas

ALS. Endorsed as read 19 May 1774. At that meeting the Associates "Agreed that the Revd. Mr. Bracken's Assistance in inspecting the School be requested." Minutes, 2:67. Such a letter to Bracken has not been found.

1. The Rev. John Bracken (1745–1818) was rector of Bruton Parish from 1773 until his death. He was master of the grammar school at the Col-

lege of William and Mary 1775–79 and president of the College 1812–14. Rutherfoord Goodwin, "The Reverend John Bracken (1745–1818), Rector of Bruton Parish and President of William and Mary College in Virginia," *HMPEC* 10 (1941): 354–89.

[Francis Hopkinson and Edward Duffield to Rev. John Waring]

[Philadelphia, 3 May 1774]

Read a Letter from Messrs. Hopkinson & Duffield 3d. May 1774 wherein They say they have purchased the Lot of Ground formerly recommended to the Associates and drawn for the Purchase Money which with Charges amounts to Five Hundred and Seventy five Pounds Sterling. And further they desire Instructions in what manner the Land shall be disposed of. That the Deed for the Land is in their Hands, which shall be recorded, and afterward forwarded to the Associates. They say Mr. Hopkinson had left Philadelphia & on that Acct. cou'd no longer assist the Associates, & that Mr. Duffield intended very soon to retire into the Country, & therefore requested that some other person might be appointed Inspector of the Negroe School in their Stead.

Letter not found. Extract from Minutes, 2:68 (meeting of 1 September 1774). After the reading of this letter,

> The Treasurer reported that he had accepted & paid Messrs. Hopkinson & Duffields Draft for Five hundred & Seventy five pounds but had not as yet received the Deed for the Land. That He wrote to the Revd. Mr. Coombe of Philadelphia to request him to superintend the Negroe School, & desired Dr. Franklin also to write to him on the same Subject but had hitherto receivd no Answer, only Mr. Duffield in his Letter of Advice about the School Mistress's Salary dated 20 May 1774 says Mr. Coombe hath not as yet joind Us in any of the Associates Business.
>
> The Treasurer saith further that 10th. June last He wrote to Mr. Duffield & requested to know what immediate Profit the Land brings in, & that as He must be a more competent Judge in what manner to dispose of the Land to the best Advantage The Associates will always be thankful to Him for any Information & Advice He may favour Them with. (Minutes, 2:69)

Waring's letters to Coombe and Duffield, and Franklin's letter to Coombe have not been found.

Edward Duffield to Rev. John Waring

Philada. May 20th. 1774

Sir,

I have drawn on you of this date for Ten pounds Sterling in favour of Mr. Thomas Barton[1] or Order, being for half a years Salary due the Mistress of the Negroe Charity School in this City, which I doubt not you will duly honour. Mr. Hopkinson (who resides in the Country) not being in Town at this time occasions my signing this Draught alone. Mr. Coombe[2] hath not as yet joined us in any of the Associates business.

I am Sir your most Obedient Humble Servant

Edwd. Duffield

N.B. It appears by the Account of the Negroe Charity School rendered this day by the Mistress thereof, that there are at present

  2 at their Needles & Spelling
  1 at Knitting, Needle, & Testament
  7 at Spelling
  3 in the Testament
  1 at Needle & Testament
  1 in the Psalter
10 in the Alphabet
  1 in Fables
  1 at Sampler & Testament
  3 in the Primer
30

Three of the above Children are free & the rest of them are slaves.

ALS. This letter was mentioned at the Associates' meeting of 1 September 1774. Minutes, 2:69.

1. Not identified.
2. For the Rev. Thomas Coombe see Biographical Appendix.

Rev. George Bisset to Rev. John Waring

[Newport, 21 May 1774]

Revd. Sir

I hereby advise you that I have drawn upon you for ten Pound Sterling in favor of Mrs. Mary Brett for one half years Salary due to her the 1st. of april last as mistress of the Negroe School. I have nothing particular to write you concerning said School but that after its usual intermission in the winter it has now encreased again very fast. I did hope to have seen it continued during the winter but it could not be effected, the causes I have already mentioned will have their effects in spite of opposition especially when confirmed by long custom. There are at present 38 as appears by a list now before me which I would have sent inclosed if I had seen any propriety in transmitting to so great a distance a long catalogue of names with which you must be intirely unacquainted. I am told by the woman that she could get more than 40 during the summer but that I humbly conceive is the largest number which one person can instruct properly. As far as I can I will endeavor to watch over your school so as to moderate in some degree the ill effects of that intermission which is so disgraceful to this Town & any directions which you may be pleased to send me shall be faithfully complied with.

I am with great respect Revd. Sir Your very humble & obedient Servant

Geo: Bisset

Newport May 21st. 1774

ALS. Endorsed as read 1 September 1774. See Minutes, 2:69–70.

Rev. George Bisset to Rev. John Waring

Newport Rhode Island July 18th. 1774

Revd. Sir

This is to advise you that I have this day drawn a bill for ten Pounds sterling in favor of Mrs. Mary Brett mistress of the Negroe school in this Town for one half years salary due the 8th. of April last.

I am with respect Revd. Sir Your very humble Servant

Geo. Bisset

ALS. Endorsed as read 5 December 1774.

[Rev. Thomas Coombe to Rev. John Waring]

[Philadelphia, 21 September 1774]

The Revd. Mr. Coombe in a Letter dated 21 September 1774 says He is sincerely disposed to bear his part in any Undertaking that has the happiness of the meanest Individual for its Object, & in particular, it will give him pleasure to be made any way useful to the benevolent designs of the Associates. He desires to have a Coadjutor join'd with him, will visit the School & occasionaly transmit an Account of it to the Associates; He says the Deed from Thomas Lawrence to the Associates hath been delivered to Him, which he will immediately have recorded, & afterwards, if thought proper shall be forwarded to the Associates.

Letter not found. Extract from Minutes, 2:71 (meeting of 2 March 1775). After reading this letter the Associates "Agreed that Thanks be returnd to Mr. Coombe for his charitable Concurrence, that he be requested to send the Deed when recorded, but previously to have an attested Copy, & also to have an accurate plan of the Ground taken and transmit the Same with the Deed, & to reserve a Copy of Said Plan for the Use of the Associates Attorneys there." The letter to Coombe has not been found.

Rev. Samuel Auchmuty to Rev. John Waring

New York September the 28th. 1774

Revd. Sir

I am ashamed of my long silence, occasioned chiefly by me being out of Town, riding about for my Health, which has been greatly impaired by my close application to the Duties of my Function. At present, I thank God, I am better than I have been for twelve months past. I hope therefore to be a better corrispondent for the time to come.

I am now to inform you, that the School, (which I have not neglected) continues full. Several of the Children read very well, and know the whole of their Catechise. They attend the Church constantly on Sundays and often on week days. The mistress continues her usual diligence, but is in a very declining state of Health. I fear we shall soon lose her. Upon inquiry, I have the pleasure to find, that those that have been brought up in the School behave remarkably well. I have drawn upon you for a Year's Salary due the 22d. instant. The Numbers that have been at the School, I cannot exactly say, as I ordered the mistress to keep the account, and only stay in Town till I finish this hasty Letter. Upon my return as the approach of winter will confine me to the City, I will make it my bussiness to draw up a particular account of the School from its first institution, & forward to you; provided the dismal & shocking situation we are now in, does not grow worse and worse, & finally end in a civil War.

As you are, I find by your last favor, no Stranger to American Affairs, I will just give you a hasty detail of our dismal situation. The Congress, (as they call themselves) are now siting at Philadelphia, and

I may venture to say will enter into very rash, and unwarrantable Resolves, such as I fear will make the madness of the People (if possible)
greater than it is at present. The four Eastern provinces, Massachusetts, Connecticut, New Hampshire, Rhode Island are seized with
such a fit of madness in general, that they are ready to rush like a
Horse that has no understanding, into the Battle. They already are
in Arms, & threaten the Kings Troops to drive them out of Boston
where they are strongly encamped. A Vain threat, which will be fatal
to them tho' they are numerous, should they attempt it. The Southern
provinces are, if possible, higher in their expressions, and will go
great lengths in iniquity. In this province and the Jersey's we are yet
tollerably quiet, but I fear our *Demagogues*, as soon as the Kings Troops
leave us, which will be in a few days, as the General & the Regiment
are under Orders to repair to Boston immediately, will give us great
uneasiness.[1] In short, no man now, dares say he is a Friend to Government, without being sure of being insulted; if not *feathered and tarred*.
God only knows what will become of the Episcopal Clergy especially
in Connecticut Government. Several already are obliged to fly, and
leave their all behind them. In regard to myself and my Assistants in
this City, I have the pleasure to find that our Congregations will not
suffer the least insult to be offered to us without properly resenting of
it. Tho' the Sons of Liberty, (sedition I mean) know my sentiments
they are honest enough to say, that as they have for many Years experienced my candid, & open, and upright conduct, however I may differ from them in regard to Government, they will suffer no insult to
my Person; they well know however that the members of the Church
here are very numerous, wealthy and in high esteem & attached to
me. Pray do not let this hasty Letter go out of your hands. In order to
save postage I must not turn over, but only add that I am, with sincere
esteem & Respect, Your Much Obliged & Affectionate Brother.

S: Auchmuty

P.S. Best respects to Sir James Jay. I have not been favored with a line
from him this four months.

ALS. Sent "per Packet." Endorsed as read 2 March 1775 and answered 28
January 1775. See Minutes, 2:72–73. Waring's reply has not been found.

1. Major-General Frederick Haldimand (1718–91) held the chief command in New York following the departure for Boston of General Thomas
Gage in 1773. On 5 September 1774 Gage ordered Haldimand to join him in
Boston as soon as possible with all available troops from New York. Haldimand was in Boston from late fall 1774 until mid-June 1775. Late in 1775 he
returned to England, ostensibly to give information on the state of the colonies but probably because he was Swiss and was not wanted as commander-in-

chief in America after Gage's resignation in August 1775. Allen French, "General Haldimand in Boston, 1774–1775," *Proceedings of the Massachusetts Historical Society* 66 (1936–41): 80–95; John R. Alden, *General Gage in America* (Baton Rouge, 1948), pp. 214, 221; *DNB*.

Rev. Samuel Auchmuty to Rev. John Waring

New York October the 20th. 1774

Revd. and very worthy Sir,

Hearing of a Vessell's sailing to morrow morning I now set myself down to inform you, that I wrote to you the 29th. of last month,[1] and then drew upon you for the Salary which was due to the mistress of the Negro School the 22d. I also informed you that she was in a declining State, & would not, I feared live long. My opinion of her condition has turned out too true; she dyed Yesterday, and this Evening I shall bury her. She was faithful in the discharge of her Duty, and a good Christian. I cannot take it upon myself appoint another Mistress, especially considering the distracted situation we are in at present, till I hear further from you. Far be it from me to fling the least Obstacle in the way against the continuance of the School; but my Conscience obliges me to inform you, that the possessors of Slaves in this City are opulent, and well able to put their Negro Children to School, and pay for it: but whether they will in general do their duty (some I know will) if the institution is dropt I doubt greatly.

The future welfare of the poor Negro's has been one of the principal Objects of my attention for a number of years. From ten Communicants which I found when I first took the charge of them, I now with pleasure can see, at one time, near Sixty, and I constantly visit them in their sickness, Baptize numbers of them in the course of a Year, and perform the burial service over those that have behavied like Christians. Besides, the Sunday Evening Lecture which the Society, for the propagation of the Gospel has ordered, I have at the request of a Number of good Christians opened another at the house of an amiable Man, Mr. Gerarde G. Beekman a merchant of opulence among us, on Thursday Evening.[2] This Lecture I attend occasionally. One of the blacks, a sincere good man in my absence reads such parts of the Church Service as I have directed, & then such Sermons as I order, best adapted to their Capacities. By this means, by the consent of their Masters & Mistresses, I keep them together & if any of them behaves amiss, they are immediately reprimanded before the rest. This Method keeps them in an excellent Order: Now if the worthy Associates should for the reason already given, chuse to drop the School, and bestow part of the Salary they now give, to some honest good Christian, who would constantly attend upon the poor Slaves at their Meetings, read for them & visit them when sick, and make it his bussiness to inform me of every thing relating to the conduct of those that are Christians, I can'ot help thinking their Money would be better bestowed; especially when I consider that these Negro's blessed with an able Instructer would, (as indeed many of them are now) soon become qualified to instruct their own Children. Do not imagine, worthy Sir, that I propose this measure to ease myself of any burden. I love the poor Blacks—they are grateful and I will never cease while it pleases God to enable me, to give them every Assistance both to their present & future happiness, in my power.

I dare say little about politic's. A dreadful Cloud hangs over us. God, the Sovereign Ruler of all Events, only knows where it will fall. I greatly fear a civil war. You will soon find the source from whence our troubles have taken their rise. Oliverian Principles, & Oliverian Steps are become too predominant. The Church Clergy in the Eastern Governments are greatly to be pitied. They already suffer persecutions. I dare no more.

Pray remember us in your prayers, and be assured that I am Your Affectionate Brother & Much Obliged Servant,

Samuel Auchmuty.

P.S. I should be glad to be favored *by you* with a candid & impartial account of the light we stand in with the Inhabitants of our Mother Country, in general: (The Ministry excluded). One Mr. Peters the Society's Missionary at Hebron in Connecticut, after being mob'd several times, his private papers seized, his House plundered &c. &c. is by this time in London.[3] I wish you could see him, he is a rough Diamond. You may depend upon what he says. Dr. Hind[4] will inform you of his abode.

ALS. Sent "Favored by Mr. De Wint." Endorsed as read 2 March and answered 4 March 1775. At the meeting of 2 March the Associates "Agreed that it be recommended to Dr. Auchmutys Consideration whether it may not be most eligible to appoint some serious good Christian Man to be a Schoolmaster for the Benefit of Such Negroe Children as shall appear to Him to be proper Objects, and who may also instruct the adult Negroes on Thursdays at their Meetings, visit the Sick &c. agreably to the Doctors proposals provided the Salary doth not exceed Twenty pounds a Year, but this Scheme is entirely submitted to the Doctors Judgement, & that He be requested to adopt such a plan as he shall think will best answer the Intention of the Associates." Minutes, 2:73−74. Waring's reply has not been found.

1. Auchmuty's letter was dated 28 September 1774, above.

2. For Gerard G. Beekman (1719−97) see Philip L. White, *The Beekmans of New York in Politics and Commerce, 1647−1877* (New York, 1956), chap. 6.

3. The Rev. Samuel.Peters (1735–1826), a native of Hebron, Connecticut, and a graduate of Yale College, was ordained by the bishop of London in 1759. He served as S.P.G. missionary at Hebron from that year until he sailed for England in October 1774. Peters first incurred the wrath of the patriots when, in August 1774, he was charged with sending false and malicious reports to England. The Sons of Liberty forced him to promise never again to send such reports. In a sermon of 4 September 1774 Peters exhorted his audience not to take up arms in rebellion; two days later he was visited by a mob. Peters took refuge in Boston a few days later, from where he wrote to Auchmuty of his travails. His letter of 1 October 1774, which was intercepted and published in the *Boston Evening Post* on 24 October, described the mob attacks on Connecticut Anglicans: "The Sons of Liberty have almost killed one of my church, tarred and feathered two, abused others, and on the 6th Day destroyed my windows and rent my cloathes . . . Pray loose no time, nor fear worse times than attend. . . ." Peters did not sail for England until 25 October. Weis, *Colonial Clergy New England*, p. 163; Dexter, *Yale Graduates* 2:482–87; Bridenbaugh, *Mitre and Sceptre*, p. 325; Annette Townsend, *The Auchmuty Family of Scotland and America* (New York, 1932), p. 62.

4. The Rev. Richard Hind, D.D. (c. 1716–1790), rector of St. Anne's, Westminster, was secretary of the S.P.G. 1773–78. Foster, *Alumni Oxonienses*; Frank J. Klingberg, *Anglican Humanitarianism in Colonial New York* (Philadelphia, 1940), p. 31n.

Robert Carter Nicholas to Rev. John Waring

[Williamsburg,] Virginia 17th. November 1774

Revd. Sir.

I have to advise you of the Death of Mrs. Wager, the Mistress of the Negro School at Williamsburg. I could wish to have revived the Charity upon such Terms as would be agreeable to you & the rest of the worthy Associates of Dr. Bray, but seeing no Prospect of it at present, I have discontinued the School,'till I can receive your farther Directions. The Acct. of what I am in Advance you will receive inclosed, Balance in my favour £11.17.2, for which I have drawn on you in favour of Messrs. Norton & Sons.

Wishing you & the rest of the Associates every Felicity, I remain very respectfully, Revd. Sir, Your most obedient Servant

Ro. C. Nicholas

ALS. Endorsed as read 2 March and answered 11 March 1775. Also endorsed: "Agreed that Thanks be returned to Robt. C. N. for his long Series of Charitable Services, that they acquiesce in his Opinion to discontinue the School at present, & that he be informed the Associates will at any time be very thankful to him for his Directions how their pious Intentions may be most effectualy promoted." See Minutes, 2:71–72. Waring's reply has not been found.

Enclosure
Account

[Williamsburg, 17 November 1774]

The Associates of Dr. Bray

Dr.

1773

April 1	To Quarters Salary due this day	£ 5.	.
July 1	To ditto . . . . ditto	5.	.
October 1	To ditto . . . . ditto	5.	.

1774

January 1	To ditto . . . . ditto	5.	.
April 6	To ditto	5.	.
July 2	To ditto . . . . ditto	5.	.
	To paid Mr. Blair a Years Rent		
	due 25th December 1773.	10.	.
August 20	To ditto paid for 7½ Months		
	to the time of Mrs. Wager's death	6.	5.
	To paid Mat: Hatton her Son in Law		
	for Balance of Salary[1]	1.13.4	
		£47.18.4	
	To Balance	15. 8.4	

Cr.

1773

December	By my Exchange to Norton & Son	£25.	
	30 per Cent	7.10.	
		£32.10.	
	Balance	15. 8.4	
		47.18.4	
	By my Exchange to Norton & Son	£11.17.2	
	30 per Cent	3.11.1½	
		15. 8.3½	

Errors Excepted 17th. November 1774.

Ro. C. Nicholas

ADS.

325

1. Mathew Hatton, sometimes known as Mathew Watts Hatton, was a Williamsburg carpenter and joiner. Stephenson, "Negro School in Williamsburg," p. 6.

[Rev. Thomas Coombe to Rev. John Waring]

[Philadelphia, 10 February 1775]

The Revd. Mr. Coombe of Philadelphia in a Letter dated 10th. February 1775 saith He hath not been wanting in Attention to the School, & hath the Satisfaction to inform the Associates that it continues full, & is very faithfully taken care of by the Mistress.

Letter not found. Extract from Minutes, 2:74 (meeting of 4 May 1775).

[Rev. George Bisset to Rev. John Waring]

[Newport, 12 April 1775]

Read a Letter from Mr. Bisset of Newport Rhode Island dated 12 April 1775, wherein he saith "the Negroe School goes on pretty nearly in the same way he formerly described. Last Summer It was as full as coud be expected, in Winter It hath been entirely the Reverse, & untill Masters are realy in earnest about the Instruction of the Young Blacks & untill a Mistress can be found as attentive to her Duty as to the Profit annexed, He utterly despairs of seeing Effects worthy of the Generosity of the Associates. As to what depends upon himself He promises all the Attention which the Care of a large Parish will admit of and advises that the Churchwardens & Vestry be requested by the Associates to take upon themselves the Care & Inspection of the School jointly with Him. This, He doubts not woud engage them to exert themselves much in favour of the School."

Letter not found. Extract from Minutes, 2:75–76 (meeting of 5 October 1775).

[Rev. Thomas Coombe to Rev. John Waring]

[Philadelphia, 18 July 1775]

Read a Letter from Mr. Coombe of Philadelphia dated 18 July 1775 wherein he saith the School continues full & the Mistress discharges her Duty with diligence & a reasonable Degree of Success. By a Postscript it appears that on the 20th. May there were 9 Negroe Children in the Alphabet, 7 in Spelling, 4 in reading, 5 in Reading & Sewing, 2 at the Needle, 2 Needle & Knitting, 1 Sampler.

Letter not found. Extract from Minutes, 2:77 (meeting of 7 March 1776).

Cessation of Activities in America

[London, 1 April 1777]

The pious Designs of the Associates in supporting Negroe Schools on the Continent of America being at present interrupted by the unhappy Disputes between great Britain and her Colonies, and there being little Prospect of resuming the same, till an amicable Accommodation shall take place

Agreed, that in order to answer the pious Intention of our Association it will be adviseable to adopt some other Plan of Charity of a similar Nature, and this Board are of Opinion, the Establishment and Support of Schools in England for the Instruction of poor Children in such Places as shall appear to stand most in need of such charitable Institutions will best correspond with the Intentions of this Society.

Minutes, 2:78–79 (meeting of 1 April 1777).

BIOGRAPHICAL APPENDIX

ARNOLD, REV. JONATHAN (1700/01–1751), of Haddam, Connecticut, graduated from Yale College (A.B. 1723) and served as minister of the Congregational Church in West Haven, Connecticut, 1725–34. He succeeded in that church the Rev. Samuel Johnson, who had converted to Anglicanism in 1722. Under Johnson's influence, Arnold, too, converted to Anglicanism. He took communion from Johnson in April 1734 and in May or June was dismissed by the West Haven church. Johnson wrote to an English correspondent on 18 August 1734: "A worthy gentleman, one Mr. Arnold, has lately left them [Congregationalists] and come over to us; he had been my successor; he only wants to be encouraged by the Society to come over for ordination; in the meantime will do all the good he can in a lay capacity." In 1735, Arnold sailed to England, where he was ordained in February 1735/36, appointed S.P.G. missionary to Connecticut, and granted an honorary A.M. by Oxford University. He served in Connecticut 1736–40 and was then transferred to Staten Island, where he served from 1740 until he was dismissed by the S.P.G. in 1745. Arnold seems to have lacked discretion and to have been of "a very unsteady disposition." Whitefield's encounters with Arnold were so acrimonious that Whitefield wrote to the secretary of the S.P.G. that Arnold "is unworthy of the name of a minister of Jesus Christ." Following his dismissal from the service of the S.P.G. Arnold went to Virginia, where he was minister of Fredericksville Parish, Albemarle County, from 1747 until his death. Arnold's career in Virginia must have been as contentious as his earlier career, for he was described as "mere mad Arnold" by Landon Carter.

Thomas Bradbury Chandler to the Rev. Philip Bearcroft, secretary of the S.P.G., 6 November 1752, S.P.G. MSS., B20, no. 102; Fulham Papers, 42:1, 29; Dexter, *Yale Graduates* 1:274–77; Gundersen, "Anglican Ministry in Virginia," p. 255; Schneider and Schneider, *Samuel Johnson* 1:84.

AUCHMUTY, REV. SAMUEL (1721/22–1777), a native of Boston, was a son of Robert Auchmuty, judge of the Massachusetts Vice Admiralty Court, and a nephew of James Auchmuty, dean of Armagh. He was a graduate of Harvard College (A.B. 1745, A.M. 1746) and was ordained by the bishop of London in March 1747. Auchmuty was then appointed S.P.G. catechist to the Negroes of New York and assistant to the Rev. Henry Barclay, rector of Trinity Church, New York. He became minister of St. George's Chapel in 1752 and succeeded Barclay as rector of Trinity Church in 1764. Auchmuty was governor of King's College 1759–64 and was a strong advocate of an American episcopate. He was S.P.G. catechist until his increased duties as rector forced his resignation in 1764. He was elected a member of the S.P.G. in 1765. Auchmuty, who administered the Associates' New York Negro school from 1760 until 1774, remained a Loyalist after the outbreak of the Revolution.

Sibley and Shipton, *Harvard Graduates* 11:115–27; Fulham Papers, 42:1, 31; S.P.G. Journals, 16:258 (meeting of 25 January 1765); *DAB*.

BACON, REV. THOMAS (c. 1700–1768), of the Isle of Man, was ordained a priest and arrived in Maryland in 1745. He was curate in St. Peter's Parish, Talbot County, until the death of the incumbent in 1746, when Bacon succeeded as rector. He published *Two Sermons, Preached to a Congregation of Black Slaves* . . . (London, 1749), and *Four Sermons, upon the Great and Indispensable Duty of All Christian Masters to Bring Up Their Negro Slaves in the Knowledge and Fear of God* (London, 1750), the latter published by the S.P.G. Bacon left St. Peter's in the summer of 1758 to become curate in All Saints Parish, Frederick County. With the death of the incumbent later that year, Bacon became rector of the parish in 1759 and served there until his death. Bacon was active in establishing charity schools in both of his parishes, and he published a compilation of Maryland laws in 1765. The Associates wrote to Bacon in 1761, authorizing him to open a Negro school in Maryland for thirty children, and in April of that year sent him 152 books for the school ("Catalog of Books," p. 71). Bacon communicated the letter to the vestry of All Saints Parish for their consideration, but a school under the auspices of the Associates was apparently never opened.

Minutes, 1:147, 148, 150 (meetings of 5 February, 2 April, 7 May 1761); *Maryland Historical Magazine* 6 (1911): 271–72; *DAB*; Rightmyer, *Maryland's Established Church*, p. 158; J. A. Leo Lemay, *Men of Letters in Colonial Maryland* (Knoxville, Tenn., 1972), pp. 313–42.

BAKER, REV. THOMAS (b. 1733), a native of Suffolk, England, kept a school there before coming to Virginia as tutor to the children of Jonathan Watson in the late 1760s. Baker also came to help Watson purchase lands, as he was skilled in surveying and agriculture. Although he lacked knowledge of Greek and Latin, Baker sailed to England for ordination in the summer of 1769. He was licensed for Virginia in August 1769 and received the King's Bounty the following month. Baker returned to Virginia in February 1770 and applied for Kingston Parish, Gloucester County.

Fulham Papers, 14:141–42, 25:173–84; Weis, *Colonial Clergy Va., N.C., S.C.*, p. 3.

BARNETT, REV. JOHN, was ordained deacon in March and priest in May 1765. He was then licensed for North Carolina and received the King's Bounty, and he was elected an Associate on 23 May 1765. He arrived in North Carolina on 26 October and was taken into the family of Governor William Tryon until provision could be made for him to be placed in a parish. Barnett served St. Philip's Parish, Brunswick County, from 1766 until 1 December 1768, when he transferred to St. George's Parish, Northampton County. He remained in Northampton County until 1771. His successor there, the Rev. Charles Taylor, reported to the S.P.G. on 20 August 1771 that Barnett had "fled into Virginia, being charged with Crimes, too base to be mentioned." Barnett was minister of St. Thomas's Parish, Orange County, Virginia, from 1771 until his resignation in 1772.

Minutes, 1:226 (meeting of 23 May 1765); S.P.G. MSS., B5, no. 42; Malone, "North Carolina Anglican Clergy," pt. 2, pp. 399–401; Weis, *Colonial Clergy Va., N.C., S.C.*, pp. 58–59; Gundersen, "Anglican Ministry in Virginia," p. 256.

BARON, REV. ALEXANDER (d. 1759), a native of Aberdeen, Scotland, was educated at Marischal College and the University of Aberdeen. He came to South Carolina in 1748 as schoolmaster of a British man-of-war, and he was appointed headmaster of the Charleston free school in January 1749. Baron traveled to England for ordination in 1753, and while in England he indicated that he "was willing to use his kind Endeavours towards the Conversion of the Negroes, and desired the Associates to send him some Books." In July Waring gave Baron 597 books. (See "Catalog of Books," p. 2.) Baron returned to South Carolina and served as rector of St. Paul's Parish, Colleton District, 1754–58. He then removed to St. Helena's Parish, Beaufort District, where he served as minister until his death.

South-Carolina Gazette (Charleston), 30 January 1749; Minutes, 1:83–84 (meeting of 17 August 1753); Weis, *Colonial Clergy Va., N.C., S.C.*, p. 72.

BEAUFAIN, HECTOR BERENGER DE (1697–1766), a native of Orange, France, immigrated to the Huguenot settlement at Purrysburg, South Carolina, in 1733. He later moved to Charleston, where he was collector of the customs from 1742 until his death. He was a member of the Commons House of Assembly 1743–45, a member of the Council 1747–56, a fellow of the Royal Society of London, and a member of the Charles Town Library Society. Beaufain was both wealthy and benevolent; in 1753 he advanced £2,500 to relieve poor Protestants arriving in the colony, and by his will he left £500, as well as his house and its furnishings, to the poor.

Arthur H. Hirsch, *The Huguenots of Colonial South Carolina* (Durham, N.C., 1928), pp. 218–19; Kenneth Coleman, "Agricultural Practices in Georgia's First Decade," *Agricultural History* 33 (1959): 196; Walter B. Edgar and N. Louise Bailey, eds., *Biographical Directory of the South Carolina House of Representatives*, vol. 2 (Columbia, S.C., 1977), pp. 65–66.

BISSET, REV. GEORGE (d. 1788), was educated in England and came to Newport, Rhode Island, in 1767, where he served as assistant minister and master of Mr. Kay's grammar school. He was installed as minister of Trinity Church on 28 October 1771 and served there until October 1779, when he left for New York City and the protection of the British lines. Bisset was a fellow of Rhode Island College (later Brown University) from 1771 to 1784. He was married to Penelope, the daughter of James Honyman, judge of the Rhode Island Vice Admiralty Court. In 1780 Mrs. Bisset petitioned the Rhode Island General Assembly, "representing that she was left by her . . . husband with one child, at the time the British troops evacuated Rhode Island." Her request for permission to join her husband in New York was granted. Bisset resided in New York until 1784, when he went to London. He was minister of St. John's Church, New Brunswick, from 1786 until his death.

Fulham Papers, 23:230; John R. Bartlett, ed., *Records of the Colony and State of Rhode Island and Providence Plantations, in New England*, 10 vols. (Providence, 1856–65), 9:93; Lorenzo Sabine, *Biographical Sketches of Loyalists of the American Revolution, with an Historical Essay*, 2 vols. (Boston, 1864), 1:230–31; Weis, *Colonial Clergy New England*, p. 33; *Historical Catalogue of Brown University, 1764–1904* (Providence, 1905), p. 27.

BOUCHER, REV. JONATHAN (1737/38–1804), a native of England, came to Virginia in 1759 to take a position as tutor to a family in Port Royal. He returned to England in 1762 for ordination, and he was minister of Hanover Parish, King George County, 1762–64 and of St. Mary's Parish, Caroline County, 1764–70. In both these Virginia parishes Boucher conducted boarding schools for young boys. He left Virginia in 1770 when he accepted a call from Saint Anne's Church in Annapolis, Maryland. He later became minister of Queen Anne's Parish, Prince Georges County, Maryland, and he finally left the colonies for England in 1775 after strenuously opposing the Revolutionary movement. Boucher was elected a member of the S.P.G. in 1771.

S.P.G. Journals, 19:25 (meeting of 19 April 1771); *DAB*; Boucher, *Reminiscences of an American Loyalist*; Anne Y. Zimmer, *Jonathan Boucher, Loyalist in Exile* (Detroit, 1978).

BROWNE, REV. MARMADUKE (1731−71), son of the Rev. Arthur and Mary (Cox) Browne, was educated at Trinity College, Dublin (A.B. 1754). He was ordained by the bishop of London and served at Queen's Chapel, Portsmouth, New Hampshire, from 1755 to 1760 as assistant to his father, who was minister there 1736−72. Browne succeeded the Rev. Thomas Pollen (see entry below) as S.P.G. missionary at Newport, Rhode Island, and as minister of Trinity Church, Newport, in December 1760. He served there until his death on 19 March 1771. Browne was a fellow of Rhode Island College (later Brown University) from 1765 to 1771.

Historical Catalogue of Brown University, 1764−1904 (Providence, 1905), p. 26; Weis, *Colonial Clergy New England*, pp. 42−43.

BRYAN, HUGH (1700−53), of Beaufort County, South Carolina, was a religious mystic and the chief Carolina disciple of the Rev. George Whitefield. Bryan had been captured by Indians as a boy and kept in slavery for many years, an experience that left him eccentric. He preached to black slaves and prophesied that they would revolt and win their freedom, actions for which he was chastised by the Commons House of Assembly in 1742. Bryan was a deacon of Stoney Creek Independent Congregational Church from 1743 until his death.

M. Eugene Sirmans, *Colonial South Carolina: A Political History, 1663−1763* (Chapel Hill, N.C., 1966), pp. 231−32; *South Carolina Historical and Genealogical Magazine* 37 (1936): 106, 38 (1937): 21, 22, 31. David T. Morgan, Jr., "The Great Awakening in the Carolinas and Georgia, 1740−1775," Ph.D. diss., University of North Carolina, 1967, p. 145.

CHAUNCY, REV. CHARLES (1705−87), of Boston, graduated from Harvard College (A.B. 1721, A.M. 1724) and served as minister of the First Church (Congregational) in Boston from 1727 until his death. Chauncy opposed Whitefield during the Great Awakening, and in the 1760s he was one of the principal opponents of the Anglican attempts to establish an American episcopate.

DAB; Edward M. Griffin, *Old Brick: Charles Chauncy of Boston, 1705–1787* (Minneapolis, Minn., 1980).

COLMAN, REV. BENJAMIN (1673–1747), a native of Boston and a graduate of Harvard College (A.B. 1692, A.M. 1695), resided in England from 1695 until 1699, where he became acquainted with leading Nonconformist ministers, met Dr. Thomas Bray, and was ordained by the London Presbytery. Colman returned to Boston to become minister of the new Brattle Street Church, which was "recon'd midway between the Church of England and the Dissenters, some of the Fundamental Articles of it being, that no man shall be deny'd communion with them for being a Church of England man, that the Scriptures shall be read publickly every Lords Day, and the Lords Prayer used at their morning and even Prayers without offense to the Congregation." Colman was a commissioner of both the Edinburgh Society for Propagating Christian Knowledge among the Indians and the Society for the Propagation of the Gospel among the Indians in New England, and he was a slave owner who spent many hours instructing his slaves. A man of latitudinarian religious beliefs, Colman supported the Great Awakening and welcomed George Whitefield to his pulpit, and he acted as a liaison between New England's Congregational clergy and English Churchmen and Dissenters.

Sibley and Shipton, *Harvard Graduates* 4:120–37; Bridenbaugh, *Mitre and Sceptre*, p. 78; *DAB*.

COOMBE, REV. THOMAS (1747–1822), a native of Philadelphia, was a graduate of the College of Philadelphia (later the University of Pennsylvania) (A.B. 1766, A.M. 1768). He traveled to England in 1768 and was ordained by the bishop of London in 1769. Coombe returned to America to become assistant minister of the United Congregations of Christ Church and St. Peter's, Philadelphia, in November 1772. Coombe administered the Associates' Philadelphia Negro school from 1774 until at least July 1775. Although in that month he delivered a sermon advocating the cause of the colonies, Coombe could not in conscience adopt the principles of the Declaration of Independence, and in 1777 he was arrested and confined by order of the president and Council of Pennsylvania on "the general charge of having evinced a disposition inimical to the cause of America." In July 1778 he resigned from the United Congregations and went to England. Coombe was later a prebendary of Canterbury, chaplain in ordinary to the king, and rector of St. Michael's Queenhithe and Trinity the Less, London.

Lorenzo Sabine, *Biographical Sketches of Loyalists of the American Revolution, with an Historical Essay*, 2 vols. (Boston, 1864), 1:334; Weis, *Colonial Clergy Middle Colonies*, pp. 199–200; *DAB*.

CORAM, THOMAS (1668?–1751), English philanthropist, lived in Massachusetts from about 1693 to 1704 as a shipbuilder. After returning to England Coram became involved in various charitable and colonizing projects. He sought unsuccessfully to settle disbanded soldiers and unemployed artisans in the region between New England and Nova Scotia. He also proposed the establishment of a foundling hospital and was supported in this effort by Dr. Thomas Bray, who wrote *A Memorial Concerning the Erecting in the City of London or the Suburbs Thereof, an Orphanotrophy or Hospital for the Reception of Poor Cast-off Children or Foundlings* . . . [London, 1728] on behalf of the proposal. The Foundling Hospital was finally chartered in 1739. Coram, who was an Associate and a charter trustee of Georgia, was also concerned with the education of Indians in New England. Coram and his wife lodged at the parsonage house occupied by the Rev. Samuel Smith and his wife from late in 1736. After the death of his wife in 1740, Coram continued to reside with the Smiths until at least 1749.

H. B. Fant, "Picturesque Thomas Coram, Projector of Two Georgias and Father of the London Foundling Hospital," *GHQ* 32 (1948): 77–104; *DNB*; *DAB*.

D'ALLONE, ABEL TASSIN, SIEUR (d. 1723), was a Huguenot refugee from France who by 1680 was at the Hague as secretary to Princess Mary of Orange. When Mary became queen of England in 1689, D'Allone was retained in the office and moved to England. In April 1689 he was made principal secretary and master of requests to the queen. On Mary's death in 1692 William kept D'Allone in office. He served for several months in 1697–98 as a *chargé d'affaires* in Paris, and in November 1698 he was appointed William's secretary for Dutch correspondence. After William's death in 1702 D'Allone returned to Holland. He hoped to receive appointment as an ambassador but instead became secretary of state for war.

David C. A. Agnew, *Protestant Exiles from France, Chiefly in the Reign of Louis XIV; or, The Huguenot Refugees and Their Descendants in Great Britain and Ireland*, 3d ed., 2 vols. ([London], 1886), 2:207–10.

DAWSON, REV. THOMAS (1713–60), matriculated at Queen's College, Oxford, in 1732. He came to Virginia and became master of the Indian school at the College of William and Mary in 1738. Dawson traveled to England for ordination in 1740 and returned to Virginia to resume his position at the Indian school, which he held until 1755. He was rector of Bruton Parish Church 1743–59, commissary of the bishop of London in Virginia 1752–60, president of the College of William and Mary 1755–60, and a member of the Council 1755–60.

Weis, *Colonial Clergy Va., N.C., S.C.*, p. 14; Mary R. M. Goodwin, "The President's House and the Presidents of the College of William and Mary, 1732–1975," typescript, 1975, in Research Library, Colonial Williamsburg Foundation.

DE ROSSET, LEWIS HENRY (d. 1786), the son of a Swiss doctor who settled in Wilmington, North Carolina, was a wealthy and respected merchant. He was a justice of the peace of New Hanover County, and he served in the lower house of the North Carolina Assembly for Wilmington 1747–53 and in the Council 1753–75. He invested part of his fortune in a plantation called Red Banks, on the northeast bank of Cape Fear about eight miles above Wilmington. De Rosset was a staunch supporter of the Church of England in North Carolina and a Loyalist; he emigrated to England in 1779.

N.C. Col. Recs. 4:1254, 5:18, 10:106–7; Greene, *Quest for Power*, p. 489; Jackson Turner Main, *The Upper House in Revolutionary America, 1763–1788* (Madison, Wisc., 1967), p. 252; Kemp P. Battle, *Letters and Documents, Relating to the Early History of the Lower Cape Fear*, James Sprunt Historical Monographs, 4 (Chapel Hill, 1904), p. 21.

DUCHÉ, REV. JACOB, JR. (1737/38–1798), was a graduate of the first class of the College of Pennsylvania (1757). He then traveled to England, where he attended Cambridge University for a year and was ordained deacon. Duché returned to Philadelphia in 1759 to become a teacher of oratory at the college and assistant minister of the United Congregations of Christ Church and St. Peter's. After the death of the rector, the Rev. Robert Jenney, Duché traveled to England for priest's orders and returned to become co-minister (with Sturgeon) of the United Congregations under the new rector, the Rev. Richard Peters. Following Sturgeon's resignation in July 1766 Duché was sole minister until he succeeded Peters as rector in 1775. He was married to Elizabeth Hopkinson, sister of Francis Hopkinson (see entry below). Duché was chaplain to the Continental Congress at the beginning of the Revolution but soon had a change of heart and became a Loyalist. He sailed for England in 1777 and did not return to America until 1792.

DAB.

DUFFIELD, EDWARD (1720–1801), was a Philadelphia clockmaker and watchmaker, a member of the American Philosophical Society, and an executor of Franklin's will. He was also a vestryman of Christ Church from 1756 to 1772 and an administrator of the Associates' Philadelphia Negro school from 1768 to 1774.

Franklin Papers 7:211n; *PMHB* 19 (1895): 520.

EARL, REV. DANIEL (d. 1790), a native of Bandon, Ireland, was a schoolmaster in Bertie County, North Carolina, from about 1751 until 1756, when he traveled to England for ordination. Earl was ordained in August and was licensed and received the King's Bounty in September 1756. He returned to North Carolina early in 1757 to become a schoolmaster in Edenton and assistant to the Rev. Clement Hall of St. Paul's Parish, Chowan County. Earl was the only schoolmaster in the colony in 1757, and his employers in Edenton agreed to allow him to officiate there on those Sundays when Hall was obliged to travel to remote chapels. The vestry therefore appointed Hall reader with a salary of forty shillings per annum in January 1757. Following Hall's death, the vestry on 24 February 1759 elected Earl minister of the parish at an annual salary of £100. The S.P.G. then, on 18 May 1759, appointed Earl missionary to St. Paul's Parish. Earl continued as S.P.G. missionary and as minister of St. Paul's Parish until 1783.

S.P.G. Journals, 14:45–47, 148 (meetings of 21 April 1758, 18 May 1759); *North Carolina Historical and Genealogical Register* 1 (1900): 607; Malone, "North Carolina Anglican Clergy," pt. 1, pp. 150–53; Weis, *Colonial Clergy Va., N.C., S.C.*, p. 62.

ELLIS, HENRY (1721–1806), was governor of Georgia 1757–60. He was successful in building up the defenses of the colony, and he aided in the establishment of the Anglican Church in Georgia. Ellis, who was interested in scientific and geographical research and was a fellow of the Royal Society, was governor of Nova Scotia 1761–63.

DAB; *DNB*; William W. Abbot, *The Royal Governors of Georgia, 1754–1775* (Chapel Hill, N.C., 1959), chap. 3; Tom Waller, "Henry Ellis, Enlightenment Gentleman," *GHQ* 63 (1979): 364–76.

EVERARD, THOMAS (d. 1784), a Williamsburg attorney, was clerk of the York County Court 1745–84. He was mayor of Williamsburg 1766–67 and 1771–72, and in 1769 Everard became a vestryman of Bruton Parish and a trustee for founding a lunatic asylum in Williamsburg. He served on the town's Committee of Safety during the Revolution. He was a slave owner who had at least fifteen slaves baptized. Everard's daughter Frances married the Rev. James Horrocks.

Hening, *Statutes* 8:378–80; *WMQ*, 1 ser. 3 (1894–95): 180, 16 (1907–08): 37,

42; *Tyler's Quarterly* 8 (1926–27): 264; *Virginia Gazette* (Purdie & Dixon), 4 December 1766, 5 December 1771; *John Norton & Sons*, p. 510; Goodwin, *Historical Sketch of Bruton Church*, p. 155.

FRANKLIN, BENJAMIN (1706–90), was resident in England as Pennsylvania agent from 1757 to 1762 and from 1764 to 1775. Perhaps as a result of Waring's letter of 24 January 1757 acquainting Franklin with the existence and purpose of the Associates, Franklin met Waring shortly after his arrival in London. Franklin was elected an Associate on 2 January 1760 and served as chairman of the Associates 1760–62. He frequently attended the monthly meetings during his London residency.

Minutes, 1:128, 132, 134, 147 (meetings of 2 January, 6 March 1760, 5 March 1761); Richard I. Shelling, "Benjamin Franklin and the Dr. Bray Associates," *PMHB* 63 (1939): 282–93.

FRANKLIN, DEBORAH (READ) (1708–74), daughter of John and Sarah Read, married Benjamin Franklin in 1730.

Franklin Papers 1:lxii.

GARDEN, REV. ALEXANDER (1685–1756), was a native of Scotland who arrived in Charleston, South Carolina, in 1719. He was appointed rector of St. Philip's Church, Charleston, in that year, and in 1726 he became commissary of the bishop of London for North and South Carolina and the Bahama Islands. Garden administered the S.P.G. Negro school in Charleston from its establishment in 1743 until his retirement as rector in 1753. He then returned to England, intending to remain there the rest of his life, but his involvement with South Carolina missionary work brought him back to Charleston, where he died on 27 September 1756.

Frank J. Klingberg, *An Appraisal of the Negro in Colonial South Carolina: A Study in Americanization* (Washington, D.C., 1941), pp. 101–22; Weis, *Colonial Clergy Va., N.C., S.C.*, p. 78.

GAVIN, REV. ANTHONY (1689–1750), was a Spanish Catholic priest who fled to England about 1715 and converted to Anglicanism. In June 1717 he was given £15 by the Commission for the Relief of Poor Proselytes, of which Bray was a member. He preached to a Spanish congregation in London and held various livings in Ireland before he was licensed for Virginia in April 1735. He received the King's Bounty for Virginia on 17 June 1735, and upon his arrival in Henrico Parish he produced letters from Governor Gooch and Commissary James

Blair recommending that he be accepted as minister. The vestry suspended a decision until Gavin had read and preached satisfactorily.
This being accomplished on Sunday, 2 September 1735, he was unanimously accepted. Gavin remained as minister of Henrico Parish until
1736, when he moved to St. James's Parish, Goochland County. After
St. James's Parish was divided in 1744, he continued as minister of St.
James–Northam Parish until his death. Throughout his ministry Gavin
preached in both English and French to the Huguenot congregation
at Manakintown, King William Parish. Gavin was the author of *A
Master-Key to Popery; Containing . . . a Discovery of the Most Secret Practices of the Secular and Regular Romish Priests in Their Auricular Confession*
(Dublin, 1724), the third edition of which was reprinted in Newport,
Rhode Island in 1773.

Rawlinson MSS., D839, fol. 47, Bodleian Library, Oxford; Fulham Papers,
42:32; Hening, *Statutes* 5:267; Perry, *Historical Collections: Virginia*, pp. 360–
61; *HMPEC* 17 (1948): 212, 229; R. A. Brock, *The Vestry Book of Henrico Parish,
Virginia, 1730–'73* (Richmond, 1874), p. 17.

GILES (OR GYLES), REV. SAMUEL (d. 1766), taught mathematics at King's
College (later Columbia University) 1760–61. He was awarded an
honorary A.B. by the college in May 1764. Giles sailed to England for
ordination, and in December 1765 he was licensed by the bishop of
London for Pennsylvania. He was to serve as S.P.G. missionary at
Dover, in Kent County on the Delaware. In February 1766 the Associates gave 192 books to Giles, "to enable him more effectualy to promote the Instruction of the Negroes in his Parish." (See "Catalog of
Books," p. 128.) Giles was lost at sea in April 1766 in a shipwreck near
the entrance to Delaware Bay.

S.P.G. Journals, 16:481 (meeting of 15 November 1765); George W. Lamb,
comp., "Clergymen Licensed to the American Colonies by the Bishops of
London, 1745–1781," *HMPEC* 13 (1944): 135; M. Halsey Thomas, comp.,
Columbia University Officers and Alumni, 1754–1857 (New York, 1936), p. 317;
A History of Columbia University, 1754–1904 (New York, 1904), p. 28; Perry,
Historical Collections: Pennsylvania, pp. 416–17.

GOOCH, SIR WILLIAM (1681–1751), of Yarmouth, England, was lieutenant governor of Virginia from 1727 to 1749. He was greatly interested in promoting the Established Church in Virginia but was toler-
ant toward dissenting denominations, as is evidenced by his certificate
in this collection (dated 18 September 1734, enclosed in Ziegenhagen
to [Smith], 3 May 1735) in favor of Virginia's German Protestants.
Gooch participated in the assault on Cartagena during the War of
Jenkins' Ear, and he was created a baronet in 1746. He resigned the

governorship of Virginia in 1749 because of declining health and returned to England, where he died.

DAB.

HALES, ROBERT, brother of the Rev. Stephen Hales, worked with Bray for the conversion and education of colonial slaves even before the establishment of the Associates. He was named one of the original trustees of D'Allone's bequest in January 1723/24, but he left the trust at the time of the enlargement of the Associates in 1729/30. Hales was a clerk to the Privy Council.

Assignment of Trustees of Mr. D'Allone's Bequest, 15 January 1729/30, above.

HALES, REV. STEPHEN (1677–1761), one of the four original Associates, was educated at Corpus Christi College, Cambridge (A.M. 1703, B.D. 1711) and was created D.D. by diploma from Oxford in 1733. Hales was perpetual curate of Teddington, Middlesex, from 1709. He was a charter trustee of Georgia, a fellow of the Royal Society, and a founder of the Society for the Encouragement of Arts and Manufactures and Commerce. Hales was the author of *A Friendly Admonition to the Drinkers of Brandy, and Other Spirituous Liquors* (London, 1734), *A Description of Ventilators* (London, 1743), and *A Treatise on Ventilators* (London, 1758).

DNB; A. E. Clark-Kennedy, *Stephen Hales, D.D., F.R.S.: An Eighteenth Century Biography* (Cambridge, Mass., 1929); D. G. C. Allan and R. E. Schofield, *Stephen Hales: Scientist and Philanthropist* (London, 1980).

HENDERSON, REV. JACOB (1681–1751), was born in Glenary, Ireland, and educated at Glasgow. He was ordained in 1710 and after serving various parishes in Delaware and New Jersey he was inducted as rector of the church at Annapolis in March 1713/14. In March 1716/17 he became rector of Queen Anne Parish, Prince Georges County, which he served until his death. Henderson was commissary of the bishop of London for the Western Shore of Maryland 1714/15–1723 and for the whole colony 1729–34. He was the first colonial to be elected a member of the S.P.G.

Rightmyer, *Maryland's Established Church*, pp. 188–89.

HENRY, REV. PATRICK (d. 1777), a native of Aberdeen, Scotland, attended Marischal College, Aberdeen, 1713–16 and 1717–18, receiving an M.A. Henry was licensed for Virginia and received the King's Bounty for Virginia in July 1732. He was minister of St. George's Parish, Spotsylvania County, 1733–34; of St. Martin's Parish, Hanover

County, 1734–36; and of St. Paul's Parish, Hanover County, 1737–77. Henry participated in the Parsons' Cause and protested against the Two-Penny Act, which his nephew of the same name defended in a famous speech in 1763.

Fulham Papers, 42:32; Gundersen, "Anglican Ministry in Virginia," p. 276; Weis, *Colonial Clergy Va., N.C., S.C.*, pp. 24–25; Brydon, *Virginia's Mother Church*, 2:296, 314.

HOLT, REV. ARTHUR (c. 1696–1742), was born in Virginia and educated in England at Sedbergh School and Christ College, Cambridge. He was ordained deacon in 1718 and priest one year later. Holt was an assistant in St. Michael's Parish, Barbados, before becoming rector of St. John's Parish (1727–28) and Christ Church Parish (1728–33), Barbados. He left for Maryland in the summer of 1733 because of his wife's poor health. He was minister of All Faith's Parish, St. Mary's County, from February to October 1734 and was minister of St. Luke's Parish, Queen Anne's County, from 1734 until his death.

Venn, *Alumni Cantabrigienses*; Rightmyer, *Maryland's Established Church*, p. 190; Fulham Papers, 3:168–69, 172–73, 236–37, 16:31–34, 41–42.

HOPKINSON, FRANCIS (1737–91), was a Philadelphia lawyer, poet, composer, and political leader. He was a member of the American Philosophical Society and was an administrator of the Associates' Philadelphia Negro school from 1768 to 1774. He was a vestryman of Christ Church 1769–73 and 1788–91. Hopkinson, who had a home and practiced law at Bordentown, New Jersey, represented New Jersey in the Continental Congress and was a signer of the Declaration of Independence.

DAB; *PMHB* 19 (1895): 521.

HUNTER, WILLIAM (d. 1761), printer of the *Virginia Gazette* (Williamsburg) from 1751 until his death, was joint deputy postmaster general with Benjamin Franklin from 1753 to 1761. He also served as official printer for the colony.

WMQ, 1 ser. 7 (1898–99): 12; Lawrence C. Wroth, *The Colonial Printer* (Charlottesville, 1964), pp. 43, 67.

JOHNSON, REV. JOSIAH (d. 1773), was licensed for Virginia in July 1766. He was master of the grammar school at the College of William and Mary 1767–72 and rector of Bruton Parish 1772–73.

Weis, *Colonial Clergy Va., N.C., S.C.*, p. 27.

JOHNSON, REV. SAMUEL (1696–1772), leader of the Church of England movement in New England, had formerly been a Congregationalist minister. He was born in Guilford, Connecticut, and graduated from the Collegiate School in Saybrook, Connecticut (later Yale College). Johnson taught school at Guilford and served as a tutor at Yale for several years before being ordained pastor of the West Haven Congregational Church in 1720. After coming to doubt the legitimacy of his ordination and the validity of the "New England Way," Johnson, along with Timothy Cutler, rector of Yale, and several others, conformed to the Church of England in 1722 and sailed to England for ordination. He returned as S.P.G. missionary to Stratford, Connecticut, and served there from 1723 until he became the first president of King's College (later Columbia University) in 1754. He resigned the presidency in 1763 and returned to Stratford, where he served as missionary and rector of the Anglican church until his death. Johnson was elected a member of the S.P.G. in 1758 and an Associate of Dr. Bray in 1760. He received a D.D. degree from Oxford in 1743.

Joseph J. Ellis, *The New England Mind in Transition: Samuel Johnson of Connecticut, 1696–1772* (New Haven, 1973); S.P.G. Journals, 14:102 (meeting of 17 November 1758); Minutes, 1:135 (meeting of 3 April 1760).

LEWIS, FIELDING (1725–82), of Fredericksburg, Virginia, represented Spotsylvania County in the House of Burgesses 1760–68. He was also a vestryman of St. George's Parish, a justice of the peace, and a colonel in the county militia. Lewis administered the Associates' Fredericksburg Negro school from 1765 to 1770. During the Revolution Lewis was commissioned by Virginia to superintend the manufacture of arms in Fredericksburg, and he was chairman of Spotsylvania County's Revolutionary committee. Lewis was married to George Washington's sister Betty.

Executive Journals of the Council 6:74; Rev. Philip Slaughter, *History of St. George's Parish, in the County of Spotsylvania, and Diocese of Virginia* (New York, 1847), p. 64; *DAB*.

MARSHALL, REV. MUNGO (d. 1758), received the King's Bounty for Virginia in 1744. He was minister of St. Thomas's Parish, Orange County, from 1745 until his death. Marshall was married to Lucy, sister of the Rev. James Marye, Jr.

Weis, *Colonial Clergy Va., N.C., S.C.*, p. 35; Brock, *Huguenot Emigration to Virginia*, p. 184.

MARYE, REV. JAMES, JR. (1731–80), attended the College of William and Mary in 1754 and went to England for ordination in 1755. He was licensed for Virginia on 27 December 1755 and received the King's Bounty three days later. His letter of 2 August 1760 indicates that he held a living in southern or eastern Virginia from a year after his arrival until he became minister of St. Thomas's Parish, Orange County, sometime after 1758. Marye remained at St. Thomas's until he succeeded his father as minister of St. George's Parish, Spotsylvania County, in January 1768, where he remained until his death.

Weis, *Colonial Clergy Va., N.C., S.C.*, pp. 35–36.

MILLER, REV. EBENEZER (1703–63), a native of Milton, Massachusetts, and a graduate of Harvard College (A.B. 1722), converted to Anglicanism after studying divinity. Miller traveled to England in 1726 to obtain ordination and a missionary appointment from the S.P.G. to Braintree, whose Anglican inhabitants had raised £100 to pay for his trip. He was ordained a deacon in June 1726 and granted an A.M. by Oxford University in July 1726, but because of his age he was not ordained a priest until July 1727. Miller received his missionary appointment from the S.P.G. in late August and returned to perform his first service in Braintree on Christmas Day 1727. Except for a two-year trip to England from 1746 to 1748 (during which Oxford conferred on him a D.D. by diploma), Miller served the Anglican congregation of Braintree continually until his death.

Fulham Papers, 42:9, 31; Sibley and Shipton, *Harvard Graduates* 7:93–100.

MUNRO, REV. HARRY (1730–1801), a native of Scotland, was educated at the universities of St. Andrew's and Edinburgh. He was ordained a minister of the Church of Scotland in 1757, and he served as a chaplain to a Highland regiment in North America during the French and Indian War. The Rev. Samuel Auchmuty wrote to the S.P.G. that Munro sought ordination as an Anglican minister: "After a serious and studious inquiry into the Constitution and Government of the Church of England, He, (to the great mortification and Disappointment of the Dissenters, who were very fond of him) declared that he could not in Conscience continue any longer amongst them." Auchmuty recommended Munro to Col. Frederick Philipse III, of the manor of Philipsburg, near present-day Yonkers, New York, as a suitable candidate for minister to the manor. Philipse wrote the S.P.G. on 23 October 1764, asking that the Society appoint Munro missionary to Philipsburg. Munro carried Philipse's letter to England, was ordained by the bishop of London in February 1765, and received an appointment from the S.P.G. He arrived at Philipsburg on 20 May 1765 and served as a missionary there until he quarreled with Philipse and left in 1768 for Albany, where he was rector of St. Peter's Church and

S.P.G. missionary. During the early years of the Revolution Munro served as a chaplain to the British forces in America. He returned to England in 1778 and in 1783 went to Scotland, where he died.

S.P.G. MSS., B2, no. 14, B3, no. 255; Weis, *Colonial Clergy Middle Colonies*, p. 280; *DAB*.

NELSON, WILLIAM (1711–72), a prominent merchant and planter of Yorktown, Virginia, represented York County in the House of Burgesses 1742–45, was a member of the Council 1745–72, and served as acting governor of the colony 1770–71. He was a strong supporter of the Church of England in Virginia, and he was the father of Governor Thomas Nelson. In April 1762 the Associates shipped seventy-eight books to Nelson for a projected Negro school in Yorktown ("Catalog of Books," p. 81).

Emory G. Evans, "The Nelsons: A Biographical Study of a Virginia Family in the Eighteenth Century," Ph.D. diss., University of Virginia, 1957; John C. Van Horne, ed., *The Correspondence of William Nelson as Acting Governor of Virginia, 1770–1771* (Charlottesville, 1975); *DAB*.

NICHOLAS, ROBERT CARTER (1728–80), a graduate of the College of William and Mary, was a prominent Williamsburg lawyer. He served as a burgess for York County 1756–61 and for James City County 1766–76, and was the treasurer of the colony from 1766 until the Revolution. Nicholas, who was a delegate to the Virginia Conventions of 1775 and 1776, was a moderate who opposed the Declaration of Independence despite his close friendship with Thomas Jefferson. Nicholas was a staunch Anglican who supported the church establishment, and he administered the Associates' Williamsburg Negro school from 1762 until it was closed in 1774.

Mason Papers 1:lxxxiii; Greene, *Quest for Power*, p. 472; *DAB*.

OTTOLENGHE, JOSEPH (c. 1711–1775), a native of Casale, Italy, went to England in 1732 to marry a cousin, but was disappointed in his suit. Ottolenghe was attracted to Christianity through reading the New Testament, and after converting from Judaism was baptized according to the rites of the Church of England in February 1734/35. Ottolenghe attended the meeting of the Associates of 14 January 1750/51, when he was hired as catechist to the Negroes in Georgia at an annual salary of £25. One month later the S.P.G. voted to supplement Ottolenghe's salary by £15 per annum. He served as catechist for the S.P.G. from 1751 until 1759, and for the Associates from 1751 until 1761. From shortly after his arrival in the colony, Ottolenghe played an important role in the silk industry. He had become acquainted with the culture of silk in his native Piedmont, where the industry was carried on extensively. In March 1752 he took charge of the reelers of silk at the Savannah filature, under the superintendence of Pickering Robinson. When in March 1753 Robinson decided to return to England because of poor health, Ottolenghe succeeded him as superintendent of the silk culture, serving in that capacity until 1766. Ottolenghe was also an active public servant, being a Savannah representative in the Commons House of Assembly 1755–66, a vestryman of Christ Church Parish, and a justice of the peace.

John C. Van Horne, "Joseph Solomon Ottolenghe (c. 1711–1775): Catechist to the Negroes, Superintendent of the Silk Culture, and Public Servant in Colonial Georgia," *Proceedings of the American Philosophical Society*, 125 (1981): 398–409.

PARKER, JAMES (c. 1714–1770), of Woodbridge, New Jersey, was apprenticed in 1727 for eight years to the printer William Bradford of New York. In May 1733, with twenty months of his indenture remaining, Parker ran away and shortly found employment with Benjamin Franklin in Philadelphia. He established the *New-York Weekly Post-Boy* in 1743, opened the first permanent printing office in New Jersey at Woodbridge in 1751, and established the *Connecticut Gazette* (New Haven) in 1755. At various times during his career Parker served as public printer to New York and New Jersey, printer to Yale College, postmaster of New Haven, and controller and secretary of the Post Office in North America. Although an Anglican and a lay reader in Woodbridge's Trinity Church, Parker published the writings of Dissenters, including such controversial works as William Livingston's *Independent Reflector* (1752–53).

DAB; Franklin Papers 2:341n.

PERCIVAL, JOHN (1683–1748), first earl of Egmont, attended Westminster School and Magdalen College, Oxford, but left the university in 1701 before taking a degree. He was a fellow of the Royal Society, and he served during his career as a member of both the Irish and English Houses of Commons and as a privy councillor of Ireland. Percival was created first earl of Egmont in the Irish peerage in 1733. He was one of the original Associates of Dr. Bray and was the first president of the Georgia Trustees.

DNB.

POLLEN, REV. THOMAS (born c. 1702), attended Corpus Christi College, Oxford (A.B. 1721, A.M. 1724), and became curate of St. Antholin's, London, and rector of Little Bookham, Surrey. He served in

Glasgow, Scotland, before being appointed S.P.G. missionary to Newport, Rhode Island, in January 1754. Pollen was minister of Trinity Church, Newport, from 1754 until he resigned in 1760 to accept a parish in Jamaica. Pollen had been dissatisfied with his situation in Newport for some time before leaving for Jamaica. He had written to the S.P.G. on 21 July 1757 asking to be removed to South Carolina because of the difficulties he was having in receiving his pay from the church.

S.P.G. Journals, 4:2–3 (meeting of 16 December 1757); Foster, *Alumni Oxonienses*; Weis, *Colonial Clergy New England*, p. 166.

READING, REV. PHILIP (1719–78), son of a London minister, was educated at Winchester College 1731–37 and at University College, Oxford. He came to Pennsylvania in the early 1740s as a tutor to a private family and served for three years before returning to England for ordination. He was licensed for Pennsylvania and received the King's Bounty in April 1746. Reading was S.P.G. missionary at Appoquinimy, Delaware, from 1746 until his death. He also served Augustine Parish, Cecil County, Maryland, from 1769 to 1776. In 1765 Reading was offered the ministry of the Anglican church at Trenton, New Jersey, by the vestry and churchwardens, and he asked the S.P.G. for permission to accept the position. The Society granted permission, but Reading apparently never settled in Trenton. A charter member of the Corporation for the Relief of Widows and Children of Clergymen in the Communion of the Church of England in America and a trustee of Wilmington Academy, Reading was the author of *The Protestant's Danger, and the Protestant's Duty. A Sermon, on Occasion of the Present Encroachments of the French. Preached at Christ-Church, Philadelphia, on Sunday, June 22, 1755* (Philadelphia, 1755). Reading translated into English Count Zinzendorf's *Epistola ad Bonos Pensilvaniæ Cives Christo non inimicos . . .* (Philadelphia, [1742]); the translation appeared in Franklin's Pennsylvania Gazette on 7 April 1743. Reading remained loyal to the crown during the Revolution and closed his church on 28 July 1776 after refusing to eliminate prayers for the king from his service.

S.P.G. Journals, 16:494–96 (meeting of 20 December 1765); Fulham Papers, 42:12,32; Thomas Frederick Kirby, *Winchester Scholars* (London, 1888), p. 237; Foster, *Alumni Oxonienses*; Nelson Waite Rightmyer, *The Anglican Church in Delaware* (Philadelphia, 1947), pp. 39–43; Weis, *Colonial Clergy Md., Del., Ga.*, p. 81; Harold Hancock, "The New Castle County Loyalists," *Delaware History* 4 (1951): 316; Elizabeth Waterson, *Churches in Delaware During the Revolution* (Wilmington, 1925), pp. 27–29; E. Miriam Lewis, ed., "The Minutes of the Wilmington Academy, 1777–1802," *Delaware History* 3 (1948–49): 194.

RHONNALD, REV. ALEXANDER, was for several years master of Eaton's Charity School in Hampton, Virginia (see Rhonnald to Waring, 27 September 1762, note 3, above). He then went to England for ordination and was licensed for Virginia in August 1759 and received the King's Bounty in May 1760. He became minister of Elizabeth River Parish, Norfolk County, in 1762 and was gone by 1766.

Weis, *Colonial Clergy Va., N.C., S.C.*, p. 42; Gundersen, "Anglican Ministry in Virginia," p. 295.

SLOANE, REV. SAMUEL (c. 1740–1807), a native of Pennsylvania, received an A.B. in 1761 from the College of New Jersey (later Princeton University). He was ordained in 1765 and received the King's Bounty for Maryland in 1766. In February 1766 the Associates gave Sloane 335 books "to enable him more effectualy to promote the Instruction of the Negroes in his parish" ("Catalog of Books," p. 128). Sloane was minister of St. Paul's Parish, Kent County, 1766–67 and of Worcester Parish, Worcester County, 1768–70. He then served as minister of Coventry Parish, Somerset County, from 1770 until his resignation in 1776, although he continued to give services until 1785.

Rightmyer, *Maryland's Established Church*, p. 212; Weis, *Colonial Clergy Md., Del., Ga.*, pp. 63–64.

SMITH, REV. CHARLES (c. 1711–1773) was ordained deacon in September 1740 and priest the following month. He served as minister of Elizabeth River Parish, Norfolk County, Virginia, from 1743 until 1 May 1761, when the parish was divided into Elizabeth River, St. Bride's, and Portsmouth parishes. Smith then became minister of Portsmouth Parish and continued there until his death.

Fulham Papers, 42:13, 33; Hening, *Statutes* 7:416–19; Weis, *Colonial Clergy Va., N.C., S.C.*, p. 47.

SMITH, REV. SAMUEL (1701–58), matriculated at the Merchant Taylors' School in 1717. He entered Trinity Hall, Cambridge, in 1720 and received an LL.B. in 1727. Smith was an assistant to Dr. Thomas Bray at St. Botolph's and became a member and the first secretary of the Associates in 1730. In 1731 he wrote an official account of Bray, published in 1746 as *Publick Spirit, Illustrated in the Life and Designs of Thomas Bray*. Smith was a charter trustee of Georgia and was rector of All Hallows, London Wall, from 1736 to 1758. The Associates received £6.6.2 from Smith's estate to be applied to the instruction of Negroes.

Minutes, 1:175 (meeting of 13 May 1762); *Ga. Col. Recs.* 1:28; Venn, *Alumni Cantabrigienses*; Verner W. Crane, "Dr. Thomas Bray and the Charitable Colony Project, 1730," *WMQ*, 3 ser. 19 (1962): 50n, 59.

STEHELIN, REV. JOHN PETER (d. 1753), a German divine resident in England, was a fellow of the Royal Society and minister of the French church in Leicesterfields. He was the author of *Traité Contre la Transubstantiation; ou, Extrait de Plusieurs Sermons Prononcés dans la Chapelle Françoise de Hammersmith* (London, 1727). Stehelin became a subscribing member of the S.P.C.K. in 1747. His obituary described him as "a perfect master of 17 languages."

Gentleman's Magazine 23 (1753): 344; *An Account of the Society for Promoting Christian Knowledge* (London, 1748), p. 19; S. Austin Allibone, *A Critical Dictionary of English Literature, and British and American Authors, Living and Deceased, from the Earliest Accounts to the Latter Half of the Nineteenth Century*, 3 vols. (Philadelphia, 1859–71), 2:2234.

STERLING, REV. JAMES (1701–63), of Ireland, was a graduate of Trinity College, Dublin (A.B. 1720, A.M. 1733). He received the King's Bounty for Maryland in 1737 and served as minister of All Hallow's Parish, Anne Arundel County, 1737–39; St. Anne's Church, Annapolis, 1739–40; and St. Paul's Parish, Kent County, 1740–63. In April 1762 the Associates shipped seventy-eight books to Sterling for a projected Negro school at Chester ("Catalog of Books," p. 81). Sterling was an author and poet as well as collector of the customs at Chester 1752–63.

DAB; Weis, *Colonial Clergy Md., Del., Ga.*, p. 64.

STEWART, REV. ALEXANDER (c. 1723–1771), was a native of Lisburn, Ireland, and attended Trinity College, Dublin (A.B. 1744). He served as a curate in the parish of Loughgeel, Diocese of Conner, 1749–53 and was then transferred to the Diocese of London. Stewart was licensed for North Carolina and received the King's Bounty in June 1753, but he did not depart England until a year later, when he sailed to America as chaplain to Governor Arthur Dobbs of North Carolina. He served as rector of St. Thomas's Parish, Beaufort County, from 1754 to 1770.

Malone, "North Carolina Anglican Clergy," pt. 1, pp. 153–56; *N.C. Col. Recs.* 7:492–96; George D. Burtchaell and Thomas U. Sadleir, eds., *Alumni Dublinienses: A Register of the Students, Graduates, Professors, and Provosts of Trinity College, in the University of Dublin* (London, 1924), p. 781.

STIRLING, ELIZABETH (WAITE) (1688–1736), of Boston, was a sister of Eunice (Waite) Coram, wife of Thomas Coram (for whom see entry above).

Boston Weekly News-Letter, 3 May 1736; *New-England Historical and Genealogical Register* 31 (1877): 424–25.

STURGEON, REV. WILLIAM (c. 1722–1770), son of a Congregational and Presbyterian minister, graduated from Yale College in 1745. After graduation he was a schoolmaster at Rye, New York, but soon conformed to the Church of England and declared himself a candidate for orders by the fall of 1746. In July of that year the vestry of Christ Church, Philadelphia, had received a letter from the S.P.G. offering to support a catechist to the city's Negroes at a salary of £30 per annum. In December the Rev. Henry Barclay, rector of Trinity Church, New York, recommended Sturgeon to the vestry of Christ Church for the position. The vestry nominated Sturgeon to the S.P.G., and he sailed to England and received orders in May 1747. He was licensed for Pennsylvania the following month and on 30 October 1747 was inducted as assistant minister of Christ Church and catechist to the Negroes. He served as assistant minister of Christ Church (after 1758 the United Congregations of Christ Church and St. Peter's) until 1762, when he became co-minister with the Rev. Jacob Duché, Jr., under the Rev. Richard Peters, the rector. He resigned on 31 July 1766 because of ill health. A prejudice against him because of "the place and manner of his education" prevented his advancement, and the Rev. William Smith described him as "but an unengaging preacher, averse to public bustle, and of but indifferent abilities, though otherwise a man of much apparent piety, that has taken much pains in his office." Sturgeon was apparently not satisfied with his situation in Philadelphia, for in 1757 he asked the S.P.G. to transfer him to the mission at Oxford, Pennsylvania, but the Society refused his request. Sturgeon was dismissed by the S.P.G. as catechist in 1763 (see Sturgeon to Waring, 15 August 1764, note 2, above), and in 1766, after resigning as assistant minister of the United Congregations, he asked to be restored to the favor of the Society and appointed missionary to Oxford or Burlington, New Jersey. The S.P.G. did not comply with Sturgeon's request, and he remained in Philadelphia until his death. Sturgeon married Hannah Denormandie (c. 1727–1769) of Philadelphia in 1749.

Sturgeon to the Rev. Daniel Burton, secretary of the S.P.G., 1 September 1766, S.P.G. MSS., B21, no. 285; S.P.G. Journals, 14:32–33, 17:178 (meetings of 24 February 1758, 21 November 1766); Fulham Papers, 42:32; Dexter, *Yale*

Graduates 2:61–63; Dorr, *Historical Account of Christ Church*, pp. 89–91, 93, 157; Richard I. Shelling, "William Sturgeon, Catechist to the Negroes of Philadelphia and Assistant Rector of Christ Church, 1747–1766," *HMPEC* 8 (1939): 388–401.

THOMPSON, REV. JOHN, a native of Scotland, received an A.M. degree from Edinburgh University. He was ordained a Presbyterian minister by the presbytery of Lewes, Delaware, in 1739 but shortly thereafter conformed to the Church of England and sailed to England for ordination, which he received from the bishop of London on 4 November 1739. On 30 November 1739 Thompson was given £10 worth of books by the Associates "as an Incouragement to Diligence in discharging his Office, but particularly in promoting the Conversion of the Negroes." Thompson received the King's Bounty for Maryland but went instead to Virginia, where he was minister of St. Mark's Parish, Orange County, from 1740 to 1772. In 1742 he married the widow of Governor Alexander Spotswood.

Minutes, 1:54–55 (meeting of 18 February 1745/46); Meade, *Old Churches* 2:78–79; Weis, *Colonial Clergy Va., N.C., S.C.*, pp. 50–51; *HMPEC* 17 (1948): 217, 247.

UPCHER, REV. ABBOT (1722–70), was educated at St. Catharine's College, Cambridge (A.B. 1745/46), and was rector of St. Gregory's and St. Peter's, Sudbury, Suffolk. He was elected an Associate on 5 February 1767.

Minutes, 1:255; Venn, *Alumni Cantabrigienses*.

VERELST, HARMAN, served as secretary and accountant to the Associates from 1735 until 1754. He also served as accountant of the Georgia Trustees from 23 August 1732 until the surrender of the charter to the crown in 1752. From 1736 Verelst received an annual salary of £150 from the trustees for his services.

Minutes, 1:8, 92 (meetings of 2 June 1736, 25 September 1754); Egmont, *Diary* 3:75; *Ga. Col. Recs.* 1:576, 2:4; Trevor R. Reese, "Harman Verelst, Accountant to the Trustees," *Georgia Historical Quarterly* 39 (1955): 348–52.

WALLER, BENJAMIN (1716–86), a graduate of the College of William and Mary, practiced law in James City County, Virginia. He was a burgess for the county 1744–61, a vestryman of Bruton Parish from 1744, and clerk of the General Court 1745–76. Waller was a member of the Williamsburg Committee of Safety in 1774, and he served as a judge of the state admiralty and general courts 1776–85. Waller had at least thirty-nine of his slaves baptized.

Mason Papers 1:cv; Goodwin, *Historical Sketch of Bruton Church*, p. 157.

WARING, REV. JOHN (c. 1716–1794), a native of Foord, England, was educated at Shrewsbury School and at St. John's College, Cambridge (A.B. 1737/38, A.M. 1741). He was ordained by the bishop of London in February 1740/41. Waring was elected an Associate in 1748/49, and in 1754 he became secretary. He served as secretary until 1779, when he retired because of "his constant Engagements." Waring was also elected a member of the S.P.G. in 1763. His obituary described him as a clerk in orders of St. James's Parish, Westminster.

Fulham Papers, 42:15; Minutes, 1:68, 92, 2:84 (meetings of 16 March 1748/49, 25 September 1754, 23 June 1779); S.P.G. Journals, 15:405 (meeting of 23 September 1763); *Gentleman's Magazine* 64 (1794): 966; Venn, *Alumni Cantabrigienses*.

WESLEY, REV. JOHN (1703–91), of Lincolnshire, England, was educated at the Charterhouse and at Christ Church College, Oxford (A.B. 1724). He was ordained a deacon in 1725, elected a fellow of Lincoln College, Oxford, in 1726, and became a priest in 1728. While at Lincoln (1726–32), from which he received the A.M. in 1726/27, Wesley and his brother Charles organized the Holy Club of Methodists, which came to include the Rev. Benjamin Ingham and Charles Delamotte (see [Wesley to Associates, c. 25 February 1736/37], notes 1, 3, above), the Rev. Thomas Broughton, later secretary of the S.P.C.K., and the Rev. George Whitefield. In the company of his brother Charles, and of Ingham and Delamotte, Wesley sailed to Georgia in October 1735 and arrived in early February 1735/36. The Georgia Trustees had appointed Wesley missionary to the colony on 10 October 1735, and the S.P.G. financially supported Wesley's ministry. He stayed in Georgia less than two years, however, primarily owing to a dispute that arose out of his repelling from communion a woman he had unsuccessfully courted. Wesley departed Georgia in December 1737 and arrived in England in February 1737/38. He resigned his appointment to Georgia on 26 April 1738. Wesley's Georgia sojourn had exposed him to the Moravians, who gave him a new view of the importance of evangelical doctrine. Upon his return to England, Wesley began his evangelical ministry as the founder of Methodism.

DNB; Coleman, *Colonial Georgia*, pp. 148–49; David T. Morgan, "John Wesley's Sojourn in Georgia Revisited," *GHQ* 64 (1980): 253–62.

YATES, REV. WILLIAM (1720–64), of Virginia, attended the College of William and Mary. He was ordained by the bishop of London in March 1745 and was licensed for Virginia the following month. Yates served for a time as principal of the Peasley School, Gloucester County. He was minister of Abingdon Parish, Gloucester County, 1750–59 and rector of Bruton Parish, Williamsburg, from 1759 until his death. He succeeded the Rev. Thomas Dawson as president of William and Mary in 1761.

Fulham Papers, 42:16, 33; Brydon, *Virginia's Mother Church* 2:321, 336; Weis, *Colonial Clergy Va., N.C., S.C.*, p. 56.

ZIEGENHAGEN, REV. FREDERICK MICHAEL (1694–1776), a native of Pomerania, came to London in 1722. In 1724 Ziegenhagen became a subscribing member of the S.P.C.K. He was court preacher at the Chapel of St. James's.

Gentleman's Magazine 31 (1761): 601, 46 (1776): 94; *An Account of the Society for Promoting Christian Knowledge* (London, 1745), p. 45; VMHB 14 (1906–07): 150.

ZOUBERBUHLER, REV. BARTHOLOMEW (1719–66), was born in St. Gall, Switzerland, and was educated in Charleston, South Carolina, from 1737 to 1745. He left South Carolina for England in 1745 for the purpose of being ordained with the expectation of returning to Orangeburg, South Carolina. Zouberbuhler was ordained by the bishop of London as deacon in September and as priest in October 1745, and in November the Georgia Trustees appointed him English minister in Savannah. He was allowed a stipend of £50 per annum by the S.P.G. and received the King's Bounty in February 1745/46. Zouberbuhler was also to preach occasionally in German and French to the inhabitants of Savannah and the surrounding areas. Zouberbuhler returned to England in 1748 "to represent to the Trustees his Inability of discharging the great Duty required from him, for the Stipend allowed him by the Incorporated Society, and the Offer that was made him of a Living in Carolina." The Trustees thereupon allowed him £50 per annum in addition to his stipend from the S.P.G. Zouberbuhler returned to Georgia in 1749, bringing with him the library of the Rev. William Crowe (see Hales to Verelst, 21 June 1749, note 1, above). He served as minister at Savannah from 1746 until his death. Zouberbuhler's will stipulated that the use, rents, profits, and future increase of the forty-three slaves on his "Beth Abram" plantation were to be used for employing a person properly qualified to instruct the Negroes in the principles of the Church of England. All the slaves born on the plantation were to be baptized, and any of the male children who had been instructed and who desired to teach other Negroes were to be manumitted for that purpose.

Ga. Col. Recs., unpub., 33:311–12, 412; *Georgia Gazette* (Savannah), 17 December 1766; Fulham Papers, 10:122–23; Edgar L. Pennington, "The Reverend Bartholomew Zouberbuhler," *GHQ* 18 (1934): 354–63; Weis, *Colonial Clergy Md., Del., Ga.*, p. 92.

THE ASSOCIATES OF DR. BRAY,
1723/24–1776

For a list of the Associates appointed by the Rev. Thomas Bray in
1723/24, and of those who became members at the time of the enlargement of the Associates in 1729/30, see the Introduction, pp. 5,
10–11 above. Following is a list of Associates elected to membership
up to the American Revolution.

Name	Date of election	Minute Book ref.
Rev. Thomas Wilson	19 Mar 46/47	1:59
Rev. John Berriman	16 Mar 48/49	1:68
Rev. William Best	16 Mar 48/49	1:68
Rev. Thomas Skinner	16 Mar 48/49	1:68
Rev. Leonard Twells	16 Mar 48/49	1:68
Rev. John Waring	16 Mar 48/49	1:68
Peter Dobree, merchant	17 Aug 53	1:84
Rev. Thomas Ashton	29 Oct 56	1:98
Peter LeKeux	29 Oct 56	1:98
Rev. Mr. Wells (or Welles)	29 Oct 56	1:98
John Spiller, dyer	15 Dec 56	1:100
Joseph Waring, brewer	2 Mar 57	1:102
Joshua Readshaw, merchant	4 May 57	1:103
John Moore	5 Apr 58	1:114
Rev. George Dixon, D.D.	5 Jul 58	1:116
Rev. Mr. Dixon	5 Jul 58	1:116
Thomas Nixon	5 Jul 58	1:116
Samuel Waring	7 Mar 59	1:121
Benjamin Franklin	2 Jan 60	1:128
Richard Morrall (or Morhall)	2 Jan 60	1:128
Rev. John Parfect	7 Feb 60	1:132
John Jones	6 Mar 60	1:133–34
Samuel Johnson	3 Apr 60	1:135

Rev. [Brooke?] Heckstall	4 Dec 60	1:144−45
Rev. Henry Owen, D.D.	4 Dec 60	1:144−45
Anthony Bacon, merchant	2 Apr 61	1:148
Thomas Triquet	2 Apr 61	1:149
Rev. Juckes Egerton	Jun 61	1:155
William Strahan	Jun 61	1:155
Joseph Waring, Jr.	Jun 61	1:155
George Garratt	3 Dec 61	1:163
Rev. Edward Yardley	4 Mar 62	1:173
Thomas Powys	13 May 62	1:175
Rev. William Worthington, D.D.	7 Apr 63	1:189
James Collinson of Lancaster	12 May 63	1:191
William Franks	12 May 63	1:191
Charles Coster	2 Jun 63	1:192
Rev. Herbert Mayo	2 Jun 63	1:192
Rev. Thomas Negus, D.D.	2 Feb 64	1:201
Thomas Beach	5 Apr 64	1:208
Edmund Pepys	5 Apr 64	1:208
Rev. William Smith, D.D.	5 Apr 64	1:208
William Powell, LL.D.	3 May 64	1:210
Rev. Hopton Haynes	Jun 64	1:212
Rev. John Moore	Jun 64	1:212
Rev. John Barnett	23 May 65	1:226
Rev. Thomas Coker	23 May 65	1:226
Rev. Peter Grand	23 May 65	1:226
Thomas Wyckelyffe, merchant	23 May 65	1:226
Rev. John Richards, D.D.	6 Feb 66	1:239
Tristram Huddleston Jervis	24 Jul 66	1:245
Christopher Dawson	5 Feb 67	1:255
Rev. Humphrey Thomas	5 Feb 67	1:255
Rev. Abbot Upcher	5 Feb 67	1:255
John Waring, surgeon	5 Feb 67	1:255
Edward Waring, M.D.	5 Feb 67	1:255
Sir John Shaw, Bart.	5 May 68	2:7
Francis Waring	(election not recorded in Minutes; he is listed in *Account*, 1769, between Shaw and Denison)	
Rev. William Denison, D.D.	16 Jun 68	2:11
Rev. Furneval Bowen	1 Feb 70	2:34
Rev. William Clements	1 Feb 70	2:34
Rev. John Douglas, D.D.	1 Feb 70	2:33
Rev. [Michael?] Hallings	1 Feb 70	2:34

Rev. Robert Markham, D.D.	1 Feb 70	2:34
Timothy Ravenhill	1 Feb 70	2:34
James Mitchell	5 Apr 70	2:37
Rev. John Gustavus Burgmann	2 Sep 73	2:63
George Wolff, merchant	6 Jan 74	2:64
Edward Lyttleton	7 Mar 76	2:77
Rev. Thomas Lyttleton	7 Mar 76	2:77
Rev. Andrew Etty	2 May 76	2:77
Rev. [Samuel?] Kettilby	(election not recorded; attended 5/2/76, 4/1/77)	

INDEX

Note on the Editor

John C. Van Horne, a native of Illinois, holds degrees
from Princeton University and the University of Virginia. At present he is Librarian of the Library Company of Philadelphia and associate editor of the Papers of Benjamin Henry Latrobe at the American
Philosophical Society. His previous publications include, as editor, *The Correspondence of William Nelson as
Acting Governor of Virginia, 1770–1771*, and, as co-
editor, *The Journals of Benjamin Henry Latrobe, 1799–
1820*; *Latrobe's View of America, 1795–1820*; and *The
Correspondence and Miscellaneous Papers of Benjamin
Henry Latrobe* (3 vols.). He has also written numerous
articles and book reviews for scholarly journals.

BOOKS IN THE SERIES BLACKS IN THE NEW WORLD